DATE DUE			
JUN 19 1998			

JOHN DEWEY

THE MIDDLE WORKS, 1899–1924

Volume 2: 1902–1903

Edited by Jo Ann Boydston
With an Introduction by Sidney Hook

Carbondale and Edwardsville
SOUTHERN ILLINOIS UNIVERSITY PRESS
London and Amsterdam
FEFFER & SIMONS, INC.

CENTER FOR EDITIONS OF
AMERICAN AUTHORS
AN APPROVED TEXT
MODERN LANGUAGE
ASSOCIATION OF AMERICA
®

*Editorial expenses for this edition have been met in
part by grants from the National Endowment for the
Humanities. Publishing expenses have been met in part
by grants from the John Dewey Foundation and from Mr.
Corliss Lamont.*

Library of Congress Cataloging in Publication Data

Dewey, John, 1859–1952.
   The middle works, 1899–1924.

   Bibliography: p.
   Includes indexes.
   CONTENTS: v. 1. 1899–1901.—v. 2. 1902–1903.
   1. Dewey, John, 1859–1952. 2. Education—Philosophy.
LB875.D34 1976   370.1′092′4   76–7231
ISBN 0–8093–0754–5 (v. 2)

The Middle Works, 1899–1924

Advisory Board

Lewis E. Hahn, *Chairman, Southern Illinois University*
Joe R. Burnett, *University of Illinois*
S. Morris Eames, *Southern Illinois University*
Vernon A. Sternberg, *Southern Illinois University Press*

Textual Consultant

Fredson Bowers, *University of Virginia, Emeritus*

CONTENTS

INTRODUCTION

By Sidney Hook

The writings of John Dewey during the period covered by this volume embrace most of the themes that were to receive a much more elaborate treatment in subsequent major works. The most conspicuous exception is the relation between art and experience and the nature of the consummatory experience. Nonetheless, the breadth of Dewey's concerns, especially when contrasted with the activities of other professional philosophers, is very impressive. These concerns must be assessed in connection with his active and vigorous interest in public affairs, his immersion in administrative planning and operations—not only of departmental affairs but of far-reaching pioneer educational experiments.

One particular aspect of John Dewey's intellectual output during these years is especially noteworthy and not known except to some scholars. I am referring to Dewey's contributions to the history of philosophy, his analysis of philosophical ideas and movements in J. M. Baldwin's large two-volumed *Dictionary of Philosophy and Psychology*. Specialists in the different fields are in the best position to judge the significance and validity of his treatment of the various topics, but no informed reader can fail to be impressed by the range, compactness, and clarity of his exposition. Today there is a comparative neglect of the history of philosophy, but in Dewey's time it was considered the natural introduction to the subject. Although in future writings Dewey made infrequent incursions into the history of philosophy, they were always undertaken, as his essays on Locke, Hobbes, and James show, with an eye on some important contemporary problem whose difficulties could in part be traced to the persistent influence of traditional but questionable assumptions. One life-long critic of Dewey once complained that Dewey approached the problems of philosophy as if they had never been discussed by other thinkers of the past. The only thing true about this observation is that Dewey preferred not to introduce his analysis of a philosophical problem with the usual lengthy history of other people's opinions about it, in which as often as not the problem gets lost. The profound truth is that all of Dewey's analyses of problems were drenched with a consciousness of their historical contexts as well as the history of prior relevant thought about them. There is hardly a chapter in any of his major works in which some peripheral historical aside or reference does not light up an aspect of the subject under discussion.

Indeed, as this volume shows, one of the perennial philosophical interests of John Dewey was the nature of history, the character and logic of historical judgment, and the bearing of knowledge of the past upon the understanding of the present. As contemporary literature continues to reveal, these are still open and much discussed questions. In virtue of his early philosophical allegiance, Dewey was already intellectually sensitized to the phenomenon of historical development. Although by the time he wrote the essays that introduce this volume he had outgrown and repudiated the Hegelian and neo-Hegelian philosophy, he was not prepared to accept the traditional Cartesian and Kantian dualisms that Hegel sought to overcome and which made mysteries of interactions in terms of which the unity of the human organism develops. In addition, the emergence and acceptance of the theory of organic evolution reinforced his belief in the principle of continuity—which according to Charles Peirce represented the chief clue to the Hegelian system—and the universality of process. To Dewey this meant that all phenomena had a dimension of historicity that was pertinent to the understanding of their function and organization.

Reliance upon the historical approach gave rise to two types of problems with which Dewey concerned himself directly and indirectly in much of his subsequent writing. The first was the bearing of history on ethical judgment. Is the validity of an ethical practice and the moral judgment of it in any way affected by the historical circumstances and conditions under which it came into existence? If morality is objective, how can it be relative to the times or the events of the past? If slavery is morally wrong, can we ever say that it was historically justified without contradicting ourselves?

What could "justified" mean over and above causally determined? But if one admits that good and bad, the justified
and unjustified, are all causally determined, what is the
relevance of the causal determination to the moral evaluation? It may be true that in the past the necessities of survival in a hunting economy explain the practice of infanticide. The dominant tradition in Dewey's day, however,
regarded that practice as immoral whenever and wherever
it occurred. The scientific historical approach may succeed
in laying bare the precise circumstances, the necessary and
sufficient conditions, for the emergence of infanticide or any
other social practice, but—so it is alleged—it can furnish no
conclusion that can possibly guide us in making valid moral
judgment. At most it can establish the facts—the inescapable
facts—of historical relativity. It cannot establish the fact of
moral relativity. On this position historical considerations
are altogether irrelevant in determining what is right and
wrong, what ought or ought not to be.

The difficulty of this latter view, according to Dewey, is
that it tends to cut off the rational approach to morality at
its source, and to absolutize as an infallible intuition (sometimes as a divine commandment) the moral judgments of a
given society. It tends to sanctify the moral status quo and
to obstruct moral growth. And above all it gives no clue except by resort to authority or intuition—ultimately declared
self-certifying—as to how the moral judgment was reached.
To say that the historical approach can give us only descriptive data but that ethics is normative is to suggest that we
can determine what should be or should have been in complete independence of what is or has been. But the essence
of reasonableness is to take note of the conditions in which
moral demands, judgments, and expectations are made. After
all it makes no sense morally to condemn a person for not
doing what it is physically or psychologically impossible for
him to do, and not much more sense to judge him for not
doing something it is highly improbable in the light of the
circumstances that he will do. But what is possible or probable in the way of human behavior is something that is the
subject of historical inquiry. How can one reasonably assess,
for example, the moral validity of capital punishment at any

time without determining the historical facts about the number and frequency of capital crimes, the probable deterrent effect of different types of punishment, the efficiency and probity of the system of judicial inquiry and a number of other factual phenomena of the past and present?

Despite some critics, Dewey nowhere and at no time contends that what is morally valid can be *logically deduced* from what is or has been. But in accordance with common-sense judgments of morality, he insists that the study of the antecedent conditions out of which a particular moral practice arose and of its consequences is not only relevant to the question of its continuing validity but essential to any claim for its rationality. For only such inquiry, together with certain other values that are not in question or dispute in the specific situation, can supply the good reasons for its continuance or discontinuance. Among these good reasons, as Dewey's subsequent writings on ethics make clear, are certain normative elements embodied in the pattern of moral life at the time moral action is taken. But from first to last in the record of his writings on ethical judgment, he insists on the direct influence of historical inquiry on human conduct. For in the concrete situations in which moral decisions must be made "moral judgments are judgments of ways to act, of deeds to do, of habits to form, of ends to cultivate. Whatever modifies the judgment, the conviction, the interpretation, the criterion, modifies conduct. To control our judgments of conduct, our estimates of habit, deed, and purpose, is in so far forth to direct conduct itself" (p. 38).

There is a second recurrent difficulty which Dewey's emphasis upon the importance of historical or genetic inquiry must face. Although for Dewey the historical method is an expression of the scientific or experimental method applied to history, many of his critics regard it as irrelevant to scientific method in virtue of its quest for origins, beginnings, and developments of things. They assert that the application of the historical or genetic method to the study of the nature of any phenomenon is a stupendous lapse into the genetic fallacy—the confusion of the questions of validity with questions of origin. Some even go so far as to suggest that there is a logical flaw in the whole developmental and evolutionary point of view if we are concerned with understanding the nature of things. For if it is asserted that our grasp of anything is dependent upon our ability to explain how "it"—whatever "it" may be—got that way, the retort comes—"How can we intelligibly answer the question 'How did it get that way?', unless we already know or understand the nature of the 'it'." If the past has influenced or causally determined the present, then the nature of the present can presumably be experimentally determined in the present without reference to its history or development. The historical approach can provide interesting information about the past, but any truth about the present must be tested by what can be observed about the present. From this point of view the present is more likely to be a key to what happened in the past than the past a key to the present.

On occasion Dewey would dismiss this latter criticism as a purely dialectical argument, although he himself on occasions resorts to dialectical arguments in rejecting other positions. What is more pertinent from Dewey's point of view is that this criticism disregards the empirical evidence that our knowledge of what has entered into the development of a situation enables us to understand and control it in a way that no horizontal cross-section, regardless of the minute histological details of the analysis, succeeds in doing. Here is one of the many ways in which Dewey's interest in and concern with child development and the educational process influenced his larger theoretical concerns, not only in trying to understand the child but the adult as well, not only in trying to understand present-day beliefs but social institutions and practices. Dewey insists that what is given or presented is not "self-explanatory" or "self-contained," that the problem we seek to resolve—whether it is one of child discipline or adult neurosis, the drug culture or the weakening of the family bond—is one into the character of which historical elements have entered constitutively. Insight into or discovery of these historical elements provides the most effective approach in coping with the phenomenon. If the canons of scientific method grow out of successful practices in resolving problems and difficulties, the ever growing use of the historical case-method in human affairs, including medicine, should lead not to the rejection of what has happened in the past as a weighty determinant of outcomes in the present and as possibly relevant to the future but to the realization of a more adequate formulation of what the historical method consists in. To be sure, the mere fact that something occurred in the past is not sufficient to account for its survival or influence in the present: otherwise there would be no historical change; yet, except possibly for mutational changes, what develops in the present is never free of the influence of the past. This is especially true in personal and social experience. It does not follow that for Dewey the more things change, the more they remain the same. He would maintain that they often remain the same because of our failure to do something about them, a failure sometimes resulting from our blindness to the relatively new possibilities of the present. He agreed with the oft-cited dictum of Santayana that those who forget the past are doomed to repeat it, but he was just as much aware of the fact that those who live in the past or see only the past in the present, the old Adam in every fresh birth, are often overwhelmed by the future to whose novelties their tendency to reduce present to the familiar past has blinded them. In the end we all die, but that does not tell us anything about the myriads of ways in which we can live and die.

If the historical development of a phenomenon is integral to its nature, and if the nature of a phenomenon is relevant to the value judgments we express in our relations to it, then, argues Dewey, the history and origin of a phenomenon may not after all be matters of indifference to its value.

We cannot take a present case of parental care, or of a child's untruthfulness, and cut it into sections, or tear it into physical pieces, or subject it to chemical analysis. Only through history, through a consideration of how it came to be what it is, can we unravel it and trace the interweaving of its constituent parts (p. 9).

This historical study does not make our moral judgments about the quality of parental care or about the nature of the child's untruthfulness less acceptable, but it does affect our judgment of what should be *done* to make the parents' or child's future behavior more desirable. The genetic or historical method gives rise to the genetic fallacy, according to Dewey, only when causes are regarded as ontologically superior to effects, and the moral quality we assign to them is automatically endowed with a moral excellence over the qualities assigned to effects or consequences. Knowledge of causes enables us to understand why these things happen and to suggest ways of controlling them, positively or negatively, but they do not exalt the moral quality of the cause over everything else. The moral quality of self-sacrifice is not necessarily reduced by knowing how it came about. As Dewey uses the term "genetic" or "historical" method, it is cognitively identical with what later he called the functional method. His brilliant use of the functional method is illustrated in the much neglected essay, "The Interpretation of Savage Mind," in which he shows how the pervasive values of a culture grow out of the mode of production in a nomadic society, without necessarily endorsing the values that are "natural" to that society. Moral judgment is usually inserted in the social process at the points where functional adjustment breaks down and it is necessary to choose or construct other values. In his later ethical writings, Dewey makes more explicit what the encompassing moral values are that should guide our judgment. These values would enable us to judge a perfectly functioning social order in the light of the historical alternatives and the concrete possibilities of development open to it. It turns out that for Dewey every moral value or principle worthy of reflective support is not an intuition vouchsafed from on high—"timeless" or "absolute" or "ultimate"—but rooted in the nature of developing, and therefore historical, man and society. Like Hegel, but without his metaphysical idealism, he opposes both intuitionism and the traditional empiricisms whose judgments merely affirm or condemn the existing order but do not reconstruct it. The first approach leaves us helpless against "engrained moral prejudice and class interests masquerading as natural morality and eternal intuitions." Of the second approach, traditional empiricism, he says in a naturalistic version of the Hegelian dialectic that its fundamental fallacy "is found in its failure to recognize negative elements in experience as a stimulus to building up a new experience which transcends the old, because involving its revision in such a way as to make good its needs and lacks. But it is just such change that the historic or genetic method is concerned with."

It should be clear by now that there is still a great deal to be mined from these early middle works of Dewey. This is true not only with respect to his theory of moral judgment but to his theory of knowledge or epistemology, a phrase or term he tried to avoid because of its misleading associations. For Dewey, the traditional theory of knowledge developed out of the problem of "the wholesale relation of thought at large to reality in general." Dewey denies that there is a genuine problem of knowledge, because for him there is no such thing as thought at large or reality in general. Common sense and science start from specific problems and seek specific solutions whose conclusions may be generalized and brought to bear on the conduct of inquiry into the other problems. The distinctions that arise in the course of inquiry are all functional and do not reflect "ontological divisions in the realm of being." Thinking takes its point of departure from an experience of felt difficulty in a situation "whose parts are actively at war with each other—so much so that they threaten to disrupt the situation, which accordingly for its own maintenance requires deliberate redefinition and re-relation of its tensional parts. This redefining and re-relating is the constructive process termed thinking."

Every informed reader will find here *in nuce*, and throughout Dewey's chapter devoted to the criticism of Lotze, some of the leading ideas developed and greatly amplified in Dewey's *Logic: The Theory of Inquiry*. At this stage of his thinking about thinking, Dewey was moving toward greater clarity, not yet aware of formidable counter movements emerging in philosophy that would seek to relegate all of his inquiries to the field of psychology, and whose mathematical-formal approach would set the tone and style for future work in logic. The kind of questions and criticisms that naturally arise among traditional logicians who regard logic as a theory of proof rather than of inquiry, Dewey was to grapple with later.

Although he does not use the term "pragmatism" to char-

acterize his position, it is implied in almost every page of his
criticism of Lotze. "The test of validity of idea is its functional or instrumental use in effecting the transition from a
relatively conflicting experience to a relatively integrated
one." The correspondence theory of truth in all its traditional forms is rejected. The truth of an idea or theory depends not on its agreement with an antecedently existing
reality but on the "adequacy of [its] performance" in bringing
into existence a new state of affairs in which the situation
that provoked thought is reconstituted.

There are other writings in this volume that have the
impact of contemporaneity. Although the language of his
essay "The Child and the Curriculum" reflects the academic
and popular idioms of the turn of the century, the ideas expressed, particularly about the necessity or indispensability
of organized subject-matter in the curriculum, are highly
relevant to present concerns. His discussion of "The School
as Social Centre" in its account of the social scene, the decline of legitimate educational and parental authority, its
emphasis upon the necessity for a quest of new sources and
forces of moral authority, not only for the young and immature, but for the adults, sounds like a muted preview of
some of our own problems.

Dewey was one of the great protagonists of the American public school. He claims that its role in assimilating the
cultural differences of different groups and races is "one of
the most remarkable exhibitions of vitality that the world
has ever seen." Yet he was well aware of the loss that resulted from a too precipitate and mechanical assimilation.
This was the loss in what we today would call the sense of
ethnicity. Sometimes the products of the public schools lost
or turned against "the positive and conservative value of
their own native traditions, their own native music, art, and
literature." It is highly improbable that Dewey would be
pleased today with the state of the public schools in our chief
metropolitan centers or with current tendencies toward a
multi-racial polarized community with conflicting rather
than complementary centers of social and moral authority.
But we can be certain that he would not content himself
merely with deploring the situation; he would be seeking

ways of reconstructing it. In his own educational experience
he never confronted the problem of wide-scale violence in
the public schools. He was aware, however, that students
who were stubborn disciplinary cases could disrupt the educational experience of others and was not opposed to measures that would prevent them from engaging in persistent
disorder. But he was insistent that such students receive
special educational treatment. He was as critical of unin-
telligent permissiveness in the classroom as he was of the
arbitrary authoritarian regimens to which it was a reaction.

Dewey was suspicious not only of traditional dualisms
but of easy contrasts of high level abstractions employed to
characterize broad points of view, like optimism and pessimism, individualism and collectivism, liberalism and conservatism, freedom and authority, and many others. He was
primarily concerned with problems and believed that an
antecedent commitment to one point of view often interfered
with an accurate statement of the problem and its resolution.
He dreaded doctrinaire positions because they overlooked
or denied the complexity of human affairs whose recognition,
on the other hand, was no excuse for apathetic despair. His
essay on "Academic Freedom," published at a time when,
because of denominational, political, and social influences,
freedom of teaching and inquiry was observed largely in the
breach in many American institutions of higher education,
is a good illustration of Dewey's sense of realism. He states
clearly and in an unqualified fashion the ideal of academic
freedom in describing the ideal of the university:

To investigate truth; critically to verify fact; to reach conclusions
by means of the best methods at command, untrammeled by external fear or favor, to communicate this truth to the student; to
interpret to him its bearing on the questions he will have to face
in life . . . (p. 55).

He realized, however, that because of the strength of
religious sentiment reflected in hostility to biological evolutionary doctrine and the weakness of public recognition of
the scientific and scholarly character of the social disciplines
at the time, this ideal of academic freedom would gradually
make its way despite episodic set backs. Not content with
stressing the ideal of academic freedom to the community

which underwrote its support, he also stressed the importance of professional responsibility on the part of those who
claimed the benefits of academic freedom. Those who were
with justification demanding that their freedom of inquiry
be protected and guaranteed regardless of how heretical their
conclusions were, were demanding something that no other
group in a democratic community could reasonably be expected to enjoy. There can be no legal restriction upon the
right of a citizen not to patronize the butcher, the baker, the
candlestick maker, the lawyer, the physician, or businessman
whose views he abominates, even though the exercise of this
right may have serious economic consequences for those
against whom it is directed. In rightfully demanding an im-
punity from such retaliatory action from his fellow citizens,
the teacher is demanding what is central to academic freedom and tenure and something no other profession in our
society can reasonably expect to enjoy. Therefore the teacher's responsibility to live up to the integrity of the educational process and not to subvert it by intellectually and
morally dishonest procedures, or even to offend legitimate
sensibilities by gratuitously abrasive and offensive manners,
is for Dewey part of the ethical dimensions of academic freedom. In subsequent years when Dewey helped organize the
American Association of University Professors, whose first
president he became, his emphasis upon the responsibilities
as well as the rights of the teacher's academic freedom was
recognized in its statement of principles.

Although uncommitted to any social or economic doctrine like that of capitalism or socialism, Dewey was extremely sensitive to and articulate about the devastating
effects of the existing social and economic order on the
quality of the personal life of the men and women affected
by it. His unvarying and primary interest was in the enrichment of individual personal experience. He judged all institutions by the impact they had on the quality of the lives of
individual persons. His trenchant criticism of both capitalism
and, later, socialism as *operating* systems was inspired by his
conviction that they failed to provide sufficient opportunities
for ordinary persons, who lacked the advantages of inherited
natural and social privileges, to develop themselves. He had

the same faith as the poet, Gray, that among the multitudes was many a "mute and inglorious Milton" whose inability to create and enjoy the works of the spirit was due more to lack of opportunity than to the absence of genetic potential. This Jeffersonian faith in experience and the common man pervades everything he wrote in educational and social philosophy. "The evils of the unearned increment are as nothing," he declares, "beside those of the undiscovered resource." His reference here is to the human resource, and to the untapped resources in every human being. He called upon the democratic community to recognize that it was "a natural and necessary part" of its obligation not only to furnish the schooling and instruction required for the intellectual, personal, and moral growth of its children but just as much "to provide such opportunities for adults as will enable them to discover and carry to some point of fulfillment the particular capacities that distinguish them" (p. 92). Dewey's objections to unearned increment, it should be noted in passing, did not flow from a belief in an egalitarianism that leveled everyone down to the same plane of achievement and reward. He felt that where the rewards of life were not commensurate with effort and merit they tended, except in unusual cases, to affect adversely the possibilities of desirable growth on the part of the recipients of such unearned increment. He also believed that increases in the value of land and capital that could be attributed not to individual enterprise and ingenuity but to the growth of the community should be used for social purposes and the enrichment of cultural life.

Today the conception of democracy as a way of life is still regarded as a rhetorical flourish in many quarters proud of their hard-headedness. To them and to many others, democracy is merely a form of uncoerced political behavior which determines who shall govern over others. From the outset of his career democracy to Dewey meant more than a merely political process. It was a moral ideal supreme among other ideals in evaluating social institutions. Capitalism and socialism may as systems of production be judged by their efficiency; as systems of distribution they may be judged by some principle of justice; but as systems of human relations, as cultures, they may also be evaluated, according to Dewey, by the ideal of community. He speaks of "social-ism of the intelligence and of the spirit" and conceives of the ideal school and society as engaged in the "promotion of this socialism of the intangible things of art, science, and other modes of social intercourse." To Dewey this ideal of the community provides a set of criteria that makes him a constructive critic of all types of existing society, since it enables him to say in which direction they should move to become better or worse. "To extend the range and the full-ness of sharing in the intellectual and spiritual resources of the community is the very meaning of the community."

To some there are other meanings of community and if we are to go beyond definition by stipulation, Dewey must offer grounds and evidence for the adequacy of his concep-tion. It would be no exaggeration to say that he attempted to do this in one way or another, sometimes directly, sometimes indirectly, in almost everything he subsequently undertook. From first to last, he was convinced, recognizing the diffi-culties, that it was possible to find a method which would provide a warrant for our judgments of good or bad, right and wrong, comparable to those of the sciences that would enable us to speak with objective, rational authority about social practices and institutions. More than this it was un-reasonable to ask or expect.

How far Dewey succeeded in achieving what he set out to do is still an open question.

Essays

THE EVOLUTIONARY METHOD AS APPLIED TO MORALITY

I. Its Scientific Necessity

I propose in the following papers to deal with the problem of the application of historical method, the group of ideas centering in the term Evolution, to the problem of Morality. A direct study of the development of moral customs or moral theories is not intended. There are questions of method which (in the present state of discussion) seem to be inevitable antecedents to the ultimately more interesting and more important treatment of the actual and concrete moral facts. Difficult as it is to draw any line in the discussion of such a comprehensive matter as evolution, I shall endeavor to steer clear of purely metaphysical problems, however significant they may be in themselves, and confine myself to those aspects of evolutionary theory which have a direct bearing upon the problem of method.

While I shall be compelled to begin with certain very general features of the idea of evolution, I shall attempt to observe the limit just laid down: not carrying the analysis any further than is needful to get surety and clearness in dealing with the method of interpreting morality. The more general discussion is rendered indispensable because we are met at the outset with a *caveat*. We are warned off before we begin. We are told that the nature of moral facts and of evolution is such as to make it impossible to get help from this source.

The argument runs as follows: Facts of morality are of a spiritual nature. The phenomena of conscience are data of value, not of history. To them applies the distinction of degree, higher and lower, not of time, earlier and later. What they are and mean in themselves, not their temporal setting,

[First published in *Philosophical Review* 11 (1902): 107–24, 353–71.]

is the problem. To confound such distinctions is not only to get no help in understanding morality, but to go positively astray; it is to obscure that difference of value which is the unique factor in the case; and to explain away, not to explain, the essential reality. That an historical statement of any spiritual value is a *hysteron proteron*; that analysis of quality or intrinsic character, and tracing of genesis are distinct processes, have become fixed articles in the creed of the contemporary idealist. And no opportunity is lost to rehearse the creed. Many writers would have it that to discuss mind or morality in terms of the historical series, is to evidence such ignorance of rudimentary philosophical distinctions as to argue total unfitness for the task undertaken.

It is this wholesale denial of the possibility of using a given method with any fruitful and positive result, that makes it necessary to ask: What do we intend *in* science by inquiry into origins? and what do we secure *for* science by stating any matter in genetic terms? Is any purpose fulfilled by this mode of attack which is not within the competent jurisdiction of other methods? Possibly the method is abused in practice by its opponents because it is abused in theory by its upholders. The latter may think that through the use of the evolutionary method something is done which is not done, and which cannot be done; and fail to bring out the deep and large service that as matter of fact is rendered. Anyway, before we either abuse or recommend genetic method we ought to have some answers to these questions: Just what is it? Just what is to come of it and how?

An apparently circuitous mode of approach to these questions may be found most direct in the end. I see no way to get an adequate answer without taking up the nature of experimental method in science, and pointing out in what sense it also is a genetic method.

The essence of the experimental method I take to be control of the analysis or interpretation of any phenomenon by bringing to light the exact conditions, and the only conditions, which are involved in its coming into being. Suppose the problem to be the nature of water. By "nature" we mean no inner metaphysical essence; its "nature" is found only by experiencing it. By nature, in science, we mean a knowledge for purposes of intellectual and practical control. Now, water simply as a given fact resists indefinitely and obstinately any direct mode of approach. No amount of scrutiny, no amount of observation of it as given, yields analytic comprehension. Observation but complicates the problem by revealing unsuspected qualities that require additional explanation.

What experimentation does is to let us see into water in the process of making. Through generating water we single out the precise and sole conditions which have to be fulfilled that water may present itself as an experienced fact. If this case be typical, then the experimental method is entitled to rank as genetic method; it is concerned with the manner or process by which anything comes into experienced existence.

Even those willing to admit this, would probably refuse to go further, and hold that the experimental method is in a true sense an historical or evolutionary method. A consideration of the reasons for refusing to take this step will throw light upon the problem. A strictly historical series is unique, not only in any one of its constituent members, but in the particular place it occupies in the series. Its own context is indispensable to its historic character. Now, in the physical world, with which the experimental sciences deal, acts or pairs of terms are not thus limited to any particular temporal part of the series. They occur and recur; and suffer no change of quality by reason of dislocation from a given context. Water is made over and over again, and, so to speak, at any date in the cosmic series. This deprives any account of it of genuinely historic quality.

Another consideration which gives us pause is that the main interest in physical science does not concern the individual case, but certain further and more general results which at once emerge and absorb attention. We have the common saying that the physical sciences are not interested in individual cases as such, but only in general laws. The particular case is taken simply as a sample, or specimen, or instance. It has no worth in itself, but only as a sample. It is only a more or less imperfect illustration of the general relation which is the true object of regard.

An examination of these reasons will, however, lead us

to the conclusion that while in the end we shall still have ground to consider the value of experiment as applied to the physical world to be genetic rather than strictly historical, yet this is due to an abstraction which we have introduced for our own purpose—that of more adequate control. The serial order, taken in itself or as reality, is strictly historical, and it is only by an intellectual abstraction (justified from the end it subserves), that we get pairs of facts which may show up at any point in the series; and thus get ground for attributing to them a generalized or non-historic meaning. Their existence, though not their working value, remains historic.

The problem of origins is, even in the case of the physical world, a strictly specific or individualized matter. We have no way of getting at the origin of water in general. Experiment has to do with the conditions of production of a specific amount of water, at a specific time and place, under specific circumstances: in a word, it must deal with just *this* water. The conditions which define its origin must be stated with equal definiteness and circumstantiality. We have a specific situation in which at a given point in time a particular fact does not present itself, and then another point at which it is found. The problem is just the discovery of the individual conditions which have made the difference at the two historical periods. It is these conditions which define to us the emerging or manifestation of the new fact, and which constitute its "origin." The question is a perfectly determinate, that is, individualized, one. What facts must be present in order that another fact may show itself? Any scientist can easily say today that by causation he means simply a relation of definite antecedence and consequence. Not every scientist, however, seems to have learned the full meaning of the proposition; viz., that the value of the conception is historical, a question of defining the conditions under which a given phenomenon develops.

Moreover, the particular water with which the experimenter actually deals never, as matter of fact, shows itself twice; it never recurs. It has just as much exclusive uniqueness as is possessed by the career of Julius Caesar or Abraham Lincoln. That particular portion of water could never have presented itself at any other portion of the world's history, any more than the life of one of the individuals named could have been lived in exactly the same way at any other epoch. To deny this is simply to fall into the error of the mediaeval realist whom the average scientist is so fond of ridiculing. It is to admit the existence of some generic water which is no water in particular, and yet all waters in general.

Yet, you say, there is a difference. Certainly; but it is a difference of interest, or purpose, not of existence, physical or metaphysical. Julius Caesar served a purpose which no other individual, at any other time, could have served. There is a peculiar flavor of human meaning and accomplishment about him which has no substitute or equivalent. Not so with water. While each portion is absolutely unique in its occurrence, yet one lot will serve our intellectual or practical needs just as well as any other. We can have substitution without loss. Water from the nearest faucet may slake thirst as well as that from the Pierian spring. And what is of more importance to our immediate problem, any one case serves just as well as any other to demonstrate that which is of scientific interest: the process by which water is made, and by which a great body of other and quite dissimilar substances are called into being. We do not care scientifically for the historical genesis of this portion of water: while we care greatly for the insight secured through the particular case into the process of making any and every portion of water. It is this knowledge of process of generation that constitutes the controlled interpretation which is the aim of science.

Hence our final scientific statement assumes the generalized form we are familiar with in physical science, instead of the individualized form we demand of historical science. Hence also the apparent disruption and dislocation from context in the stream of serial reality. The modern logician has correctly apprehended the abstract character of this disjointed result when he says that all universal statements are hypothetical: announcing that when or if certain conditions are given, then certain consequences result, but not categorically asserting the actual existence of the fact as to either antecedent or consequent. When the logician recognizes the full significance of this statement, and of its counterpart that every categorical proposition is enunciated of an individual, he will be ready to admit that statements arrived at by experimental science are of an historical order. They take their rise in, and they find their application to, a world of unique and changing things: an evolutionary universe.

This abstract or hypothetical character should not disguise from us, however, the supreme value of the genetic statement arrived at by experimental science. It reveals to us a process which is operating continuously. Through knowledge of this process, we are enabled to get both intellectual and practical control of great bodies of fact which otherwise would be opaque and recalcitrant. Knowing the process, we can analyze, we can understand, the phenomena of water whenever and however they present themselves. The control, moreover, extends beyond just the water itself. Knowledge of process of genesis becomes an instrument of investigation into, and control over, impure waters; so that we can measure the amount and nature of deviation from the standard. It becomes an active factor, a useful tool in investigating fluids which are not water, and chemical compounds which are not even fluid. There is no putting a limit to the ramifications and applications of the theoretical and technological control afforded us by laying hold of an operative process. It applies not only to what the empirical logician is fond of calling "common" elements and "resembling" cases; but aids us equally in dealing with apparent divergences and discrepancies. Holding the process in its more generic features, we can follow it into its refinements and modifications. By the cumulative method, by bringing together our knowledge of varying processes and of the particular sequence or course of events in each, entire regions otherwise utterly unexplorable are interpreted, and made amenable.

Lest the reader begin to suspect that we have left the matter of the value of evolutionary ideas comprehending morality, let us turn abruptly to that field. I shall endeavor to point out that there is more than analogy, there is an exact identity, between what the experimental method does for our physical knowledge, and what the historical method in a narrower sense may do for the spiritual region: the region of conscious values. My aim is to show that the historical method reveals to us a process of becoming, and thereby brings under intellectual and practical control facts which utterly resist general speculation or mere introspective observation.

History, as viewed from the evolutionary standpoint, is not a mere collection of incidents or external changes, which something fixed (whether spiritual or physical) has passed through, but is a process that reveals to us the conditions under which moral practices and ideas have originated. This enables us to place, to relate them. In seeing where they came from, in what situations they arose, we see their significance. Moreover, by tracing the historical sequence we are enabled to substitute a view of the whole in its concrete reality for a sketchy view of isolated fragments History is for the individual and for the unending procession of the universe, what experiment is to the detached field of physics. We cannot apply artificial isolation and artificial recombination to those facts with which ethical science is concerned. We cannot take a present case of parental care, or of a child's untruthfulness, and cut it into sections, or tear it into physical pieces, or subject it to chemical analysis. Only through history, through a consideration of how it came to be what it is, can we unravel it and trace the interweaving of its constituent parts. History offers to us the only available substitute for the isolation and for the cumulative recombination of experiment. The early periods present us in their relative crudeness and simplicity with a substitute for the artificial operation of an experiment: following the phenomenon into the more complicated and refined form which it assumes later, is a substitute for the synthesis of the experiment.

The value of the earlier stages of any historic evolution is, I repeat, like that of the artificial isolation of a physical fact from its usual context. The transformation of this logical advantage into a matter of superior excellence in the order of existence, is the root of the materialistic fallacy. It is this unjustifiable transference which calls out those protests referred to early in this paper; which have led the idealists to protest against the industry of explaining conscious facts in evolutionary terms. It is assumed that the earlier fact somehow sets the standard of reality and of worth for the entire series. In practice, though not in express formulation, it is assumed that the earlier stages, being "causal," somehow are an exhaustive and adequate index of reality, and that consequently all later terms can be understood only when reduced to equivalent terms. It is this supposed reduction of the later into the earlier, that the idealist rightly holds is not to explain but to explain away; not to analyze but to ignore and deny.

The procedure is the counterpart of the Greek and mediaeval theories of the universe, in assigning differences of value to different parts of space. We have ceased regarding the celestial universe as of higher rank in the hierarchy of being than the terrestrial. Homogeneity of existence in space has become such an integral part of the working apparatus of the modern scientist that he can hardly put himself into the older attitude. Nevertheless, he is quite likely to fall into exactly the same sort of fallacy, when it comes to time instead of space. The earlier is regarded as somehow more "real" than the later, or as furnishing the quality in terms of which the reality of all the later must be stated.

There is, indeed, a point of view from which the earlier in time is of greater value; but it is that of method, not of existence. That which is presented to us in the later terms of the series in too complicated and confused a form to be unravelled, shows itself in a relatively simple and transparent mode in the earlier members. Their relative fewness and superficiality makes it much easier to secure the mental isolation needful.

The fallacy of the standard character of the earlier is so entrenched and widespread that it can hardly be dismissed with brief mention. The simple fact of the case is that the genetic method, whether used in experimental or historical science, does not "derive" or "deduce" a consequent from an antecedent, in the sense of resolving it, or dissolving it, into what has gone before. The later fact in its experienced *quality* is unique, irresolvable, and underived. Water is water with all its peculiar characteristics, *after* the presence of oxygen and hydrogen gas has been shown to be a necessary condition of its generation as much as before. A statement of the conditions under which a given thing shows itself in existence, does not detract one iota from the individual properties of that thing; it does not alter them. This is as true of water or any physical product as it is of the sense of obligation or of any spiritual product. It is not the quality, but the coming into existence with which science deals directly. What is "derived" is just the appearance of the quality, its emerging into experience. The value of apprehending it in terms of its antecedent conditions is, as repeatedly stated, that of control: intellectual control—the ability to interpret both obviously allied facts and divergent facts, showing the same *modus* operating under different conditions; and practical control, ability to get or to avoid an experience of a given sort when we desire.

The fallacy assumes that the earlier datum has some sort of fixity and finality of its own. Even those who assert most positively that causation is a simple matter of antecedent and consequent, are still given to speaking as if the antecedent supplied the sole stamp of meaning and reality to the consequent. If, for example, the earlier stage shows only social instincts on the part of the animal, then, somehow or other, the later manifestations of human conscience are only animal instincts disguised and overlaid. To attribute any additional meaning to them, is an illusion to be banished by a proper scientific view. Now, the earlier fact is no more a finished thing, or completely given reality, than is the later. Indeed, the entire significance of the experimental method is that attention centres upon either antecedent or consequent simply because of interest in a process. The antecedent is of worth because it defines one term of the process of becoming; the consequent because it defines the other term. Both are strictly subordinated to the process to which they give terms, limits.

The analogy with the terms of an algebraic series is more than a metaphor. The earlier terms do not develop the later ones. The earlier term is just as incomprehensible in itself as is the later one. Taken together, they constitute elements in a problem which is solved by discovering a continuous process or course which, individualized by the limiting terms, shows itself first in one form and then in the other. The interest in the generation of water does not terminate with the discovery of H_2 and O. We have also gained significant facts with reference to the H_2 and the O in knowing that when they come together they give water. To know that about them is to know *them* through and in a process, exactly as analyzing water into them explains water in genetic terms. Excepting as H and O are known in this "effect" (and, of course, in other similar ones), they are absolutely unknown—they are an algebraic X and Y.

The reason this matter is not clear to the popular consciousness, as well as to the expert writer, is because an older, purely metaphysical conception of causation survives, according to which the cause is somehow superior in rank and excellence to the effect. The effects are regarded as somehow all inside the womb of cause, only awaiting their proper time to be delivered. They are considered as derived and secondary, not simply in the order of time, but in the order of existence. Materialism arises just out of this fetich-like worship of the antecedent. Writers who ought to know better tell us that if we only had an adequate knowledge of the "primitive" state of the world, if we only had some general formula by which to circumscribe it, we could deduce down to its last detail the entire existing constitution of the world, life, and society. It is pretty clear, however, that in order to have this adequate knowledge of primitive phenomena as "cause," we should have to know everything that has come after as "effect." We do not know what it is as "cause" (that is we do not know it at all), excepting as we know it through its "effects." The entire novel of a penny-a-liner may possibly be deduced from its first chapter, but hardly that of an artist. Our adequate knowledge of the earlier constitution of the stellar universe depends upon the degree in which we are familiar with what as a matter of fact has come since. So the comprehensive world-formula about the operation of certain forces depends absolutely upon the empirical knowledge that as matter of fact certain results take place when certain conditions are present. The formula is a mere summary or shorthand record of the entire historical series—so much for its magic power in deduction and derivation. The mode of reasoning is tautological. Since we know the nature of the antecedent only through the specific consequence, adequate knowledge of primitive conditions can mean nothing else but a complete knowledge of the whole thing from beginning to end. It is surprising how *a priori* the average empiricist becomes the moment he takes himself to the adoration of causes. He surrenders his belief in a reality apprehended through experience, in behalf of a notion of the superior metaphysical excellence of what he mentally constructs as a bygone existence. He regards the later terms of experience not as real in their experienced character, but as something to be deduced or derived from a reality adequately given in what he is pleased to denominate cause.

So much time has been spent upon the fallacy involved in supposing that the early forms of an historical series are superior to the later, that before passing on I must recur to the proposition on its positive side. It still remains true that the statement of any event or historical series, in terms of its earlier members, has an advantage for science: its logical superiority consists in presenting the matter in so simplified a form that we can detach and grasp separately elements which are wholly lost in the confused complexity of the mature phases. We can single out a particular fact from its company of associates, and give it more exact and more exclusive attention. This is what is meant by saying that history does for moral matters, for matters of conscious value, what experimentation does for physical things: it gives control by furnishing relative isolation.

This also establishes the significance of the later members of the series. Starting with the earlier ones as our clue, we can trace each successive degree of complication as it introduces itself. Having found conditions operating historically by themselves, we can see what happens when these conditions come together. We can refer the more complicated fact to the combination of conditions. Here we have the counterpart of the synthetic recombination, or cumulative method of experiment. We put together the separate threads coming from different sources, and see how they are woven into a pattern so extensive and minute as to defy the analysis of direct inspection.

We should be prepared, from our foregoing discussion,

to see how this superiority and logical value is also given
ontological significance. Just as the materialist isolates and
deifies the earlier term as an exponent of reality, so the
idealist deals with the later term. To him it is the reality of
which the first form is simply the appearance. He contrasts
the various members of the series as possessing different
degrees of reality, the more primitive being nearest zero. To
him the reality is somehow "latent" or "potential" in the
earlier forms, and, gradually working from within, transforms them until it finds for itself a fairly adequate expression. It is an axiom with him that what is evolved in the
latest form is involved in the earliest. The later reality is,
therefore, to him the persistent reality in contrast with which
the first forms are, if not illusions, at least poor excuses for
being. We are all familiar with these applications of the
Aristotelian metaphysics to the evolutionary process. We are
not concerned here with the metaphysical problems involved,
though they are serious enough: as the notion that the real
somehow chooses an imperfect mode or vehicle of expression
for itself, and only after a long series of more or less abortive
attempts succeeds in showing itself as the reality. It is
enough for present purposes to note that we have here
simply a particular case of the general fallacy just discussed—the emphasis of a particular term of the series at
the expense of the process operative in reference to all terms.

Both the earlier and the later are simply limits which
define the process in question. They are the framework
which gives it outline; they are the terms which characterize
the problem to be attacked. The introduction of more detailed
intermediate terms, together with a statement of their exact
temporal and quantitative relations to each other, fill out the
outline. They give us finally a complete whole, constituted
by members standing in orderly and consecutive relations to
each other.

Just as experiment transforms a brute physical fact into
a relatively luminous series of changes, so evolutionary
method applied to a moral fact does not leave us either with
a mere animal instinct on one side, or with the spiritual
categoric imperative on the other. It reveals to us a single
continuing process in which both animal instinct and the

sense of duty have their place. It puts us in possession of a concrete whole.

The analogy with modern biological interests is significant. There was a time when units of fixed structure seemed alone to have importance. They, by simple physical juxtaposition and combination, were supposed to account for all more complex forms and functions. For logical purposes it makes no difference whether these units are "cells" with relation to the organism as a whole, or brain "centres" with reference to certain neural functions. Some peculiar property was supposed to be resident in these units, which somehow controlled or explained other activities and structures. Now, morphology is ceasing to lord it over physiology; and physiology is ceasing to be a mere matter of certain functions. It is a chemico-physical process operating wherever we have organized structure and the performance of function that is the subject of scientific attention. The problem is to discover and analyze this process, and then trace its different modes of operation as it presents itself under a variety of conditions; these conditions being stated definitely through experimental control. Just as the biologist is surrendering the attempt to locate his reality in one spot rather than another, in the cell as such, or the brain centre as such, so the moralist must cease trying to find the key to his problem in the animal instinct as such; and as the biologist has ceased taking a function as ultimate and self-explanatory, so the moralist must cease discussing the refined moral consciousness of civilization as final. He must turn to the moralizing process which operates continuously, and endeavor to account for its different manifestations under differentials of condition historically presented.

This whole matter may indeed be summed up in terms of the conception of causation. If we assume the meaning of this notion to be a relation of antecedent and consequent, we cannot play fast and loose with it. The cause is not merely an antecedent; it is *what* it is *as* antecedent, and cannot be regarded as real when severed from that which succeeds it. The same holds of the consequent—it is what it is only as a term in the series. But we do more than place the antecedent and consequent. We get the continuous reality. And then

the entire series, the defined and historic event, is itself
employed to interpret and construct a larger realm of experience. Through the series we better apprehend the universe. It is that which is characterized by and through such
a history. The historic consequence is a predicate of a new
subject.

We get a more thorough and adequate experience of the
antecedents, H and O, and of the consequent, water, in finding out how water is generated. But we do not stop at this
point. The entire sequence to which both antecedence and
consequence belong, becomes an important factor in realizing
the nature of the world in which such an event takes place.
Our drama becomes in turn a significant episode in a larger
drama. So in moral matters we comprehend both the animal
instinct and the human categorical imperative when we place
them as limiting terms of a single continuous history. But
over and above this, we understand better the universe,
knowing that it is of a kind to be marked by such a history.
It is in the light of such a more ultimate judgment, made
possible by the evolutionary method, that we see how limited
is the view that tells us that history can only speak of certain
external things that have happened to morality; can trace
its outward fortunes, but reveal nothing of its nature. It
shows us morality in the position which it occupies in the
universe; in the situations that demand it.

Having found in the apprehension of process the reality
which eludes us when we look for it either in earlier or later
terms, we have to be careful to avoid a further error, viz.:
*the confusion of continuity of process with identity of con-
tent.* The following quotations illustrate the error to which
I refer: We may "raise the single inductive inquiry, What
acts have men everywhere and at all times considered right
or wrong respectively, and what acts have some considered
right or indifferent and others wrong? Tables of agreement
and difference can be drawn up to show what mankind at
least has regarded as the essential content of the moral
law. . . . For the rich harvest which this treatment of the
moral field is sure to yield, we shall have to wait until the
spirit of science has exorcised the spirit of speculation from
our contending schools of ethics" (Schurman, *The Ethical*

Import of Darwinism, pp. 205, 206). "The science of historical ethics is still too young to have established what moral principles are ultimate and fundamental—that is, what principles man everywhere and at all times has considered binding" (*Ethical Import*, pp. 255–56).

The implication of the quotations is that the scientific method is concerned with the abstraction of a certain common and unchanging content—that it is on the lookout for some duty or duties that have been regarded at all times and in all places as equally binding. I seize upon this conception because it is sufficiently near the proposition just presented to make it worth while to indicate the difference between them. I have insisted that the scientific method is concerned with the discovery of a common and continuous process, and that this can be determined only historically. The notion now propounded is that science is concerned with a common content or structure of beliefs, and this can be apprehended historically. I do not find, however, that it is identity of content which is important, either theoretically or practically. On the contrary, the method of comparison and abstraction which leaves us with simply a fixed common element apart from all diversity and variety, gives a mere *caput mortuum*, rigidly static, arbitrary, a residuum without explanation. Practically, it gives us no leverage for what is the most important thing—control.

Doubtless it is true that other historical sciences have passed through a "comparative" period in which the discovery of a common element of structure was taken to be the object of search; but the other sciences have left that point of view far behind. The comparative anatomist knows very well that external similarity is no guarantee of identity of function, or of homologous organs; and that like functions may be exercised through modes of structure which externally are characterized by the most profound and extensive differences. The same is true of the comparative philologist. It is only in the region of consciousness, in discussing myths, rites, institutions, and moral practices, that the idea persists that the important thing is to hit upon some structure which is everywhere alike. The advance which has taken place in the biological and quasi-biological sciences is sure to take place in the social sciences as well. What the biologist instinctively searches for (given as data a variety of different forms or species, with the problem of tracing their relationship) is first a common ancestor. This furnishes a point of departure and supplies one limiting term of the series under consideration. The present differentiated forms furnish the other limiting term. The problem is to discover the single process which, operating under definitely different conditions, has manifested itself in these specifically different outward forms. Knowledge of differences is just as important as that of the generic identity of the process. The function of locomotion is a mere abstraction, excepting as we can trace and define its performance through environmental conditions that give rise equally to the legless snake, the fins of the fish, the wings of the bird, and the legs of the quadruped. It is only through insight into diversification that the hold upon the process becomes vital and concrete. Similarly in morals. Supposing (which does not seem to be the case) that an identical belief regarding the duty of parental care, or of conjugal fidelity, could be discovered in human societies at all times and places. This would throw no light whatsoever upon the scientific significance of that phenomenon. On the other hand, an adequate knowledge of historical facts might throw great light upon the ethics of family relations, exhibited in complete neglect of children as well as in self-sacrificing devotion to their welfare, and in all stages of regard and disregard of personal faithfulness as between husband and wife. The very differences of belief become significant when they can be referred to varying conditions which have brought them about.

Just one word on the practical side. The common and rigidly fixed content gives no help regarding the future. It gives no indication of the method of progress in any desired direction. There is no way of turning it over into a mode of control of future experience, either in corporate action or individual education. It is just a bare isolated final fact. If any use at all could be made of it, the tendency would be to lower the working standard of moral action in all more advanced societies. By hypothesis, it furnishes only the duty which is common to the lowest with the highest. The essence of moral struggle and of moral progress lies, however, precisely in that region where sections of society, or groups of individuals, are becoming conscious of the necessity of ideals of a higher and more generalized order than those recognized in the past. To fix upon that which has been believed everywhere, and at all times "as the essential content of the moral law," would give practical morality a tremendous set-back.

The previous discussion may be summarized as follows: The object of science is primarily to give intellectual control—that is, ability to interpret phenomena—and secondarily, practical control—that is, ability to secure desirable and avoid undesirable future experiences. Second, experiment accomplishes this in physical sciences. It takes an unanalyzed total fact which in its totality must simply be accepted at its face value, and shows the exact and exclusive conditions of its origin. By this means it takes it out of its opaque isolation and gives it meaning by presenting it as a distinct and yet related part of a larger historic continuum. Third, the discovery of the process becomes at once an instrument for the interpretation of other facts which are explainable by reference to the process operating under somewhat different conditions. Fourth, the significance of conscious or spiritual values cannot be made out by direct inspection, nor yet by direct physical dissection and recomposition. They are, therefore, outside the scope of science except so far as amenable to historic method. Fifth, history gives us these facts in process of becoming or generation; the earlier terms of the series provide us with a simplification which is the counterpart of isolation in physical experiment; each successive later term answers the purpose of synthetic recombination under increasingly complex conditions. Sixth, a complete historical account of the development of any ethical idea or practice would not only enable us to interpret both its cruder and more mature forms, but—what is even more important—would give us insight into the operations and conditions which make for morality, and thus afford us intellectual tools for attacking other moral facts. Seventh, in analogy with the results flowing in physical sciences from intellectual control, we have every reason to suppose that the successful execution of this mode of approach would yield also fruit in practical control: that is, knowledge of means by which individual and corporate conduct might be modified in desirable directions. If we get knowledge of a process of generation, we get knowledge of how to proceed in getting a desired result.

I have endeavored in this paper simply to show that either morality must remain outside the sphere of science, or be approached and attacked by the historical method. This is what I mean by the "necessity" of this method. It still remains open to an objector to take the first of the alternatives, and hold that morality is not open to any sort of scientific treatment, and that it is essential to its existence as morality that it should not be so treated. In other words, I have not as yet discussed directly the question of what the bearing of the application of the historical method, as scientific mode of approach, is upon the value or validity of distinctively moral phenomena. To that problem, accordingly, my next article will be devoted. What does this method do for morality as morality, and how? I shall endeavor to show that the method not only does not destroy distinctively ethical values, but that it supplies them with an added sanction.

II. Its Significance for Conduct

In a preceding paper,[1] I attempted to show that only by the use of evolutionary ideas, that is, the historical method, can morality be brought within the domain of science. That discussion, however, did not develop the implied bearings of the presented theory upon distinctively moral values and validities. If we suppose for the moment that scientific treatment would follow the general lines indicated, what would be the influence of such a treatment upon morality as such? Would it leave moral quality unaffected—just where it was? Would it lessen or destroy the moral meaning as such? Or would it intensify and expand ethical significance, giving an added meaning and an added sanction?

1. *Philosophical Review*, March 1902.

Before directly taking up these questions, it is necessary to dispose of a certain ambiguity and confusion. I am convinced that in much recent discussion about validity or objective value, writers have taken up indiscriminately two different standpoints, and passed unwittingly from one problem to another and quite different matter. One question is this: What is the validity of the moral point of view as such? Or, in the form which contemporary thought makes most urgent: How is the validity of the moral point of view, with its insistence upon standards, ideals, responsibilities, to be reconciled with the validity of the scientific point of view and its insistence upon the presented, upon facts, upon the causal? A distinct question is the following: How is the validity of a given moral point of view or judgment determined? This judgment about capital punishment is morally valid; that one is ethically incompetent. This point of view regarding temperance, expansion, the silver question, or ganized charity, etc., is true—that is, has superior objective value—compared with some other point of view. Or, the judgment "I should follow my artistic bent, even if it interferes with existing filial relations," is correct.

Now, ethical science is primarily concerned with problems of validity in the latter sense. It belongs to logic, to the theory of points of view, the categories, and of the methods that develop these points of view, to discuss the validity of morality *überhaupt*. The scientist as such is not directly concerned with matters of ultimate validity; neither, however, is he taken up with mere presented facts. His fundamental and interesting problem is that of ways of passing upon questions of specific validity; ways of determining the respective values of this or that particular judgment. The extent to which philosophical writers adopt and repeat the propositions of empirical writers, developed before objective science had made much headway, is surprising. It is not bare description of given facts that constitutes the work of the scientist; but discovering, testing, and elaborating adequate modes of *finding out what is really given*; adequate modes of describing and defining what is thus laid bare.

This ought to be too trivial, too commonplace to mention, but current arguments against the use of historical methods in ethics indicate the need not only of mention but of stress. The opponent argues thus: It is of course true that morality has a history; that is, we can trace different moral practices, beliefs, customs, demands, opinions, in various forms of outward manifestation. We can say that here such and such moral practices obtained, and then gave way in this point or that. This indeed is a branch of history, and an interesting one. As history it is mere truism to say that it will receive scientific treatment just in the degree in which all the resources of historic method are called into action. But when this is said and done the result remains history, not ethics. What ethics deals with is the moral worth of these various practices, beliefs, etc.; and this question of worth is a totally different matter from existence in a temporal series, and from the accurate description of serial order. The historian of ethics can at most supply only data; the distinctive work of the ethical writer is still all to be done. And we may imagine the objector going on to add the stock phrases: History is descriptive, it deals with the given, the actual, the phenomenal. Ethics is normative, it wants to know about the standard, the ideal, that which ought to be, whether or no it is or ever has been.

In my judgment the objector is here entangled in the looseness and vagueness of his own analysis. He has not discriminated the two meanings of validity. He is arguing that because a genetic or historic account does not determine *ab initio* the moral point of view as such, therefore it is not necessary to the right determination of questions of specific value—an obvious *mutatio conclusionis*.[2]

Because history does not create off-hand, so to speak,

2. There is of course a more fundamental problem: whether the validity of the moral categories *as such* can be adequately treated apart from that of specific validities. There is at least a working presumption that the logic which deals with the question of validity and truth in general must get its material by considering the specific criteria and modes of verification used in settling matters of truth and worth in particular instances. It is difficult to see, for example, just how the logic of the theoretic sciences can discuss the possibility of the intellect reaching truth at large, severed from the problem of the methods which the special sciences use in discriminating truth from error in their own special provinces.

moral validity, it hardly follows that an adequate knowledge of historical development is not quite indispensable to the successful pursuit of the task of deciding upon validity in this and that special case. At times it would seem as if the objector went even further in his confusion; it would almost appear that he confounds history as an objective succession of events with history as the rational account and interpretation of these events; history as bare fact and history as method. It might be true that objective history does not create moral values as such, and yet be true that there is no way of settling questions of valid ethical significance in detail apart from historical consideration. In any case, whatever deserves the name of history is more than an inventory of practices, beliefs, and opinions. It is concerned with the origin and development of these customs and ideas; and with the question of their mode of operation after they have arisen. The described facts—yes; but among the facts described are precisely certain conditions under which various norms, ideals, and rules of action have originated and functioned. A continual pigeon-holing of such consideration as mere "description" becomes irritating when it assumes that the description cannot go beyond the *prima facie* and obvious appearance of the material dealt with; that it just goes heaping up more and more such unexplained and uninterpreted data. This no more supplies the general content of historic science than the first appearance of the world to our senses is the significant content of physical science. All this is only material to be described; not the described material. Its worth is to furnish data and present problems, suggest working hypotheses, and supply the material through which they may be tested.

The historic method is a method, first, for determining how specific moral values (whether in the way of customs, expectations, conceived ends, or rules) came to be; and second, for determining their significance as indicated in their career. Its assumptions are that norms and ideals, as well as unreflective customs, arose out of certain situations, in response to the demands of those situations; and that once in existence they operated with a less or greater meed of success (to be determined by study of the concrete case).

We are still engaged in forming norms, in setting up ends, in conceiving obligations. If moral science has any constructive value, it must provide standpoints and working instrumentalities for the more adequate performance of these tasks. Are we to say that the urgent problem of the present right determination of standards and aims can be solved when we cut loose from a consideration of the past? Shall we say that a defined and critical knowledge of the origin, history, and destiny of such matters in the past life of humanity is aside from the mark in our present situation?

To adopt such a standpoint, even by implication, is to commit ourselves to two assumptions: first, that while there may have been rationality in past moral beliefs and practices, there is no such rationality as to the present and the future. In other words, it is assumed that while moral attitudes of mankind have hitherto arisén in relation to a definite situation, the present is quite in the air, and hence judgment of it cannot be directed. Secondly, it is assumed that a knowledge of how norms and moral endeavors have been brought about in the past throws no light upon the intrinsic process of moralization. For my part, I am not presumptuous enough to venture upon such notions; I would have those who deny moral significance to the historical method show how we may guide and control the formation of our further moral judgments if we forego inquiry into the process of their formation as historically set before us.

In these introductory words, I do not suppose myself to have shown that the historic method has a settled moral significance that at once facilitates conduct and gives it an added sanction by introducing more rationality; but I hope at least to have cleared up somewhat the real point at issue, and to have shown the irrelevancy of some of the current, rather peremptory, modes of disposing of the genetic standpoint in morals.

The problem of the best method of arriving at correct judgments on points of moral worth, necessarily traverses ground covered by the time-honored and time-worn theories of intuitionalism and empiricism. Even at the risk of threshing old straw, it will be advisable to compare the evolutionary method with these other points of view. In such a comparison, however, it is to be borne in mind that the sole point under review is that of the logical relationship of the theory examined to the meaning and sanction of our moral judgments. The question is not whether or no there are intuitions; whether or no they can be utilized in special cases, or whether or no all supposed intuitions can be accounted for as products of associative memory. The problem is not one of fact but of value. It is a logical problem. If we suppose such necessary and universal beliefs as go by the name of "intuition" to exist, does such existence settle anything regarding the validity of what is believed, either in general or in part? It is a question of the relation of the intuition to fact— to the moral order in reality. Under what conditions alone, and in what measure or degree, are we justified in arguing from the existence of moral intuitions as mental states and acts to facts taken to correspond to them?

The reply already hinted at is that the mere existence of a belief, even admitting that as a belief it cannot in any way be got rid of, determines absolutely nothing regarding the objectivity of its own content. The worth of the intuition depends upon genetic considerations. In so far as we can state the intuition in terms of the conditions of its origin, development, and later career, in so far we have some criterion for passing judgment upon its pretentions to validity. If we can find that the intuition is a legitimate response to enduring and deep-seated conditions, we have some reason to attribute worth to it. If we find that historically the belief has played a part in maintaining the integrity of social life, and in bringing new values into it, our belief in its worth is additionally guaranteed. But if we cannot find such historic origin and functioning, the intuition remains a mere state of consciousness, a hallucination, an illusion, which is not made more worthy by simply multiplying the number of people who have participated in it.

Put roughly we may say that intuitionalism, as ordinarily conceived, makes the ethical belief a brute fact, because unrelated. Its very lack of genetic relationship to the situation in which it appears condemns it to isolation. This isolation logically makes it impossible to credit it with objective validity. The intuitionalist, in proclaiming the necessity of his content, proclaims thereby its objective reference; but in asserting its non-genetic character he denies *any* reference whatsoever. The genetic theory holds that the content embodied in any so-called intuition is a response to a given active situation: that it arises, develops, and operates somehow in reference to this situation. This functional reference establishes in advance some kind of relationship to objective conditions, and hence some presumption of validity. If the "intuition" persists, it ,is within certain limits because the situation persists. If the particular moral belief is really inexpugnable, it is just because the conditions which require it are so enduring as to persistently call out an attitude which is relevant to them. The probability is that it continues in existence simply because it continues to be necessary in function.

The presumption or probability, however, must not be pushed too far. It is a well-known fact that habits endure and project themselves after the conditions which originally generated them pass over, and that under such circumstances the habits become sources of error and even of hallucination. Indeed the most generic psychological statement that we have of illusions is that a psycho-physical disposition in conformity with the state of the case in the great majority of instances asserts itself by the principle of habit, when some of the conditions are radically different, and thus produces a judgment whose content does violence to the facts of the particular case.

The point of the genetic method is then that it shows relationships, and thereby at once guarantees and defines meaning. We must take the history of any intuition or attitude of moral consciousness in both directions: both *ex parte ante* and *ex parte post*. We must consider it with reference to the antecedents which evoked it, and with reference to its later career and fate. It arises in a certain context, and as a reaction to certain circumstances; it has a subsequent history which can be traced. It maintains and reinforces certain conditions, and modifies others. It becomes a stimulus which provokes new modes of action. Now when we see how and why the belief came about, and also know what else came about because of it, we have a hold upon the worth of the belief which is entirely wanting when we set it up as an isolated intuition. Pure intuitionalism is often indeed undistinguishable from the crassest empiricism. The "intuition" is declared to be a content of "reason," but reason is a mere label. The ordinary relation and criteria of rationality are expressly eliminated. Quite likely we have deified the results of a merely accidental history or series of circumstances. The only way to introduce reasonableness is to analyze in detail the course of events from which the intuition results, and to trace in further detail the influences that radiate from it. There is much ground for John Stuart Mill's basis of opposition to intuitionalism—that it tends to perpetuate prejudice and sanctify conservatism by calling them eternal truths of reason, and thus to erect barriers in the way of moral progress.

A given belief or intuition represents, as regards its content, a cross-section of an historic process. No wonder it becomes meaningless and obstructive when the static section is taken as if it were a complete and individualized reality. Any morphological section becomes significant in itself, and heuristic with reference to further scientific activity, just in the degree in which it is employed along with other cross-sections, before and after, in constructing a continuous process or life-history.

Every intuitionalist admits that as matter of fact the supposed content of the intuitions has in some cases at least varied from time to time. This point is familiar as an objection of fact against intuitionalism. Its logical significance is however even more important.

This admission condemns, as a nugatory pretense, the claim to objective validity on the part of every intuition. If we are mistaken in one case, we may be in others, since by definition any standard outside the intuition as such is excluded. Either everything that appears to the individual as final and authoritative is such, or else such appearance lacks competency in any case. Intuitionalism is Protagorean in its belief that man's ideas are the measure of moral realities. If the intuitionalist falls back upon the notion of the inexpugnable, he falls back simply upon a question of bare fact. How much time is to be allowed? Certainly the life of the individual occupies but a brief span in the continuity of conscious social life in which it is imbedded. Beliefs that are inexpugnable for a given individual, or for a series of generations, or even for an entire nationality, finally fade away. According to the test of inexpugnableness this would show that they were never intuitions, and hence never objectively valid—*ex hypothesi*. Viewed in this way, the contents of our present moral beliefs become objects of suspicion. Intuitionalism at one stroke transforms itself into scepticism. What guarantee have we that our present "intuitions" have more validity than hundreds of past ideas that have shown themselves by passing away to be empty opinion or indurated prejudice? In denying genesis and history to have objective worth, we make the whole history of moral belief an illusion—a vain shew. The same logic that makes necessary the rejection of former moral ideas as not really intuitions, and hence of no moral worth at all, cuts the ground out from under any and every moral belief.

On the other hand, the genetic theory ascribes a certain positive moral validity to any belief that has arisen as a persistent response to a situation, while at the same time it enables us to measure, through tracing its later career and destiny, the range of worth attaching to it. The genetic method grades worth, instead of compelling us either to consecrate or damn it *in toto*. Take as a special and test case the matter of the value of human life. Savage tribes almost universally practice infanticide. They do so not only without a thought of its immorality, but in many cases, and up to a certain extent, in recognition of a supposed obligation. Their moral "intuitions" inform them that the welfare of the older and vigorous members of a group is to be preferred to that of the decrepit and feeble—that the latter are a burden to the well-being of the community, and hence to be eliminated. Now the theory which denies a certain positive value genetically measured to this belief, by its own dialectic also deprives us of any reason for attributing positive ethical significance to the moral aspirations of today. A theory which regards infanticide in the light of a reaction to its own set of historic conditions may, by investigating these conditions, give a relative justification to the idea. It may also, by tracing its later and continuing effects, finally condemn it. It may see how its persistence left a group stranded on a lower level, and how its passing away coincided with and conditioned a more complex and richer social order. The investigation may, indeed it should, reveal principles of the moralizing process which give better control of the moral beliefs and practices of today.

Infanticide arises in nomadic peoples; the tribes are nomadic just because the necessity of getting food keeps them on the move from place to place. This very necessity makes impossible the settled abode with the ties and attachments which spring up about it. It keeps all the institutional relations of life loose and superficial. Moreover, to a nomadic people everything that has to be carried about is a burden. Every infant is not only such a burden, but is an additional drain upon the scanty food resources of his community. Moreover, the burden of transportation falls upon the woman, and the woman is already laden with all the camp equipment and utensils. The food supply is so precarious that the older babies, in order to make sure of life, are long suckled at the breast, frequently for four or five years. To try and feed the new baby is possibly to starve the old. Moreover, in the encampment the woman has many duties put upon her in order that the man may be free to hunt. These duties can hardly be adequately performed if many little children are demanding attention.

Needless to say, the question is not one of justifying infanticide. The genetic or historic consideration reveals, however, that in the rough the same sort of moral process is at work in the savage society as in the civilized. The fundamental question in any case is the paramount conditions of social existence. Let the social situation be such that more value comes to life from preserving and caring for the tender, helpless, and feeble, than from ignoring them, and their nurture will be a moral duty. Let this preservation become a tax, and even a threat against the integrity of the community life, and an opposite belief and practice are set up.

The same method which gives a relative justification to the "intuition," also forbids its continuance. Such justification as it gets is in its relativity to a given type of social life.

That type, however, is so crude and undeveloped as compared with other forms we are familiar with, that it cannot be tolerated. The demand for doing away with infanticide is just the same as its justification: that it is consistent with a certain type of life. It not only arises within it, but tends to perpetuate it.

Now if we turn our gaze to the present social life we find precisely the same situation. Our moral code does not permit us intentionally to expose, nor willfully to destroy, the infant and the aged. It does permit us, however, to condemn hundreds and thousands of little children, as well as grown people, to sickly, stunted, and defective lives, physical as well as mental. To be sure this state of things is attacked as immoral by many social reformers, but the general attitude is one of comparative indifference, sometimes indeed of irritation with the visionaries who endeavor to stir up dissatisfaction, or even of indignation with them as imperiling the foundations of society. Not that the condemnation of children to a partial life is in and of itself a necessary pillar of society, but that it is a necessary incident of a whole industrial order which cannot be attacked without shaking society. In other words, there is at bottom a belief simply in the necessity of these things to the conservation and maintenance of the established social type. And this is precisely the reason the savage would appeal to in defense of his infanticide if he were capable of reflective thought. Very much the same thing can be said about our practice of war, and the necessity that war implies the offering up a sacrifice of so many thousands of human lives every year. Such things are simply "necessary"; and hence our impatience with or contempt for those who proclaim their radical immorality. Hence our zeal in idealizing, and in imputing moral qualities of patriotism, bravery, etc.

The point here, as in the case of infanticide, is neither merely to glorify nor condemn the thing in and of itself, but rather to get back to the general movement of society which produces these particular ethical symptoms; and in turn to trace in more detail their historic consequences, realizing in detail to what extent they tend to perpetuate undeveloped and inadequate social forms.

The illustration suggests that the import of the argument is wider than just the question of intuitionalism. The problem is the criterion for the validity of any moral idea prevalent in society at a given time. The conclusion is that a genetic treatment places any such belief in relation both to the circumstances which generate it, and the effects which it produces, and thereby gets us out of the region of mere opinion, sentimentality, and prejudice. This possibility of objective judgment is the scientific phase of the matter. But the fact, that this control of judgment of the worth or lack of worth in current moral beliefs at once modifies the beliefs and determines the development of new ones, shows that the scientific method has of itself a moral value: it determines and enforces fundamental moral motives and sanctions. It is an intrinsic factor in controlling the formation of moral judgments, and this is a part of the evolution of moral ideals and standards.

The relation of the genetic method to empiricism, so far as the matter of moral validity is concerned, requires attention. Fortunately, the notion that intuitionalism and empiricism exhaust the alternatives no longer universally obtains. We are getting aware that it is quite possible to conceive ideas and values as arising in and with reference to experience; and yet hold that empiricism, being just one mode of logical interpretation, gives a faulty and distorted account of them. Fortunately, moreover, (for our argument is already getting too long) it is not necessary to examine the whole scope of empirical method. Only two points concern us here: one, the relation of the empirical method to the genetic method; the second, a comparison of their bearings upon the question of determining worth in our ethical judgments.

Empiricism is no more historic in character than is intuitionalism. Empiricism is concerned with the moral idea or belief as a grouping or association of various elementary feelings. It regards the idea simply as a complex state which is to be explained by resolving it into its elementary constituents. By its logic, both the complex and the elements are isolated from an historic context. The genetic method determines the worth or significance of the belief by considering the place that it occupied in a developing series; the empirical method by referring it to its components. Elementary feelings or sensations, as the empiricist deals with them, have no inherent or intrinsic time reference at all. Such reference is a purely external matter that attaches to the accidental way in which one of these elements happens to fall in with others; accidental because its position of antecedence or consequence is something lying wholly outside of the element itself. While the genetic method finds quality or meaning to be essentially a function of position in the historic series, the empirical method holds that reality and hence validity can be got at only by dissolving the bonds of temporal connection, and getting to a residual experience which is self-existent and self-sufficing.

The empirical and the genetic methods thus imply a very different relationship between the moral state, idea, or belief, and objective reality. From the genetic standpoint, the moral idea is essentially an attitude that arises in the individual in response to the practical situation in which he is involved. It is the estimate the individual puts upon that situation. It is a certain way of conceiving it or interpreting it with reference to the exigencies of action. Accordingly, it operates as a method of reconstructing the situation through the act indicated. It arises as a response to a stimulus, and its worth is found in its success, as response, in doing the particular work demanded of it, not in the extent to which it parallels or reproduces the precise conditions which evoke it. The idea of withdrawing the hand may be an adequate response to the perception of a flame. The idea, however, is not an impression of the object. In like manner the notion of giving an accused man a chance to justify himself may be an adequate response to the stimulus of capture and presumed guilt. And yet it in no way depends for its reality upon being a mere impress of the existing state of affairs. The test of its worth is its capacity to regulate the various factors entering into the situation. The empirical theory holds that the idea arises as a reflex of some existing object or fact. Hence the test of its objectivity is the faithfulness with which it reproduces that object as copy. The genetic theory holds that the idea arises as a response, and that the test of its validity is found in its later career as manifested with reference to the needs of the situation that evoked it.

The difference again may be stated as follows: The empirical method holds that the belief or idea is generated by a process of repetition or cumulation; the genetic method by a process of adjustment. We need only refer to Spencer's account of the way in which various impressions consolidate themselves into moral beliefs or intuitions to see how completely the process is conceived as one of sheer accumulation. This, moreover, lies not in Spencer's personal wish to conceive it that way, but rather in the logic of empiricism itself. Each experience being separate and isolated, due to an impression received from an existent thing, all that remains is for the various images of these experiences to pile up on each other in such a way that the like elements continually reinforce one another, while the unlike ones fade, blur, and are finally effaced. Empiricism can conceive a given experience only as a summation of elements. Here is where its weakness lies, as its intuitional opponents have always felt practically, though they have not always seized the logical point. If a moral belief is simply an accumulation through repeated associations of previously given elements of experience without any essential modification or reconstruction of them, then one of two things is certain: either the original state was inherently ethical in quality—and thus the contention of the intuitionalist is virtually admitted—or else the empiricist is trying to generate the ethical by telescoping into one another purely non-ethical elements. Here is the vulnerable point in empiricism—by its logic change of quality in passage from generating elements to final product must be explained away. It is illusion. But the essence of an historic process is precisely qualitative change in a process, that, as process, is continuous.

The empiricist is compelled to regard an idea as simply an accumulation of particular experiences, because he regards the original experience as an impression whose worth lies in its pictorial accuracy. If we regard the "first" term as a reaction or response, while it is thoroughly and genuinely empirical in character (in the sense of arising wholly within and because of experience and not from any extraneous *a priori* source), yet its business as response is to transcend, not barely to repeat, the quality of experience as previously given or constituted. Its further development consists in such elaborating and transforming of the response as makes it more adequate. Instead of bare consolidation of ready-made elements, there is a series of tentative adjustments which gradually perfect an adaptation.

The logic of the moral idea is like the logic of an invention, say a telephone. Certain positive elements or qualities are present; but there are also certain ends which, not being adequately served by the qualities existent, are felt as needs. Facts as given and needs as demands are viewed in relation to each other because of their common relationship to some process of experience. Tentative reactions are tried. The old "fact" or quality is viewed in a new light—the light of a need—hence is treated in a new way and thereby transformed. The operative factor is the reaction that, while called out in and by experience, transcends by modifying what is already given, instead of simply repeating it and accumulating more qualities of the same sort.

This logical objection can be brought into closer connection with facts by considering the relation of a moral belief to a biological instinct, or a well-formed social custom, which has not yet been brought into the ethical sphere; the empiricist who turns evolutionist without appreciation of the inherent disparity of his logic and the realities of a historic process, holds that conscious customs are generated by the persistence of biological habits, and that moral practices form the cumulative effect of the customs. But more instinctive acts simply make instinct more instinctive; more acts of habit just harden an original custom. It is only through *failure* in the adequate working of the instinct or habit— failure from the standpoint of adjustment—that history, change in quality or values, is made. Simple repetition of acts of caring for the young, however long continued, would not awaken a consciousness of obligation, or of virtue, or of any moral value, as long as the acts were habitually performed— just because there would be no need for a transformation. In so far as definite acts are repeated and consolidated, the original habit or instinct of doing certain things in a certain way is just strengthened. We do not think we "ought" to breathe, though the habit offers a typical instinct of an accumulatively consolidated act. Not by repetition, but by the failure of the purely biological methods of caring for the young, did any new or different attitude need to arise. Some failure of instinct created the demand for a conscious attention to the nurture of the young. Only through this conscious attitude and its tension *against* some instinct could an ethical adaptation arise out of a physiological adaptation. Experience as it *has* been, experience in its given or constituted form, as such, is absolutely insufficient in generating any moral belief. Either it is so coherent that the moral attitude is unnecessary, or it is so incoherent as to require the moral attitude *as* something different, and *because* different from itself. It is precisely the breakdown which serves as stimulus for qualitatively unlike modes of response, which, in so far as it is maintained in the medium of conscious attention, may be called ethical. The fundamental fallacy of empiricism is found in its failure to recognize negative elements in experience as a stimulus to building up a new experience which transcends the old, because involving its revision in such a way as to make good its needs and lacks. But it is just such change that the historic or genetic method is concerned with.

From this point of view, Huxley's contention of the essential difference and even opposition between the moral and natural gets an intelligible meaning. As I have endeavored to show elsewhere,[3] his claim is not true in the sense that the moral process is to be opposed to the natural process as such. It is valid in that the mere presentation, repetition, or accumulation of the natural just as it is or has been (as a *given* state, the only way in which the empiricist recognizes it) cannot generate anything approximating a moral attitude. It is the lack of adequate functioning in the given adjustments that supplies the conditions which call out a different mode of action; and it is in so far as this is new and different that it gets its standing by transforming or reconstructing the previously existing elements. It is this need and effort of reconstruction which creates the feeling of antagonism or opposition between the old, the natural order, and the new or ethical order—the order which demands that a way of

3. *Monist*, Vol. VIII, p. 321, "Evolution and Ethics" [*Early Works of John Dewey*, 5:34–53].

conceiving or interpreting the situation cease to be *mere* idea, and become a practical construction.

The relevancy of this radical incapacity of the empirical method to deal with historic change, to the question of our grounds for accepting or criticizing moral judgments is obvious—to empiricism the given is the real, and the given is that which resists further analysis. Undoubtedly ethical empiricism has been of great value in the actual development of morality in the last century. It has resolved into "elements" many habits and beliefs around which was gathered an emotional sanctification in such a way as greatly to facilitate their practical breaking-up. It has shown mere custom, prejudice, factitious association, class-interest to be operative in institutions, laws, ways of acting, that claimed moral worth, and has thus been a potent, perhaps the most potent force, in releasing certain tied-up impulses and rendering them available for future organization.

But even this service has had three marked restrictions. Empiricism has had no particular direction to give in furthering the positive organization. It has set free certain tendencies, but the consequent movement of these tendencies has been left again to circumstance and dominant interest. Potent in criticism, empiricism is helpless in construction. In the second place, it has no way of discriminating in its reduction of complete states, practices and ideas into "elements." All ideas and ideals alike give way to its dissolving touch. It is no accident that John Stuart Mill, whose mind was inherently organic and constructive, felt his habit of "inveterate analysis" as a sceptical and destructive influence, and sought to counteract its baneful influence by finding "indissoluble associations," by falling back upon certain "natural" social feelings of an organizing sort, and by nourishing his ideals upon the historic interpretations of Comte and the "German School." It was always open to any writer of less positive and serious moral consciousness, to subject the best working ideas of humanity to the same treatment that, in the hands of James Mill and Jeremy Bentham, was so effective against engrained moral prejudice and class interests masquerading as natural morality and eternal intuitions. And thirdly, thereby, empiricism always and inevitably generates intuitionalism. Someone must come to the rescue of the threatened ideals; and so they are vehemently reasserted as inherently and unrelatedly valid. When dogmatism is necessary in order to protect from dissolution ideas that appear requisite to the better life of humanity, dogmatism may be accounted due; and it arrives with an impetus derived from shock with the theory it opposes. Thus arbitrary reactions and oscillations are substituted for a gradual and controlled development of moral opinion and practice.

Empiricism is thus as absolutistic in its logic as is intuitionalism. Complex ideas, beliefs, practices, are indeed relative, made through associations of elements. But the elements are just *given*, they are fixed, absolute; they are objective determinations, not critical points of a process. And the associations which yoke them are all externally determined also; they are not continuities of an historic growth. The contrast comes out strongly when we compare the typical empiricist's mode of dealing with some apparently absurd custom of a remote people, enforced by that people as sacred obligation, with the historian's treatment of it. The empiricist makes of it a freak, an excrescence from external chance combinations; the historian sees it embedded in the life of the people, historically knit together with its whole body of memories and traditions; carrying, as well as carried by, customs which are involved in the whole scheme of social life. It is not an accident, but a logical necessity, that the historic method arose partly at least in reaction from the arbitrary absolutism of empiricism which made a *tabula rasa* of institutions, customs, organized beliefs, and left in their place untimed, unrelated elements, open to any possible conjunction but demanding none. The historic method is as critical as empiricism; it destroys by explaining, by laying bare, by setting the fact dealt with in its whole context; and mayhap condemning it by showing how obsolete is that situation. But, at the same time, it justifies—relatively. The situation was a reality, it existed in its own time and place, and the fact in question was an integral part of it.

This then is the case for the moral significance of the genetic method: it unites the present situation with its accepted customs, beliefs, moral ideals, hopes, and aspirations, with the past. It sees the moral process as a whole, and yet in perspective. Whatever then can be learned from a study of the past, is at once available in the analysis of the present. It becomes an instrument of inquiry, of interpretation, of criticism as regards our present assumptions and aspirations. Thereby it brings their constitution and formation out into the light as far as may be. It eliminates surds, mere survivals, emotional reactions, and rationalizes, *so far as that is possible at any given time*, the attitudes we take, the ideals we form. Both empiricism and intuitionalism, though in very different ways, deny the continuity of the moralizing process. They set up timeless, and hence absolute and disconnected, ultimates; thereby they sever the problems and movements of the present from the past, rob the past, the sole object of calm, impartial, and genuinely objective study, of all instructing power, and leave our experience to form undirected, at the mercy of circumstance and arbitrariness, whether that of dogmatism or scepticism. To help us see the present situation comprehensively, analytically, to put in our hands a grasp of the factors that have counted, this way or that, in the moralizing of man, that is what the historic method does for us. If our moral judgments were just judgments *about* morality, this might be of scientific worth, but would lack moral significance, moral helpfulness. But moral judgments are judgments of ways to act, of deeds to do, of habits to form, of ends to cultivate. Whatever modifies the judgment, the conviction, the interpretation, the criterion, modifies conduct. To control our judgments of conduct, our estimates of habit, deed, and purpose, is in so far forth to direct conduct itself.

Thus the contention of the previous paper as to the scientific necessity of the genetic or evolutionary method, and of the present paper as to its practical moral significance turn out to be one. Whatever gives scientific control gives of necessity also practical assistance; just because the standpoint is one of continuity of process that knows no separation of past from present.

INTERPRETATION OF SAVAGE MIND

The psychical attitudes and traits of the savage are more than stages through which mind has passed, leaving them behind. They are outgrowths which have entered decisively into further evolution, and as such form an integral part of the framework of present mental organization. Such positive significance is commonly attributed, in theory at least, to animal mind; but the mental structure of the savage, which presumably has an even greater relevancy for genetic psychology, is strangely neglected.

The cause of this neglect I believe lies in the scant results so far secured, because of the abuse of the comparative method—which abuse in turn is due to the lack of a proper method of interpretation. Comparison as currently employed is defective—even perverse—in at least three respects. In the first place, it is used indiscriminately and arbitrarily. Facts are torn loose from their context in social and natural environment and heaped miscellaneously together, because they have impressed the observer as alike in some respect. Upon a single page of Spencer,[1] which I chanced to open in looking for an illustration of this point, appear Kamschadales, Kirghiz, Bedouins, East Africans, Bechuanas, Damaras, Hottentots, Malays, Papuans, Fijians, Andamanese—all cited in reference to establishing a certain common property of primitive minds. What would we think of a biologist who appealed successively to some external characteristic of say snake, butterfly, elephant, oyster and robin in support of a statement? And yet the peoples mentioned present widely remote cultural resources, varied environments and distinc-

1. *Sociology*, I, 57.

[First published in *Psychological Review* 9 (1902): 217–30. Reprinted in *Philosophy and Civilization* (New York: Minton, Balch and Co., 1931), pp. 173–87.]

tive institutions. What is the scientific value of a proposition thus arrived at?

In the second place, this haphazard, uncontrollable selection yields only static facts—facts which lack the dynamic quality necessary to a genetic consideration. The following is a summary of Mr. Spencer's characterizations of primitive man, emotional and intellectual:

He is explosive and chaotic in feeling, improvident, childishly mirthful, intolerant of restraint, with but small flow of altruistic feeling,[2] attentive to meaningless detail and incapable of selecting the facts from which conclusions may be drawn, with feeble grasp of thought, incapable of rational surprise, incurious, lacking in ingenuity and constructive imagination.[3] Even the one quality which is stated positively, namely, keenness of perception, is interpreted in a purely negative way, as a character antagonistic to reflective development. "In proportion as the mental energies go out in restless perception, they cannot go out in deliberate thought."[4] And this from a sensationalist in psychology!

Such descriptions as these also bear out my first point. Mr. Spencer himself admits frequent and marked discrepancies (e.g., Sociology, I, 56, 59, 62, 65, etc.), and it would not be difficult to bring together a considerable mass of proof-texts to support the exact opposite of each of his assertions. But my point here is that present civilized mind is virtually taken as a standard, and savage mind is measured off on this fixed scale.

It is no wonder that the outcome is negative; that primitive mind is described in terms of "lack," "absence": its traits are incapacities. Qualities defined in such fashion are surely useless in suggesting, to say nothing of determining, progress, and are correspondingly infertile for genetic psychology, which is interested in becoming, growth, development.

The third remark is that the results thus reached, even passing them as correct, yield only loose aggregates of unrelated traits—not a coherent scheme of mind. We do not

2. *Sociology*, I, 59, 60, 63, 69, 71.
3. *Sociology*, I, 79, 82, 85–87.
4. *Sociology*, I, 77.

escape from an inorganic conglomerate conception of mind by just abusing the "faculty" psychology. Our standpoint must be more positive. We must recognize that mind has a pattern, a scheme of arrangement in its constituent elements, and that it is the business of a serious comparative psychology to exhibit these patterns, forms or types in detail. By such terms, I do not mean anything metaphysical; I mean to indicate the necessity of a conception such as is a commonplace with the zoologist. Terms like articulate or vertebrate, carnivor or herbivor, are "pattern" terms of the sort intended. They imply that an animal is something more than a random composite of isolated parts, made by taking an eye here, an ear there, a set of teeth somewhere else. They signify that the constituent elements are arranged in a certain way; that in being co-adapted to the dominant functions of the organism they are of necessity co-related with one another. Genetic psychology of mind will advance only as it discovers and specifies generic forms or patterns of this sort in psychic morphology.

It is a method for the determination of such types that I wish to suggest in this paper. The biological point of view commits us to the conviction that mind, whatever else it may be, is at least an organ of service for the control of environment in relation to the ends of the life process.

If we search in any social group for the special functions to which mind is thus relative, occupations at once suggest themselves.[5] Occupations determine the fundamental modes of activity, and hence control the formation and use of habits. These habits, in turn, are something more than practical and overt. "Apperceptive masses" and associational traits of necessity conform to the dominant activities. The occupations determine the chief modes of satisfaction, the standards of success and failure. Hence they furnish the working classifications and definitions of value; they control the desire processes. Moreover, they decide the sets of objects and relations that are important, and thereby provide the

5. We might almost say, in the converse direction, that biological genera are "occupational" classifications. They connote different ways of getting a living with the different instrumentalities (organs) appropriate to them, and the different associative relations set up by them.

content or material of attention, and the qualities that are interestingly significant. The directions given to mental life thereby extend to emotional and intellectual characteristics. So fundamental and pervasive is the group of occupational activities that it affords the scheme or pattern of the structural organization of mental traits. Occupations integrate special elements into a functioning whole.

Because the hunting life differs from, say, the agricultural, in the sort of satisfactions and ends it furnishes, in the objects to which it requires attention, in the problems it sets for reflection and deliberation, as well as in the psychophysic coordinations it stimulates and selects, we may well speak, and without metaphor, of the hunting psychosis or mental type. And so of the pastoral, the military, the trading, the manually productive (or manufacturing) occupations and so on. As a specific illustration of the standpoint and method, I shall take the hunting vocation, and that as carried on by the Australian aborigines. I shall try first to describe its chief distinguishing marks; and then to show how the mental pattern developed is carried over into various activities, customs and products, which on their face have nothing to do with the hunting life. If a controlling influence of this sort can be made out—if it can be shown that art, war, marriage, etc., tend to be psychologically assimilated to the pattern developed in the hunting vocation, we shall thereby get an important method for the interpretation of social institutions and cultural resources—a psychological method for sociology.

The Australian lives in an environment upon the whole benign, without intense or violent unfavorable exhibition of natural forces (save in alternations of drought and flood in some portions), not made dangerous by beasts of prey, and with a sufficient supply of food to maintain small groups in a good state of nutrition though not abundant enough to do this without continual change of abode. The tribes had no cultivated plants, no domesticated animals (save the dingo dog), hence no beasts of burden, and no knowledge or use of metals.[6]

6. All these points are important, for the general hunting psychosis exhibits marked differentiations when developed in relation to

Now as to the psychic pattern formed under such circumstances. How are the sensory-motor coordinations common to all men organized, how stimulated and inhibited into
relatively permanent psychic habits, through the activities
appropriate to such a situation?

By the nature of the case, food and sex stimuli are the
most exigent of all excitants to psycho-physic activity, and
the interests connected with them are the most intense and
persistent. But with civilized man, all sorts of intermediate
terms come in between the stimulus and the overt act, and
between the overt act and the final satisfaction. Man no
longer defines his end to be the satisfaction of hunger as
such. It is so complicated and loaded with all kinds of technical activities, associations, deliberations and social divisions
of labor, that conscious attention and interest are in the
process and its content. Even in the crudest agriculture,
means are developed to the point where they demand attention on their own account, and control the formation and
use of habits to such an extent that they are the central
interests, while the food process and enjoyment as such is
incidental and occasional.

The gathering and saving of seed, preparing the ground,
sowing, tending, weeding, care of cattle, making of improvements, continued observation of times and seasons engage
thought and direct action. In a word, in all post-hunting
situations the end is mentally apprehended and appreciated
not as food satisfaction, but as a continuously ordered series
of activities and of objective contents pertaining to them.
And hence the direct and personal display of energy, personal
putting forth of effort, personal acquisition and use of skill
are not conceived or felt as immediate parts of the food
process. But the exact contrary is the case in hunting. There
are no intermediate appliances, no adjustment of means to
remote ends, no postponements of satisfaction, no transfer

ferocious beasts; in relation to a very sparse or very abundant
food supply; in relation to violently hostile natural forces; and
when hunting is pursued in connection with various degrees of
agriculture or domesticated herds or flocks. For economy of
space, I have omitted reference to the few portions of Australia
where the food supply (generally fish in such circumstances) is
sufficiently abundant to permit quasi-permanent abodes, though
the psychological variations thus induced are interesting.

of interest and attention over to a complex system of acts and objects. Want, effort, skill and satisfaction stand in the closest relations to one another. The ultimate aim and the urgent concern of the moment are identical; memory of the past and hope for the future meet and are lost in the stress of the present problem; tools, implements, weapons are not mechanical and objective means, but are part of the present activity, organic parts of personal skill and effort. The land is not a means to a result but an intimate and fused portion of life—a matter not of objective inspection and analysis, but of affectionate and sympathetic regard. The making of weapons is felt as a part of the exciting use of them. Plants and animals are not "things," but are factors in the display of energy and form the contents of most intense satisfactions. The "animism" of primitive mind is a necessary expression of the immediacy of relation existing between want, overt activity, that which affords satisfaction and the attained satisfaction itself. Only when things are treated simply as *means*, are marked off and held off against remote ends, do they become "objects."

Such immediacy of interest, attention and deed is the essential trait of the nomad hunter. He has no cultivated plants, no system of appliances and tending and regulating plants and animals; he does not even anticipate the future by drying meat. When food is abundant, he gorges himself, but does not save. His habitation is a temporary improvised hut. In the interior, he does not even save skins for clothes in the cold of winter, but cooks them with the rest of the carcass. Generally even by the water he has no permanent boats, but makes one of bark when and as he needs it. He has no tools or equipment except those actually in use at the moment of getting or using food—weapons of the chase and war. Even set traps and nets which work for the savage are practically unknown. He catches beast, bird and fish with his own hands when he does not use club or spear; and if he uses nets he is himself personally concerned in their use.

Now such facts as these are usually given a purely negative interpretation. They are used as proofs of the incapacities of the savage. But in fact they are parts of a very positive psychosis, which taken in itself and not merely measured

against something else, requires and exhibits highly specialized skill and affords intense satisfactions—psychical and
social satisfactions, not merely sensuous indulgences. The
savage's repugnance to what we term a higher plane of life
is not due to stupidity or dullness or apathy—or to any other
merely negative qualities—such traits are a later development
and fit the individual only too readily for exploitation as a
tool by "superior races." His aversion is due to the fact that
in the new occupations he does not have so clear or so intense a sphere for the display of intellectual and practical
skill, or such opportunity for a dramatic play of emotion.
Consciousness, even if superficial, is maintained at a higher
intensity.[7]

The hunting life is of necessity one of great emotional
interest, and of adequate demand for acquiring and using
highly specialized skills of sense, movement, ingenuity,
strategy and combat. It is hardly necessary to argue the first
point. Game and sport are still words which mean the most
intense immediate play of the emotions, running their entire
gamut. And these terms still are applied most liberally and
most appropriately to hunting. The transferred application of
the hunting language to pursuit of truth, plot interest, business adventure and speculation, to all intense and active
forms of amusement, to gambling and the "sporting life,"
evidences how deeply imbedded in later consciousness is the
hunting pattern or schema.[8]

The interest of the game, the alternate suspense and
movement, the strained and alert attention to stimuli always
changing, always demanding graceful, prompt, strategic and
forceful response; the play of emotions along the scale of
want, effort, success or failure—this is the very type, psychically speaking, of the drama. The breathless interest with

7. For good statements by competent authorities of the Australian's
   aversion to agriculture, etc., see Hodgkinson, *Australia, from Port
   Macquarie to Moreton Bay*, p. 243; and Grey, *Two Expeditions*,
   II, 279.
8. See Thomas's "The Gaming Instinct," *American Journal of
   Sociology*, Vol. VI, p. 750. I am indebted to Dr. Thomas
   (through personal conversation as well as from his articles) for
   not only specific suggestions, but for the point of view here presented to such an extent that this article is virtually a joint contribution.

which we hang upon the movement of play or novel are re-
flexes of the mental attitudes evolved in the hunting vocation.

The savage loses nothing in enjoyment of the drama
because it means life or death to him.[9] The emotional interest
in the game itself is moreover immensely reinforced and
deepened by its social accompaniments. Skill and success
mean applause and admiration; it means the possibility of
lavish generosity—the quality that wins all. Rivalry and
emulation and vanity all quicken and feed it. It means sexual
admiration and conquests—more wives or more elopements.
It means, if persistent, the ultimate selection of the individual for all tribal positions of dignity and authority.

But perhaps the most conclusive evidence of the emotional satisfactions involved is the fact that the men reserve
the hunting occupation to themselves, and give to the women
everything that has to do with the vegetable side of existence
(where the passive subject-matter does not arouse the
dramatic play), and all activity of every sort that involves the
more remote adaptation of means to ends—and hence,
drudgery.[10]

The same sort of evidence is found in the fact that, with
change to agricultural life, other than hunting types of action
are (if women do not suffice) handed over to slaves, and the
energy and skill acquired go into the game of war. This also
explains the apparent contradiction in the psychic retrogres-
sion of the mass with some advances in civilization. The
gain is found in the freed activities of the few, and in the
cumulation of the objective instrumentalities of social life,
and in the final development, under the discipline of subjection, of new modes of interest having to do with remoter
ends—considerations, however, which are psychologically
realized by the mass only at much later periods.

As to the high degree of skill, practical and intellectual,

9. Though some writers even say that the savage's interest in the
   game of hunting is so great that he hunts for the excitement
   rather than for food. See Lumholtz, *Among Cannibals,* p. 161
   and p. 191.
10. This collateral development of a different mental pattern in
    women is a matter of the greatest significance, in itself, in its
    relation to subsequent developments and in relation to present
    mental interests.

stimulated and created by the hunting occupation, the case is equally clear—provided, that is, we bear in mind the types of skill appropriate to the immediate adjustments required, and do not look for qualities irrelevant because useless in such a situation.

No one has ever called a purely hunting race dull, apathetic or stupid. Much has been written regarding the aversion of savages to higher resources of civilization—their refusal to adopt iron tools or weapons, for example, and their sodden absorption in routine habits. None of this applies to the Australian or any other *pure* hunting type. Their attention is mobile and fluid as is their life; they are eager to the point of greed for anything which will fit into their dramatic situations so as to intensify skill and increase emotion. Here again the apparent discrepancies strengthen the case. It is when the native is forced into an alien use of the new resources, instead of adapting them to his own ends, that his workmanship, skill and artistic taste uniformly degenerate.

Competent testimony is unanimous as to the quickness and accuracy of apprehension evinced by the natives in coming in contact even for the first time with complicated constructive devices of civilized man, provided only these appliances have a direct or immediate action-index. One of the commonest remarks of travelers, hardly prepossessed in favor of the savage, is their superiority in keenness, alertness and a sort of intelligent good humor to the average English rustic. The accuracy, quickness and minuteness of perception of eye, ear and smell are no barren accumulation of meaningless sense detail as Spencer would have it; they are the cultivation to the highest point of skill and emotional availability of the instrumentalities and modes of a dramatic life. The same applies to the native's interest in hard and sustained labor, to his patience and perseverance as well as to his gracefulness and dexterity of movement—the latter extending to fingers and toes to an extent which makes even skilled Europeans awkward and clumsy. The usual denial of power of continued hard work, of patience and of endurance to the savage is based once more upon trying him by a foreign standard—interest in ends which involve a long series of means detached from all problems of purely personal adjustment. Patience and persistence and long-maintained effort the savage does show when they come within the scope of that immediate contest situation with reference to which his mental pattern is formed.

I hardly need say, I suppose, that in saying these things I have no desire to idealize savage intelligence and volition. The savage paid for highly specialized skill in all matters of personal adjustment, by incapacity in all that is impersonal, that is to say, remote, generalized, objectified, abstracted. But my point is that we understand their incapacities only by seeing them as the obverse side of positively organized developments; and, still more, that it is only by viewing them primarily in their positive aspect that we grasp the genetic significance of savage mind for the long and tortuous process of mental development, and secure from its consideration assistance in comprehending the structure of present mind.

I come now to a brief consideration of the second main point—the extent to which this psychic pattern is carried over into all the relations of life, and becomes emotionally an assimilating medium. First, take art. The art of the Australian is not constructive, not architectonic, not graphic, but dramatic and mimetic.[11] Every writer who has direct knowledge of the Australian corroborees, whether occasional and secular, or state and ceremonial, testifies to the remarkable interest shown in dramatic representation. The reproduction by dances, of the movements and behavior of the animals of the chase is startling. Great humor is also shown in adapting and reproducing recent events and personal traits. These performances are attended with high emotional attacks; and all the accompaniments of decoration, song, music, spectators' shouts, etc., are designed to revive the feelings appropriate to the immediate conflict-situations which mean so much to the savage. Novelty is at a distinct premium; old songs are discarded; one of the chief interests at an intertribal friendly meeting is learning new dance-songs; and acquisition of a new one is often sufficient motive for invitation to a general meeting.

11. There are of course pictures, but comparatively speaking, few and crude. Even the carvings, if originally pictorial, have mostly lost that quality, and become conventional.

The ceremonial corroborees are of course more than forms of art.[12] We have in them the sole exception to the principle that the activities of the hunter are immediate. Here they are weighted with a highly complicated structure of elaborated traditional rites—elaborated and complicated almost beyond belief.[13] But it is an exception which proves the rule. This apparatus of traditionary agencies has no reference to either practical or intellectual control, it gets nowhere objectively. Its effect is just to reinstate the emotional excitations of the food conflict-situations; and particularly to frame in the young the psychic disposition which will make them thoroughly interested in the necessary performances.[14]

It is a natural transition to religion. Totemism and the abundance of plant and animal myths (especially the latter) and the paucity of cosmic and cosmogonic myth testify to the centering of attention upon the content of the combat, or hunting situation. It would be absurd to attempt in a parenthesis an explanation of totemism, but certainly any explanation is radically defective which does not make much of the implication of tribe and animal in the same emotional situation. Hunter and hunted are the factors of a single tension; the mental situation cannot be defined except in terms of both. If animals got away, it is surely because they try; and if they are caught it is surely because after all they are not totally averse—they are friendly. And they seal their friendliness by sharing in one of the most intense satisfactions of life—savory food to the hungry. They are, as a matter of fact, co-partners in the life of the group. Why then should they not be represented as of close kin? In any case, attention and interest centre in animals more persistently than in anything else; and they afford the content of whatever concentrated intellectual activity goes on. The food taboos, with

12. It is, of course, a historic fact that the actual origin of dramatic art (through the Greeks) is in mimetic dances of a festival and ceremonial sort.

13. The best account is of course Spencer and Gillen. Certain ceremonies take weeks.

14. Not, of course, that all these ceremonies are initiatory in character; on the contrary, many are "magical," intended to promote the productivity of their chief food-supplies. But even these were conducted in dramatic fashion, and in such way as to reproduce the emotional disposition involved in the actual occupational life.

their supernatural sanctions, certainly create tensions, or reinstate conflict-situations, in the mind; and thus serve to keep alive in consciousness values which otherwise would be more nearly relegated to the mechanically habitual, or become sensuous, not idealized or emotionalized.

I turn now to matters of death and sickness, their cause, and cure, or, if cure is hopeless, their remedy by expiation. Here the assimilation to the psychosis of the hunting activity is obvious. Sickness and death from sickness are uniformly treated as the results of attacks of other persons, who with secret and strange weapons are hunting their victim to his death. And the remedy is to hunt the hunter, to get the aid of that wonderful pursuer and tracker, the medicine man, who by superior ability runs down the guilty party, or with great skill hunts out the deadly missile or poison lodged in the frame of his victim.

If death ensues, then we have the devices for tracking and locating the guilty party. And then comes actual conflict, actual man-hunting. Death can be avenged only by the ordeal of battle—and here we have the explanation of the wars and war-like performances of which so much has been made. It is, however, now generally admitted that the chief object of these war-like meetings is to reinstate the emotion of conflict rather than to kill. They are, so to speak, pyschological duels on a large scale—as one observer says, they are fights with "a maximum of noise, boast, outward show of courage and a minimum of casualties."[15] But the maneuvering, throwing and dodging that take place are a positive dramatic exercise in the utilities of their occupational pursuits.

Finally, as to marriage, and the relations between the sexes. What was said concerning the impossibility of an adequate account of totemism applies with greater force to the problem of the system of group relationships which determine marital possibilities. It is clear, however, that the system of injunctions and restrictions serves to develop a scheme of inhibitions and intensified stimuli which makes sex-satisfaction a matter of pursuit, conflict, victory and

15. Horn, *Expedition*, Part Four, p. 36.

trophy over again. There is neither complete absence of inhibition, which, involving little personal adjustment, does not bring the sexual sensations into the sphere of emotion as such; nor is there a system of voluntary agreement and affection, which is possible only with a highly developed method of intellectual control, and large outlooks upon a long future. There is just the ratio between freedom and restraint that develops the dramatic instinct, and gives courtship and the possession of women all the emotional joys of the hunt—personal display, rivalry, enough exercise of force to stimulate the organism; and the emotion of prowess joined to the physical sensations of indulgence. Here, as elsewhere in the hunting psychosis, novelty is at a premium, for the mind is dependent upon a present or immediate stimulus to get activity going. It requires no deep scientific analysis to inform us that sex relations are still largely in the dramatized stage; and the play of emotion which accompanies the enacting of the successive stages of the drama gives way to genuine affection and intelligent foresight only slowly through great modifications of the whole educative and economic environment. Recent writers, I think, in their interest on the institutional side of marriage (for we are going through a period of reading back Aryan legal relationships just as we formerly read back Aryan theogonies and mythologies) have overlooked the tremendous importance of the immediate play of psychic factors congruous to hunting as such.[16]

In conclusion, let me point out that the adjustment of habits to ends, through the medium of a problematic, doubtful, precarious situation, is the structural form upon which present intelligence and emotion are built. It remains the ground-pattern. The further problem of genetic psychology is then to show how the purely immediate personal adjustment of habit to direct satisfaction, in the savage, became transformed through the introduction of impersonal, generalized objective instrumentalities and ends; how it ceased to be immediate and became loaded and surcharged with a

16. For a statement doing justice to the psycho-physic factors involved, see Thomas, "Der Ursprung der Exogamie," *Zeitschrift für Socialwissenschaft,* Vol. V, p. 1.

content which forced personal want, initiative, effort and satisfaction further and further apart, putting all kinds of social divisions of labor, intermediate agencies and objective contents between them. This is the problem of the formation of mental patterns appropriate to agricultural, military, professional and technological and trade pursuits, and the reconstruction and overlaying of the original hunting schema.

But by these various agencies we have not so much destroyed or left behind the hunting structural arrangement of mind, as we have set free its constitutive psycho-physic factors so as to make them available and interesting in all kinds of objective and idealized pursuits—the hunt for truth, beauty, virtue, wealth, social well-being, and even of heaven and of God.

ACADEMIC FREEDOM

In discussing the questions summed up in the phrase academic freedom, it is necessary to make a distinction between the university proper and those teaching bodies, called by whatever name, whose primary business is to inculcate a fixed set of ideas and facts. The former aims to discover and communicate truth and to make its recipients better judges of truth and more effective in applying it to the affairs of life. The latter have as their aim the perpetuation of a certain way of looking at things current among a given body of persons. Their purpose is to disciple rather than to discipline —not indeed at the expense of truth, but in such a way as to conserve what is already regarded as truth by some considerable body of persons. The problem of freedom of inquiry and instruction clearly assumes different forms in these two types of institutions. An ecclesiastical, political, or even economic corporation holding certain tenets certainly has a right to support an institution to maintain and propagate its creed. It is a question not so much of freedom of thought as of ability to secure competent teachers willing to work under such conditions, to pay bills, and to have a constituency from which to draw students. Needless to say, the line between these two types of institutions is not so clear-cut in practice as it is in theory. Many institutions are in a state of transition. Historically, they are bound by ties to some particular body of beliefs, generally to some denominational association. Nominally, they still owe a certain allegiance to a particular body. But they are also assuming many strictly university functions and are thereby accepting obligations to a larger world of scholarship and of society. In these respects the institution imposes upon its teaching corps not merely a right, but a duty, to maintain in all ways the uni-

[First published in *Educational Review* 23 (1902): 1–14.]

versity ideal of freedom of inquiry and freedom of communication. But, in other respects, while the historical denominational ties are elongated and attenuated, they still remain; and through them the instructor is to some extent bound. Implicit, if not explicit, obligations are assumed. In this situation, conflict between the two concerns of the university may arise; and in the confusion of this conflict it is difficult to determine just which way the instructor is morally bound to face. Upon the whole it is clear, however, that the burden falls upon the individual. If he finds that the particular and local attachment is so strong as to limit him in the pursuit of what he regards as essential, there is one liberty which cannot be taken away from him: the liberty of finding a more congenial sphere of work. So far as the institution is frank in acknowledging and maintaining its denominational connections, he cannot throw the burden back upon it. Nevertheless he, and those who are like-minded, have the right to deplore what they consider as a restriction, and to hope and labor for the time when the obligation in behalf of all the truth to society at large shall be felt as more urgent than that of a part of truth to a part of society.

But it cannot be inferred that the problem is a wholly simple one, even within the frankly announced denominational institutions. The line in almost any case is a shifting one. I am told that a certain denominational college permits and encourages a good deal of instruction in anatomy and physiology because there is biblical authority for the statement that the human body is fearfully and wonderfully made, while it looks askance upon the teaching of geology because the recognized doctrine of the latter appears to it to conflict with the plain statements of Genesis. As regards anatomy and physiology, an instructor in such an institution would naturally feel that his indebtedness was to the world of scholarship rather than to his own denomination, and here conflict might possibly arise. Or a teacher of history might find a conflict existing between the supposed interests of his denomination and the historical facts as determined by the best research at his command. Here, again, he would find himself naturally pulled in two different directions. No possible tie to what his own institution specially stands for can impose upon him the obligation to suppress the truth as he sees it. I quote such cases simply to indicate that, while in a general way there is a line of demarcation between the two types of institutions referred to, and consequently the problem of academic freedom does not arise so definitely in one type, yet even in the latter, because all things shift, the question, after all, may assert itself.

In the subsequent discussion I shall confine myself exclusively to institutions of the university type. It is clear that in this sphere any attack, or even any restriction, upon academic freedom is directed against the university itself. To investigate truth; critically to verify fact; to reach conclusions by means of the best methods at command, untrammeled by external fear or favor, to communicate this truth to the student; to interpret to him its bearing on the questions he will have to face in life—this is precisely the aim and object of the university. To aim a blow at any one of these operations is to deal a vital wound to the university itself. The university function is the truth-function. At one time it may be more concerned with the tradition or transmission of truth, and at another time with its discovery. Both functions are necessary, and neither can ever be entirely absent. The exact ratio between them depends upon local and temporal considerations rather than upon anything inherent in the university. The one thing that is inherent and essential is the idea of truth.

So clear are these principles that, in the abstract, no theoretical problem can possibly arise. The difficulties arise from two concrete sources. In the first place, there is no gainsaying the fact that some of the studies taught in the university are inherently in a much more scientific condition than others. In the second place, the popular or general recognition of scientific status is much more widespread as regards some subjects than others. Upon the whole, it is practically impossible for any serious question regarding academic freedom to arise in the sphere of mathematics, astronomy, physics, or chemistry. Each of these subjects has now its definite established technique, and its own sphere within which it is supreme. This is so as fact; and it is generally so recognized by all persons of influence in the community. Consequently, there is no leverage from which to direct an attack upon academic freedom in any of these subjects. Such, of course, was not the case a few centuries ago. We know the storm that raged about astronomy. We know that it is only through great trial and tribulation that the sciences have worked out such a definite body of truth and such definite instrumentalities of inquiry and verification as to give them a position assured from attack.

The biological sciences are clearly in a transitional state. The conception of evolution is a test case. It is safe to say that no university worthy of the name would put any limitation upon instruction in this theory, or upon its use as an agency of research and classification. Very little sympathy could be secured for an attack upon a university for encouraging the use of this theory. Many of the smaller colleges, however, would be shaken to their foundations by anything that seemed like a public avowal of belief in this doctrine. These facts would seem to mean that the more influential sections of the community upon which the universities properly depend have adjusted themselves to the fact that biology is a science which must be the judge of its own methods of work; that its facts and tests of fact are to be sought within its own scientific operations, and not in any extraneous sources. There are still, however, large portions of society which have not come to recognize that biology is an established science, and which, therefore, cannot concede to it the right to determine belief in regions that conflict with received opinions, and with the emotions that cluster about them.

There is another group of sciences which, from the standpoint of definitive method and a clearly accepted body of verified fact, are more remote from a scientific status. I refer especially to the social and psychological disciplines, and to some phases of linguistic and historical study—those most intimately associated with religious history and literature. Moreover, the public recognition of the scientific status attained lags behind the fact. As compared with mathematics or physics we can employ the term "science" only in a tentative and somewhat prophetic sense—the aspirations, the tendencies, the movement are scientific. But to the public at large the facts and relations with which these topics deal are still almost wholly in the region of opinion, prejudice, and accepted tradition. It has hardly dawned upon the community as a whole that science really has anything to say upon matters in the social and psychological sphere. The general public may be willing enough to admit in the abstract the existence of a science of political economy, sociology, or psychology, but when these dare to emerge from a remote and technical sphere, and pass authoritative judgment upon affairs of daily life,—when they come in contact, that is, with the interests of daily life,—they meet with little but scepticism or hostility or, what is worse, sensational exploitation.

It is out of these two facts—the backwardness of some of our sciences and failure of the general public to recognize even the amount of advance actually made—that the concrete problems of academic freedom arise. The case may be stated as follows: On behalf of academic freedom it may be urged that the only way in which the more backward subjects can possibly reach anything like the status of mathematics and mechanics is by encouraging to the utmost freedom of investigation, and the publication, oral and printed, of the results of inquiry. It may be urged that the very failure on the part of the public to recognize rightful jurisdiction for scientific methods and results is only the more reason for unusual frankness and fullness of expression. Because the public is so behind the scientific times, it must be brought up. The points of contact, it may be urged, between the social and moral sciences and social needs, are even more numerous and more urgent than in the case of the mathematical and physical sciences. The latter have secured their independence through a certain abstractness, a certain remoteness from matters of social concern. Political economy, sociology, historical interpretation, psychology in its various possible applications, deal face-to-face with problems of life, not with problems of technical theory. Hence the right and duty of academic freedom are even greater here than elsewhere.

Per contra, it may be pointed out that, in so far as these subjects have not reached a scientific status, an expression of opinion on the part of a university instructor remains after all nothing but an expression of opinion, and hardly entitled to any more weight than that of any other reasonably intelligent person. It, however, is almost certain to be regarded as an official judgment. It thus commits and possibly compromises the institution to which the instructor belongs. The sphere of ideas which has not yet come under recognized scientific control is, moreover, precisely that which is bound up most closely with deep-rooted prejudice and intense emotional reaction. These, in turn, exist because of habits and modes of life to which the people have accustomed themselves. To attack them is to appear to be hostile to institutions with which the worth of life is bound up.

John Stuart Mill, with characteristic insight, somewhere points out that the German easily tolerates and welcomes all kinds of new ideas and new speculations because they exist in a region apart; they do not affect, excepting indirectly, the practical conduct of life. With the Englishman it is different. He is instinctively uneasy in the presence of a new idea; the wider the scope of the idea, the more readily uneasiness turns to suspicion and hostility. He recognizes that to accept the new idea means a change in the institutions of life. The idea is too serious a matter to be trifled with. The American has certainly inherited enough of the Englishman's sense for the connection of theory and practice to be conservative in the matter of the public broaching (and under modern conditions even classroom discussion is quasi-public) of ideas which lie much beyond the bounds of the domain publicly allotted to science.

Wherever scientific method is only partially attained the danger of undue dogmatism and of partisanship is very great. It is possible to consecrate ideas born of sheer partisanship with the halo of scientifically established belief. It is possible to state what is currently recognized to be scientific truth in such a way as to violate the most sacred beliefs of a large number of our fellow-men. The manner of conveying the truth may cause an irritation quite foreign to its own substance. This is quite likely to be the case whenever the negative rather than the positive aspect is dwelt upon; wherever the discrepancy between the new truth and established

institutions is emphasized, rather than the intrinsic significance of the new conception. The outcome is disintegrating
instead of constructive; and the methods inevitably breed
distrust and antagonism.

One might, for example, be scientifically convinced of
the transitional character of the existing capitalistic control
of industrial affairs and its reflected influences upon political
life; one might be convinced that many and grave evils and
injustices are incident to it, and yet never raise the question
of academic freedom, although developing his views with
definiteness and explicitness. He might go at the problem in
such an objective, historic, and constructive manner as not to
excite the prejudices or inflame the passions even of those
who thoroughly disagreed with him. On the other hand,
views at the bottom exactly the same can be stated in such
a way as to rasp the feelings of everyone exercising the
capitalistic function. What will stand or fall upon its own
scientific merits, if presented as a case of objective social
evolution, is mixed up with all sorts of extraneous and
passion-inflaming factors when set forth as the outcome of
the conscious and aggressive selfishness of a class.

As a result of such influences the problem of academic
freedom becomes to a very large extent a personal matter. I
mean that it is a matter of the scholarship, judgment, and
sympathy of the individual in dealing with matters either
only just coming within the range of strict scientific treatment, or, even if fairly annexed to the scientific domain, not
yet recognized by contemporary public opinion as belonging
there. All sorts of difficulties arise when we attempt to lay
down any rules for, or pass any judgment upon, the personal
aspects of the matter. Such rules are likely to be innocuous
truisms. We can insist upon one hand that the individual
must be loyal to truth, and that he must have the courage of
his convictions; that he must not permit their presumed un-
popularity, the possibly unfavorable reaction of their free
expression upon his own career, to swerve him from his
singleness of devotion to truth. We may dwell upon the
dangers of moral cowardice and of turning traitor to the
cause in which every scholar is enlisted. We may indicate the
necessity of the use of common sense in the expression of

views on controverted points, especially points entering into
the arena of current religious and political discussion. We
may insist that a man needs tact as well as scholarship; or,
let us say, sympathy with human interests—since "tact"
suggests perhaps too much a kind of juggling diplomacy with
the questions at issue.

It is possible to confuse loyalty to truth with self-
conceit in the assertion of personal opinion. It is possible to
identify courage with bumptiousness. Lack of reverence for
the things that mean much to humanity, joined with a
craving for public notoriety, may induce a man to pose as a
martyr to truth when in reality he is a victim of his own
lack of mental and moral poise. President Harper, in a clear
and comprehensive discussion in his Convocation Address of
December, 1900,[1] points out so clearly the sources of personal
failure of this sort that I make no apology for quoting his
words:

(1) A professor is guilty of an abuse of privilege who promul-
gates as truth ideas or opinions which have not been tested
scientifically by his colleagues in the same department of research or investigation. (2) A professor abuses his privilege who
takes advantage of a class room exercise to propagate the partisan
views of one or another of the political parties. (3) A professor
abuses his privilege who in any way seeks to influence his pupils
or the public by sensational methods. (4) A professor abuses his
privilege of expression of opinion when, although a student
and perhaps an authority in one department or group of departments, he undertakes to speak authoritatively on subjects which
have no relationship to the department in which he was appointed to give instruction. (5) A professor abuses his privilege
in many cases when, although shut off in large measure from
the world and engaged within a narrow field of investigation,
he undertakes to instruct his colleagues or the public concerning
matters in the world at large in connection with which he has
had little or no experience.

Now, while all university men will doubtless agree with
President Harper when he says "freedom of expression must
be given to members of a university faculty, even though it
be abused, for the abuse of it is not so great an evil as the
restriction of such liberty," yet it is clear that the presence of

1. See *University* [of Chicago] *Record*, Vol. V, p. 377.

these personal elements detracts very much from the simplicity and significance of an issue regarding academic freedom. For reasons into which I cannot fully go, I am convinced
that it is now well-nigh impossible to have raised, in any of
the true universities of this country, a straight out-and-out
issue of academic freedom. The constantly increasing momentum of scientific inquiry, the increasing sense of the
university spirit binding together into one whole the scattered members of various faculties throughout the country,
the increased sensitiveness of public opinion, and the active
willingness of a large part of the public press to seize upon
and even to exaggerate anything squinting towards an in-
fringement upon the rights of free inquiry and free speech—
these reasons, among others, make me dissent most thoroughly from the opinion sometimes expressed that there is a
growing danger threatening academic freedom.

The exact contrary is, in my judgment, the case as regards academic freedom in the popular sense, that is to say,
of dictatorial interferences by moneyed benefactors with
special individual utterances.

It does not follow, however, that there is no danger in
the present situation. Academic freedom is not exhausted in
the right to express opinion. More fundamental is the matter
of freedom of work. Subtle and refined danger is always more
to be apprehended than a public and obvious one. Encroach-
ments that arise unconsciously out of the impersonal situation are more to be dreaded than those coming from the
voluntary action of individuals. Influences that gradually
sap and undermine the conditions of free work are more
ominous than those which attack the individual in the open.
Ability to talk freely is an important thing, but hardly
comparable with ability to work freely. Now freedom of work
is not a matter which lends itself to sensational newspaper
articles. It is an intangible, undefinable affair; something
which is in the atmosphere and operates as a continuous
and unconscious stimulus. It affects the spirit in which the
university as a whole does its work, rather than the overt
expressions of any one individual. The influences which
help and hinder in this freedom are internal and organic,
rather than outward and personal.

Without being a pessimist, I think it behooves the community of university men to be watchful on this side. Upon the whole, we are pretty sure that actual freedom of expression is not going to be interrupted at the behest of any immediate outside influence, even if accompanied with the prospective gift of large sums of money. Things are too far along for that. The man with money hardly dare directly interfere with freedom of inquiry, even if he wished to; and no respectable university administration would have the courage, even if it were willing, to defy the combined condemnation of other universities and of the general public.

None the less the financial factor in the conduct of the modern university is continually growing in importance, and very serious problems arise in adjusting this factor to strict educational ideals. Money is absolutely indispensable as a means. But it is only a means. The danger lies in the difficulty of making money adequate as a means, and yet keeping it in its place—not permitting it to usurp any of the functions of control which belong only to educational purposes. To these, if the university is to be a true university, money and all things connected therewith must be subordinate. But the pressure to get the means is tending to make it an end; and this is academic materialism—the worst foe of freedom of work in its widest sense.

Garfield's conception of the college as a bench with a student at one end and a great teacher at the other, is still a pious topic of after-dinner reminiscence; but it is without bearing in the present situation. The modern university is itself a great economic plant. It needs libraries, museums, and laboratories, numerous, expensive to found and to maintain. It requires a large staff of teachers.

Now the need for money is not in itself external to genuine university concerns; much less antagonistic to them. The university must expand in order to be true to itself, and to expand it must have money. The danger is that means absorb attention and thus possess the value that attaches alone to the ultimate educational end. The public mind gives an importance to the money side of educational institutions which is insensibly modifying the standard of judgment both within and without the college walls. The great event in the history of an institution is now likely to be a big gift, rather than a new investigation or the development of a strong and vigorous teacher. Institutions are ranked by their obvious material prosperity, until the atmosphere of money-getting and money-spending hides from view the interests for the sake of which money alone has a place. The imagination is more or less taken by the thought of this force, vague but potent; the emotions are enkindled by grandiose conceptions of the possibilities latent in money. Unconsciously, without intention, the money argument comes to be an argument out of proportion, out of perspective. It is bound up in so many ways, seen and unseen, with the glory and dignity of the institution that it derives from association an importance to which it has in itself no claim.

This vague potentiality, invading imagination and seducing emotion, checks initiative and limits responsibility. Many an individual who would pursue his straight course of action unhindered by thought of personal harm to himself, is deflected because of fear of injury to the institution to which he belongs. The temptation is attractive just because it does not appeal to the lower and selfish motives of the individual, but comes clothed in the garb of the ideals of an institution. Loyalty to an institution, *esprit de corps*, is strong in the university, as in the army and navy. A vague apprehension of bringing harm upon the body with which one is connected is kept alive by the tendency of the general public to make no distinction between an individual in his personal and his professional capacity. Whatever he says and does is popularly regarded as an official expression of the institution with which he is connected. All this tends to paralyze independence and drive the individual back into a narrower corner of work.

Moreover, a new type of college administration has been called into being by the great expansion on the material side. A ponderous machinery has come into existence for carrying on the multiplicity of business and quasi-business matters without which the modern university would come to a standstill. This machinery tends to come between the individual and the region of moral aims in which he should assert himself. Personality counts for less than the apparatus through which, it sometimes seems, the individual alone can accomplish anything. Moreover, the minutiae, the routine turning of the machinery, absorb time and energy. Many a modern college man is asking himself where he is to get the leisure and strength to devote himself to his ultimate ends, so much, willy-nilly, has to be spent on the intermediate means. The side-tracking of personal energy into the routine of academic machinery is a serious problem.

All this, while absorbing some of the energy which ought to find outlet in dealing with the larger issues of life, would not be so threatening were it not for its association with the contemporary tendency to specialization. Specialization, in its measure and degree, means withdrawal. It means preoccupation with a comparatively remote field in relatively minute detail. I have no doubt that in the long run the method of specialization will justify itself, not only scientifically, but practically. But value in terms of ultimate results is no reason for disguising the immediate danger to courage, and the freedom that can come only from courage. Teaching, in any case, is something of a protected industry; it is sheltered. The teacher is set somewhat one side from the incidence of the most violent stresses and strains of life. His problems are largely intellectual, not moral; his associates are largely immature. There is always the danger of a teacher's losing something of the virility that comes from having to face and wrestle with economic and political problems on equal terms with competitors. Specialization unfortunately increases these dangers. It leads the individual, if he follows it unreservedly, into bypaths still further off from the highway where men, struggling together, develop strength. The insidious conviction that certain matters of fundamental import to humanity are none of my concern because outside of my *Fach*, is likely to work more harm to genuine freedom of academic work than any fancied dread of interference from a moneyed benefactor.

The expansion of the material side of the modern university also carries with it strong tendencies towards centralization. The old-fashioned college faculty was pretty sure to be a thorough-going democracy in its way. Its teachers were selected more often because of their marked individual traits than because of pure scholarship. Each stood his own and for his own. The executive was but *primus inter pares*. It was a question not of organization or administration (or even of execution on any large scale), but rather of person making himself count in contact with person, whether teacher or student. All that is now changed—necessarily so. It requires ability of a very specialized and intensified order to wield the administrative resources of a modern university. The conditions make inevitably for centralization. It is difficult to draw the line between that administrative centralization which is necessary for the economical and efficient use of resources and that moral centralization which restricts initiative and responsibility. Individual participation in legislative authority and position is a guarantee of strong, free, and independent personalities. The old faculty, a genuine republic of letters, is likely to become an oligarchy—more efficient from the standpoint of material results achieved, but of less account in breeding men. This reacts in countless ways upon that freedom of work which is necessary to make the university man a force in the working life of the community. It deprives him of responsibility, and with weakening of responsibility comes loss of initiative.

This is one phase of the matter—fortunately not the whole of it. There has never been a time in the history of the world when the community so recognized its need of expert guidance as today. In spite of our intellectual chaos, in spite of the meaningless hullabaloo of opinion kept up so persistently about us by the daily press, there is a very genuine hunger and thirst after light. The man who has the word of wisdom to say is sure of his audience. If he gets his light out from under the bushel, it carries a long way. From this point of view there are strong influences working to free the university spirit, the spirit of inquiry and expression of truth, from its entanglements and concealments. The need being imperative, the stimulus is great. A due degree of courage, a due measure of the spirit of initiative and personal responsibility is the natural response. With the decay of external and merely governmental forms of authority, the demand grows for the authority of wisdom and intelligence. This force is bound to overcome those influences which tend to withdraw and pen the scholar within his own closet.

An immediate resource counteracting the dangers threat-

ening academic freedom, is found also in the growth of in-
tercollegiate sentiment and opinion. No fact is more significant than the growing inclination on the part of scientific
associations to assume a right and duty to inquire into what
affects the welfare of its own line of inquiry, however and
wherever it takes place. This is the growth of the corporate
scientific consciousness; the sense of the solidarity of truth.
Whatever wounds the body of truth in one of its members
attacks the whole organism. It is not chimerical to foresee a
time when the consciousness of being a member of an
organized society of truth-seekers will solidify and reinforce
otherwise scattered and casual efforts.

Given that individual initiative whose permanent weakening we can scarcely imagine in an Anglo-Saxon community: and two forces, the need of the community for guidance
and the sense of membership in the wider university to which
every inquirer belongs, will assuredly amply triumph over
all dangers attacking academic freedom.

THE UNIVERSITY OF CHICAGO SCHOOL OF EDUCATION

The School of Education was generously endowed by Mrs. Emmons Blaine through her interest in educational progress, especially as that was represented by Colonel Francis W. Parker in the old Cook County Normal School. It was her large-minded purpose that he should have an opportunity to carry out the great work that he had undertaken, free from conventional, financial, and political complications. Her foundation, under the direction of Colonel Parker, took form in the Chicago Institute. The building strikes of the years 1900–1901 prevented the erection of a building; and during the spring of 1901 negotiations were carried on which resulted in the incorporation of the Chicago Institute in the University of Chicago, as the professional school of education in the latter. The sad and premature death of Colonel Parker in the spring of 1902 led to a consolidation of the undergraduate work of the Department of Education in the university with that of the School of Education, so that the former head of the Department of Education became the director of the school.

The aim of the school remains the training of teachers—teachers thoroughly interested in educational progress, and competent not only in class-room instruction, but to foster the general spread of whatever is best in elementary education. All training schools for teachers naturally have many of their purposes in common; but past history, traditions, and local circumstances give every institution a stamp of its own. It was inevitable, in the case of a personality as progressive, vigorous, and devoted as that of Colonel Parker, that this impress should be unusually pronounced. The school, as he was accustomed to say, was founded as an exponent of the "new education," devoted to the complete development, physical, mental, and moral, of the child.

[First published in *Elementary School Teacher* 3 (1902): 200–203.]

The School of Education, in its original form, was concerned with the training of elementary-school teachers; and, so far as the professional work is concerned, only the training upon that side has as yet been organized. Plans are now under way, however, for grouping the college courses which are especially adapted to the needs of secondary-school teachers, and for combining those with such courses in education as will enable the university to undertake the professional training of teachers of that class.

Upon the side of schools for children, affording models of demonstration, laboratories for investigation and verification, and for acquiring the necessary technical command of modes of teaching, the school is already unusually well equipped. The Chicago Institute brought with it a complete elementary school from the kindergarten through the eighth grade. This serves especially as a school of observation and practice as to the actual technique of class management and instruction. The professional work of those who are in training for elementary-school teachers is closely connected with this practice school. The combination with the Department of Education brought in an elementary school whose especial province is the application of psychological method to problems of the curriculum, and the development of a distinct body of psychological principles which may be put at the disposal of teachers in such a way as to enable them to direct more intelligently their own thinking and practice. The department had also under its charge two secondary schools, representing the essential problems and factors of high-school education. The Chicago Manual Training School is an almost classic example of the claims and functions of manual training and technological work; while the former South Side Academy was a typical example of the academic school conducted along the lines of linguistic and scientific training.

The School of Education thus has at command all the factors which, in their cooperative interaction, are requisite for a complete educational scheme. If anything be needed to complete the chain, it is found in the fact that within the university organization the work of the freshman and sophomore years has been arranged in a distinctive form—

that of the Junior College—because it is felt that this work connects quite as closely with secondary-school work as with that of college training proper. It is believed and hoped that with the new buildings the existing gaps and overlappings between secondary and collegiate education may be completely done away with, and the work of the one gradually blend and fuse with that of the other. Taking this work in connection with that of the Senior Colleges, and of the graduate and professional schools, it is thought that the University of Chicago may be able to do something significant and important in the way of providing the working model of an economic and efficient unification of the various parts of the educational system.

The work of the professional students may be classed under three heads: First, they pursue courses in academic lines calculated to increase and strengthen their scholarship; and particularly to put them in command of the intellectual standpoint and method which are absolutely indispensable in genuine culture. It is a commonplace that the functions of elementary education have been seriously impaired by the lack of adequate training in subject-matter on the part of many of its teachers. From this lack, evils at opposite extremes have resulted. On one side, because of the narrow horizon and equipment of the teachers, the material of the curriculum was frequently restricted and hardened into the relatively few and mechanical elements within the teacher's reach. On the other side, teachers who have felt the poverty-stricken and devitalizing character of this material have struck out in new directions and introduced a large variety of new materials which have been found to appeal to the interests of the children. But, as the consequences proved, the teachers were often so lacking in scientific and historical knowledge, and in thorough intellectual discipline, as not to be able to control the introduction of these new factors and to secure their proper adjustment to one another. The intimate association of collegiate and professional work seems to be absolutely necessary to secure that variety of material and method, together with system and arrangement, which is necessary to the full and yet orderly growth of child nature. As time goes on, an ever-increasing intimacy of union between college and professional work may reasonably be expected.

In the second place, the professional student discusses and sees tested principles of education. Upon the pedagogical side it is also easy to detect two extreme evils, which it is desirable to avoid. At one extremity there is pedagogical instruction of a purely theoretic nature, ending too often in the acquisition of a glib terminology and of rigid formulae which modify the language of the would-be teacher, but have little effect in illuminating and interpreting his endeavor. At the other extreme is instruction which puts the teacher in command of an arsenal of immediate practical devices which may be employed in securing attention and hearing recitations in various subjects—devices, however, which are not interpreted to the teacher in terms of their scientific relation to principles of growth. Such devices may at first appear to add to the direct efficiency of the teacher in the schoolroom; but in the long run they reveal their narrowness and lack of scientific basis in failure to promote the growth of intellectual initiative on the part of the teacher, and in failure to cooperate with his own common sense in dealing with both the unusual and the ordinary problems of the schoolroom. As an assistance in avoiding both of these unfortunate results, the work of the professional students is based upon instruction in psychology, having for its aim, not the acquisition of technical distinctions together with precepts for educating various faculties, but insight into the conditions and modes of healthful growth, and of whatever impedes or arrests that growth. These principles are then tested, both negatively and positively, by the study of children with a view to making the theory concrete and definite through recognition of its particular applications; and the practice is enlightened, enlarged, and liberated through personal appreciation of its animating purposes and scientific base.

In the third place, the professional students work upon subject-matter with reference to its use in secondary and elementary schools. This aspect of their study represents a union of the two previous factors. It depends on some adequate understanding of the subject-matter as that stands in the minds of experts and specialists in a particular branch.

Its successful execution requires insight into the general principles of mental growth, and into the particular embodiments of those principles exhibited in individual children of different ages and temperaments. Consequently, in addition to the academic studies pursued in the colleges, and the studies in psychology and educational principles, there is a considerable group of studies in geography, history, nature study, etc.; where the future teacher studies these topics in the light of the selection and organization of subject-matter which, upon one side, is adequate from the side of scholarly information and training and, upon the other, is adapted to children's needs and powers at a given age.

It is proposed in the pages of this journal to publish from time to time discussions of psychological and social conditions, and processes of growth; and statements, derived from the actual work of both the Laboratory and Elementary Schools, of the way in which these principles find concrete expression in the selection and use of subject-matter with children.

The University of Chicago Bulletin of Information
Volume 2, Number 4, October 1902

THE UNIVERSITY OF CHICAGO SCHOOL OF EDUCATION

Fees for Matriculation, Tuition, etc.

Each student upon entering any branch of the University pays a matriculation fee of $5; this sum is paid but once, and secures membership in the University as a whole. The tuition fee is $40 per quarter of twelve weeks. Upon graduation there is a graduation fee, including Diploma, of $5. For other expenses, see *Circular of Information of the Colleges*.

Admission

Students may be admitted as either regular or unclassified students.

1. Admission to regular standing in the School of Education is granted to students who offer any fifteen of the units accepted for admission to a Junior College of the University. (See below.) A unit means a course of study comprising not less than 150 hours of prepared work. It corresponds essentially to a course of study running through one year, in which classes meet four times weekly. Two hours of laboratory work are regarded as equivalent to one hour of prepared class-room or recitation work. These units admit without examination, upon presentation of properly certified documents, (*a*) graduates of universities and colleges; (*b*) students who have taken courses in approved colleges or normal schools, provided they have honorable dismissal from the same; (*c*) graduates of high schools, normal schools, and academies affiliating or cooperating with

the University. Others are admitted who pass the required examinations in some fifteen units and who fulfill the requirements of age, moral character, etc.

The following subjects are accepted for admission by the University, with the values assigned:

Civil Government . . . . ½ unit

History:

    History of Greece . . . . ½ unit
    History of Rome . . . . ½ unit
    Mediaeval History . . . . ½ unit
    Modern History . . . . ½ unit
    History of the United States, ½ unit or 1 unit, according to the length and thoroughness of the course.
    History of England, ½ unit or 1 unit, according to the length and thoroughness of the course.

Greek . . . . 2 units

    If Greek is offered for admission, the minimum which will be accepted is two units. This includes the reading of four books of the *Anabasis*, with exercises in composition. Six books of the *Iliad* or *Odyssey* represent the third unit of Greek.

Latin . . . . 4 units

    If Latin is offered for admission, the minimum which will be accepted is two units. The two units cover the reading of the usual amount of Caesar's *Gallic War*, or its equivalent, with the work preliminary thereto. The third unit of Latin is represented by a year's work in *Virgil* or *Ovid* (or equivalent), and the fourth unit by a year's work in *Cicero*, or equivalent. Latin composition is also required for the completion of four units.

French . . . . 3 units

    Each full year of high-school or academic work in French will constitute a unit. A student may offer one, two, or three units of French.

German . . . . 3 units

    Each full year of high-school or academic work in German will constitute a unit. A student may offer one, two, or three units of German.

English . . . . 2 units

Mathematics:

    Algebra to Quadratic Equations . . . . 1 unit
    Algebra through Quadratic Equations, ½ unit (in addition to the above).
    Plane Geometry . . . . 1 unit
    Solid Geometry . . . . ½ unit

Physics . . . . 1 unit
> The student's laboratory notebook in Physics must be presented.

Chemistry . . . . 1 unit

Geology . . . . ½ unit

Physiography, ½ unit or 1 unit, according to the length and thoroughness of the course.

General Biology . . . . 1 unit

Zoology . . . . 1 unit

Botany . . . . 1 unit

Physiology . . . . ½ unit

For fuller statement of the exact character of the admission work, see the *Circular of Information* of the University, the *Departments of Arts, Literature, and Science: The Colleges.*

2. Admission to the School of Education, but not to regular standing, is also granted (*a*) to teachers of at least one year's successful experience, when recommended by the Director and the Dean of the School of Education; (*b*) to graduates of high schools and academies not in affiliation or cooperation with the University, provided such high schools and academies have standard four-year courses such as are accepted by the leading state universities; (*c*) to students who have had, in private schools, courses which are fully equivalent to those mentioned under (*b*).

Students admitted under the terms of the preceding paragraph are unclassified students. Applicants for admission as unclassified students must present official testimonials or certificates showing the amount and kind of work which they have done. When the work of unclassified students has been shown to be satisfactory, they shall be given regular standing in the School of Education, provided they present the requisite number of admission credits.

3. Unclassified students are also admitted to special work upon the same terms as in the Colleges of the University. A full statement may be found upon page 72 of the *Annual Register*. In general these conditions are, to be at least twenty-one years of age, and to satisfy the instructor in any particular branch of study of ability to pursue that particular branch with success. Unclassified students of this

type are permitted to work along special lines without reference to the course as a whole, when the recommendation of some special teacher has received the approval of the Director. They receive no diploma, however; and in case they wish to transfer themselves to the roll of regular students, have to fulfill all the regular requirements of admission, and of prescribed work.

4. Students may be admitted with advanced standing when part of the work already done is equivalent to some part of that required for a diploma. In general, college graduates may expect advanced credit in courses in subject-matter, and normal school graduates in pedagogical courses.

Professional Work: Two Years' Course

Four distinct lines of work are offered, either directly under the School of Education, or through this School in cooperation with colleges of the University.

The first covers a two years' course, at the end of which a diploma is granted to those successfully completing it. This course is intended to train teachers for engaging in general elementary-school work. This course requires eighteen Majors of work, viz., three Majors for each of the six quarters making up the two years' course. Most of this work is prescribed and is taken in the School of Education proper. Two Majors, to be taken as a rule during the second year, are elective and are taken in the colleges. In addition to the three regular Majors, work is required in Physical Culture, and also in some one or more of the Arts. The term *Arts* covers instruction in Music, Drawing and Painting, Clay-Modelling, Cooking and Manual Training. In addition to work in the Arts, some time is spent in observation, or in actual practice in the practice school, when the student is properly qualified to engage in such work with profit to himself and to a class of pupils.

The actual arrangement of work in the two years' course is as follows:[1]

---

1. This is subject to change in details.

	First Year	Second Year
Psychology and Education	2 Mj.	2 Mj.
History	1½ Mj.	1 Mj.
Nature Study	1 Mj.	1½ Mj.
Geography	1½ Mj.	1 Mj.
Mathematics	1 Mj.	1 Mj.
Speech and Oral Reading	1 Mj.	½ Mj.
Home Economics	0 Mj.	1 Mj.
College Electives	1 Mj.	1 Mj.

Special Courses

Courses are also arranged covering a longer time, the amount depending upon previous professional, general and specialized training, and leading to a diploma. The special courses give training for special teachers in Kindergarten Teaching, Manual Training, Fine Arts, Domestic Science and Art, Physical Culture, Music, Oral Speech and Reading, as well as in any regular study, such as Geography, History, Nature Study. In general, the work of the first year is mainly identical with that of students who are preparing for general teaching; in the second year this time is about equally divided between the two, while the later years are devoted more particularly to specialization. These courses also make provision for a considerable amount of free electives in the colleges. While they are elective, they are to be so chosen as to harmonize with the particular subject in which the student is preparing to specialize as a teacher. These special courses will be fully organized in the autumn of 1903, and a detailed descriptive circular will be issued in the spring of 1903.

Courses are provided which lead to both a Bachelor's degree in the College and a teacher's certificate in the School of Education. They include systematic training for teachers and supervisors in elementary schools. Courses will also be specially arranged for those wishing to engage in secondary teaching. In either case, the certificates have reference to specialized teaching. For secondary teachers, for example, they will be given in ancient languages; modern languages; English; physics and mathematics; organic science; history and social science; commerce, etc. The course of study will include (a) the required work for the degrees of A.B., Ph.B., or S.B.; (b) such additional work in the subject in which the student intends teaching as is necessary for adequate equipment; (c) courses in the theory and practice of teaching; (d) free electives. A special detailed descriptive circular will be issued in the spring of 1903.

Graduate Work

In the case of persons already holding college degrees, ample provision is made for graduate work leading to the masters' and doctors' degrees, respectively. These degrees are granted by the faculty of the University having graduate work in charge, upon recommendation of the Department of Philosophy and the School of Education. All the resources of the School of Education are available for students entering upon such graduate work; so there is unusual opportunity for a combination of advanced work in educational theory and history and various phases of practical application. In cases where the candidate has not received training in the modern psychological standpoint and method, he will be expected to do the undergraduate work in this subject in addition to his graduate work. A variety of courses is offered in the science and philosophy of education; in the history of education, as regards both the theory of pedagogy and development of the school as an institution; and in problems of school organization and administration. The courses leading to these advanced degrees are intended to prepare persons to assume responsible positions, as school principals, superintendents, directors of professional studies in normal schools, and teachers of psychology and education in both normal schools and colleges. For further information regarding these courses, see the program of philosophy and education. For details of graduate work, see the *Circular of Information* of the University; *The Graduate Schools*.

Connected Schools

The professional work of the School of Education is made concrete in the system of schools connected with it, which cover the period from kindergarten to preparation for college, technical school, and life. This system includes the University Laboratory School, University Elementary School, University Secondary School, and the Chicago Manual Training School. Through these, as a medium, the professional student is brought into contact with problems of educational method, subject-matter, organization, and administration, and is enabled to test, interpret, criticize, and verify the principles he has learned.

While the University undertakes the teaching of children, only because of the necessary connection of laboratory work and demonstration with instruction in theory, these schools offer, to a limited number of children, unusual educational advantages. These are: (1) expert direction, (2) continuity, and (3) variety and flexibility.

The schools, in their various parts, are under the supervision of those who have no ends to serve excepting those connected with the best possible development of educational theory and practice. Children may enter at four years of age and remain under the same general system of instruction and administration until ready for college or for life. With the elimination of overlappings and the introduction of necessary connecting links, it is expected to shorten this period of education by at least two years for the average student. This shortening, however, will not be at the expense of the variety of materials and methods needed for pupils at this age. The ordinary elementary curriculum is reinforced by work in the various arts of expression and construction, as well as by much more subject-matter in history and science than can be successfully introduced into ordinary schools. The Secondary School provides a wide and flexible scheme of courses, Academic, Scientific, Commercial and Technical.

Individual pupils may be so carefully and consecutively watched as gradually to discover their particular capacities and bent, thus opening the way to that later specialization in vocation or study for which they are best fitted. At the same time the variety of pursuits and studies is such as to prevent narrowness from premature specialization, and to render unnecessary elective work before the pupil has the experience and training to make him capable of exercising it wisely.

Publications

Two educational journals are edited by the School of Education and published by The University of Chicago. One, the *School Review*, covers the field of secondary education; the other, the *Elementary School Teacher*, is devoted to primary education, and publishes material directly derived from the work of the elementary schools conducted under its direction. Both are published ten times a year. All correspondence should be addressed to the University Press.

Each school publishes a circular giving information as to terms of admission, tuition, etc. Apply to The University of Chicago, stating which one is desired.

The Building

The permanent building of the school is now erecting on Scammon Court, between Kimbark and Monroe avenues, facing the Midway Plaisance. It is of stone, with a frontage of 350 feet, and a depth, at the east and west wings, of 162 feet. The main part is four stories high; the extreme wings are two stories. Passenger and freight elevators are provided. The building provides amply for class-rooms for elementary and pedagogic work, and also for all forms of work in construction and expression, such as drawing, modelling, music, manual training, cooking, etc. Scientific laboratories are numerous and well equipped and arranged. Lighting and ventilation are of the most approved type. It is hoped the building will be ready for use by the Summer Quarter, 1903. It will be ready in any event by the Autumn Quarter. Plans are also making for the speedy erection of shops for the Manual Training School, which will be models for this form of secondary-school work. It is expected they will also be ready in the autumn of 1903.

THE SCHOOL AS SOCIAL CENTRE[1]

According to the character of my invitation to speak to you, I shall confine myself to the philosophy of the school as a social centre. I accept the invitation with pleasure, but at the same time I do not feel that the philosophical aspect of the matter is the urgent or important one. The pressing thing, the significant thing, is really to make the school a social centre; that is a matter of practice, not of theory. Just what to do in order to make the schoolhouse a centre of full and adequate social service, to bring it completely into the current of social life—such are the matters, I am sure, which really deserve the attention of the public and that occupy your own minds.

It is possible, however, and conceivably useful to ask ourselves: What is the meaning of the popular demand in this direction? Why should the community in general, and those particularly interested in education in especial, be so unusually sensitive at just this period to this need? Why should the lack be more felt now than a generation ago? What forces are stirring that awaken such speedy and favorable response to the notion that the school, as a place of instruction for children, is not performing its full function—that it needs also to operate as a centre of life for all ages and classes?

A brief historic retrospect will put before us the background of the present situation. The function of education, since anything which might pass by that name was found among savage tribes, has been social. The particular organ or structure, however, through which this aim was subserved,

1. An address delivered before the National Council of Education, Minneapolis, Minn., July, 1902.

[First published in *Elementary School Teacher* 3 (1902): 73–86, and in *Proceedings and Addresses* of the National Educational Association, 1902, pp. 373–83.]

and the nature of its adjustment to other social institutions, has varied according to the peculiar condition of the given time. The general principle of evolution—development from the undifferentiated toward the formation of distinct organs on the principle of division of labor—stands out clearly in a survey of educational history. At the outset there was no school as a separate institution. The educative processes were carried on in the ordinary play of family and community life. As the ends to be reached by education became more numerous and remote, and the means employed more specialized, it was necessary, however, for society to develop a distinct institution. Only in this way could the special needs be adequately attended to. In this way developed the schools carried on by great philosophical organizations of antiquity —the Platonic, Stoic, Epicurean, etc.—then came schools as a phase of the work of the church. Finally, with the increasing separation of church and state, the latter asserted itself as the proper founder and supporter of educational institutions; and the modern type of public, or at least quasi-public, school developed. There are many who regard the transfer of this educational function from the church to the state as more than a matter for regret; they conceive of it as a move which, if persisted in, will result disastrously to the best and permanent interests of mankind. But I take it we are not called upon today to reckon with this class, large and important as it may be. I assume that practically all here are believers in the principle of state education—even if we should not find it entirely easy to justify our faith on logical or philosophical grounds. The reason for referring to this claiming by the state of the education function is to indicate that it was in continuance of the policy of specialization or division of labor.

With the development of the state has come a certain distinction between state and society. As I use these terms, I mean by "state" the organization of the resources of community life through governmental machinery of legislation and administration. I mean by "society" the less definite and freer play of the forces of the community which goes on in the daily intercourse and contact of men in an endless variety of ways that have nothing to do with politics or government or the state in any institutional sense. Now, the control of education by the state inevitably carried with it a certain segregation of the machinery of both school administration and instruction from the freer, more varied, and more flexible modes of social intercourse. So true is this that for a long time the school was occupied exclusively with but one function, the purveying of intellectual material to a certain number of selected minds. Even when the democratic impulse broke into the isolated department of the school, it did not effect a complete reconstruction, but only the addition of another element. This was preparation for citizenship. The meaning of this phrase, "preparation for citizenship," shows precisely what I have in mind by the difference between the school as an isolated thing related to the state alone, and the school as a thoroughly socialized affair in contact at all points with the flow of community life. Citizenship, to most minds, means a distinctly political thing. It is defined in terms of relation to the government, not to society in its broader aspects. To be able to vote intelligently, to take such share as might be in the conduct of public legislation and administration—that has been the significance of the term.

Now our community life has suddenly awakened; and in awakening it has found that governmental institutions and affairs represent only a small part of the important purposes and difficult problems of life, and that even that fraction cannot be dealt with adequately except in the light of a wide range of domestic, economic, and scientific considerations quite excluded from the conception of the state of citizenship. We find that our political problems involve race questions, questions of the assimilation of diverse types of language and custom; we find that most serious political questions grow out of underlying industrial and commercial changes and adjustments; we find that most of our pressing political problems cannot be solved by special measures of legislation or executive activity, but only by the promotion of common sympathies and a common understanding. We find, moreover, that the solution of the difficulties must go back to a more adequate scientific comprehension of the actual facts and relations involved. The isolation between state and society, between the government and the institutions of family, business life, etc., is breaking down. We realize the thin and artificial character of the separation. We begin to see that we are dealing with a complicated interaction of varied and vital forces, only a few of which can be pigeon-holed as governmental. The content of the term "citizenship" is broadening; it is coming to mean all the relationships of all sorts that are involved in membership in a community.

This of itself would tend to develop a sense of some-thing absent in the existing type of education, something defective in the service rendered by the school. Change the image of what constitutes citizenship and you change the image of what is the purpose of the school. Change this, and you change the picture of what the school should be doing and of how it should be doing it. The feeling that the school is not doing all that it should do in simply giving instruction during the day to a certain number of children of different ages, the demand that it shall assume a wider scope of activities having an educative effect upon the adult members of the community, has its basis just here: We are feeling everywhere the organic unity of the different modes of social life, and consequently demand that the school shall be related more widely, shall receive from more quarters, and shall give in more directions.

As I have already intimated, the older idea of the school was that its primary concern was with the inculcation of certain facts and truths from the intellectual point of view, and the acquisition of certain forms of skill. When the school became public or common, this notion was broadened to include whatever would make the citizen a more capable and righteous voter and legislator; but it was still thought that this end would be reached along the line of intellectual instruction. To teach children the Constitution of the United States, the nature and working of various parts of govern-mental machinery, from the nation through the state and the county down to the township and the school district—to teach such things was thought to prepare the pupil for citizenship. And so some fifteen or twenty years ago, when the feeling arose that the schools were not doing all that they should be doing for our life as a whole, this consciousness expressed itself in a demand for a more thorough and extensive teaching of civics. To my mind the demand for the school as a social centre bears the same ratio to the situation which confronts us today as the movement for civics bore to the conditions of half a generation ago. We have awakened to deeper aspects of the question; we have seen that the machinery of governmental life is, after all, but a machinery and depends for its rightness and efficiency upon underlying social and industrial causes. We have lost a good deal of our faith in the efficacy of purely intellectual instruction.

Some four specific developments may be mentioned as having a bearing upon the question of the school as a social centre. The first of these is the much-increased efficiency and ease of all the agencies that have to do with bringing people into contact with one another. Recent inventions have so multiplied and cheapened the means of transportation, and of the circulation of ideas and news through books, magazines, and papers, that it is no longer physically possible for one nationality, race, class, or sect to be kept apart from others, impervious to their wishes and beliefs. Cheap and rapid long-distance transportation has made America a meeting-place for all the peoples and tongues of the world. The centralization of industry has forced members of classes into the closest association with, and dependence upon, each other. Bigotry, intolerance, or even an unswerving faith in the superiority of one's own religious and political creed, are much shaken when individuals are brought face-to-face with each other, or have the ideas of others continuously and forcibly placed before them. The congestion of our city life is only one aspect of the bringing of people together which modern inventions have induced.

That many dangers result from sudden dislocations of people from the surroundings—physical, industrial, and intellectual—to which they have become adapted; that great instability may accompany this sudden massing of heterogeneous peoples, goes without saying. On the other hand, these very agencies present instrumentalities of which advantage may be taken. The best as well as the worst of modern newspapers is a product. The organized public library with its facilities for reaching all classes of people is an effect. The popular assembly and lyceum is another. No educational system can be regarded as complete until it adopts into itself the various ways in which social and intellectual intercourse may be promoted, and employs them systematically, not only to counteract dangers which these same agencies are bringing with them, but so as to make them positive causes in raising the whole level of life.

Both the demand and the opportunity are increased in our large cities by the commingling of classes and races. It is said that one ward in the city of Chicago has forty different languages represented in it. It is a well-known fact that some of the largest Irish, German, and Bohemian cities in the world are located in America, not in their own countries. The power of the public schools to assimilate different races to our own institutions, through the education given to the younger generation, is doubtless one of the most remarkable exhibitions of vitality that the world has ever seen. But, after all, it leaves the older generation still untouched; and the assimilation of the younger can hardly be complete or certain as long as the homes of the parents remain comparatively unaffected. Indeed, wise observers in both New York and Chicago have recently sounded a note of alarm. They have called attention to the fact that in some respects the children are too rapidly, I will not say Americanized, but too rapidly de-nationalized. They lose the positive and conservative value of their own native traditions, their own native music, art, and literature. They do not get complete initiation into the customs of their new country, and so are frequently left floating and unstable between the two. They even learn to despise the dress, bearing, habits, language, and beliefs of their parents—many of which have more substance and worth than the superficial putting on of the newly adopted habits. If I understand aright, one of the chief motives in the development of the new labor museum at Hull House has been to show the younger generation something of the skill and art and historic meaning in the industrial habits of the older generations—modes of spinning, weaving, metal-working, etc., discarded in this country because there was no place for them in our industrial system. Many a child has awakened to an appreciation of admirable

qualities hitherto unknown in his father or mother for whom
he had begun to entertain a contempt. Many an association
of local history and past national glory has been awakened
to quicken and enrich the life of the family.

In the second place, along with the increasing intercourse and interaction, with all its dangers and opportunities, there has come a relaxation of the bonds of social
discipline and control. I suppose none of us would be willing
to believe that the movement away from dogmatism and
fixed authority was anything but a movement in the right
direction. But no one can view the loosening of the power
of the older religious and social authorities without deep
concern. We may feel sure that in time independent judgment, with the individual freedom and responsibility that go
with it, will more than make good the temporary losses. But
meantime there is a temporary loss. Parental authority has
much less influence in controlling the conduct of children.
Reverence seems to decay on every side, and boisterousness
and hoodlumism to increase. Flippancy toward parental and
other forms of constituted authority waxes, while obedient
orderliness wanes. The domestic ties themselves, as between
husband and wife as well as in relation to children, lose
something of their permanence and sanctity. The church,
with its supernatural sanctions, its means of shaping the
daily life of its adherents, finds its grasp slowly slipping
away from it. We might as well frankly recognize that
many of the old agencies for moralizing mankind, and of
keeping them living decent, respectable, and orderly lives,
are losing in efficiency—particularly those agencies which
rested for their force upon custom, tradition, and unquestion-
ing acceptance. It is impossible for society to remain purely
a passive spectator in the midst of such a scene. It must
search for other agencies with which it may repair the loss,
and which may produce the results which the former methods are failing to secure. Here, too, it is not enough for
society to confine its work to children. However much they
may need the disciplinary training of a widened and enlightened education, the older generation needs it also. Besides, time is short, very short, for the average child in the
average city school. The work is hardly more than begun

there, and unless it is largely to go for naught the community must find methods of supplementing it and carrying it further outside the regular school channel.

In the third place, the intellectual life, facts, and truths of knowledge, are much more obviously and intimately connected with all other affairs of life than they ever have been at any previous period in the history of the world. Hence a purely and exclusively intellectual instruction means less than it ever meant before. And, again, the daily occupations and ordinary surroundings of life are much more in need of interpretation than ever they have been before. We might almost say that once there was a time when learning related almost wholly to a world outside and beyond that of the daily concerns of life itself. To study physics, to learn German, to become acquainted with Chinese history, were elegant accomplishments, but more or less useless from the standpoint of daily life. In fact, it is just this sort of idea which the term "culture" still conveys to many minds. When learning was useful, it was only to a comparatively small and particularly select class in the community. It was just something that the doctor or lawyer or clergyman needed in his particular calling, but so far away from and above the mass of mankind that it could only awaken their blind and submissive admiration. The recent public lament regarding the degradation of the teacher's calling is, to my mind, just a reminiscence of the time when to know enough to be a teacher was something which of itself set off the individual in a special class by himself. It fails to take account of the changes which have put knowledge in common circulation, and made it possible for every man to be a teacher in some respect unto his neighbor.

Under modern conditions, practically every sphere of learning, whether of social or natural science, may impinge at once, and at any point, upon the conduct of life. German is not a fact, knowledge of which makes a distinction between a man and his fellow, but a mode of social and business intercourse. Physics is no longer natural philosophy —something concerned with remarkable discoveries about important but very remote laws; it is a set of facts which, through the applications of heat and electricity to our ordinary surroundings, constantly come home to us. Physiology, bacteriology, anatomy concern our individual health and the sanitation of our cities. Their facts are exploited in sensational if not scientific ways in the daily newspapers. And so we might go through the whole schedule of studies, once so foreign and alien, and show how intimately concerned they now are with commonplace life. The simple fact is that we are living in an age of applied science. It is impossible to escape the influence, direct and indirect, of the applications.

On the other hand, life is getting so specialized, the divisions of labor are carried so far, that nothing explains or interprets itself. The worker in a modern factory who is concerned with a fractional piece of a complex activity, present to him only in a limited series of acts carried on with a distinct portion of a machine, is typical of much in our entire social life. The old worker knew something of his process and business as a whole. If he did not come into personal contact with all of it, the whole was so small and so close to him that he was acquainted with it. He was thus aware of the meaning of the particular part of the work which he himself was doing. He saw and felt it as a vital part of the whole, and his horizon was extended. The situation is now the opposite. Most people are doing particular things of whose exact reasons and relationships they are only dimly aware. The whole is so vast, so complicated, and so technical that it is next to out of the question to get any direct acquaintanceship with it. Hence we must rely upon instruction, upon interpretations that come to us through conscious channels. One of the great motives for the flourishing of some of the great technical correspondence schools of the present day is not only the utilitarian desire to profit by preparation for better positions, but an honest eagerness to know something more of the great forces which condition the particular work one is doing, and to get an insight into those broad relations which are so partially yet tantalizingly hinted at. The same is true of the growing interest in forms of popular science, which forms a marked portion of the stock in trade of some of the best and most successful of our modern monthly magazines. This same motive added much to the effectiveness of the university-extension movement, particularly in England. It creates a particular demand for a certain type of popular illustrated lecture. Unless the lives of a large part of our wage-earners are to be left to their own barren meagreness, the community must see to it, by some organized agency, that they are instructed in the scientific foundation and social bearings of the things they see about them, and of the activities in which they are themselves engaging.

The fourth point of demand and opportunity is the prolongation, under modern conditions, of continuous instruction. We have heard much of the significance of prolonged infancy in relation to education. It has become almost a part of our pedagogical creed that premature engagement in the serious vocations of life is detrimental to full growth. There is a corollary to this proposition which has not as yet received equal recognition. Only where social occupations are well defined and of a pretty permanent type can the period of instruction be cut short at any particular period. It is commonly recognized that a doctor or a lawyer must go on studying all his life if he is to be a successful man in his profession. The reason is obvious enough. Conditions about him are highly unstable; new problems present themselves; new facts obtrude. Previous study of law, no matter how thorough and accurate the study, did not provide for these new situations. Hence the need of continual study. There are still portions of the country where the lawyer practically prepares himself before he enters upon his professional career. All he has to do afterward is to perfect himself in certain finer points, and get greater skill in the manipulation of what he already knows. But these are the more backward and unprogressive sections where change is gradual and infrequent, and so the individual prepared once is prepared always.

Now, what is true of the lawyer and the doctor, in the more progressive sections of the country, is true to a certain extent of all sorts and degrees of people. Social, economic, and intellectual conditions are changing at a rate undreamed of in past history. Now, unless the agencies of instruction are kept running more or less parallel with these changes, a

considerable body of men is bound to find itself without the
training which will enable it to adapt itself to what is going
on. It will be left stranded and become a burden for the
community to carry. Where progress is continuous and certain, education must be equally certain and continuous. The
youth at eighteen may be educated so as to be ready for the
conditions which will meet him at nineteen; but he can
hardly be prepared for those which are to confront him when
he is forty-five. If he is ready for the latter when they come,
it will be because his own education has been keeping pace
in the intermediate years. Doubtless conversation, social intercourse, observation, and reflection upon what one sees going
on about one, the reading of magazines and books, will do
much; they are important, even if unorganized methods of
continuous education. But they can hardly be expected to do
all, and hence they do not relieve the community from the
responsibility of providing, through the school as a centre, a
continuous education for all classes of whatever age.

The fourfold need, and the fourfold opportunity, which
I have hastily sketched, defines to some extent the work of
the school as a social centre.

It must provide at least part of that training which is
necessary to keep the individual properly adjusted to a rapidly changing environment. It must interpret to him the
intellectual and social meaning of the work in which he is
engaged: that is, must reveal its relations to the life and
work of the world. It must make up to him in part for the
decay of dogmatic and fixed methods of social discipline. It
must supply him compensation for the loss of reverence and
the influence of authority. And, finally, it must provide means
for bringing people and their ideas and beliefs together, in
such ways as will lessen friction and instability, and introduce deeper sympathy and wider understanding.

In what ways shall the school as a social centre perform
these various tasks? To answer this question in anything like
detail is to pass from my allotted sphere of philosophy into
that of practical execution. But it comes within the scope of
a theoretical consideration to indicate certain general lines.
First, there is mixing people up with each other; bringing
them together under wholesome influences, and under con-

ditions which will promote their getting acquainted with the
best side of each other. I suppose, whenever we are framing
our ideals of the school as a social centre, what we think of
is particularly the better class of social settlements. What
we want is to see the school, every public school, doing something of the same sort of work that is now done by a settlement or two scattered at wide distances through the city.
And we all know that the work of such an institution as
Hull House has been primarily not that of conveying intellectual instruction, but of being a social clearing-house. It is
not merely a place where ideas and beliefs may be exchanged, not merely in the arena of formal discussion—for
argument alone breeds misunderstanding and fixes prejudice
—but in ways where ideas are incarnated in human form and
clothed with the winning grace of personal life. Classes for
study may be numerous, but all are regarded as modes of
bringing people together, of doing away with barriers of
caste, or class, or race, or type of experience that keep people
from real communion with each other.

The function of the school as a social centre in pro-
moting social meetings for social purposes suggests at once
another function—provision and direction of reasonable
forms of amusement and recreation. The social club, the
gymnasium, the amateur theatrical representation, the con-
cert, the stereopticon lecture—these are agencies the force
of which social settlements have long known, and which are
coming into use wherever anything is doing in the way of
making schools social centres. I sometimes think that recreation is the most overlooked and neglected of all ethical
forces. Our whole Puritan tradition tends to make us slight
this side of life, or even condemn it. But the demand for
recreation, for enjoyment just as enjoyment, is one of the
strongest and most fundamental things in human nature. To
pass it over is to invite it to find its expression in defective
and perverted form. The brothel, the saloons, the low dance-
house, the gambling den, the trivial, inconsiderate, and
demoralizing associations which form themselves on every
street corner, are the answer of human nature to the neglect,
on the part of supposed moral leaders, of this factor in
human nature. I believe that there is no force more likely

to count in the general reform of social conditions than the practical recognition that in recreation there is a positive moral influence which it is the duty of the community to take hold of and direct.

In the third place, there ought to be some provision for a sort of continuous social selection of a somewhat specialized type—using "specialized," of course, in a relative sense. Our cities carried on evening schools long before anything was said or heard of the school as a social centre. These were intended to give instruction in the rudiments to those who had little or no early opportunities. So far they were and are good. But what I have in mind is something of a more distinctly advanced and selective nature. To refer once more to the working model upon which I am pretty continuously drawing, in the activities of Hull House we find provision made for classes in music, drawing, clay-modelling, joinery, metal-working, and so on. There is no reason why something in the way of scientific laboratories should not be provided for those who are particularly interested in problems of mechanics or electricity; and so the list might be continued. Now, the obvious operation of such modes of instruction is to pick out and attract to itself those individuals who have particular ability in any particular line. There is a vast amount of unutilized talent dormant all about us. Many an individual has capacity within himself of which he is only dimly conscious, because he has never had an opportunity for expressing it. He is not only losing the satisfaction of employment, but society suffers from this wasted capital. The evils of the unearned increment are as nothing beside those of the undiscovered resource. In time, I am confident, the community will recognize it as a natural and necessary part of its own duty—quite as much as is now giving instruction to little children—to provide such opportunities for adults as will enable them to discover and carry to some point of fulfillment the particular capacities that distinguish them.

In conclusion, we may say that the conception of the school as a social centre is born of our entire democratic movement. Everywhere we see signs of the growing recognition that the community owes to each one of its members

the fullest opportunity for development. Everywhere we see
the growing recognition that the community life is defective
and distorted excepting as it does thus care for all its constituent parts. This is no longer viewed as a matter of charity,
but as a matter of justice—nay, even of something higher
and better than justice—a necessary phase of developing and
growing life. Men will long dispute about material socialism,
about socialism considered as a matter of distribution of the
material resources of the community; but there is a socialism
regarding which there can be no such dispute—socialism of
the intelligence and of the spirit. To extend the range and
the fullness of sharing in the intellectual and spiritual resources of the community is the very meaning of the community. Because the older type of education is not fully adequate to this task under changed conditions, we feel its lack
and demand that the school shall become a social centre. The
school as a social centre means the active and organized
promotion of this socialism of the intangible things of art,
science, and other modes of social intercourse.

Miscellany

IN REMEMBRANCE
FRANCIS W. PARKER

Education in the sphere of the common public schools has had two great leaders: Horace Mann and F. W. Parker. Both came at periods when a leader was necessary. In Horace Mann's day public-school education was chaotic and in the true democratic sense of the term practically non-existent. His intellectual insight, enthusiasm, and executive force brought about a revolution in a single generation. Colonel Parker came when the idea of the common schools had received universal recognition; but there was little social enthusiasm, little moral idealism, embodied in the system. The external machinery was there, but it needed to be taken possession of by the spirit of life. It was Colonel Parker more than any other one man who insisted that the magnificent machinery which American democracy had created should also be made effective for the moral aims of democracy. The timeliness of his work is evidenced by his success. The proposal of means and ends twenty-five years ago made Quincy a storm centre in education and aroused ridicule all over the country. Now they are practically taken for granted, so far at least as their general spirit is concerned, in all of the better schools of the country. Colonel Parker had a magnificent faith in the child and in the community. His aggressiveness sprang from this faith. The event has justified him, as it rebukes the time server and preachers of expediency, who are ready to compromise ultimate ends by cowardly surrender to the pressure of the moment. Colonel Parker was a loyal and devoted soldier in the battle of humanity for growth and freedom.

[First published in *Journal of Education* 55 (1902): 199.]

IN MEMORIAM:
COLONEL FRANCIS WAYLAND PARKER[1]

This is neither the time nor the place to attempt a review of the educational philosophy or the educational work of Colonel Parker. But our noble and single-minded friend obeyed above most men the scriptural injunction; he loved and did with his whole mind and his whole soul. Hence it is as impossible to speak of his personality apart from his educational work as it is to speak of his educational work apart from his personality. He was fortunate in the complete identification of his whole being, his whole personality, with the work to which he devoted himself.

Thus there are three things in his educational work which come to me because they are characteristic of his personality, because they belong to the man. Colonel Parker was upon the program of the educational meeting which was held in the city last week, but was kept away by his sickness. The title of his speech was "Education into Citizenship." If there could have been anything more characteristic than this of Colonel Parker's attitude toward education, it was the subtitle: "Relating Especially to Dependent and Defective and Backward Children." His last address sums up the man, his recognition of the social element in education, of that which makes it a real force in community life; and the outgoing of his heart to all those who, being helpless, needed peculiarly tender care. Much as he did for education in the way of improving and reforming its methods of teaching and its administration, the essence of what he did was greater than any specific contribution; it was to inspire the teacher and the child in the schoolroom with his own affectionate and sympathetic personality. He renewed the old lesson as to the

1. From stenographic report.

[First published in *Elementary School Teacher* 2 (1902): 704–8. Reprinted as "Francis W. Parker" in *Characters and Events*, ed. Joseph Ratner (New York: Henry Holt and Co., 1929), 1:95–99.]

shortcomings of all instruction until it adds devotion and love to intellectuality: "The greatest of these is love." He was accustomed to say that the social spirit of the schoolroom does more for the child than the formal instruction given; that what the children learn from contact with one another and the teacher is more than what they learn from the text-book and the lecture. If this be true, then the atmosphere and spirit of the schoolroom must be that of freedom, of confidence, of mutual interest in a common life of work and play. He was accustomed to say that all the resources of the schoolroom should be centered upon the "bad" child—resources of helpfulness and sympathy. That was most needed in the schoolroom. That which to the pedant and formalist is a barrier was to him an appeal. What he did in breaking down the despotism, formalism and the rigidity of the old-fashioned school he did, not just because of abstract theory, but because he insisted that the love and faith, which are the tokens of the highest character everywhere, find a peculiarly appropriate place in the contact of the learned and the mature with the little and the feeble.

The second thing that comes to me in the connection of his personality with his educational work is that he believed there is absolutely nothing too good for the children. Many of you, doubtless, have heard him give a talk entitled "Nature and the Child," in which he gave a poetic and idealized sketch (which I supposed to be autobiographical, although he did not say so) of a boy on a farm and his contact with nature. On that farm he studied, without being aware of it, mineralogy, geography, geology, botany, and zoology, and came in contact with nature in all her forms. He believed that what he did there himself in that undirected and casual way every child should be allowed to do, should be encouraged to do, through an educational system. Thus he did much for what is termed the enrichment of the elementary-school curriculum; not, again, just as an intellectual matter of putting in this and that study, but because he believed that whatever there is of value in the history of man and in the world of nature is the true birthright of every child born among us. To do anything by any method, by any system of administration which keeps the child from full and complete contact with these things, is a wrong against human nature and against the human spirit.

The third point in which his educational faith and his personality came together was his faith in the professional training of teachers, and in the science of education. I once heard him say that it was this thing that induced him to come out here. He gave up a position which, judged by a conventional standard, was one of superior dignity and importance. But in the position which he occupied he felt that he was getting away from the children. The more he had to do with such a position, the more also he realized that the future of education depends upon the training of the teacher. His belief in the unrealized possibilities of the art of teaching was sublime. It is an inspiration to all teachers everywhere —just as it has been to those who have come immediately under his personality. Just as he believed that there was nothing in the world of nature or art too good for the child, so he believed that there was nothing in the personality of another, no element of the human spirit, which should not be called forth in the art of educating, of developing the latent possibilities of the human soul. It was that moral goal, that moral ideal, the possibility of a fuller development, which inspired him in the work he did with teachers.

The great lesson that comes home to me from Colonel Parker's life, the great lesson that I feel that I ought to call especially to the attention of the younger people here present, is what it means really to attain success in life. Colonel Parker never temporized, he never used little expediencies or policies. He never got lost in the smaller things of life; he kept his eyes steadily on the great things, and he fought onward with all the vigor of his personality for those things which are enduring, invisible, and worth while. He waged warfare against opposition; the opposition that came from those who could not get beyond the things they could see and touch, and who, consequently, had attached themselves to the mechanical and formal. The opposition was sometimes active and virulent; more often that of indifference and inertia—harder to face than the active sort. But he never wavered a moment; he never compromised; he never sacrificed the spirit to the letter. As a result, more than the usual measure of success came to him.

Twenty-five years ago, in Quincy, Massachusetts, the work he undertook was an object of derision, as well as of sympathy, all over the country. He was a pioneer, and to many he seemed a faddist, a fanatic. It was only twenty-five years ago; and yet the things for which he then stood are taken today almost as a matter of course, without debate, in all the best schools of this country. Afterward, in Chicago, he waged, against untoward influences, the battle of the professional training of teachers; he fought to keep away every political and personal influence that might in any way lower the standard of the school. Every year he had to wage the battle over again, and every year he simply made his appeal to the people, to the democracy, in which was his trust. His faith in human nature was rewarded. Every year forces rallied about him, and, working with him, won his battles against the combined ranks of political and personal enemies. He gave years of struggle to the elevation of the education of the child and of the teacher; and in his last years, with full poetic justice, with more than the recognition that comes to most pioneers and apostles in this world, his beneficent friend crowned his work with that generous gift which brought within sight—alas, not within grasp—a realization of his lifelong dreams. These things came to him not because he sought them, but because he sought the things which he considered permanently worthy and desirable. And with these other successes came to him the love and loyalty of devoted and attached friends. He was fortunate above most in winning to himself the loyal assistance and unflinching confidence of others.

When a great life has passed away, we get a better perspective of the things that are really worth while; the smaller things, the temporary things, drop back where they belong; and the qualities that ennoble life—faith, courage, devotion to ideals, an end to fight for and to live for—stand out in their supreme significance. Our friend's physical presence has left us, but his spirit remains, reinforced and multiplied. It abides not only in this university community and in this city community, but it lives on in the heart and in the work of every teacher throughout this broad land who has been touched by a truer perception of the high ideal and calling of the teacher.

DISCUSSION OF "WHAT OUR SCHOOLS OWE TO CHILD STUDY" BY THEODORE B. NOSS

[John Dewey, professor of philosophy and education, University of Chicago.]—I would emphasize, first, the last statement in Professor Noss's paper.* The chief thing child study has done is that it has regenerated the peculiar thing named "pedagogy and psychology for teachers," a great deal that formerly went by this name being very remote. The first pedagogical doctrine, "from the concrete to the abstract," was often disregarded by pedagogs themselves. The concrete for the teacher is the mind of the child, not mind in general, but a particular mind, a particular spirit in an individual child. Child study has led us to base methods on the actual characteristics of the actual concrete being under instruction. Classifications used to be laid down of the various faculties of the mind: memory, imagination, reasoning, and rules given for training each. There was smooth sailing when these were considered only theoretically; but when the rules were applied to children it was discovered that the latter were not faculties, but live beings. A person from Mars might study purely theoretical pedagogy, and still not be able to identify a human being. Analysis is carried so far that it would not put one in touch with faculties when bound together in a human being. Independent of some exaggeration about particular truths discovered by child study, it has served to put emphasis in training a child upon the right basis. The teacher who really knows the subject to be taught and the nature of the individual mind which is dealt with can develop his own devices with better results than he could attain by learning particular recipes having not much to do with the child. Child study has put into proper perspective the sort of train-

* *Middle Works of John Dewey*, 2:379–82.

[First published in *Proceedings and Addresses* of the National Educational Association, 1902, pp. 719–20.]

ing which the teacher needs, and has brought a vitalizing element into the work. We teachers are the most conscientious class in the world; often too conscientious in following types of pedagogical recommendations which bring no adequate return. Child study vitalizes the truths grasped after.

Child study has brought about a different conception of education itself. One of the late advances in education was the doctrine of drawing out instead of pouring in. But the thing drawn out was expected to be knowledge, as though the child had swallowed the world, and methods must be applied to draw out of him what he has swallowed. Conceive little children in the home or at play. They don't sit around waiting to have things drawn out, but are all activity, full of intensity, zeal, restlessness. Child study makes prominent the activities of the child and tries to find the line along which these activities can direct themselves.

Child study brings out the significance of development in education. We have always talked about this, comparing the child to the acorn, but it has been treated in a poetical rather than a scientific way. We recognize particular characteristics which are prominent at different periods of growth, and which must be treated in different ways. Child study has done much in bringing out the defining and leading characteristics of different epochs. Biologists talk about a culture medium. According to different media they get different results in lower and even in higher forms of life; and this control of the nature of living things is as scientific as the action of machinery. The skill of the horticulturist in transforming grains and fruits is not guess-work or haphazard, for he knows the conditions necessary for such transformation. There is certainty that this can ultimately be done in human development when conditions for growth are better known. To say that there are laws governing the movement of planets, laws of chemistry, metals, etc., and that mind has no laws of its own to be made use of, is absurd.

To ridicule child study, which has its excrescences, is to say that mind has no laws which can be discovered. The time will come when one of the two or three important facts which educational history will mention about this period will

be its recognition that the embodied mind of boys and girls
has laws which can be discovered, and the laws discovered
give a basis for directing a growth which will give the richest
and best results.

MEMORANDUM TO PRESIDENT HARPER ON COEDUCATION

President W. R. Harper,

My dear Sir:

In voting "No" upon the proposition submitted to the Senate, involving separate recitation rooms and laboratories for Junior College women, I respectfully submit the following reasons:

1. At the outset it was a matter of choice to adopt or not to adopt coeducation. Having adopted it, the University assumed certain responsibilities. These extend to the cause of woman's education here and elsewhere. Therefore the effect of the proposed move upon the cause of coeducation must be taken into account. Action in accordance with it would be generally regarded by the public as evidence that coeducation as hitherto conducted had been a failure. To put this stigma upon coeducation is to deal the most severe blow at the cause of the collegiate education of women that it has met in the present generation. The action would be everywhere quoted as proof that coeducational institutions regretted coeducation and were beginning to move backward. To disguise this blow under the name of an advance in the administration of coeducation would, in the long run, deceive no one. Moreover the action would satisfy no one. While antagonizing the friends of coeducation, so strong in the middle west, it would none the less be regarded by the opponents of coeducation as an unworthy evasion of the main issue.

2. As matter of fact the move would be an attack upon coeducation within the University itself. I have taught mixed classes for the past sixteen years including sophomore as well as advanced work. Beginning with a prejudice against

[Dewey to Harper, 9 January 1902, Presidents' Papers, 1899–1925, (Copy), Department of Special Collections, University of Chicago Library.]

coeducation, I observed the matter scientifically, as a psychologist, as well as personally. My mature and firm conviction is that co-instruction is intellectually beneficial as well as morally helpful. In view of this it is not surprising that the specific argument of senators in favor of separate instruction were accompanied by expressions of distrust against coeducation as such. Moreover, co-instruction is indispensable as a safeguard. To set up physical contiguity and social contact between young men and women without the checks and compensation of meeting in class room and laboratory, is wantonly to invoke difficulty and to invite danger. If the proposed move be taken I hope that the friction, undesirable and disagreeable complications arising, approaching scandal, will be seen to be due to the abandonment of the very essence of coeducation; I am afraid, however, that they will be charged to the cause of coeducation and urged as a reason for going still further.

3. The natural policy would be to meet whatever defects exist in the present situation by additional provision of a positive sort for both men and women, and especially for men. A relaxing of close supervision of the men's social life, sports, etc.; the introduction of more initiative and responsibility into their lives, would do much to attract and hold strong men. To make good the existing weak places in instruction and research would do the rest. Given the sort of life and work that young men want, and the kind of man that will be kept away from the University simply because he will have to associate upon equal terms with his equals, is not the kind that the University wants or needs. To divert energy and money away from the needed strengthening of certain obvious weak points in the present situation simply to create and foster a "corporate consciousness" (better described as a consciousness of sex distinctions) is superfluous as it is harmful.

The same holds as regards work for women. While it is certainly illogical to argue that the presence of women keeps away men, and at the same time plead for additional facilities for women which will induce more to come, yet discussion (which has not yet been had upon this topic) might show that certain great improvements are possible as regards courses more particularly adapted to the presumed needs of women. If this should appear, after mature consideration, then the needed provision should be made in a positive and constructive way, not by introducing restriction and arousing ill feeling, sex divisions and continued attention to sex matters. It is clear that this would be also much more economical.

4. Any plan calling for removal of Junior College work (whether of men or of women) from the control and influence of the more advanced instruction and research, is a step backward.

5. Experience justifies the belief that separate instruction would lead gradually but surely to lowering the standard of scholarship in teaching women.

6. The proposition is highly objectionable in form: a. It is ambiguous; it does not state whether separate instruction for women is to be compulsory or elective; b. It is loosely drawn; without saying whether or no the same policy is to be extended to the women of the Senior Colleges it creates conditions which would inevitably tend to bring that about. We should soon find ourselves in a dilemma. The feelings, prejudices and customs engendered in the two years of separation would either require continued separation, or else surround coeducation in the Senior Colleges with continual and embarrassing friction—facts which would be quoted against coeducation as such. c. It is coupled in an obnoxious way with a financial condition. Discussion and legislation regarding a fundamental and radical educational change should be on a basis, and conducted on a plane where there cannot be the slightest suspicion of consideration about gifts of money influencing judgment.

For such reasons I record my vote in the negative.

Respectfully yours,
John Dewey

Head of the Depts.
of Philosophy and Education

LETTER TO A. K. PARKER ON COEDUCATION

The University of Chicago
Chicago, July 25, 1902

Dr. A. K. Parker, Recorder
University of Chicago
Dear Sir:

Upon the proposition to separate as far as possible the men and women in instruction in the Junior Colleges I record my vote in the negative and append herewith the following reasons:

I. THE REASONS PROFFERED IN SUPPORT OF THE MEASURE ARE NOT SUFFICIENTLY WEIGHTY, BEING LARGELY MUTUALLY CONTRADICTORY, OR ELSE IRRELEVANT.

The burden of proof in this matter rests with the affirmative, not with the negative. The University has stood committed, since its inception, to a certain principle and policy of action. This was adopted at the outset deliberately and with a full knowledge of the meaning and consequence of what was done. Through this action a situation has been created, involving relations of trust and of reasonable expectation on the part of the University to the community, the faculty, and the body of students. Only the most weighty reasons can justify a change of policy in a fundamental manner, and then only after there is a general understanding on the part of the community as well as of the faculty of what is contemplated, and after every effort has been taken to secure the proposed measure from such misinterpretation as will damage the University. Such departure from an established principle also clearly demands, both in equity and for its own success, a much larger majority within the faculty than would be needed to justify any measure along established lines, or any measure in a purely new and hitherto untried direction.

In support of the statement that the reasons for the proposed change are not of a sufficiently serious and weighty character I submit the following:

(1) There is a fundamental ambiguity in the proposition. Is its character educational or administrative? When it is urged that the present measure suffers from the same objection as the proposition upon which the Senate voted in the winter, namely of tying up an educational principle with the prospects of additional material prosperity for the University, (save that buildings are now substituted for the million and a half dollars of the other proposition,) it is replied that the existing proposition is in reality what it is in name: namely, a purely educational matter. On the other hand, when it is urged that no adequate reasons of a strictly educational sort exist, and that such as are proffered are really in the nature of subversion of coeducation, it is replied that the measure is essentially one of administrative detail in the general expansion of the University, simply indicating the lines along which such expansion may most successfully proceed. And particular arguments continually shift from one point of view to the other.

In this connection it may be noted that the present proposition comes to the Senate as the seventh of a series of motions passed by the Junior College faculty, the other six relating wholly to the matter of architectural program and material development; also that both of the two forms in which the matter has been before the Senate have been formulated and submitted to the Senate from outside its own body, and, consequently, it has never had any opportunity for positive constructive consideration of alternative schemes. Such discussion and formulation might be expected to develop plans which would relieve present difficulties more economically and more effectively than the present scheme; which would not raise in any way the sex issue with all its attendant dangers; and which would directly secure desirable results in departmental development, only remotely touched upon by the proposal before us. Such plans might, for instance, direct some portion of the large funds necessary for the triplication of recitation halls, laboratories, and libraries into the erection of departmental buildings, either singly or in groups. This would equally well relieve the present congestion; and would have the additional advantage of keeping the elementary and Junior College work in intellectual contact with the higher and research work—a condition upon which alone the former can obtain its maximum efficiency.

(2) The measure receives a cordial and respectable element of support from those persons who are inherently and constitutionally opposed to coeducation. It is frankly welcomed by them on the ground "that a half of a loaf is better than no bread"; and because they expect and intend that in its future operation it will extend itself to upper class work as well. On the other hand, it is presented as a distinct forward step in the administration of coeducation, necessary to the full realization of that idea.

(3) It is supported by arguments not always offered as against coeducation as such, but which, if valid, certainly apply to its very essence. Such arguments are:

That boys and girls are distracted each by the presence of the opposite sex; thinking more of each other than of their work, the latter suffers; that the boys are too gallant to compete with the girls, and so fall behind in scholarship; that the girls are so much brighter and quicker at this period that the boys cannot compete, anyway, and become discouraged; that instructors have to be so courteous in the presence of women students that they cannot apply to the men the measures of stern discipline required; that boys' and girls' minds and tastes are so much unlike that they need to have different modes of instruction.

If such arguments have any force, they apply to the fundamental principle and policy of coeducation. On the other hand if the proposed measure does not attack coeducation, all such arguments must be eliminated. If they are eliminated, very much of what has been said in faculty meetings in favor of the measure, and a very considerable portion of the votes in its favor, would have to go also.

(4) The argument that the separation will give opportunity for the growth of a more distinctively feminine and a

more distinctively masculine college life, respectively, implies, in my judgment, the most profound, because most subtle, of all the attacks upon the coeducational principle. The fundamental reason for coeducation is that by association in intellectual inquiry and discussion men and women become acquainted with each other's points of view, ideas, and methods of work, and learn mutual sympathy and respect; and that such intellectual sympathy and respect is a profound factor in the proper social and moral attitude of the sexes to each other. The adjustment of individuals of different sexes to each other must presumably be made at some period of life. Deliberately to suppress the most favorable conditions for a right adjustment, made in an objective way upon an intellectual basis; deliberately to encourage the formation of habits of isolated feeling, thinking, and acting (under the name of a distinctively masculine and feminine life) is to cut at the idea of coeducation at its very roots. The argument implies that the proper basis of the relation of the sexes is the life of amusement and recreation, instead of that of serious pursuit of truth in mutual competition and cooperation. The proposed measure thus takes away the chief safeguard of coeducation and leaves all its weak points exposed and multiplied. Quadrangles contiguous to each other for social purposes and absolutely remote for intellectual purposes are a standing invitation to silliness, flirtations, and even scandal. When such results come, as they surely will, will they be attributed to their original cause or used as arguments for going further along the path of separation?

(5) It is argued that when women first come to college, away from home, they need a period of rest and shelter in which to get adjusted to new surroundings; and that later on, they can stand the strain of being in the same class with men. Why should this period be two years, rather than three months or three years? The simple fact is that nineteen-twentieths of the students come from schools where they have been in continual association with each other, without even the thought of the possibility of any different arrangement; and that the first difficulties and embarrassments will arise, when, after two years' separation, they are again brought abruptly into contact with each other, with habits

fixed by separation, with spurious questions in their minds raised by it, and with positive prejudices engendered in the minds of many against any such association at all. Moreover, the expressions of the most mature women of the University, its alumnae, show that their experience has not taught them the need of any such artificial protection, but that, on the contrary, they resent its implications.

(6) Other arguments are crowding and close physical contact in Cobb Hall; the undue amount of visiting alleged to exist there; the monopolizing of stairs and halls by the girls, etc. These arguments are so logically irrelevant that they would not even be mentioned were it not for the positive evidence that they have had great weight in arousing momentary irritation with the present situation and a reaction in favor of some change. Clearly, such matters will be remedied by any scheme of building expansion; and as soon as any such scheme is under way, a large part of the genuine opposition to the present system will die out from lack of material to feed upon.

(7) The argument that there is danger of so great an increase in the number of women as will make the institution a female seminary, and the other argument that the change will be so attractive to parents and to women as to draw here many who would otherwise go to woman's colleges, may be left to deal with each other. It may be worth while to call attention, however, to the fact that ten years' experience in one of the few colleges which have adopted the proposed policy—namely, Colby College—shows under this régime a doubling of the number of women and a positive falling off in the number of men. It is also pertinent to add that the development of the professional schools, the addition of advantages appealing particularly to men, and, still more, the educational development of an advanced type of work, will almost surely attract such numbers of men as will entirely shut out the anticipated danger.

II. WHATEVER THE ACTUAL INTENTION AND DESIRE, THE PROPOSED MOVE WILL, AS A MATTER OF FACT, AFFECT VERY UNFAVORABLY THE CAUSE OF COEDUCATION BOTH AT THE UNIVERSITY AND ELSEWHERE.

(1) It will inevitably be quoted both in this country

and abroad as proof that coeducation has been a failure at the University of Chicago, and that some drastic remedy has been needed. As a matter of fact, in a German newspaper of Vienna, during last winter, the statement was made, in a conspicuous way, that coeducation had been abolished at the University of Chicago because it was such a failure there; and this fact was seriously used in that city as an argument against further educational privileges to women. Taken in itself, this fact may be dismissed as trivial; but it is indicative of what will inevitably happen. Surely the University is under some moral obligation to the cause of woman's higher education not to take a step which can everywhere be used by those opposed to such education.

(2) The move will tend to lower the level of instruction of women in the University. It will be impossible to keep both sides evenly balanced; and experience as well as reflection shows which side will suffer. Gradually but surely the women will get, I will not say the relative failures, but the less forcible and less taxing and more emotional teachers. Few if any men teachers maintain the same method and standard, teaching women alone, that they maintain with men alone, or with men and women together.

(3) The proposed move is an undeserved reflection upon the conduct of our men and women students. It will be regarded everywhere as an indication that the past conduct of the college men and women in relation to each other has been so foolish or so immoral as to require condemnation. Doubtless, no such criticism is intended; but with equal certainty the inference will be drawn.

(4) The tendency of a separation would be to introduce an undesirable spirit of aristocracy into the university; attracting a class of men and women more interested in social diversion, and with the wealth necessary to indulge in it, rather than those of a disposition to serious work. There is the more reason to anticipate such danger in so far as the proposed change is based upon the idea that the University, since located in a wealthy and socially advanced city, must develop a type of institution in accordance with its own surroundings, rather than that of the more democratic state universities.

(5) The scheme is sure to accomplish just what it is

supposed to obviate—the fixing of attention upon sex matters. It at once draws the attention of students coming to the
University to the matter of sex as a fundamental consideration in determining the instruction they are to receive.
While for other reasons, optional sections in which men and
women may recite together, if they so choose, are preferable
to a purely coercive scheme, yet as regards the matter of
concentrating attention upon sex as a basis of college work
such provision is to be deprecated.

(6) The limits of the scheme are so undefined that in
many important respects I do not know the exact nature of
the measure upon which I am voting. In the January Convocation address some change was suggested in the way
of extending wider privileges of choice to both men and
women. Amendments in the Senate to the effect that optional
sections should be provided, as far as possible, in which men
and women might recite together, and that the measure
should apply only to required, not to elective Junior College
work, were voted down, apparently by the same members
who are supporting the main proposition. The limits of the
measure are also uncertain. In form it applies only to Junior
College work, but the line between Junior College and Senior
College work is an administrative rather than an educational one—that is to say, large numbers of Senior College
and even graduate students are constantly taking Junior
College work. The natural tendency will be either for the
Senior College work to encroach upon the Junior in such a
way as to break down the proposed scheme in its execution; or else, in order to secure the measure in its Junior
College application, to extend it further into Senior College
work. Moreover, it is possible for this separation to be extended throughout the entire Senior College without legislative act bearing directly upon the question. The development
of Junior College work to the point of giving a Bachelor's
degree, the reservation of the Senior College for professional
and quasi-professional work, are already broached. Add to
this the possibility of continual transfer, especially in departments heartily favoring the scheme and not heartily
supporting the principle of coeducation, of Senior College
electives to the Junior College, and the whole thing is done.

III. There will be administrative difficulties of a nature to provoke continual friction. The assignment of instructors to the men and women sections, respectively; the coercion of departmental instructors who are in favor of coeducation, and who believe that no such thing as coeducation without co-instruction is possible, or, (if there is no coercion) the granting of freedom of choice, creating continual odious comparisons and contrasts of different departments, indicate some of the difficulties.

IV. The experiment of building up a Junior College as a distinctive feature of the university system is a most important educational matter, and one which may be expected to exercise, if it has a fair chance, a wide influence. Is it not a mistake to complicate and make more difficult its success, and to obscure the interpretation of the results reached by it, through attempting to build up at the same time two junior colleges and by introducing a further experiment along sex lines?

V. Either the experiment will not cost any more money than any other scheme of development, in which case the quality of work will inevitably suffer, or else it will be decidedly more expensive, and all this additional expense will be diverted from present needs in the development of departments.

VI. THE PROPOSED MEASURE PUTS THE UNIVERSITY BEFORE THE COMMUNITY AND THE COUNTRY IN THE LIGHT OF RAISING THE SEX ISSUE.

There is no one point upon which public sentiment is so deeply and extensively sensitive as upon the question of sex. Even the labor question shrinks beside it. Admitting for the sake of argument that many or even most of the previous statements are not well grounded, it still remains a fact that after an institution has taken a certain policy regarding the relation of the sexes that policy cannot be changed without leaving in the minds of a large part of the community the belief either that it is calculated to work harm to the interests of women; or else, as a matter of fact, irrespective of intention, will have that result. Such a situation is full of peril. No university, however great its financial resources, can contemplate with equanimity a move which makes it the

centre of acrimonious discussion and which tends to lessen
its command of the moral confidence of the community.

Respectfully yours,

(Signed) John Dewey

Reviews

ANALYTICAL PSYCHOLOGY

A Practical Manual by Lightner Witmer. Boston and London: Ginn & Co., 1902.

Very few recent books in philosophy or psychology appeal to a more definite need than this book or meet it more adequately. It is "a series of experiments which can be performed by untrained students," with little explanation on the part of a teacher, and without costly apparatus. As such it affords a most valuable supplement to any of the good textbooks in psychology already in use. It may, of course, be used also as an independent manual and introductory manual, as the experiments cover such topics as apperception, attention, association, space-perception, and analysis of sensation (the last under three well conceived headings), and in that order. But I believe its largest usefulness will be found when employed by both teacher and student to reinforce, illustrate and make concrete the principles found in more theoretic works. I quote with hearty approval Dr. Witmer's words: "This Manual can render no more gratifying service than that of diverting those who are destined to become teachers from an unwholesome subservience to psychological and pedagogical authorities toward a confident self-dependence upon their own powers of observation and reflection." And I add that the book is most admirably qualified to perform this task. It shows upon every page marks of adaptation to the teacher's and student's needs. Properly used in normal schools, I anticipate that it will become a most important adjunct to preparation for teaching. It strikes the happy mean between mere general theory and a complicated and minute experimentation which, not illustrating general principles, has little value for the teacher.

[First published in *School Review* 10 (1902): 412.]

THE WORLD AND THE INDIVIDUAL

Gifford Lectures, Second Series: Nature, Man, and the Moral
Order by Josiah Royce, Ph.D. New York: Macmillan Co.;
London: Macmillan and Co., 1901.

In this volume Professor Royce develops the general
theory of Being elaborated in the first series of Gifford
Lectures, by applying it to a number of particular problems
that arise in connection with human experience as human.
The sub-title of the book indicates the general character of
the problems taken up: Nature, Man, and the Moral Order.
For the purposes of review, at least, we may sub-divide Mr.
Royce's discussion somewhat differently, putting together the
first three chapters under the head of the explanation of certain phases of our intellectual organization of experience;
grouping chapters four and five together as an account of
nature as such; and placing the last five under the general
heading of the self and the individual with special reference
to the moral problems involved. The modulation between
these divisions, however, is subtle, and, in particular, throughout the discussion of the self there is a continuous blending
of the treatment of the individual as related to nature on one
side, and to moral action on the other.

The primary problem as to intellectual experience is to
justify, in spite of particular facts to the contrary, the conception that it is a revelation, however mysterious, fragmentary, and illegible in detail, of the unity which is whole,
perfect, and absolute, a unity in which Being is entirely
identified with Meaning. The problem is constituted by the
fact that our experience is decidedly limited, not complete;
that in it meaning is divorced from being; and that such
meanings or ideas as we have, seem to be resisted and determined by facts which are alien, stubbornly resistant, and
compulsory—where meaning *seems* to be determined by a
reality which is anything but meaning. The solution of the
problem is in the recognition that this stubborn other does

[First published in *Philosophical Review* 11 (1902): 392–407.]

not resist and force our will and meaning, in so far as they
are genuine and adequate, but because of their limitations
and fragmentariness. Through the very resistance is furnished the material of a fuller purpose and a completer
realization. Our recognition of facts is not a matter of taking
note of something wholly outside us, but is rather an
acknowledgment by will of its own basis or presuppositions,
and of what is necessary to its own completeness. Or, "a
fact, then, is at once that which my present will implies and
presupposes, and that which, for this very reason, is in some
aspect Other than what I find myself here and now producing, accomplishing, attaining" (p. 28). Hence the twofold aspect of facts as experienced by us. Their most universal character is "a synthesis of their so-called 'stubborn'
or 'foreign' character, with their equally genuine character as
expressions of our own purpose" (p. 30). Reality is to us an
"Ought." It is that which the will ought to recognize; but
"ought" no more here than in morality is identical with
coercion. That which the will ought to recognize is just its
own complete self. The particular facts which seem to limit,
constrain, and determine us, thereby enable "us even now to
accomplish our will better than we could if we did not acknowledge these facts" (p. 41). Here is the possibility of
reconciling empiricism with idealism. The present will or
meaning, being limited, must continually wait upon instruction from beyond its present self in order to find out
what it really is; it cannot anticipate in detail, much less
mold the world of fact to its own present meaning. But the
start is with meaning, and every fact empirically won serves
in the further appreciation of what Meaning really means. It
depends upon and points to a perfected embodiment of idea
in reality. And this is idealism.

In carrying out the principle of learning from the Other,
what our own will is or means, we find ourselves committed
to the principle of putting to one side for the time our present
purpose, and devoting ourselves to its completion through
the search for fact as such. This search manifests itself in
the act of attention which discriminates. The act of attention
distinguishes for us the fact which is just now acknowledged,
from the "rest of the universe." But this distinction does not

isolate. The very discrimination of the present fact implies that we also acknowledge in a general way the rest of the universe as real. Our interest is partial, but this very partiality implies that in the very withdrawal of attention it still acknowledges the rest of the universe as there, and hence as something which ought to be attended to. "And every least shifting of our conscious momentary attention is one of the small steps whereby we continually undertake to make good the original sin, as it were, with which our form of consciousness is beset" (p. 58).

Hence we get a series of discriminations. Each act of attention is discrete, but it implies a further succession of attentions or discriminations in which its own deficiencies shall be made good. It demands continuity, though the only way in which it can reach it is through the discrete points of a series. Hence all discrimination takes the form also of classification or relationship. We attempt to find something which is "between" the two discrete terms with which we are dealing, in virtue of which they may be identified. So far as this search succeeds, the succession of our acts finds itself expressed in an objective series which becomes a complex order-system. We have law precisely because within the series of changes "some definable characters of the objects that are undergoing the transformation do not vary" (p. 94).

Facts that are thus related to one another as an ordered series of discrete elements constitute the World of Description. It is an abstract, not a real world, just because in this process of discriminations we have set aside for the time the will or purpose (whose active acknowledgment constitutes the World of Appreciation, not Description), and set ourselves simply to finding the possible contents of some or any will. Because of this abstractness the objects of the World of Description may be stated in any order, while the acts of a will of necessity present themselves in an irreversible series. But the world of discriminated and ordered facts nevertheless presupposes the will to discriminate. The objective world of the scientist, however free within itself of any consecutive series of realized purposes, still presupposes the volitional series of acts by which the scientist observes and constructs it. We thus have reason at least for suspecting that the series of contents which the descriptive attitude is endeavoring to make into a continuum by interpolating connecting links, is after all but an image or reflex of the world of self-representative acts in which a complete will expresses itself.

The conception that the world of facts is present as the object of attention, meets a difficulty in the character of time. How can the past and the future be in any sense present? The key to the reply is found in the fact that even in perceptual time, in time as actually experienced by us, there is given a serial whole within which are distinguished time differences of former and latter. A succession comes to us as a present whole, present in the sense that it is known all at once. Our time experience is not that of a mathematically indivisible instant, but rather of a passage or transition from predecessors to successors. Succession is a movement from something towards its desired fulfillment. "Our temporal form of experience is thus peculiarly the form of the Will as such. . . . Every part of a succession is present in so far as when it is, that which is *no longer*, and that which is *not yet*, both of them stand in essentially significant relations to this present" (pp. 124–25). Conceptual time, the world as a temporal succession, presents exactly the same features. "We conceive the past as leading towards, as aiming in the direction of the future, in such wise that the future depends for its meaning upon the past, and the past in its turn has its meaning as a process expectant of the future" (p. 132). Time as such is finite, because it marks the movement of the imperfect towards its own perfection. But the temporal world *as a whole* is at the same time an eternal world. A finite idea must appear as essentially temporal because in its very fragmentariness it is aiming or moving towards its own completion. But since the fulfillment exists, since indeed the nature of being is to be fulfillment, the temporal world is present as completely realized to the absolute, and in this complete presentation is eternal. In a temporal process as such each event of the series excludes former and latter elements. But all the members of an "experienced succession are *at once* to any consciousness which observes the whole succession as a whole" (pp. 138–39).

By the nature of the case, the entire temporal succession

is present to the Absolute, and hence the absolute experience does, for *all* time, what our consciousness does for some portion of time; it has presented to it at once all distinctions of past, present, and future. The eternal order is thus nothing essentially different from the temporal; it is just the essential order in its entirety, taken as known once for all by the Absolute.

As already stated, the World of Description is the result of our attempt, when we recognize the inadequate content of our will, to find out *how* the will is expressed in the facts of universal experience. The World of Appreciation is our recognition of *what* it is our will even now seeks. We learn that our will demands not merely contents to be appreciated, but other wills than ours. Hence the World of Description is never a whole truth: it must be interpreted in terms of the World of Appreciation.[1]

Our belief in the reality of nature "is inseparably bound up with our belief in the existence of our fellow-men" (pp. 165–66). Nature is the common realm of human experience: the real object is simply that which is common to my fellow and myself. It is thus essentially a social tool—that which serves as the common basis of definite acts of cooperation. The so-called rigidly uniform natural laws are just more generalized means of conceiving and socially communicating definite plans of action. The discovery of mechanical laws of nature has been a condition for the organization of definite social customs. Because we conceive nature as a socially significant tool, then that aspect of nature in which it

---

1. I do not find, however, in Professor Royce's discussion, any basis for a distinction between the problem of *what* our will intends, and *how* the will is expressed. To know what the will intends is precisely to know how it is embodied. This is the very point of the distinction and relation of the inner and outer meaning. The World of Description arises (see particularly p. 310) just because not knowing enough of our purpose we cannot set about directly expressing it. On the other hand, the criterion that he sets up for the reality of persons, viz.: that our fellows furnish us with a needed supplement to our own meanings, that they are local centres for imparting meanings to us (pp. 172–74), holds equally well of all our knowledge of, and intercourse with, objects. According to this theory, either all things ought to be persons (because they too are embodiments of meanings which help make up the fulfillment), or else all persons ought to be things—simply supplementary agencies in filling out the meaning already partially possessed by us.

is most serviceable socially, viz., that of suggesting unvarying laws, has come to be taken as an essential characteristic of nature. This mechanical conception then is no axiom, or even an empirically established generalization; it possesses its present authority because of our social interest in discovering uniformity as the basis of social cooperation. We must guard ourselves against letting this social interest blind us to other aspects of nature, or make us believe that nature is simply and only an unvarying uniformity. To regard nature as just a treasure-house of purely mechanical laws, is to be anthropomorphic—it is to take our social need as final.

In discovering the human motive which is at the basis of our assumption of mechanical law, we soften the ordinary dualism between mind and matter. The conception of evolution still further breaks down this dualism. Evolution bridges the apparent gulf between mind and matter, and thereby forces upon us the question: what is the real link that unites these extremes? Professor Royce begins his answer to this question by pointing out that the laws of our World of Description are not literal truths of experience, but ideal constructions, "convenient conceptions whereby we summarize observed facts" (pp. 215–16). They are in marked contrast with some other generalizations that are *literal* statements—such as that an organism grows old but never grows young. A significant difference between these symbolic and literal laws is that the former describe reversible processes, the latter irreversible. The former are true of matter only; while laws of irreversible processes are common to matter and to mind. It is in the region of the abstract and ideal constructions that we find the difference between mind and matter emphasized; it is in the more literal, actual, and directly observable ones that we find a process common to material and mental phenomena. Secondly, both material and mental facts involve a tendency of one part to communicate with another. Ideas assimilate other ideas; in material nature the so-called wave movements institute a like propagation. Again, both the material and the mental worlds show a tendency to the formation of habits. Physical nature tends to fall into rhythms. These rhythms, however, are not absolutely permanent; if we take a long enough time span, they pass away or decay. It is suggested that apparently fixed natural processes have after all only the same relative stability which habits have in conscious beings. Perhaps "the inner nature of things is not so much ideally constant as merely relatively stable, so that in the fluent life of our consciousness, we directly know a process of which the apparently absolute stability of the conceived material processes is really only another instance, whose inner fluency is concealed from us by the longer intervals of time demanded for important changes to take place" (p. 223).

Finally, the process of evolution itself is common to both mental and material nature. The outcome of these four points of community is to suggest an impression and an hypothesis. The impression is that the contrast ordinarily made between material and conscious processes "depends merely upon the accidents of the human point of view" (p. 224). The hypothesis is that the material processes in their reality are just as conscious as are those which go on in ourselves; but go on at such different rates from ours that there is no free communication between theirs and ours. Nature is to be regarded as the phenomenal sign of a vast conscious process; a finite consciousness in which, as in our own, there is a play between habit and novelty; between the irrevocable which is left behind, and the repeated or persistent. On this basis, the "fluent inner experience, which our hypothesis attributes to inorganic Nature would be a finite experience of an extremely august temporal span, so that a material region of the inorganic world would be to us the phenomenal sign of the presence of at least one fellow-creature who took, perhaps, a billion years to complete a moment of his consciousness, so that where we saw, in the signs given us of his presence, only monotonous permanence of fact, he, in his inner life, faced momentarily significant change" (p. 228). Evolution is then interpreted as due "to the constant intercommunication of a vast number of relatively separate regions of this world of conscious life" (p. 229).

Every natural process, viewed from within, is the pursuit of an ideal. Hence there is no dead or merely material nature, and no evolution of mind out of matter. There is simply intercommunication through which elements or facts

that are novel in our experience arise. This continual reception and transmission occasions what we shall call growth
or development. "The essence of this Doctrine of Evolution
lies in the fact that it recognizes the continuity of man's life
with that of an extra-human realm, whose existence is hinted
to us by our experience of Nature" (p. 242).[2]

This brings us to our second main division—the human
self. Professor Royce begins by calling attention: (1) to the
ambiguity of traditional doctrines about the self, seen on one
side in exaltations of its dignity and value, and on the other
in depreciations of it through assertions of its "selfishness"
and need of regeneration; and (2) to the variability of selfhood as actually and empirically known, its change from day
to day and almost from moment to moment. This ambiguity
in theory, and instability in fact, the author finds to originate
in the fact that empirical self-consciousness depends upon a
series of contrast-effects bound up with our social experience.
The individual defines himself through the contrast of his
own desires and aims with those of others who enter into the
same social situations with him. Thus, as the other elements
vary, the self varies.

2. It may be said that we have here the basis of discrimination between persons and things which was declared in the previous
note to be lacking: the "person" is that the time rate of whose
mental process is sufficiently like our own to enable us to enter
into direct communication with it; the "thing" belongs to some
consciousness whose time rate is disparate from our own. This
may be so; but then what becomes of the previous elaborate development of the World of Description through serially recurrent
discriminative acts, and of distinction of it from the World of
Appreciation as that which being common to different consciousnesses, serves as a basis for cooperation among them? I do not,
however, consider myself a competent critic here; this whole
doctrine of "nature" is too high for me; I cannot attain unto it.
To be frank, I do not believe that such speculative constructions,
with no further basis than certain vague analogies, involving
also the highly precarious proposition that certain "truths"
about irreversible processes are much more literal and actual in
their objective validity than are mechanical laws, do anything
but bring philosophy into disrepute. It is, I believe, this sort of
thing which encourages in the man of science, as well as in the
man of common sense, the too common notion about metaphysics. In any case, it is not clear what entitles Professor Royce
suddenly to turn his back upon ideal constructions and fall back
upon literal experiences—seeing that his whole theory of Being
is based upon discounting literal experiences as fragmentary,
mere hints, glimpses, etc., etc., in favor of what, for our type of
consciousness, must be, and must remain, a wholly ideal construction.

The ambiguity in the theoretical view is due to the fact that the present self is, as finite, essentially fragmentary; it needs to be fulfilled in the Absolute self which is its own unity. The empirical principle of contrast-effects is given a rational or philosophical meaning by recognizing that, in all its diverse and chaotic changes, the self is struggling to possess or create some one principle, some finally significant contrast, which shall mark it off from all others. The most stable feature of the empirical Ego is just the *general* fact of contrast—the will to be different, or to be unique. The true self, in the Absolute, is a significantly different meaning or purpose contrasted with that of every other. Hence in the world of Absolute Being, each retains its own individuality distinct from other selves, yes, even distinct from the Absolute self. Our life plans are mutually contrasting life plans, and each can reach its own fulfillment only by recognizing this contrast both for one's self and for others. Except in the variety of unique meanings or wills the absolute will or meaning cannot exist. As finite, we are longings of which God is the conscious satisfaction; but conscious fulfillment in turn presupposes conscious longing. The divine completion demands our incompletion. A goal which is not the goal of a process is meaningless (pp. 299–304 *passim*, p. 308).

Having thus determined the place of the self in Absolute Being, Professor Royce turns to its place in the temporal world, with special reference to the problem of the emergence of new selves. The problem is the appearance of new life purposes. In explanation, Professor Royce recurs to the theory of discriminative attention by which new members are continually interpolated as intermediates between two extremes (whose unity is sought), so that a series is constructed. The empirical self in order to define itself, discriminates others from self and self from others. This happens only through imitation. But imitation is neither mere reiteration by the agent of his previous will or self, nor is it a mere repetition of the imitated self. It is a third construction of a new self, which, having assimilated to itself something from both the previous self and the other, lies, so to speak, between them. Thus the historical individual is a series of results of intermediation by which relatively unrelated selves are made more related.

Professor Royce then makes "the wholly tentative hypothesis that the process of evolution of new forms of consciousness in Nature is throughout of this same general type"
(p. 315). That is, the appearance of new selves in nature is
the same sort of thing as is the appearance of new modes of
self-definition within the same finite self. "Sexual generation
is analogous to the process of conscious imitation" (pp. 315–
16), while the process of asexual generation is like that type
of human action in which the individual, having a definite
purpose already in mind, tries it on experimentally without
imitation. We need only suppose that some of the intermediary terms resulting from the discriminating process become conscious not merely of their place in the temporal
series, but of their relation in the Absolute, to appreciate
how the discriminated contents might appear as new selves.
For in such case they will "define their own lives as in
dividually significant, conceive their goal as the Absolute"
(p. 321). As meanings relating to the Absolute, they survive
the finite experimental purposes for which they were originated.[3]

We now come to the distinctive moral problem. The
postulates of a moral order are: (1) the freedom of the self
in choosing; (2) hence the reality of moral badness as well as
of goodness—for otherwise there can be no alternatives, no
choice; (3) the possibility of real improvement in the objective order through the right choice of the individual—for
unless the choice makes a real difference in things there can
be no true freedom. But how can choice, real evil, and the
making of things better or worse, really exist in a world
which is eternally present as complete to an Absolute Being?
In such a world, must not every apparent choice be really an

3. One can hardly refrain from a question. Since by the theory
every meaning is conscious, and is related to the Absolute, how
does it happen that some are conscious of their relation, and
thus set up, on their own account, as new finite selves; while
others are unaware of this relation, and are thus taken as terms
within some finite self? Surely, all meanings as temporal are on
the same plane; and all as in the eternal are on the same plane.
Why then this invidious distinction: why do some remain only
temporal as to their consciousness, while others succeed in gaining a consciousness in relation to the eternal? Moreover, the
distinctive self is conscious of itself only *in* its own serial terms.
Why do not such terms then segregate themselves and appear as
"persons"? Professor Royce seems to have no criterion of distinction between a "self" and its own "states."

act eternally done and known in the Absolute, just as it is, with no possibility of its being otherwise? In such a world, it would seem either that there is no evil, or that evil is a means by which the Absolute wins its own perfection, and hence is in no sense the doing of the individual.

The principle of solution for these difficulties is found in "the true distinction and the true connection, between the temporal and the eternal aspects of Being" (p. 347). The finite self seeks but does not know the Absolute, which, accordingly, appears as its other. Two courses are consequently open to the fragmentary self. It may undertake to win its own unity either by obeying the world beyond, or by subjugating that to its own present narrowness. Instead of seeking perfection in rational obedience to the law of the Absolute, it may seek rather to master the world in terms of its own fragmentary insight and intention. It may then either expand into the larger whole, or endeavor to narrow the latter into its own petty compass. Here is the choice which gives significance to good and evil.

The possibility of choice is involved in the nature of attention. In so far as we attend to the ought, we can but act upon it. The essence of attention is to unite knowledge and deed. But attention involves inattention, and we may choose to ignore, to forget the Ought that is recognized. Attention can be fixed upon the private self; in excluding the ought from our attention, we prevent its direct influence upon our action. And this ignoring and forgetting is sin. Although ignorance, it is evil for it is voluntarily chosen; it comes from the will to forget (pp. 357–59 passim).[4]

To the objection that even the sinful act must contribute

4. This seems to be an unusually naïve begging of the question. The premise is that attention is "an act by which we come to know a truth, and an act by which we are led to an outward deed" (p. 355). The idea is a nascent deed; attend to it and it becomes a completed deed. Yet, Professor Royce assumes that there is no evil unless the Ought has been known and recognized. To recognize it, however, is certainly to be attentive to it. How then can we avoid acting upon it? Why, replies Professor Royce, just by being inattentive, by forgetting; we cannot get directly from attention to non-action, but we can get from attention to non-action through forgetting! But how forget? How escape from attention? It would seem to be a philosophical principle that what a given concept forbids cannot be secured simply by changing its name.

to the perfection of God, and being unique is fulfilled in the whole in a way for which no other will could provide a substitute, Professor Royce replies by returning to the definition of the temporal and the eternal order. All the temporal or finite facts as such are evil, since, "taken in themselves," they have no adequate meaning, and hence leave us searching and dissatisfied. But such searching, and hence such finite evil is necessary, because without it there can be no consciousness of finding and of fulfillment, no Absolute. But surely if a finite fact is evil, then it can work more evil. While this evil must be undone in the Absolute, yet this undoing does not flow from the evil itself, but from other wills (either of the same agent or of some other self) to thwart, and atone, and make good the evil. And while the good thus attained is doubtless higher than the good that would have existed had there been no evil, yet it comes about not because of the evil will, but because of some other will which recognizes what the evil will denies (pp. 365–66 *passim*).[5]

In lecture nine, Professor Royce considers the struggle with evil, particularly with reference to our consolation in this struggle, and its bearing upon the virtues of courage, endurance, resignation, and hope. He discusses particularly two aspects of the problem. As already stated, the finite and temporal life is, as such, essentially more or less dissatisfied, and so evil. Hence, dissatisfaction is the universal experience of every temporal being. As also already stated, the very

5. Two significant difficulties appear here. First, how can the finite will, in any *particular* case, distinguish between the act which carries it towards fulfillment, and that which narrows and limits it? It is our former difficulty: all acts are on the same plane *qua* temporal, and on the same *qua* eternal, while Professor Royce seems to take one act as *merely* temporal and another as *merely* eternal. And this suggests the second difficulty: How can any finite will be really good, if all the temporal and finite as such is evil? The distinction between the temporal order and the eternal order, which Professor Royce holds to be the key to the whole problem, is a distinction *in toto*. It applies equally to each and every act. To admit that the eternal can be realized in one fragmentary passing finite meaning, and hence make it good or better, while it is absolutely indispensable for any distinction between one idea as truer or falser than another, one act better or worse than another, is to introduce a principle which involves a complete revision of Professor Royce's fundamental notion of Absolute Being.

presence of ill in the temporal order is the condition of the perfection of the eternal order. "Were there no longing in Time there would be no peace in Eternity" (p. 386). Our comfort in the struggle is thus in realizing that the sorrows of our finitude are identically God's own sorrows, and have their purpose and meaning in the divine life as such significant sorrows; and in the assurance that God's fulfillment in the eternal order—a fulfillment in which we share—is to be won through the very bitterness of tribulation. We may know that God sorrows in and with us, and that this sorrowing contributes somehow to the ultimate perfection. The other aspect of the problem is that the concrete contents of our suffering are the outcome of some individual's finite will. "Morally evil deeds, and the ill fortune of mankind, are inseparably linked aspects of the temporal order" (p. 389). Our suffering from the results of other wills (unknown to us, and many of them doubtless extra-human) is thus a sign of our organic participation in a realm of infinite experiences in which infinite meanings are realized. And if this fact brings us sorrow, it also brings us comfort and courage. Unless one can harm another, he cannot help him; and where an individual can neither harm nor help, no significant moral task is possible. On such a basis, moral life would be a mere cultivation of "a purely vain and formal piety, as empty as it is ineffectual" (p. 403). To suffer the consequences of another's ill deed, is, if rightly interpreted, an occasion for rejoicing: in it we may "discover at least one case where our own share in the atoning work of our common humanity is clearly laid before me" (p. 392).

The final chapter discusses the union of God and man. In general, this is simply a summary of the previous discussion, especially in terms of the relation of the temporal and the eternal, with a further account of its bearing upon the question of human immortality. As in what I have to say in criticism I shall connect with the former of these points, I here take up simply the question of immortality. The finite union with the Absolute, the fact that the eternal is but the temporal process known as a whole, carries with it as a necessary consequence an immortal individual life. Individuality cannot be attained in our present finite form of consciousness.

We are real individuals only in the Absolute. Hence we must be conscious of selfhood in him, "in a form higher than that now accessible to us" (p. 445). Secondly, the very nature of death, in a universe of the type idealistically defined by Professor Royce, implies immortality. The significance of death is the passing away or defeat of a purpose or meaning before that meaning is worked out to its completeness, or is expressed with its intended individual wholeness. But every real fact is a conscious fact, and hence a defeated purpose must be known *as such*. It can be known only by some conscious being who can say: this was my purpose, but temporally I no longer seek its embodiment. And this once more means "that whoever dies with his meanings unexpressed, lives as individual, to see, in the eternal world, just his unique meaning finally expressed in a life sequent to the life that death terminated" (p. 443). In other words, the whole individual must realize the defeated purpose as an incident in his own life, and in the fulfillment of his own true purpose. In the third place, the task set upon the individual, that of performing his unique function in the absolute, is not a task which can ever be brought to an end. There is always meaning to be realized, for every new action creates a new situation which calls for a new deed.

The final summary of the whole doctrine is that "despite God's absolute unity we as individuals preserve and attain our unique lives and meanings, and are not lost in the very life that sustains us, and that needs us as its own expression. This life is real through us all; and we are real through our union with that life" (p. 452).

I confess to a certain embarrassment in concluding this review. It is absurd to attempt to criticize a subtle and comprehensive philosophical argument of four hundred and fifty pages in a few lines of a magazine article. To attempt it puts one in the rôle of a carping fault-finder. And yet Professor Royce's book, just because of its fundamental character, compels searchings of heart. One cannot read it without the stirring either of assent or dissent, and without some striving to formulate the reasons for assent or dissent. In my own case, I find the net result to be a dissent as profound as is the metaphysical theory of Being which Professor Royce presents to us. And so I shall close with a brief statement of this dissent, not as a criticism of Professor Royce, but as an expression of my own reaction.

In my review of his previous volume (*Philosophical Review*, Vol. IX, pp. 311 ff. [*Middle Works of John Dewey*, 1:241–56]), I said in effect that Professor Royce seemed to me to be attempting a self-contradictory task. On the one hand, the fragmentariness, the transitoriness of our actual experience is magnified; this is the essence of the method by which the definition of the Absolute is reached, and it affords, by contrast, the content of the definition of the Absolute. On the other hand, some kind of organic relationship is constantly supposed between the Absolute and the finite, between the complete and the fragmentary, in virtue of which alone some meaning is attachable to the latter. Without such identity, there is no basis for ascribing any valuable qualitative content to the finite. The Absolute as Absolute must, after all, include the fragmentary, and hence the fragmentary cannot be really fragmentary. Professor Royce's phrase "taken in itself" as applied to the finite is at most question-begging. Recognizing that doubtless much of his present volume has escaped me, and that my own mental medium has doubtless distorted something of what remains, I am still bound to say that my most careful study of the new volume has only strongly reinforced my conviction of the contradiction inherent in the old. On page 417 he speaks of an "ontological relation that, when rightly viewed is seen to link yourself even in all your weakness, to the very life of God, and the whole universe to the meaning of every Individual." He says, "not only in spite then of our finite bondage, but because of what it means and implies, we are full of the presence and the freedom of God." Grant all this, and what becomes of the finitude and fragmentariness of which Professor Royce makes so much? An Absolute which enters organically into the "fragmentary" consciousness is one which gives that fragmentary consciousness a *present* and *immediate* (temporal) absolute significance. Truth to tell, Professor Royce has all the time two fragmentaries: one the fragmentary as it is in us, the other as it is in his Absolute. And he vibrates back and forth between them.

On one side, he says the final meaning of our experience "can simply never be expressed *in the type of experience* which we men now have at our disposal" (p. 266). And again, "the true individual Self of any man gets its final expression in some *form of consciousness different* from that which we men now possess" (p. 269). And again, "in God, every individual Self, however insignificant its temporal endurance may seem, eternally possesses a *form of consciousness that is wholly other* than this our present flickering form of mortal consciousness"[6] (p. 435, italics mine in each case). In all these cases, it is a different type or form of consciousness which is asserted. The whole burden of at least one half the volume is this radical transcendence of the finite consciousness by the Absolute. And, on the other hand, this finite consciousness is and must be already *in* the Absolute, and the Absolute already *in* it. Professor Royce's entire metaphysics seems to me permeated with this illusion of double vision, of reduplication.

Take such a passage as that on page 381, "Any temporal fact, as such, is essentially more or less dissatisfying, and so evil. . . . In Time there is for the will, no conscious satisfaction," and contrast it with these passages from pages 411 and 427. "For our temporal life is the very expression of the eternal triumph"; and again, "Here and now, . . . is the temporal expression of a value that is unique, and that would be missed as a lost perfection of the eternal world if it were not known to God as just this finite striving. The temporal brevity of the instant is here no barrier to its eternal significance." Professor Royce seems to have two minds about time and two about eternity. On one side, the temporal process in each and every phase is equally fragmentary and finite. The eternal is simply the temporal process taken as an object of knowledge all at once. Here there is no organic relationship between eternity and any *particular* temporal portion. The other view is that the meaning of the whole time process somehow manifests itself in every member of the process. Each part of experience has an eternal meaning, because it

6. And yet our consciousness is immortal, and yet again no temporal moment is any better than any other!

really embodies in its own significance the meaning of all others, being linked to them in the Absolute.

Consider the "melody" metaphor which Professor Royce employs so much. A melody is not a present whole just because after it has been sung or played, we recall to ourselves the fact that all its successive notes make one melody. "The present knowledge of the whole" (p. 418), does not constitute the melody as melody. Otherwise the knowledge of any conceivable series of noises would constitute a melody just the moment it becomes the object of a single cognitive act. What makes the melody a melody is precisely that *no* note is "fragmentary," but each somehow carries within its own meaning, as each is experienced *in* succession, the meaning of all the other notes. To apply the metaphor in any consistent way to human experience as a temporal process, would involve the rewriting of every sentence in which Professor Royce has taken the "finitude" of our experience as indicative of some experience which is of another type or form. The notes simply do *not* make a melody in some *other* consciousness than that which is of them as they come and go. Such other type of consciousness is a bare symbol, a reminiscence that once such and such a melody was present to us in its own vital and dynamic change. And so Professor Royce's Absolute seems to me a mere pallid and formal symbol of the actual wealth and concreteness of experience as it is actually experienced.

The likeness and the difference of Professor Royce from the German transcendentalists is significant: in certain phases of his doctrine he is close to Fichte, though far enough from Hegel. But even when the likeness in doctrine is greatest, in method the difference is tremendous. The old transcendentalists were at least serious with their theory of the Absolute as the meaning and reality of present experience. They worked out the idea into a logic, a *Naturphilosophie*, and a philosophy of history. They re-read our actual thinking experience, our actual scientific consciousness, and our actual associative life in detail, in terms of that which gives them their reality. At first sight, Professor Royce, with his willingness to leave all these matters in the region of the empirical and the contingent, to be got at casually and fragmentarily, seems to be more modest—to leave more room to the actual, to the empirical scientist. But, after all, this region is left simply because, from the standpoint of the Absolute, it means so little "to us men." Surely when we are dealing with fragments, the mere size of the rubbish heap hardly matters; nor does permission to go playing freely in it amount to much. The apparently larger concession to and reverence for empirically given elements thus turn out to be mainly nominal. As a result, Professor Royce's own method seems to be essentially formal. He is dealing with Being, and with the categories of the finite, of time, of the individual, wholly at large. And not even Professor Royce's comprehensive knowledge and subtle intellect can avoid the unreal and arbitrary character that attaches to concepts which at best are only "hinted at" by the actual warp and woof of our experience as experience, and which accordingly can be only logically determined. As a consequence, Professor Royce dives arbitrarily from the region of concepts into the chaotic sea of experience, and fishes out here and there just that particular experience which is required at that time to give body and tone to thin and empty categories. Without the psychology of ideo-motor action, of intention, of imitation, without the empirical principle of irreversibility, etc., etc., his constructive thought would hardly get very far. Not that I object to his use of these empirical elements; quite the contrary. But why take these experiences rather than any other? Either our experiences, yea, even the experiences of "us men" have ultimate meaning and worth, and the "Absolute" is only the most adequate possible construing of this meaning; or else, having it not, they are not available to give content to the Absolute. But a difference of form or type between our consciousness and the Absolute, simply once for all makes metaphysical method impossible.

Contributions to *Dictionary of Philosophy and Psychology*

NATURAL [Lat. *naturalis*]: Ger. *natürlich*; Fr. *naturel*; Ital. *naturale*. In accordance with, belonging to, or derived from nature.

While the term is derived from and associated, philosophically as well as etymologically, with the term NATURE (q.v.), it has selected especially one side of the meaning of that term, namely, that which is in accordance with the course of events, that which is regular, stated, and usual. The sense of physical has thus dropped into the background, though still apparent in such phrases as natural science and natural philosophy. A double meaning, that is, a higher and a lower sense, corresponding to similar connotations of nature, still persists, however, in its ethical implication. (1) On one side, that which is regular and uniform is that which is to be expected; it is the normal, that from which as a standard all departures are measured, and is opposed to the artificial as the purely factitious and strained. As norm, the word gets a highly ideal import, often being the highest term of commendation, as in popular aesthetic judgment of a picture, or in social intercourse, in judgment of a personality. (2) In its theological use, however, it is identified with the carnal, base, or worldly—thus the term "natural man" in the writings of St. Paul, and through him in theology generally. (3) In a midway or neutral sense the term natural is simply opposed to that which is supernatural or revealed, and then may be further supplied with a good or bad sense, according to the disposition of the writer—as natural religion, natural theology. (4) It is also defined as that which belongs to men, by and from birth, as opposed to that which has been acquired historically or conferred by political authority—as NATURAL RIGHTS (q.v.) distinguished from POSITIVE RIGHTS (q.v.).

[First published in *Dictionary of Philosophy and Psychology*, Vol. 2, ed. James Mark Baldwin (New York: Macmillan Co., 1902).]

NATURAL REALISM: Ger. *natürlicher Realismus*; Fr. *réalisme naturel*; Ital. *realismo naturale*. The theory that in the fact of perception, as a veracious datum and testimony of consciousness, a knowledge both of mind and matter is indubitably given. The same as Natural Dualism. Cf. REALISM, PRESENTATIONISM (1), and COMMON SENSE.

The term is defined as used by Hamilton. See his edition of Reid, Note A, § i, and *Discussions on Philos.*, 55.

NATURALISM [Lat. *naturalis*, natural]: Ger. *Naturalismus*; Fr. *naturalisme*; Ital. *naturalismo*. (1) The theory that the whole of the universe or of experience may be accounted for by a method like that of the physical sciences, and with recourse only to the current conceptions of physical and natural science; more specifically, that mental and moral processes may be reduced to the terms and categories of the natural sciences. It is best defined negatively as that which excludes everything distinctly spiritual or transcendental. In this meaning it is about equivalent to POSITIVISM (q.v.).

NATURALISM (in art). A theory which holds it to be the true end of art to "follow nature." The rendering of a landscape or human character without subjective idealization; without omission of elements that are opposed to the personal or average taste and conscience. It is, however, distinguished from realism by implying faithfulness to the forces at work rather than minute copying of details.

NATURE [Lat. *natura*, from *nasci*, to be born or produced; an equivalent of the Gr. φύσις, from φύειν]: Ger. *Natur*; Fr. *nature*; Ital. *natura*. The word has a primary double sense, each of these meanings having in turn a number of subdivisions. (1) In the first place, nature means whatever (literally or figuratively) is born with the thing, and hence belongs originally to its own being instead of being acquired or superadded.

It thus means (*a*) the constitution, native structure, essence, or very being of a thing. Thus we speak of the nature of anything—of a horse, stone, man, star, thought, soul, God, etc. The Scholastics used the term as equivalent, objectively

or as regards the existence concerned, to essence, but as connoting more especially not the being in itself, but (*b*) considered as the active source (or principle) of the operations
by which the being realized its destined end. Here is the
transition to the second meaning.

(2) Nature is the sum total of forces which animate the
created world, or the aggregate of events and changing things
which make it up.

In this conception two quite distinct meanings are
obviously contained. In one meaning, nature is conceived
(*a*) as the dynamic agent concerned in bringing about the
changes in the world. It is at least semi-personified. Thus the
Scholastics talked of nature doing this and that; of various
forces and qualities as the various modes of the operation of
nature, etc. This use of nature, as a cause at large, was seized
upon by Comte (see POSITIVISM) as a sign of the "metaphysical" stage of thought, distinguished equally from the
theological, where God is the active cause, and the positive or
scientific, where search for efficient agents is given up, and
simple sequences and coexistences are traced. Under (2, *a*)
we again have a subdivision, according as nature is conceived as (*α*) an independent, self-active agent, as in various
forms of pantheism and mysticism, or as (*β*) a subordinate
principle, a secondary cause, intervening between God as
efficient principle and the details of existence. In its other
meaning (*b*)—under (2)—nature is regarded as simply the
name given to the sum total or phenomena in time and
space; the physical world as presented to the senses. It is expressly restricted to phenomena, in their material relations to
one another; and the idea of productive or formative agency
is excluded. It is equivalent to the physical world, the realm
of things and events with which physical science deals.

Few terms used in philosophy have a wider or a looser
use, or involve greater ambiguity. While often used as
equivalent to the mechanical and material world, as a system
of particular objects and changes, it rarely quite loses its
sense of primordial, primitive, intrinsic, or, indeed, of something dynamic and productive; and so the term is used in an
active or passive, a spiritual or material sense, about as the
writer pleases. It is not surprising, then, that historically we

find it used to mark off, in a most definite way, the world from God, and again to identify the world with God, and once more to afford a connecting principle between God and the details of the world. Its various sub-meanings can, however, best be brought out in connection with the history of the term.

It is perhaps the oldest of all formulated and general philosophic concepts—that is, in its Greek form φύσις. Aristotle expressly calls the earlier philosophers (particularly the Ionic school) physicists (φυσικοί) and physiologists (φυσιο-λόγοι) to express their preoccupation with nature as the object of philosophy. Περὶ φύσεως (concerning nature) is the putative, traditional, or actual title of the writings of Xenophanes, Melissus, Parmenides, and Heraclitus. The term began with that wide and vague sense which has always hung about it—something designating the whole world, considered not as a chaos of particular things, but as referred to some general principle for explanation or to account for its production. Thus the statement of Windelband (*Hist. of Philos.*, 73, Eng. trans.) that the "constitutive mark of the concept φύσις was originally that of remaining ever like itself," its contrary being the transient, is altogether too narrow. While the chief object of interest to the "physiologues" was what we should term the physical world, and their categories are, to us, of a physical sort (fire, air, water, etc.), yet it must be remembered that no clear distinction of mind and matter had yet been made; nature was conceived of as living and, in so far at least, as psychical; the scheme, in a word, was HYLOZOISM (q.v.), not materialism. It was with Plato that the distinction between the physical and the metaphysical was clearly stated, and thus the tendency initiated to use the term nature in a restricted sense which marked it off from the spiritual; it was the sphere of becoming, as distinct from that of being, and hence was contingent, and the object of probable knowledge only. (God as distinct from φύσις was the ὅθεν φύεται.) But it was far from being identical with what we should term nature in the purely physical sense, the term σῶμα much more nearly expressing that. Moreover, in general and in detail, a teleological explanation of nature was required by which it was subjected to the good and to reason (see NOUS). In Aristotle, this Platonic conception of nature joined with a strain derived from the Sophists, and the term got for the first time a complete, explicit statement—the term, though not the idea, being rather incidental in Plato. In their political and ethical discussions, the Sophists (Hippias, see Xenophon, *Mem.*, iv. 14 ff.) had raised the question as to whether obligation exists by nature (φύσει) or by institution or convention (θέσει or νόμῳ). This gave rise to the conception of nature as a standard or norm that could be used to justify objective validity as distinct from arbitrary assertion or merely subjective convenience. The dramatists (Sophocles, *Antigone*) had already developed the conception of a law of nature which was universal and eternal, and the ethical industry of Socrates was devoted to establishing the existence and worth of such a law-giving nature. Hence, in Aristotle we have the conception of nature as, on one hand, the system of moving, changing things so far as directed to realizing an end, or (in their totality) *the* end, the absolute good; and, on the other, as the standard by reference to which all particulars of a given class, as well as all failures, deviations, and abnormalities, are to be measured; while it is distinguished from art because its efficient cause is internal, and not external. It is in this sense, for example, that man is, by nature, a political animal, and that the state is, by nature, prior to the individual citizen.

This conception, like the rest of the Aristotelian philosophy, was reformulated by the Scholastics, and thus has become (in the popular sense of nature as at once a productive force and the standard of order and regularity) a part of the ordinary view of the world. But there are two elements involved in the Aristotelian conception; and even if we grant that his own synthesis was adequate, it was hardly possible that later writers should not emphasize one factor or the other. On the one hand, there is the mechanical element— the physical is just the realm of extended and movable bodies, being thus distinguished from both the metaphysical and the teleological (*Met.*, vi. 1, and *De Caelo*, i. 1).

In the Epicurean philosophy, this conception becomes dominant and exclusive; the teleological factor, the reason or end, which, according to Aristotle, had animated the complex of moving bodies, is absolutely eliminated; and nature is simply the sum total of the mechanical impacts and arrangements of the purely quantitative elements, the atoms. This is the view which found its classical expression in the *De rerum Natura* of Lucretius, a poem which perhaps has done more than any one other cause to give to the term its limited, purely physical, content.

But all the order and uniformity and system (orderly unity) of nature is due, according to Aristotle, to the fact that it represents the transition of the potential to completion, under the teleological influence of forms, and of the supreme FORM (q.v.), God. In it, so far as it is really nature, nothing is superfluous, nothing perverted, nothing happens just by accident. It is an organic whole (ζῶον). This aspect is emphasized by the Stoics (Strato being the connecting link, Windelband, *Hist. of Philos.*, 179), save that, denying the transcendence of form and nous, nature is regarded as self-moved, both efficiently and teleologically. Nature is not merely ordered and attracted to perfection by God; it is God. It is itself law, cause, standard, and providence. To "live in accordance with nature" is the sum of all virtue. Nature is also used by the Stoics, in a restricted sense, as the peculiar animating principle of the plant, as distinct from the ἕξις of the inorganic, the ψυχή of the animal, or the νοῦς of man (Erdmann, *Hist. of Philos.*, i. 189, trans., and Zeller, *Hist. of Gr. Philos.*).

With Plotinus, nature again assumes a definite intermediate position, established, however, on the basis of emanations, not upon a teleological one. As NOUS (q.v.) comes below the supreme and ineffable One, so nous subdivides into a higher and lower soul (ψυχή), the higher which contemplates and enjoys the rational forces (νοῖ) which make up the νοῦς: the lower, which after the archetype thus contemplated, carries them into act and thus creates the objective world. This lower soul is nature—equivalent practically to the world soul of Plato and the λόγος σπερματικός of the Stoics. In the Middle Ages three strains appear. One is the orthodox scholastic, following Aristotle, expressly defining nature as the essence of anything, so far as it operates in a regular way to bring the thing to its appointed end. Another is the mystic, which continued the Platonic and Neo-Platonic sense, but in a more pantheistic way, tending to make nature the mysterious, vital creative energy of God. The third is the Arabian interpretation of Aristotle. Averroës, like the Stoics, interpreted Aristotle so as to deny the transcendent nous; form and purpose are wholly immanent in nature. Hence the distinction of nature (*De Caelo*) into *Natura naturans*, equivalent to God, the one reality viewed as active, as form and force, and into *Natura naturata*, the world as materialized form, as effect (see Siebeck, *Arch. f. Gesch. d. Philos.*, iii. 370, for origin of this distinction). The two terms made their way both among the Mystics and the Scholastics, being adapted to their respective uses. They appeared with Cusanus and Giordano Bruno, and (probably) from them made their way into Spinoza. With him, in scholastic fashion, the nature of a thing is its essence and its idea (*Ethica*, iv. def. 8'), and so the supreme essence is also *Natura*, *Natura naturans*, or *Deus*, while the world of modified existences is *Natura naturata* (i. pr. 29, schol.). In his earlier writings he distinguishes the latter into *generalis* and *particularis*, but abandons this in the *Ethics*.

Modern thought has added no essentially new elements to the concept of nature. It has, however, clearly brought out the homogeneity of nature, its identical structure and operation in all its parts, mundane and stellar, thus effectually doing away with the ancient conception of a diversity of grades, values, and qualities, a conception which, more than any other, is the philosophical idea underlying modern science (Windelband, *Hist. of Philos.*, 402). So far as science is concerned, the mechanical conception of nature may be said to have become, through the writings of Descartes, Galileo, Hobbes, and Newton, completely victorious, as against the Platonic and Aristotelian conceptions. The problem still remains, however, whether, taken as a totality and system, nature does not demand a rational and teleological valuation; and thus at the Renaissance, in the 17th and again in the 19th century, have arisen philosophic systems which have insisted that nature as a totality or system is an expression of thought, and which have attempted, with varying degrees of success, to combine a modified Aristotelianism with the detailed results of contemporary science.

This found its most ambitious expression in the so-called *Naturphilosophie* of Oken, Schelling, and Hegel, in the early part of the 19th century. In another connection the names of Rousseau and Goethe need special mention. Rousseau's motto and warcry was "Return to Nature," and in his treatment of the idea all the various senses and ambiguities were rolled into one. Nature meant at once the historically primitive and original; that which is distinct from art and the artificial; that which is opposed to the politically instituted; and that which is normative and ideal. In formulating the opposition between nature and culture he stimulated Herder and Schiller (as well as many others), and was, indirectly, an important factor in the development of the Modern German philosophy of history and society. Goethe, moved by the discussion, was led back to Spinoza; revived Spinoza's conception of nature, giving it, however, a thoroughly dynamic and organic interpretation, and by embodying it in his poetry, as well as in his prose criticism and his scientific efforts, influenced not only the *Naturphilosophie* movement already referred to, but all modern literature and aesthetic theory.

NATURE (philosophy of): Ger. *Naturphilosophie*; Fr. *philosophie de la nature*; Ital. *filosofia della natura*. That branch of fundamental philosophy which deals with NATURE (q.v.): coordinate with theology (philosophy of God) and with rational psychology or philosophy of spirit (as philosophy of man). Often used synonymously with cosmology.

For the earlier history see NATURE. Kant first connects it expressly with the modern scientific view of the world, and defines it as the attempt to carry back the facts and forces of physical science to a limited number of forces—in his own theory, attraction and repulsion. His own philosophy is dynamic, but in a mechanical sense. Schelling emphasizes, on the side of method, the self-contained, non-empirical character of Naturphilosophie; and, in content, the dynamic-organic concept. According to Hegel, it takes up into itself all the results and methods of physics, but develops them, showing they do not have their basis in experience, but constitute a self-included, necessary whole derived from thought itself (Begriff).

The content of the system is found in the dialectic sequence which takes us from the extreme externalization of thought (space and time) to its internalization in sentient life—living and feeling organisms. With the latter, the philosophy of spirit takes up its tale, since thought is now coming to conscious recognition of itself. The philosophy of nature soon fell into disrepute, partly because of the arbitrary and artificial use made of its categories; and even more largely because the manifold results of the continually multiplying specialisms in science defied all attempts at reduction to a few fundamental principles. Spencer has revived the notion (though not the term) in his attempt to connect the phenomena of life, mind, and society by the formula of evolution, in a way which reduces all facts to terms of integration of motion and differentiation of matter. There are many signs of attempts to reinstate a philosophy of nature in connection with the idea of evolution, often in a sense quite divergent from Spencer; but the special sciences still lack organization, both themselves and in relation to one another, to an extent which makes the problem the most baffling of all the phases of philosophy today. Among recent English-speaking authors, Tyndall, Huxley, John Fiske, Cope, and Le Conte have occupied themselves particularly with the philosophic interpretation of scientific phenomena. In Germany the names of Lotze, Fechner, Haeckel, Wundt, Ostwald, and Mach are prominent.

NECESSITY [Lat. *necessitas*]: Ger. *Nothwendigkeit*; Fr. *nécessité*; Ital. *necessità*. (1) The state or condition that cannot be otherwise than it is; that must be just as it is.

(2) The principle in virtue of which the condition of the universe as a whole, or any particular part of it, is rendered, both as to its existence and quality, inevitable. Opposed to both freedom and chance, but especially, in its strictly philosophical use, to CHANCE (q.v.) or contingency. That which has the property of necessity is said to be necessary.

It is frequently used to designate the chief principle of those philosophies which admit only the principle of cause and effect, and which deny purposiveness to the universe. Technically, various forms of it have been recognized. (1)

Logical (also metaphysical) necessity: the necessity of thought in virtue of which a truth, either immediate or inferential, must be conceived in such and such a manner; thus freedom itself would be a logical necessity if it followed, in accordance with the principles of identity and non-contradiction, from conceded premises. (2) Mathematical necessity: the similar logical relationship of parts of a demonstration or construction in mathematical reasoning. (3) Physical (also natural) necessity: that which arises from laws of nature or which arises in the course of nature from the principle of causation: mechanism, the "reign of law"; invariable sequence, according to modern writers, e.g. J. S. Mill. (4) Moral necessity: that required by moral law, by the moral order of the universe; that which follows from the nature of God as a moral governor; also used in a narrower sense, as equivalent to "practical" necessity, which is neither logical nor physical, but the result of a certain need or demand regarded as of fundamental importance (see POSTULATE).

These distinctions we owe directly to Leibnitz, and they are most fully developed in his *Théodicée*. According to him there are three main types. (*a*) Metaphysical, logical, geometrical: that which cannot be otherwise than as it is without self-contradiction; absolute necessity. (*b*) Physical necessity: that of the order of nature, which might conceivably be otherwise, but which follows from the will of God, who has chosen the best world; hypothetical necessity. (*c*) Moral necessity: that which animates a moral being, even God himself, in the choice of good. Since a perfectly moral being would have a perfectly adequate conception of the good, it would by moral necessity choose it. In this sense, physical necessity depends upon moral necessity. The term is also used in a strictly logical sense, equivalent to APODICTIC (q.v.), and also to designate the opposite of those theories which assert free will (necessitarianism: see DETERMINISM, and WILL).

In the Pre-Socratics, necessity was a quasi-mythical expression for the law or order of the cosmos, as in the teaching of Parmenides that the goddess at the centre of the world is Necessity—an (apparently) Pythagorean conception which finds expression in the myth of Er (Plato, *Rep.*, Bk. X), where the entire universe is made to revolve upon an axis of necessity. Heraclitus used the idea (in the form of destiny) to account for the fact that a certain balance and system is observed in all change. With the Atomists (Leucippus) it becomes (ἀνάγκη) a definite philosophical concept; the atoms, darting about at random, impinge upon one another; from the aggregations thus formed, there is, of necessity, a whirling motion set up. With Plato (aside from incidental and non-technical use of it as equivalent to the force of proof and demonstration) necessity is the co-author, with νοῦς, of the sensible world; as irrational it is blind, indifferent to good, since νοῦς alone is the principle of ends, or of the good, and hence that which keeps the world in a state of partial non-being and which prevents its arriving at completion (*Timaeus*, 48, 56, 68). Aristotle repeats the same idea (*De An. part.*, IV. ii. 677). Matter resists form, and thus hinders NATURE (q.v.) from arriving at its actualization. (The idea seems to be that in part matter lends itself to the realization of purposes, but in part has an impetus of its own which is quite indifferent to ends.) In this indifference matter is thus contingent—it may or may not present certain traits. As such it is τύχη, chance; so that necessity in the physical sense, and chance in the teleological, are practically one and the same thing. Hence, in his logical writings necessity has quite another meaning. Of future events, we cannot make a necessary assertion; the general tendency of nature may be thwarted by chance. Hence our judgment is not of determinate truth. On the other hand, of universals, of past events, etc., any judgment is either necessarily true or false. Here the tendency comes out to identify necessity with the immanent logical rationale of any subject, that from which perfectly definite consequences follow. The Stoics fuse the various senses of necessity—that of (*a*) the source of physical world-order, (*b*) the universal of reason from which determined conclusions result, and (*c*) the natural (or temporal) causal antecedent (Zeller, *Stoics, Epicureans, and Sceptics*, 170–82, and Windelband, *Hist. of Philos.*, 181). Since the Atomists did not work out their own idea systematically, and even presupposed a more or less random movement upon which necessity supervened, we may fairly regard the Stoics as the authors of the conviction that everything, everywhere, is controlled by necessity admitting of no exception —in other words, of the idea of the universality of natural causation, which is fate. This conception is common to what is called fatalism, also, in oriental philosophies: the hypothesis of a fixed and immutable world decree.

Spinoza carries the fusion still further by expressly identifying the whole causal relationship with the logical or mathematical—the world follows from the nature of God by the same necessity that various truths follow from a geometrical definition. (It was partly in reaction from Spinoza that Leibnitz made the distinctions referred to above.) It was characteristic of the whole rationalistic school (see RATIONALISM) to identify reality with the requirements of logical necessity, as manifested in the principles of identity and non-contradiction; and if, like Leibnitz, they made a distinction between truths of reason and truths of matter of fact (which are empirical), and thus avoided the Spinozistic identification of logical relationship with natural sequence, it was a concession to common sense rather than a philosophic implication of their system. Kant introduces a new motive. On the one hand, growing natural science had given to the conception of necessity (causal relationship) in nature a solidity and concreteness which it could not have had in earlier writers; on the other hand, he rejects the dogmatic identification of the laws of being with those of logical thought. Hence his theory makes causality and thus necessity absolutely true of all nature, or the world of phenomena, by regarding causation as a category involved in the presentation of the world of sense to an experiencing subject. The source of necessity is thus found in the understanding as applied to sense; so that it may fairly be said that Kant restores in a critical and constructive way that which he had rejected in a dogmatic and formal way, namely, the origin of necessity in reason. At least, this path was followed by his idealistic successors, finding its outcome in the expression of Hegel (*Logic*, § 158), that "freedom is the truth of necessity," that is to say, that the determination of one phase of the objective world by another is at bottom but the self-determination of conscious mind, so that the necessary object, when experienced completely, appears as a cooperating factor in the development of free spiritual life.

NEO-CRITICISM: Ger. *Neo-Kriticismus*; Fr. *néocriti-cisme*; Ital. *neo-criticismo*. The revived KANTIANISM (q.v.) of the 19th century; theoretically equivalent to Neo-Kantianism, but as matter of fact used mainly for the form given to the Kantian thought in France by Renouvier, Pillon, and others.

NEO-PLATONISM: Ger. *Neuplatonismus*; Fr. *néopla-tonisme;* Ital. *neo-platonismo*. (1) The revival and transfor-mation of Platonic philosophy that took place, with Alexan-dria as its headquarters, under the influence of oriental thought. Cf. Whittaker, *The Neo-Platonists* (1901). See PATRISTIC PHILOSOPHY (2), ALEXANDRIAN SCHOOL, and SO-CRATICS (Plato).

(2) Also, the revival of Platonism that took place at Cambridge, England, in the 17th century, under the influence of Cudworth and Henry More. See CAMBRIDGE PLATONISTS.

NEO-PYTHAGOREANISM: Ger. *neupythagoreische Lehre* (K.G.); Fr. *néo Pitagoreisme*; Ital. *neo-pitagoreismo*. A system or, better, a tendency of thought which arose at Alexandria in the 1st century A.D., and which, in accordance with the tendency of the time, tried to consecrate its own teachings by identifying them with the teaching of some ancient sage.

It had its derivation from the latest period of the philoso-phy of Plato, in which the categories of the One, the Dyad, the Odd and Even, etc., were manipulated; and it emphasized the dualism of the Platonic metaphysic, transforming it into the basis of an ethical and religious asceticism. In connection with the latter it revived also the Pythagorean mysteries. It is of chief philosophic import because of its influence upon NEO-PLATONISM (q.v.) and, indirectly, upon Clement and Origen. Cf. PATRISTIC PHILOSOPHY.

NESCIENCE [Lat. *scientia*, knowledge, + the negative prefix *ne*-]: Ger. *Nichtwissen*; Fr. *nescience*; Ital. *nescienza*.

Literally, the condition of ignorance; but in a recent quasi-technical philosophical use, the theory that certain forms of reality (as God, the soul, matter in itself, etc.) are beyond our knowledge.

While often used as equivalent to AGNOSTICISM (q.v.), it is also employed to describe the philosophy of Hamilton and Mansel, who would repudiate the title of Agnostics, but who hold that only an indirect or mediate knowledge of the existence of the Absolute, akin to faith or belief rather than to thought, is possible.

NEXUS [Lat. *nexus*, a bond, from *nectere*, to bind, tie]: Ger. *Nexus*; Fr. *nexus, lien*; Ital. *nesso*. The mutual dependence of different elements of an ordered series upon one another; same as connection or relation, but containing in addition a suggestion of union into an ordered whole; most frequently used in the phrase "Causal Nexus."

NIHILISM [Lat. *nihil*, nothing]: Ger. *Nihilismus*; Fr. *nihilisme*; Ital. *nichilismo*. A term somewhat loosely used, generally by the opponents of a system, to designate its supposed tendencies; namely, to destroy existence, truth, or knowledge. In its strictest sense it means the belief that nothing is, and hence no knowledge is, possible; or that truth in knowledge and obligation in morality have no objective reality. In its contemporaneous use it generally denotes a political or social doctrine rather than a strictly philosophic one; the idea that social progress is to be looked for only in the abolition of all existing social institutions and a return to political void (e.g. Spencer's "Administrative Nihilism"—Huxley); the extreme being ANARCHISM (q.v.).

This doctrine, however, is said to be derived from the emphasis laid on the negative in Hegel's dialectic, especially from the first categories of his *Logic*, in which the dialectical identity of being and non-being is asserted.

The first pure nihilist in philosophic theory was also the last, viz. the Sophist Gorgias of Leontini, who is reported to have taught: (1) that nothing exists; (2) that if anything did exist it would be unknowable; (3) if it existed and were knowable it could not be communicated. The doctrine thus stated has no modern supporters, but certain phases of the Buddhistic doctrine of NIRVANA (q.v.) and of Schopenhauer's doctrine of the annihilation of will might be termed nihilistic. It is generally used nowadays by realists to mark their opinion of the idealistic doctrine of the external world, or, in a similar controversial way, to denote the tendency of doctrines of philosophical scepticism, such as Hume's. Fichte's words, as quoted by Sir W. Hamilton (edition of Reid's *Works*, 129, note), are often used as a proof of the nihilistic character of idealism, but in fact are employed by Fichte to express simply the logical outcome of a partial stage of development, not as a statement of his whole system.

Literature: Ueberweg, *Hist. of Philos.*, i. 76–8; Reid's *Works*, 478; Fichte, *Sittenlehre*, Werke, iv. 151. The dependence of Russian nihilism upon a development of Hegel's philosophy is asserted by Kaufmann, *Contemp. Rev.*, xxxviii. 913.

NISUS [Lat. *nitor*, to struggle, to strive]: same in the other languages. The inherent tendency in any process of change to strive against obstacles towards its appropriate end. Leibnitz uses it as a quasi-technical term. He denies the existence of mere capacity or potency, holding that reality always issues in act. This remains as nisus or active tendency when hindered from expressing itself. In modern physical terms, it is practically the equivalent of energy of position, ready to translate itself into kinetic energy (Leibnitz, *New Essays*, ii. chap. xxi. § 2, and *On the Reform of Metaphysics*).

Nisus formativus is the supposed tendency inherent in every embryonic organism to reproduce the form of its species —a term of speculative biology.

NOETIC [Gr. νοητικός, from νοητά, ideas which can be thought, not imaged, from νοῦς, reason]: Ger. *noëtisch*; Fr. *intelligible*; Ital. *noetico*.

In accordance with their general philosophical presuppositions, the early Greek writers assumed that all distinctions in existence were the counterparts of distinctions in modes of knowing and vice versa. When it was seen that certain experiences appeared to have permanent and general validity, while others had to do with the particular and changing, the tendency was to assume a superior form of knowing—reason—and an inferior—sense—and to divide the objective spheres accordingly. Heraclitus and Parmenides contributed to the distinction, but we owe its sharp formulation to Plato. With reference to his theory of ideas, he marks off sharply the incorporeal world, τόπος νοητός, the world of conceptions, from the world which is seen, τόπος αἰσθητικός, the world of perceptions. The first is the ultimate reality of which the second is but an image.

Aristotle, following Plato, uses the noun νοητά to express the essence of real beings taken in their intelligible aspect, their capacity of being rationally apprehended. As the Neo-Platonists made much of the doctrine of Nous (q.v.), so the adjective noetic played a large part in their system. The noetic cosmos (κόσμος νοητός) expressed the fact that the nous includes within itself a complete system of forms and forces as its own distinctions. Cudworth revived the term with practically the Aristotelian meaning. Sir William Hamilton used it to designate knowledge originated within the mind.

Literature: Plato, *Rep.*, vi. 507 ff.; *Phaedrus*, 246 ff.; *Phaedo*, 100 D; *Theaetetus, Symposium*; Aristotle, *De Anima*, III. iv. 12; Plotinus, *Enn.*, vi. 22; Cudworth, *Eternal and Immutable Morality*, Bk. II. i. 4, v. 2; Hamilton, *Lects. on Met.*, xxxviii. See also Martineau, *Types of Ethical Theory*, 443–5.

NOMINALISM [Lat. *nominalis*, from *nomen*, a name]: Ger. *Nominalismus*; Fr. *nominalisme*; Ital. *nominalismo*. The doctrine that universals have no objective existence or validity; in its extreme form, that they are only names (*nomina, flatus vocis*), that is, creations of language for purposes of convenient communication. See REALISM (1) for full account and history.

NON-BEING: Ger. *Nichtseiendes, Nichts* (*Nicht-sein*); Fr. *non-être* (*néant*); Ital. *non-essere*. Literally, just the absence or negation of being; but in accordance with the Greek tendency to give (unconsciously) an objective meaning to all categories of thought, non-being (μὴ ὄν, μὴ εἶναι) was assumed as existent, until it became an object of dispute among philosophic schools as to whether non-being is or is not.

The Eleatics (Parmenides, 470 B.C.), who identified it with empty space, holding that everything must be full (or that all that is, is), denied its existence. The Atomists, however (Leucippus), needing a space for their discrete particles to move in, asserted that non-being (the VOID, q.v.) was as real as being (the atoms). Plato (denying empty space as a fact) assumed a relative world of non-being (the counterpart of ignorance) as the opposite of his ideas, and, interpreting it also as space, regarded it as the matrix out of which the world was created. In not dissimilar fashion the theological doctrine of the creation of the world "out of nothing" tended to give non-being a quasi-existence, as at least the background of the divine operation. Aristotle attempted to give the term a dynamic interpretation. As all nature moves between the potential and the completed, the potential at once is and is-not. On one side, it is the medium, the matter, through which the form realizes itself; and it is also the restraint which prevents the full exhibition of form, and which is responsible for failures and deviations from the main line of development. In the Neo-Platonists, non-being becomes a highly important category. As empty space and as privation it was the responsible factor in the development of the purely physical world and also the cause of evil. It is the absolute opposite of pure being, which yet, just because it is non-being, reduces the manifestations of being to lower levels. However naïve the Greek formulation, it is obvious that through the use of this term there were gradually developed two of the most serious problems of philosophy: one on the side of cosmology, as to the existence of a vacuum, and the possibility of motion without a vacuum; the other the metaphysical and ethical problem of the significance of the negative factor in the universe, of hindrance and imperfection. It is a metaphysical problem, as well as an ethical one, because the value of the concept of growth and development (of change which is qualitative) seems to imply a passage from the potential to the actual, or from (relative) non-being to being. The problem in the former sense was revived by Descartes and in the latter by Hegel. With Hegel, becoming (Werden), process, activity are the ultimate and absolute, and thus a negative factor is as necessary as is a positive. In the famous doctrine of the identity of being and non-being is contained the assertion that the immediate or "first" being of anything negates itself, and thus passes away, and that this passing away turns out to be not complete disappearance, but a development of itself, and so a reconstitution of being upon a higher, more mediate (or significant) plane (cf. the recent development of the doctrine by Ormond, as cited below). Scotus and other mediaeval philosophers had already taught that since God creates the world out of nothing, nothing belongs to the essence of God.

Literature: Parmenides, v. 33, 35; Aristotle, *De Gen. et Corr.*, i. 8 (for Leucippus's doctrine), and also Plutarch, *Adv. Coel.*, 4. 2; Plato, *Rep.*, v. 476–9, vi. 511; *Timaeus*; Aristotle, *Physics*, iv. 2 (cf. Zeller, *Philos. d. Griechen*, iii. 603–23); *Met.*, Bk. XII; Plotinus, *Enneads*, iii. 6, 18; St. Augustine, *De Civ. Dei*, xii. 2; Scotus, *De div. Nat.*, iii. 19; Hegel, *Logic* (lesser), §§ 87–8, and *Werke*, iii. 72–3 (larger logic); Ormond, *Basal Concepts in Philos.* (1896).

NON-EGO: Ger. *Nicht-ich*; Fr. *non-moi*; Ital. *non-io*. The opposite of the Ego; the not-me; the external object; the external world. Cf. EGO.

The term is of especial significance, as a technical term, in the philosophy of Fichte; it represents the second positing (the anti-positing—Entgegensetzen; see POSIT) of the Ego as that which limits and thereby stimulates and defines the more specific activity of the Ego. See Fichte, *Werke*, i. 101–5, and Fischer, *Gesch. d. neueren Philos.*, v. 438.

NOOLOGY [Gr. *νοῦς*, reason, + *λόγος*, theory]: Ger. *Noologie*; Fr. *noologie*; Ital. *noologia* (the equivalents are suggested). That part of philosophy which deals with intuitive truths of reason; as distinct from Dianoiology, which deals with truths discursively or demonstratively established.

A term suggested by Sir William Hamilton, Reid's *Works*, note A, § v, but having no currency. Hamilton probably derived it from Kant (*Krit. d. reinen Vernunft*, 643). It is used by Crusius for psychology.

NORM and NORMATIVE (in the moral sciences): Ger. *normativ* (*normgebend*); Fr. *normatif*; Ital. *normativo*. The principle, whether truth or mode of reality, which controls action, thought, and emotion, if these are to realize their appropriate ends; the end as law. The norm of thinking is truth; of emotion, the beautiful; of volition, the good. These principles (and their corresponding philosophic disciplines) are hence termed normative. The three normative sciences are thus logic, aesthetics, and ethics.

Reference to a norm may be roughly taken to discriminate the philosophic from the natural sciences. The latter aim simply to describe phenomena and explain them in terms of laws or principles homogeneous with the facts The explaining principles are, moreover, mechanical, having to do with conditions of manifestation in time. In the philosophic sciences, facts are interpreted with reference to their meaning, or value—their significance from the position occupied, or part played, by them in the total make-up of experience. The standpoint, moreover, is teleological, since the interest is not in the conditions of origin, but in the fulfillment of purpose in realizing their appropriate values. Whether this distinction is one of objective reality, or one of standpoint and method of treatment, is, however, itself a philosophic problem. According to some writers the distinction between concepts of origin and of value has a distinct ontological reference; according to others the significance is only methodological. That is to say, to the latter there are not two spheres, one of pure phenomena, the other of ends and values; but the distinction is one of standpoint for purposes of description and explanation. Cf. ORIGIN *versus* NATURE.

The term norm is closely related to the terms criterion and standard. Criterion applies, however, more definitely to the process of judgment; it is the rule or mode of control as employed to assist judgment in making proper discriminations. A criterion of beauty is the principle employed in arriving at correct estimates or appreciations; a norm of beauty

controls (or is supposed to control) the facts themselves in
their own meaning. The criterion thus has a more subjective
connotation. The standard is the principle used to measure
value, and to lay off a scale of values. The standard of
beauty is that type or form to which the facts conform in
the degree in which the term beautiful is applicable to them.
It differs from the norm in that the objectively regulating
character of the norm is not necessarily ascribed to it. It
agrees with the criterion in referring especially to the process
of judgment or evaluation, but differs in that it takes some
objective form as its adequate embodiment or manifestation.
The criterion is the deciding principle in forming judgments;
the standard is the principle which gives content to the
adequate judgment. The norm which regulates the value
of the facts may also, of course, be the standard by which
their relative worths are measured, and the criterion by
which the individual is guided in arriving at a correct apprehension of these worths.

NOUMENON, and -AL [Gr. *νοούμενον*, anything known,
from *νοεῖν*, to perceive, know]: Ger. *Noumenon (-al)*, DING
AN SICH (q.v.); Fr. *noumène (-al)*; Ital. *numeno*. The object
of pure thought, or of rational intuition, free from all elements of sense. See PHENOMENON, and MUNDUS INTELLI-
GIBILIS.

Plato uses the term a number of times, but simply in
connection with *νοῦς* and *νοεῖν*, as the intelligible, the things
of thought, e.g. *Parmenides*, 132; *Republic*, vi. 508.

Kant uses the term generally as equivalent with thing-
in-itself; that is, the thing, as *not* object of sense; and hence
as something which can only be thought. But in his *Dialectic*
he ascribes to thought, as over and above sensuous schematism, specific functions; namely, (1) to limit the world of
sense and phenomena, by making us aware of a possible
world of reality beyond; (2) to afford an ideal of totality,
which can, indeed, never be realized, but which serves, none
the less, as a standard to suggest and to regulate, so as to
give the greatest possible completeness to experience. For
this Kant uses, indeed, the term idea rather than noumenon,
but as its basis of definition is exactly the same (the refer-

ence to reason transcending experience), it was impossible that the two should not be confused. Through the practical Reason, the world of Noumena, or Things-in-themselves, thus left open as a theoretical possibility, is found to be a practical reality in the consciousness of duty. And in the *Critique of Judgment*, the teleological principle lying at the basis of science mediates between the noumenal and the phenomenal, not indeed asserting the existence of the former, but treating the latter as if the noumenal were its ground. It was the aim of Fichte and of Kant's successors to combine systematically the objective sense of noumenon, the thing-in-itself, and the subjective—the ideal of knowledge—which Kant had brought together only in a confused way. Reinhold is conscious of this confusion, and accordingly carefully discriminates the thing-in-itself, as the source of the "matter" of our perceptions, from the noumenon, as denoting the unrealizable ideals and problems which thought sets to experience. The thing-in-itself here has more kinship with phenomena than with noumena. See Kant, *Critique of Pure Reason*, 217–26, 249–52 (Max Müller's trans.); *Proleg.*, §§ 44, 57 (in this latter, the three meanings of thing-in-itself, limit to sensibility, and ideal of rational completeness are practically identified); *Critique of Practical Reason*, Bk. I. chap. i. Pt. II; *Critique of Judgment*, 427–8 (Bernard's trans.). Kant seems to have used the term as equivalent to the ancient νοητά, which was opposed to αἰσθητά. According to Vaihinger (*Commentar zu Kant*, 117) Kant was indebted especially to Sextus Empiricus. For Reinhold, see Erdmann, *Hist. of Philos.*, ii. 479.

NOUS [Gr. νοῦς, reason, thought]: Ger. *Nus* (K.G.); Fr. *intelligence*; Ital. *nous*. Reason, thought, considered not as subjective, nor as a mere psychic entity, but as having an objective, especially a teleological, significance.

We owe the term, as a technical one, to Anaxagoras. He felt the need of a special principle to account for the order of the universe and so, besides the infinity of simple qualities, assumed a distinct principle, which, however, was still regarded as material, being only lighter and finer than the others. To it, however, greater activity was ascribed, and it acted according to ends, not merely according to mechanical impact, thus giving movement, unity, and system to what had previously been a disordered jumble of inert elements. It is probable, however, that he limited its importance to the stellar heavens; or, at least, used it only when mechanical principles failed. Diogenes of Apollonia identified nous with air, and extended its action to organic bodies. Plato generalized the nous of Anaxagoras, proclaiming the necessity of a rational (teleological) explanation of all natural processes, and making nous also a thoroughly immaterial principle. As the principle which lays down ends, nous is also the Supreme Good, the source of all other ends and aims; as such it is the supreme principle of all the ideas. It thus gets an ethical and logical connotation as well as a cosmological.

On the other hand, nous gets a psychological significance as the highest form of mental insight, the immediate and absolutely assured knowledge of rational things. (Knowledge and the object of knowledge are thus essentially one.) Here $νοῦς$ is distinguished from $διάνοια$ (sometimes called $ἐπιστήμη$, and sometimes $τέχνη$), which is discursive knowledge, and hence dependent upon assumptions, which cease to be such (and hence are unproved hypotheses) until carried back to the self-evident things of reason. Aristotle continues this line of thought, and practically identifies $νοῦς$ as the supreme end, and thus the unmoved mover, or source of all motion, with God, whose activity is $νόησις νοήσεως$, the thinking of thought; an expression which makes explicit and absolute the virtual assumption of Plato regarding the unity of $νοῦς$ as faculty of highest knowledge and the $νοητόν$ as the supreme object of knowledge. This divine nous is transcendent, moving the world only teleologically, not immanently nor yet causally. As transcendent it is, while immanent in human beings, yet separable from the body ($χωριστός$) and, as such, imperishable. In man, however, the $νοῦς$ assumes a dual form: the active ($νοῦς ποιητικός$), which is free and the source of all man's insight and virtue that links him to the divine ($θεωρεῖν$), and the passive ($νοῦς παθητικός$), which includes thoughts that are dependent upon perception, memory —experience as mediated through any bodily organ. Some of the Peripatetic followers of Aristotle, such as Theophrastus and Strato, appear (like his later Arabian followers) to have denied the transcendence of nous, to have given it a material and sensuous coloring, and thus to have prepared the way for the Stoics. It is with the Neo-Platonists, however, that the conception of nous becomes all-important again. The Absolute is, indeed, above all distinctions, and so cannot be regarded as, in itself, conscious or as reason. But its first distinction is into nous on one side, and being on the other. Nous thus becomes the conception for the absolute reason and subject. Moreover, it possesses a dynamic and self-differentiating quality, and is thus plural (νοῖ) as well as singular. As noi it is the source of all the dynamic principles which operate in the creation of the universe. With the Neo-Platonists the conception reaches its zenith. The distinction (of Kant, but particularly as used by Coleridge) of REASON from UNDERSTANDING (q.v.) may, however, be compared with it, but the modern distinction of the subjective from the objective inevitably gives reason a much more psychological sense than nous possessed with the ancients.

Literature: Plato, *Phaedo*, 97; *Republic*, vi. 508; and *Sophist*, 254; Aristotle, *Metaphysics*, i. 3, 984; Simplicius, *Phys.*, 33, and 225a; Plotinus, *Enneads*; Zeller, *Philos. d. Griechen*, ii. 590–2, iii. 512, 528–9.

NULLIBRISTS: Ger. *Nullibristen* (Eisler); (not in use in the other languages). A term applied to those who deny that the soul exists in space, since it is simple and immaterial.

Used by Henry More (*Enchir. met.*, 27, 1). It has no currency.

NUMBER (in metaphysics). According to the Pythagoreans, numbers constituted the essence or reality of things. They were the first and ultimate elements out of which things are composed. Plato in his later doctrine (taught orally) seems to have called the Ideas numbers. The Neo-Platonists and Neo-Pythagoreans regarded metaphysical numbers as the archetypes of arithmetical numbers, and the animating principles of things. See ONE (the).

Nicholas Cusanus and the Platonists of the early Renaissance gave great place to number in their cosmologies, being clearly influenced by the new mathematical developments. The mystics have in all ages given importance to numbers and their relations, as either prototypes or symbols of the deepest things in experience. Three (the union of the odd and even), four (the first square), seven (the sum of four and three), twelve (the product of three and four) have been especially honored.

OBJECT (-IVE; general and philosophical) [Lat. *ob*, off, over against, + *iacere*, to throw, to lie; the equivalent of Gr. ἀντικείμενον, usually translated *oppositum*]: Ger. *Gegenstand, gegenständlich, Objekt, objektif*; Fr. *objet, objectif*; Ital. *obbietto, oggetto, obbiettivo.* (1) That in which the mind's activity terminates; that towards which any mental operation is directed. But since the TERMINUS (q.v.) of intellect and of volition may be distinguished, this most general sense easily breaks up into two others. (2) That which is known, considered as giving truth and reality to the knowing process. (3) That which is the goal of impulse or choice—aim, end, ultimate purpose. But since the problem of knowledge has been chiefly as to how the external world may be known (knowledge of states of consciousness being taken as a matter of course), (4) object is often used popularly to mean "thing." (5) Combining with the philosophical sense, it then is set over against mind and consciousness as the external, often the material, world. This tendency is strengthened by the use of the word SUBJECT (q.v.) to denote mind, and is one of the two chief meanings of the adjective objective. (6) That which is known may also be distinguished from that which is only erroneously assumed or accepted—from that which we deceive ourselves into believing; hence object is used as equivalent to real. This sense is not common with the noun, but is most frequent with the adjective objective, which designates that which belongs really to any subject-matter as distinct from that which is imported or reflected into it through the prejudices, illusions, fallacies, or errors of the person observing or judging: opposed to that which is *merely* in the mind. It is (2) above made more specific. (7) Objective then comes to mean the intrinsically real, or self-subsistent, having validity in itself—e.g. "duty is objective." (8) In later scholastic philosophy, object and objective are used exclusively to denote that which exists simply and only as material of mental operations. The use is continued in Descartes and is found in Berkeley, who expressly calls the existence of objects *as perceived* their objective existence. The history of the transformation of this earlier meaning to the later ones will be found under SUBJECT. Cf. OBJECT.

OBJECTIVISM [for der. see OBJECT]: Ger. *Objectivismus*; Fr. *objectivisme*; Ital. *oggettivismo*. (1) The theory which attributes objective validity to at least some of our ideas, and thus regards the mind as capable of attaining real truth. Opposed to scepticism and to phenomenalism.

(2) The theory which tends to neglect the mental and spiritual in its theory of reality.

(3) The theory, in ethics, which conceives the aim of morality to be the attainment of an objective state (so Külpe, *Introd. to Philos.*, §§ 14 and 30). Cf. SUBJECTIVISM.

OCCAMISM: Ger. *Occamismus*; Fr. *doctrine d'Occam*; Ital. *dottrina di Occam*. The doctrine held by the followers of William of Occam, the founder of scholastic Nominalism (see REALISM). They were also called Terminists, because of the doctrine of Occam that universals are not anything really existing, but are only *termini*, predicables.

OCCASIONALISM [Lat. *occasio*, an event]: Ger. *Occasionalismus, Theorie der Gelegenheitsursache* (occasional cause); Fr. *occasionalisme, hypothèse des causes occasionnelles*; Ital. *occasionalismo*. The theory that matter and mind do not act upon each other directly, but that upon occasion of certain changes in one, God intervenes to bring about corresponding changes in the other. Each is then called the "occasional cause" with reference to the other.

The theory was developed by Geulincx and Malebranche in order to deal with the problem—arising from the extreme dualism asserted by Descartes between thought and extension—of the interaction of mind and matter in general, and of the body and soul in particular, combined with the growing difficulties felt in forming any intelligible theory of causation. The same problem was dealt with in the single-substance theory of Spinoza and the Leibnitzian doctrine of pre-established harmony. Descartes in general had asserted that all changes of matter-in-motion are to be accounted for by reference to extension, while all psychical matters are to be referred to the nature of mind. This latter theory, however it might do for clear and adequate ideas, could not explain confused ideas and the passions and emotions connected with them. Here was an exception, and God had arranged in man a coexistence of the two substances, so that a disturbance of the "animal spirits" (centring in the pineal gland) excited in the mind an unclear idea, whether sensation, passion, or emotion. This doctrine of *influxus physicus* was so obviously contradictory to the rest of the system, that the Cartesians at once set about doing away with it. With Geulincx the causal problem was the chief one; and he denies completely the possession of any efficient causality by matter. Its changes are, so to speak, only "cues" upon which God effects the real results. Malebranche adds to this point of view the epistemological one: not only can one substance not directly influence the other, but they are so heterogeneous that mind cannot know matter. We "see things in God," matter again being the occasion rather than the real object of our knowledge.

Literature: Descartes, *Principia*, § 36; *Meds.*, v and vi, *Passions de l'Âme*; Geulincx, *Ethics*, 113; *Met.*, 26; Malebranche, *Recherche de la Vérité*, vi. 2, 3; Falckenberg, Windelband, Ueberweg, Histories of Philosophy (Index of each, sub verbo).

ONE (the) [AS. *ān*, one; Gr. τὸ ἕν]: Ger. *das Eine, Eins und Viele* (one and many); Fr. *l'un* (*et le multiple*); Ital. *l'uno* (*e il molteplice*). A technical term of the Neo-Platonic philosophy denoting the absolute first principle—a principle above both Being and Thought, since these are both subject to definition and (in so far) to limitation. For the less ontological senses of the term see UNITY.

In the later oral teachings of Plato, he seems to have been much influenced by the doctrines of the Pythagoreans, and to have attempted a synthesis of their theory of numbers with his own theory of ideas. In this doctrine he identified the One with the Good, with the supreme Idea and Being (see Trendelenburg, *Platonis de Ideis et Numeris Doctrina*), and attempted to derive from it the series of other ideas. This tendency was carried still further in the Old Academy. Speusippus distinguished the One from the Good, the One being the principle of which the Good is the result; and also from reason, which is reduced to the plane of the Platonic World-soul, as moving cause (Zeller, *Philos. d. Griechen*, II. i. 851–3). In other words, the formal or logical cause was placed above both the final and the efficient. Xenocrates made the One and the Dyad the supreme ground of all existence—the One being the first or male God, the Father and Nous; while the Dyad (indefinite plurality) is the mother; from their marriage arose numbers, and the Soul is Number which is self-moving. These fantastical distinctions found a fertile soil in Neo-Pythagoreanism and Neo-Platonism, and it is in the latter that the One becomes the supreme category. With Plotinus, the Absolute is entirely ineffable and incomprehensible; and can be described only as simple relation of Being to itself, excluding all distinction and all relativity, to express which the term the One, or the Only One, is chosen. From this the whole hierarchy of subordinate beings and distinctions radiate or emanate, without either efficient or purposive activity upon its part. Jamblicus desired to make the One still more transcendent and ineffable, and accordingly distinguished between the First One and the Second One, which is interposed between it and plurality, and is the source of further emanations. Proclus carries the doctrine to its end by declaring that the Absolute, since undefinable and unknowable, cannot be called even the One except figuratively. From it, however, proceeds a plurality of Ones, which are simple and supersensuous, and through which emanation proceeds towards Being and towards Thought.

Literature: Zeller, *Philos. d. Griechen*, III. ii. 491, 521, 688, 793, 846; Plotinus, *Enneads*, VI. ix. 1.

ONTOLOGICAL ARGUMENT: Ger. *ontologisches Argument*; Fr. *argument ontologique*; Ital. *argomento ontologico*. The method of reasoning which infers the existence of God from a consideration of the content of the idea of God; ranked by Kant with the cosmological and physico-teleological as one of the three fundamental conceptions of rational theology. See RELIGION (philosophy of).

Its best representative is Descartes, who, however, unites the psychological method of St. Augustine with the purely logical one of Anselm. See SCHOLASTICISM, I.

St. Augustine, starting with the fact of doubt, infers then to the reality of the inner subject. This self-assurance involves certainty of being, of life, of feeling, and of rational perception. The certainty of being demands that reason be ruled by a principle which is its norm, which accordingly it does not itself generate, but which is above it. The idea of perfect truth thus involves the reality of perfect truth. See PATRISTIC PHILOSOPHY (6).

Anselm, on the other hand, works upon the basis of mediaeval REALISM (q.v.). The universals are the reals; and since there are grades and degrees of universality, there are all grades of reality. The most universal, God, is the most real—*ens realissimum*. If one denies the existence of God, he must have the idea of God, and that means he has the idea of one than whom nothing greater can be thought. But to be in reality and in thought is greater than to be in intellect alone. Accordingly, if one have the thought of God at all, he must think of him as existing (Proslogium). This is often known as the "Anselmian Argument." Descartes argues from the existence of doubt to that of thought; and therefrom (by immediate inference) to that of the ego, and of mental processes and ideas as bare facts at least. Such facts must have a cause; the cause must be at least equal to its effect. One has ideas of perfection, and by this principle one cannot be the cause, because one is not perfect. Only a perfect being could effect such an idea. And, again, the very idea of God, or of the infinite, involves that of necessary existence—his nature is such as to involve existence necessarily, not simply contingently, just as the idea of the triangle involves three-sidedness (*Meditations*, iii, and *Principia*, i. 14–16). In Spinoza the argument appears condensed into a definition of the Absolute—that which can be conceived only as existing. Kant attempts to show that both the cosmological and the teleological depend upon the ontological, so that if this can be shaken, all rational theology is also shaken. It is a contradiction to *think* of God as non-existent, but it does not follow that God exists. Existence is not a part of the content of thought, but rather something which controls and necessitates thought—something which is "given." Kant thus detects the essence of the whole rationalistic position in this argument—viz. the assumption that thought as such is a valid criterion of reality; while in truth, according to Kant, thought, *per se*, is only analytic of itself, and requires sense-experience to get a judgment of reality. Hegel, throwing overboard the ontological argument as an argument from *a* thought, the particular thought of God, holds that fundamentally Thought as such determines Being—or that at the root of all judgment is the presupposition of the identity of Thought and Being, or God; and that the old ontological argument may be regarded as a vague anticipation of this underlying unity.

Literature: see under THEISM, and RELIGION (philosophy of).

ONTOLOGISM [Gr. τὰ ὄντα, existing things, + λόγος, science]: Ger. *Ontologismus*; Fr. *ontologisme*; Ital. *ontologismo*. (1) The philosophical (ontological) method which proceeds from logical categories directly to reality: it is applied to the great speculative systems of which the ontological postulates are not grounded in experience.

Hume and Kant vigorously opposed ontologism. For the newer developments of the method cf. Ueberweg-Heinze, *Gesch. d. Philos.*, III. ii. (8th ed.) 328.   (J.M.B.)

(2) The theory of the school founded by Gioberti in Italy (1801–52). The doctrine, namely, that the method and principles of philosophy should be sought for in the object, not in the subject.

The theory is a reaction from the supposed subjectivism of modern thought. Gioberti held that Descartes had substituted a psychologic method (see PSYCHOLOGISM) for the true ontological, and that modern philosophy, in so far as it proceeded from an examination either of consciousness or of the process of knowing, had put philosophy further off the right track, and had logically ended in sensualism, Protestantism, and atheism. We must begin with the supreme and objective intuition of the mind: *Ens creat existentias*. While the theory originally was in the interests of Catholicism, Gioberti himself gradually modified his philosophical views in a somewhat pantheistic sense, and politically became one of the chief apostles of an independent and united Italy. Ontologism was condemned by papal authority in 1861, and again in 1862 and 1866. Aside from Gioberti's political views, this result was probably inevitable, as his original system, in presupposing an adequate intuition of absolute being, tended to subordinate theology to philosophy, and, indeed, to make revealed religion unnecessary. Gioberti and his system are of interest to Americans through their influence upon O. A. Brownson. The latter, however, endeavored to avoid the theological errors of Gioberti, and held that while his philosophy was ontological, he was not an "ontologist" in the sense reprobated by the Church.

   Literature: Ueberweg, *Hist. of Philos.* (trans. by Morris, and appendix by Botta), ii. 497–509; Louis Ferri, *L'Histoire de Philos. en Italie*, i. 387; Brownson, *Works*, ii. 126, 468 ff. (art. "Ontologism and Psychologism").

   ONTOLOGY [Gr. ὄν, ὄντος, being, + λόγος, science]: Ger. *Ontologie*; Fr. *ontologie*; Ital. *ontologia*. The doctrine or science of reality in its ultimate nature. Cf. METAPHYSICS, and PHILOSOPHY.

   Plato uses the phrase ὄντως ὄντα to express the absolutely real character of the ideas; but being interested chiefly in the question of method in regard to them, uses Dialectic, not ontology, to denote the science which deals with them. Even Aristotle, who held that since every special science has its own peculiar sphere of existence (οὐσία, or ὄν) as its object, there must be a supreme science which deals with existence in its generality, being as being, ὄν ᾗ ὄν, yet used the term "first philosophy" or philosophy to designate this science. The Scholastics, while regarding *Ens qua Ens* as the object of philosophy, yet subdivided and named it on a different basis. It was accordingly Wolff who made the term current. Philosophy is first divided into theoretical and practical; the former, called metaphysics, is again divided into a general part (ontology) dealing with being in general, irrespective of whether it is material or spiritual; and a special part dealing with the three chief forms of being, namely God, the world, and the soul (see Erdmann, *Hist. of Philos.*, ii. 223–4, and Zeller, *Gesch. d. deutsch. Philos.*, 183–8).

Wolff's identification of ontology with the logical principles of identity and contradiction had great influence (in a reactionary way) upon Kant. With Kant, ontology becomes a pretended science, since it attempts the impossible task of dealing with objects without any reference to the way in which they are given and known. Largely through his influence, ontology and ontological became terms of reproach, meaning vain attempts to deal with being apart from its presentation in consciousness (so G. H. Lewes and the English positivists generally). Sir William Hamilton defined it as the science which infers the properties of unknown being from its known manifestations—or as Inferential Psychology! (*Metaph.*, i. 124–5). The excess of emphasis upon the theory of knowing, as distinct from the theory of being, led, however, to scepticism and subjectivism, and so to a new conception of ontology as the science of the real, so far as that shall be determined through the process of knowledge: in other words, the question of the possibility of ontology is the question of the validity of knowledge.

Summing up, we may say that three stages are easily discernible. Ancient and even mediaeval philosophy are, as often said, predominatingly ontological; they are concerned with the objective, and it is assumed (naïvely or dogmatically) that being is as it is known to be, or that knowing is a process of participating in being, that it is itself a phase or factor in the structure of being. The second sense is the modern sceptical, or positivistic, in which it is assumed that being-in-itself (things as they really are) is to be sharply marked off from things in relation to us, or existence as presented through our senses, as phenomena. According to this view ontology is only the pretended and impossible theory of them. The third is the critical sense; the ancient dependence of knowing upon being is reversed; the first need is to examine the nature, possibility, and validity of knowledge, and then, through the results thus reached, go on to consider the being known. Thus ontology is no longer the general theory of being, distinct from its special forms; it is the theory of the known reality as distinct from the theory of the process of knowing. English thought probably owes to Ferrier (*Inst. of Met.*, 47–9) the clear-cut recognition of this latter distinction of ontology and epistemology.

OPINION (in philosophy). (1) Generally speaking, any idea or conception of fact, aiming at truth and regarded as probably approximating it, but confessedly not attaining certitude as regards it. It differs from HYPOTHESIS (q.v.) in not looking forward to future verification, nor aiming to serve any function of generalization or explanation. Its reference is rather to a condition of thought based upon evidence or inference not adequate to produce assured knowledge. It connotes belief, however, rather than doubt.

(2) Used in a more depreciatory sense to denote arbitrary or dogmatic preconception, e.g. a matter of *mere* opinion of unwarranted conviction.

The term now simply denotes a certain value or function of ideas taken in their objective reference; their worth as regards a standard of truth or certainty. As a technical term it is employed to translate the Greek δόξα. Parmenides distinguished τὰ πρὸς ἀλήθειαν from τὰ πρὸς δόξαν. The former designated whatever had to do with reason, and apprehended truth and being; the latter designated mere custom and blind belief, and related to appearance, non-being, error. This sense of the term is connected with the Greek δοκεῖν, meaning both to believe or think, and to seem. This sense of mere seeming or appearance is taken up by Plato. Δόξα refers to the region intermediate between being and non-being—the realm of phenomena—and is thus intermediate between mere ‾sense (αἴσθησις) and rational thought (διάνοια). It is subdivided into a higher form (πίστις, conviction; sometimes called right opinion, ὀρθή, or ἀληθὴς, δόξα) and a lower (εἰκασία, conjecture, blind guessing). The former is based on reason (it is reasonable), though unaware of its basis—not reasoned. It mediates the connection with discursive, or demonstrative, thought, and relates to those aspects of the sensible world that embody mathematical and teleological relations, which, however, cannot be stated *per se* (*Theaetetus*, 187–203; *Timaeus*, 270 ff.; and *Republic*, Bk. VI. 510). Aristotle to a considerable extent subdivides Plato's metaphysical conception into a logical and a rhetorical one. The former makes opinion a mode of judgment, hence arising in the soul as such, not from its affection by the body. As a mode of judgment, however, it does not rest upon an adequate syllogistic process, and hence does not reach demonstrative knowledge (*Anal. Post.*, Bk. I. chap. xxxiii; *Metaphysics*, vii. 15). The point of connection with Plato is in the fact that Plato related opinion to the world of change, not of being. Now, whatever changes may be otherwise than as it is, and hence it is not necessary, but contingent. On the rhetorical side, δόξα is a state of persuasion or belief, and the question of producing it is practical and psychological. Aristotle also makes much use of the conception of opinion in his ethics. All conduct relates to future, and therefore contingent, things—matters of opinion. But it is of the highest importance that these opinions should be formed in accordance with will, rather than with merely desire. Φρόνησις is the virtue of the habit of intellect in forming opinions in relation to right will. In general, δοξαστικόν, the sphere of opinion, is the probable. Plotinus makes opinion the region intermediate between imagination and reason; all knowledge of the physical world as such is opinion. It depends upon the senses, but is found only in a soul which reflects and reasons.

After the distinction between the subjective and objective was clearly established, the nature of opinion ceased to be a metaphysical problem. It simply denoted one case of the more general principle—the subjective. Consequently, in modern times, opinion hardly has a technical meaning. Hobbes uses it to denote the state of unstable and alternating ideas previous to judgment (*Leviathan*, Pt. I. chap. vii). Locke uses it in its present popular sense: the admission of something as true without assurance (*Essay*, iv. 15). Kant distinguishes matters of fact, of opinion, and of (rational) faith. The first refers to things, the existence of which can be proved either through pure reason or by exhibition in experience; the second refers to possible, but not actual, objects of experience in the world of sense, e.g. the existence of inhabitants upon Mars; the third to necessary objects of thought, but not of knowledge, i.e. God, immortality, the *summum bonum* (*Critique of Judgment*, Pt. II. § 91).

OPTIMISM and PESSIMISM [Lat. *optimus*, best, superlative of *bonus*, good, and *pessimus*, worst, superlative of *malus*, bad]: Ger. *Optimismus* and *Pessimismus*; Fr. *optimisme* and *pessimisme*; Ital. *ottimismo* and *pessimismo*. These are opposite correlative terms applied to the valuation of experience, life, and the world. Optimism is the view that the world is thoroughly good; or, that it is the best possible world. Pessimism is the view that the world is thoroughly bad; or, that it is the worst possible world. The problem is that of the relation of the world as a physical, or metaphysical, existence to its interpretation in ethical terms.

Plato, in the *Timaeus*, was the first to formulate the conception of optimism. His problem is the relation of the world as created to the demiurge, its architect. He made it, although sensible and changeable, after the pattern of the eternal and ideal; "he desired that all things should be good, and nothing bad, so far as this was attainable," and so the world, being like the fairest and most perfect of intelligible beings, is a "blessed god" (30), and a "sensible God, the greatest and best, the fairest, the most perfect possible, the image of its maker" (92). None the less, as created, as sensible, the world implies non-being, and hence evil. There is a limit set; the world is to be good, "so far as that is attainable." And in other of his writings he dwells in a somewhat gloomy spirit upon the evils thrust into the life of man by his connection with the sensible world and the material body, so that the good is reached by withdrawal from the created world (so in *Phaedo*, *Phaedrus*, parts of *Gorgias*, and the tenth book of the *Republic*). In this conception of the element of non-being in the world of experience, limiting the eternal good, Plato is the logical father of pessimism as well as of optimism. In him the Greek spirit was so strong that upon the whole the sensuous is looked upon as the plastic embodiment of the ideal, and hence as fair and good. But the elements are in unstable equilibrium, and it needs only to have the emphasis fall upon the negative limit to have a pessimistic result. The Stoics and Neo-Platonists continued the optimistic tradition of Plato, and so did the great Scholastics, following, however, in mode of statement, the Aristotelian teleology, rather than the Platonic tradition. The Epicurean and Sceptical schools were empirical rather than philosophical pessimists: they dwelt upon the actual bulk of pain and evil in the world, as confutation of the Stoic ethics.

Leibnitz repeats, in amplified form, a teleological optimism in his *Théodicée*. The world must be the best of all possible worlds, for it is the work of God. God through his wisdom knew all possibilities, and through his goodness chose the best of these possibilities, and through his power created it. Evil is of three forms: metaphysical, the expression of the necessary finitude of the world; physical, which serves to teach us law by punishing its infractions; and moral, which is a necessary phase of freedom. This optimism made its way through Wolff and others into the popular philosophy of the rationalistic enlightenment, and is seen, for example, in Pope. Like the optimism of the Stoics, it was met on empirical rather than philosophic grounds; notably by Voltaire's *Candide*, which, in its ironical treatment of Leibnitz, comes perilously near the doctrine that life is not worth living. In his *Phil. ignor.* Voltaire catalogues all the sources of woe in the world. Kant, in his early period, repeats the optimism of Leibnitz (*Versuch einiger Betrachtungen uber den Optimismus*, 1759). In his critical period Kant holds that there is a radical evil in man's nature in his tendency to make self-love—the particularistic, sensuous principle—the motive of his actions. The good principle is that of humanity, which is rational and universal.

Rousseau had already raised the question of good and evil in the historic and social life of man, in his assertion that the primitive, natural man was thoroughly good, and was rendered thoroughly evil by institutions and culture. Kant took up this problem, in connection with his notion of the twofold structure of man just referred to; he held that in the state of nature the natural propensities are good, since adapted to their end. Physically there is "Paradise," morally a state of complete innocence. But man becomes conscious of himself, has a will, departs from the natural law implanted in his instincts, and evil arises—the "Fall." Conscious desires lead to work, to the arts, to property, to civil relations, to culture. Through culture man's life ceases to be something produced by nature, and is self-produced. The conflict of nature and culture produces unhappiness, but is an ethical necessity incident to the recognition of rational law. The end of history is not the happiness of the individual, but the perfection of the whole of humanity. Conflict and suffering lead towards the latter. In short, Kant is a pessimist regarding man in his natural actuality, an optimist regarding him in his moral possibility.

Hegel seizes upon the three factors implied in the history now resumed: (1) the relation of the negative factor in creation to the Creator (where he utilizes Fichte's idea), (2) the relation of the particular and universal in man, and (3) the function of conflict and suffering in history; and attempts to make a synthesis of pessimism and optimism. Since the absolute is not a static fact or content, but a process, it involves negation, particularization, and consequent conflict and suffering within itself. But this conflict through differentiation is the dynamic of progress, and so functions for good. In a static cross-section the world is evil; in its movement (which Hegel calls "actuality") it is good.

The French Revolution introduced the positive side of the negative teaching of Rousseau. It held that a reform of economic and political conditions was all that was necessary to initiate a tendency towards the infinite perfectibility of man. Malthus's doctrine of population was purposely intended to refute this conception. As generalized and applied by Darwin, it has carried over the question of optimism and pessimism into the biological sphere. One school points to the universality of the struggle of existence as teaching the lesson of pessimism; another, the contribution made by this struggle to development as indicating an optimistic conclusion. Spencer has used the evolutionary conception to argue to the self-destructive, and hence transitional, character of evil.

Schopenhauer is the pessimistic pendant of Hegel's optimism. Will, not thought, or reason, is the absolute—the true, thing-in-itself. This will is irrational, hence objectless; there is no progress or development, but only the restless play of purposeless will. Hence the will is essentially unhappy. Since the objective world is only a picture of this will, it must be a world of suffering. This metaphysical reasoning is reinforced by psychological considerations; desire is essentially painful, and its satisfaction, pleasure, is only the removal of pain. Hence pain must preponderate in life. All experience and observation confirm this result. Von Hartmann attempts what he regards as a synthesis of Hegel and Schopenhauer. There is a logical factor and an alogical one, both attributes of the unconscious. While the will-factor makes it better that the world should not exist than exist, yet the world is the best of all possible worlds, and continually evolving to higher intensities of consciousness. Its teleology is optimistic, although from the standpoint of satisfaction the world is evil.

Current popular thought phrases the problem in the question of whether life is worth living. Interest has shifted from the theological problem to the question of intrinsic value of life. Cf. MELIORISM.

ORGANIC [Gr. ὀργανικός, pertaining to organs]: Ger. *organisch*; Fr. *organique*; Ital. *organico*. (1) Relating to that which has life, whether animal or vegetable; opposed to inanimate or inorganic. See ORGANISM (vital). But since the peculiarity of living beings is a certain relation of the parts to one another, such that they mutually act and react upon one another so as to maintain the whole in existence, it means (2) that which possesses a similar necessary relationship of whole and part; that which is systematized; that which is an internal or intrinsic means to an end, as distinct from an external or accidental one. This sense shades into teleological and is opposed to MECHANICAL (q.v.).

Historically, the identification of organic with the living comes last. Aristotle uses the term as equivalent to instrumental; even as synonymous with mechanical, i.e. the means that brings about a result. An organic body is one, whether living or not, in which heterogeneous elements make up a composite whole. This sense persists till Leibnitz, who uses

the term in a sense easily confused with the modern significance of living, but yet not the same. According to him,
that is organic all of whose parts are in turn machines, i.e.
implements adapted to ends. "Thus the organic body of a living being is a kind of divine machine or natural automaton,
because a machine which is made by man's art is not a
machine in all its parts; for example, the tooth of a brass
wheel has parts or fragments . . . which have nothing in
themselves to show the use to which the wheel was destined.
. . . But nature's machines are machines even in their
smallest parts *ad infinitum*" (*Monadology*, § 64; see also the
Princ. de la Nature, 31).

From this time on, the two elements in the conception
(that of composition of parts and of relation of means to
end) are intimately connected, and Kant welds them together in his famous definition of the organic as that in
which all the parts are reciprocally means and ends to one
another and to the whole (*Werke*, iv. 493). It is this conception of the whole as primary which marks off the conception
from the Leibnitzian, in which the distinction goes on *ad
infinitum*. This tends to change the indefinite pluralism of
Leibnitz into a systematic monism when the conception
"organic" is applied to the world at large. Cf. LIFE, ORGAN-
ISM, and SOCIAL ORGANISM.

Literature: Eucken, *Philos. Terminol.*, 26, 138, 153,
202; Mackenzie, *Introd. to Social Philos.*

ORGANISM [Gr. ὄργανον, an organ]: Ger. *Organismus*;
Fr. *organisme*; Ital. *organismo*. (1) A living being; see
ORGANISM (in Biology).

(2) A totality whose various parts or elements are related to each other according to some principle which is
derived from the whole itself, and hence is internal and not
external, necessary and not accidental. A system. Cf. OR-
GANIC.

While the Greeks use the term in quite another sense
from the moderns, the idea, even in its generalized philosophical use, was quite familiar to them. Plato regarded the
world as an animated whole—as ζῷον. With Aristotle the
end or form animates all potentiality or matter in such a
way as to keep it moving towards perfection, and thereby

gives it order. In living beings, this appears in the continual higher stages of articulation ($\delta\iota\acute{\alpha}\rho\theta\rho\omega\sigma\iota\varsigma$). Thus the form is the inner life of nature, as distinct from an external arrangement. In this sense, Aristotle applies the notion (not the term) organism, or a whole ordered and moving from an internal principle of causality, to the state, since the individual gets his social life only through his immanent connection with the whole. The Stoics expressly declare the world to be $\sigma\acute{\upsilon}\sigma\tau\eta\mu\alpha$, a living organized whole; and ethically they proclaim that the individual is not a part ($\mu\acute{\epsilon}\rho\sigma\varsigma$), but a member ($\mu\acute{\epsilon}\lambda\sigma\varsigma$) of the universe. The conception on the social side passed into Christianity in the conception of the Church as the mystic body (*corpus mysticum*) of Christ. In the Middle Ages, the paralleling of the state and the living body is common, and John of Salisbury undertakes to find a part of the body corresponding to every part of the state (see Eucken, *Grundbegriffe d. Gegenwart*, 157). Herder, in the 18th century, is most active in reviving a conception of nature as a living whole, working according to an internal principle, through a continuous series of manifestations. Kant gives the conception a clear-cut definition (see ORGANIC), but gives the idea only a subjective validity. Schelling, however, gives the term a completely objective meaning, applicable to the universe itself. Through his followers it becomes a favorite term to designate the principle of philosophies which regard the world as moving from intrinsic principles, and as producing its effects after the manner of an immanent life and intelligence (*Syst. d. trans. Idealismus*, 261).

Spencer has recently used the term in a generalized sense in recent English thought, as in his assertion that society is an organism. On discussions of this point, however, there is ambiguity—organism is sometimes used as analogous to the organs (or functions) of an animal body; at other times, in its logical sense, of a coherent whole, systematized by an internal principle. Cf. SOCIAL ORGANISM.

Literature: see ORGANIC, and SOCIAL ORGANISM.

OUTNESS [AS. *ūt*, out]: Ger. *Aussensein*; Fr. *externalité*; Ital. *esteriorità*. Distance; externality in space; externality to mind.

The term was introduced by Berkeley in his *Essay towards a new Theory of Vision* (46), also *Principles of Knowledge* (47). In each case it is used as synonymous with space and distance. Hume uses it also as equivalent to distance (*Treatise*, Bk. I. Pt. IV. § 2). So also Reid and Hutchison Stirling. Huxley: "sense of outness—no power of distinguishing between the external world and himself" (*Physiology*, § 289).

OVERSOUL: Ger. *Ueberseele*; Fr. (no exact equivalent —TH.F.); Ital. (not in use). A term used by Emerson to express the Absolute Unity, in which subject and object, the knowing and the known, are one; the total reality in which are included all parts of the universe, and all our partial, successive thoughts and acts. It connotes this absolute reality particularly as the source of all that is most universal and valuable in the experience of man: genius in his intellect, virtue in his will, and love in his emotions. See Emerson, *Essays*, "Oversoul."

PALINGENESIS [Gr. πάλιν, again, + γένεσις, becoming, birth]: Ger. *Palingenese*; Fr. *palingenèse*; Ital. *palingenesi*. (1) The doctrine that the soul passes through a succession of rebirths: METEMPSYCHOSIS (q.v.).

(2) Also sometimes used, in theological writings, to express REGENERATION (q.v.), of which it is the literal equivalent.

(3) The term has a technical philosophic significance only in the writings of Schopenhauer, who uses it to express the fact that will is untouched by death, and reappears in a new individual, until the will-to-live is completed, denied, and abrogated. He distinguishes it from metempsychosis as the vulgar doctrine that the concrete "soul" reappears, but claims it is identical with the esoteric teaching of Buddhism (Schopenhauer, *The World as Will and as Idea*, trans. by Haldane, iii. 300–301).

PANENTHEISM [Gr. πᾶν, all, + ἐν, in, + θεός, God]: Ger. *Panentheismus*; Fr. *panenthéisme*; Ital. *panenteismo*. A name given by Krause to his attempted reconciliation of theism and pantheism; the doctrine that God is neither the world, nor yet outside the world, but that the world is in him, and that he extends beyond its limits.

PANLOGISM [Gr. $\pi\hat{a}\nu$, all, + $\lambda\acute{o}\gamma os$, thought, reason]: Ger. *Panlogismus*; Fr. *panlogisme*; Ital. *panlogismo*. A term applied to philosophic systems which make thought the absolute—usually to the system of Hegel.

PANPNEUMATISM [Gr. $\pi\hat{a}\nu$, all, + $\pi\nu\epsilon\hat{v}\mu a$, spirit]: Ger. *Panpneumatismus*; Fr. *panpneumatisme*; Ital. *panpneumatismo*. A term used by v. Hartmann (only) to designate a "higher synthesis of PANLOGISM (q.v.) and PANTHELISM (q.v.), according to which the absolute is both will and thought."

PANPSYCHISM [Gr. $\pi\hat{a}\nu$, all, + $\psi v\chi\acute{\eta}$, soul]: Ger. *Panpsychismus, Allbeseelung*; Fr. *panpsychisme*; Ital. *panpsichismo*. (1) The theory that all matter, or all nature, is itself psychical, or has a psychical aspect; that atoms and molecules, as well as plants and animals, have a rudimentary life of sensation, feeling, and impulse, which bears the same relation to their movements (whether causal or parallel) that the psychical life of human beings does to their objective activities. The theory is a revival, under conditions of modern science, of ancient ANIMISM (q.v.) and HYLOZOISM (q.v.).

(2) The term is also used (as by Windelband) to designate the Arabian interpretation of Aristotle's doctrine of reason, according to which man's reason is but a special mode of an eternal, impersonal divine Reason. See AVERROISM.

Literature: Fechner, *Ueber die Seelenfrage*; Nanna, *Zend-Avesta*; Paulsen, *Introd. to Philos.* (Eng. trans.), 91, 99, 131; citations in Eisler, *Wörterb. d. philos. Begriffe*, "Pampsychismus."

PANTHEISM [Gr. $\pi\hat{a}\nu$, all, + $\theta\epsilon\acute{o}s$, God]: Ger. *Pantheismus*; Fr. *panthéisme*; Ital. *panteismo*. (1) The term has a wide and loose meaning, especially in controversial writings, where the *odium theologicum* attaches to it; in this way it is used to designate almost any system which transcends current or received THEISM (q.v.) in its theory of a positive and organic relation of God to the world.

Theism, when combined with philosophical dualism, as it is quite apt to be, tends naturally to become DEISM (q.v.), assuming an external and mechanical relation of God to the world of nature and of man. This calls out a reaction on both philosophic and religious grounds. The former reaction occurs because of the difficulties felt in an external relation of the infinite and finite. The latter is made independent, and thus the former practically becomes itself a finite. The connection between them is made one of causation and design merely. Difficulties arise from applying the category of causation to the infinite, especially as the cause is moved back indefinitely in time; while the notion of design is used in such a way as to imply that God is simply an external artificer or mechanic. The religious reaction arises because this external relation does not allow of the intimate communication of the human and divine spirits, the sense of absorption and permeation, which seem to be required by deep religious experience. Hence the attempts to bring the finite into more essential and intrinsic relations to God. If these attempts are animated particularly by the religious motive, they tend to MYSTICISM (q.v.), which is closely akin to pantheism. But, in any case, they are condemned by the deists as tending to swallow up the finite in God, or as pantheistic. As will be evident, even from this brief outline, it is a matter of the nicest balance to keep, especially in Christian theology, the theory of the relation of God as infinite to the world as finite, from leaning to pantheism on one side or to deism on the other.

(2) In its narrower and proper philosophic sense, pantheism is any system which expressly (not merely by implication) regards the finite world as simply a mode, limitation, part, or aspect of the one eternal, absolute Being; and of such a nature that from the standpoint of this Being no distinct existence can be attributed to it. The chief problem of pantheism understood in this way, i.e. as acosmism,

is to account for the appearance of self-subsistence, or separate being, belonging to the finite world.

The Eleatic school (see PRE-SOCRATICS) may be regarded as the forerunners of pantheism in their insistence upon the unity and all-comprehensiveness of true Being. The distinction between finite and infinite, God and the world, had not, however, been made sufficiently clear at this time to justify calling the system pantheism. Through Plato and Aristotle the terms of the problem, both in themselves and in their relation to each other, are made evident. NEO-PLATONISM (q.v.) and STOICISM (q.v.) are both pantheistic. The former is of a logical idealistic type, based upon Plato's theory of the relation of the One Being, *Nous*, and the Ideas; teaching that the world is simply one of a series of emanations from God, radiating from him, as light from the sun, and having its apparent distinction only through a negative element, Non-Being or Matter. Stoicism is a development of Aristotelianism under the influence of the earlier Greek cosmologists, especially Heraclitus.

Neo-Platonism, and some of the congruent ideas of the Stoics (especially of the λόγος σπερματικός), influenced the formation and development of Christian theology; and pantheistic tendencies in the latter accordingly crop out, as in Scotus Erigena (see SCHOLASTICISM) and in the mystics, like Eckhart and Boehme. The doctrines particularly influenced are those of the Trinity and Creation (the latter being a continuation of the quasi-emanistic process which finds its expression in the incarnation of the Father in the Logos, and in the activity of the Spirit); of Redemption, conceived as the necessary return to God, thus completing the circuit, whose first half is the unfolding of the world from God in creation; of religious experience, as the immediate, unhindered, ecstatic converse of the human spirit with God. AVERROISM (q.v.) gave a pantheistic interpretation of Aristotle, and is perhaps even more influential than Neo-Platonism in all the later developments of pantheism, particularly as it is more allied in content and terminology to a scientific view of nature. In Giordano Bruno, this latter motive culminates in a poetic personification of nature; and the humanistic view of the universe displaces the factor of religious experience, so important in mediaeval thought. Later John Toland presented a naturalistic pantheism, identifying God with the forces of nature.

Averroism came to Spinoza through its influence upon Jewish thought, and is by him combined with the mediaeval religious motive, the modern scientific one, and with the problem of Cartesian philosophy regarding the relation of mind and matter in a splendid synthesis which makes him the classic type of pantheistic thought. Spinoza's influence was felt first not in philosophy, but in literature, in Herder, Lessing, and above all in Goethe. Schelling revived pantheism in connection with the problem of subject and object (which had displaced the Cartesian problem of mind and matter) in his philosophy of identity. Hegel attempted here as elsewhere a synthesis of ideas in opposition to each other, viz. theism and pantheism. He adopted the monistic factor of Spinoza, but seized upon his statement that *determinatio est negatio* as the explicit definition of the root of all pantheism (or absorption of the finite into the infinite), and reversed it to mean all negation is determination: i.e. negation is ultimately positive, being the dynamic factor through which Being actualizes itself into full, concrete individuality. Hegel's system broke up into two schools, one avowedly pantheistic (as in Strauss); the other atheistic, holding that God comes to existence merely and only in the evolution of human individuals. Hartmann holds that only pantheism is henceforth philosophically possible; Hegel and Schopenhauer, holding principles which in their opposition are exhaustive of the universe, being both pantheists. But by pantheism Hartmann seems to mean especially MONISM (q.v.), an identification of terms which seems to be growing, though to be deprecated from the point of view of clearness of thought. Herbert Spencer alternates between a pantheism, in his theory of the absolute unknowable force, and a dualism, in his theory of the relation of mind and matter, subject and object.

Literature: for the most part we must rely upon works upon and by the individual authors, especially Spinoza. Jundt, *Hist. du Panthéisme populaire* (1876, confined to mediaeval pantheism and Eckhart); Jäsche, *Der Pantheismus*

(1826); most works on THEISM (q.v.) and antitheistic theories, and the introductions to philosophy (e.g. Paulsen). See also Vol. 3, *Dictionary of Philosophy and Psychology*, Bibliog. B, 2, f.

PANTHELISM [Gr. πᾶν, all, + θέλειν, to wish, will]: Ger. *Panthelismus*; Fr. *panthélisme*; Ital. *pantelismo* (de Sarlo). The doctrine that will is the basis of the universe; that it is the absolute, or, in a more limited sense, that reason (intellect) is subordinate to the will, and is to be derived from it.

The term is applied to such systems as Fichte's, with its derivation of knowing from acting, and to Schopenhauer's. See VOLUNTARISM. Cf. Falckenberg, *Hist. of Mod. Philos.* (Index), and Francesco de Sarlo, *Metafisica, scienza e moralità* (1898).

PAROUSIA [Gr. παρεῖναι, to be present]: Ger. *Parusie*; Fr. *parousie*; Ital. *parusia*. (1) A semi-technical term used by Plato to express relationship between absolute being or essence and the sensible world. It is closely allied to his more specifically technical terms participation (μέθεξις) and community (κοινωνία). The world of sense has essence and existence only through the presence of the good in it (*Politics*, 509).

(2) It is employed as a technical term by Plotinus to express the relation of soul and body. The soul is not present in the body, but is rather present to it. More strictly, Plotinus says the body is present to the soul. Through this relation, sentience and vitality are rendered to the body. By parousia the soul thoroughly animates and permeates the body without getting in any way entangled with it (Plotinus, *Enneads*, vi. 4, 12).

(3) The term is used in early Christian thought to express the relation of the Holy Spirit to the individual and the Church. It is a matter of dispute whether this use is influenced by the technical philosophical discussions.

PASSION and PASSIVE [Lat. *passio*, the trans. of Gr. πάθος, from πάσχειν, to suffer]: Ger. *Passivität* (*leidend*, *passiv*); Fr. *passion* (*passif*); Ital. *passività* (*passivo*). Generally passion is the condition of being acted upon, of being affected, receptive; opposed to action. Passive is the corresponding adjective. Technically, it has its philosophical meaning as one of the ten categories of Aristotle (*Topics* and *Categories*). See CATEGORY.

According to the theory of Trendelenburg that the categories correspond to distinctions of language, this category is derived from the passive voice of the verb. In the *Metaphysics* (xiv. 2) Aristotle generalizes the categories under three heads—essences, attributes (πάθη), and relations. As attribute, the "passion" describes what flows not from the essence or substance of the thing itself, but from the way it is acted upon by other things. Thus it comes to mere attribute in general, apart from its passive connotation. Hence the chief importance of the concept historically is in connection with the discussion of the nature of SUBSTANCE (q.v.). Among the Scholastics, the relation of the *passiones entis* to *ens* was a matter of dispute; the Thomists holding that they are real, not simply something attributed to being by thought, and are one in nature with Ens itself; while the Scotists hold that they are real, but yet, by the nature of the thing, totally different from Ens or being; while others asserted that they were the results of thought. In modern thought the term is practically given up. Cf. AFFECTION, ACCIDENT, MODE, PROPERTY, and QUALITY.

PERIPATETICS [Gr. περί, about, + πατεῖν, to walk]: Ger. *Peripatetiker*; Fr. *péripatéticiens*; Ital. *peripatetici*. A name given to the school of Aristotle, traditionally because his discussions were carried on while walking about in the Lyceum (*Diog. Laert.*, Bk. V). The modern explanation, however, is that its name is derived from a special path (περίπατος) in the Lyceum used for taking walks.

Theophrastus, Eudemus, Strato, Aristo, Diodorus of Tyre, Andronicus of Rhodes, are among the chief successive heads of the school. The term New Peripatetics is sometimes applied to the writers of the Renaissance, who, in opposition to the Arabian and Christian Aristotelianism of the Middle Ages, attempted, by returning to the original Greek text, to give an objective setting forth of his doctrine. Pomponatius (d. 1525) and Scaliger (1484–1558) are some of the greater names, most of which, however, belong to the history of scholarship rather than to that of philosophy.

PERMANENCE [Lat. *per*, through, + *manere*, to remain, persist]: Ger. *Permanenz, Beständigkeit*; Fr. *permanence*; Ital. *permanenza*. The condition of fixity, persistence, continuity, especially in time; existing unchanged through a given duration of time.

Beginning with Heraclitus and the Eleatic school, Greek philosophy was much occupied with the problem of rest and MOTION (q.v.), or of self-identity and change, the former being regarded as a sign of Being, and the latter of NON-BEING (q.v.). See also SAME AND OTHER. It was Kant who introduced the category of permanence in the modern sense. It is the critical and phenomenal counterpart of the old dogmatic, ontological conception of substance, and indicates that *quantity* of matter and energy remains unchanged, being neither increased nor diminished, in all changes of phenomena. It is thus the metaphysical counterpart of the scientific doctrine of the conservation of energy—metaphysical because derived not from observation or experience, but treated as a principle which is necessary to the having of experience (Kant, *Critique of Pure Reason*, 160–6, Müller's trans., and Preface to *Metaphysical Foundations of Nat. Sci.*). Cf. BELIEF for the consideration of permanence in the external world.

PERSEITY (1) and (2) PER SE [Lat. *perseitas, per se*, through itself]: Ger. *Perseität*; Fr. *perséité*; Ital. *perseità*. (1) Literally, the conception of self-included existence, but in its technical use the term applied to the Thomistic doctrine of the relation of good to the divine will. Cf. ST. THOMAS (philosophy of).

The Scotists held that good was the arbitrary creation of the divine will, in itself superior to it; the Thomists held that will in its adequate expression is essentially moved by the concept of the good as presented in reason, and that this relationship of reason and will holds in the divine nature as well as in the human. The *perseitas boni* is the essential rationality of the good. See Windelband, *Hist. of Mod. Philos.*, Eng. trans., 332.

PHASE [Gr. φάσις, from φάειν, to make to appear, to make visible]: Ger. *Phase*; Fr. *phase*; Ital. *fase*. One of a series of definite forms, or modes of appearance, or specific characters which one and the same subject-matter presents either successively, or from different points of view.

It is often used as synonymous with aspect, but strictly speaking is differentiated by referring to successive, instead of simultaneous, modes of manifestation. It also involves a shade less reference to the subject or percipient, "aspect" indicating a certain distinction introduced by the way the subject looks at the matter.

PHENOMENALISM [Gr. φαίνεσθαι, to appear]: Ger. *Phänomenalismus*; Fr. *phénoménisme*; Ital. *fenomenismo*. (1) The theory that all knowledge is limited to phenomena (things and events in time and space), and that we cannot penetrate to reality in itself. Cf. PHENOMENON, EMPIRICISM, AGNOSTICISM, and POSITIVISM.

(2) The theory that all we know is a phenomenon, that is, reality present to consciousness, either directly or reflectively; and that phenomena are all that there are to know, there being no thing-in-itself or object out of relation to consciousness.

This latter is the philosophy held by Shadworth Hodgson. Cf. also IMMANENCE PHILOSOPHY (q.v.). It is obvious that the two senses differ radically from each other, the first having its point in the assertion of a real but unknown thing-in-itself; the latter in its denial.

PHENOMENOLOGY [Gr. φαινόμενον, that which appears, + λόγος, doctrine, theory]: Ger. *Phänomenologie*; Fr. *phénoménologie*; Ital. *fenomenologia*. (1) Literally, the theory of appearances or manifestations; in technical use, that theory of the particular, especially historical, facts of any subject-matter which exhibits them as natural and necessary manifestations of their underlying principle. Cf. PHENOMENON.

Hegel thus used the term in his *Phenomenology of Spirit*, to express the progress of mind, individual and racial, from the lowest form of knowledge, through successive necessary stages, to the highest—absolute thought. On the obverse side, it is thus also an exposition of the extent of reason in its generalized or typical temporal stages of development. Among recent writers v. Hartmann is given to using the term to denote the exposition of a general principle with reference to a philosophic construction of historic data.

(2) Kant used the term in a different sense to denote one of the four branches of his *Metaphysic of Nature*; viz. that concerned with motion and rest as regards their modality, that is, their use as predicates of a judgment about things.

PHENOMENON [Gr. τὸ φαινόμενον, a thing that is seen, that appears]: Ger. *Phänomen, Erscheinung*; Fr. *phénomène*; Ital. *fenomeno*. (1) In Greek thought phenomena were always opposed to essences (ὄντα), and hence defined as possessing a lesser and derived form of reality. No particular gulf exists between the two; both are objective, but the phenomena are changeable and manifold, and related to sense, while essences are eternal and one, and related to reason.

(2) But in modern times the phenomenon is opposed to the THING-IN-ITSELF (q.v.) or to the NOUMENON (q.v.). They belong to radically distinct orders; the phenomenon is always relative to us, dependent upon the way the thing-in-itself affects us in sensation, or the way the mind looks at it. This is especially true in Kantian thought. The word appearance (*Schein*) is often used somewhat in this sense—for that which has the SEMBLANCE (q.v.) at least of reality.

(3) It is also used in what we may term a naturalistic or positivistic sense: it is the object or event in space or time, and as such capable of accurate observation and description; reflection based upon it is verifiable.

This third sense is also derived from Kant, but is used without any reference to the subjective factor—to the part played passively by our sensibility and actively by our understanding in the constitution of the phenomenon. The reconciliation of this third sense, which makes phenomena the data of positive science and thus objective, and the second, which defines them through reference to impressions made upon our senses (which of course would be different if our senses were different), constitutes the chief problem of the concept of "phenomena." To meet the difficulty, Kant employed his distinction of matter and form; but since, according to modern science, "matter" of objects throughout, down to its last sensuous detail, is subject to quantitative laws—since, indeed, it is just this "matter" which is the real object of science—the distinction of phenomena as related to us, in distinction from objects in themselves, seems practically to fall through.

(4) It is used in a colorless philosophic sense, as equivalent to "fact," or event—to any particular which requires explanation. And it may be questioned whether this practical, apparently non-philosophic sense is not in truth the most philosophic of all.

PHILOSOPHY [Gr. φίλος, lover, + σοφία, wisdom]: Ger. *Philosophie*; Fr. *philosophie*; Ital. *filosofia*. Four general senses may easily be distinguished: (1) The widest sense, in which it means the explanation of any set of phenomena by reference to its determining principles, whether practical, causal, or logical; theory, reasoned doctrine.

In this sense, it is in common use in English speech. Natural philosophy is physics; and we hear of the philosophy of invention, of machines, of digestion, of hair-dressing, and so on indefinitely.

(2) Used in the same wide sense, but with a clear ethical implication: the power and habit of referring all events and special facts to some general principle, and of behaving (of reacting to the events and facts) in the light of this reference; the working theory of things as exhibited in conduct. Thus we say: he took it philosophically; he is a real philosopher; his philosophy deserted him. In this second sense, there is often an implication of Stoicism in its popular meaning; that is, the reference to general principles enables one to endure or suffer calmly what would otherwise excite emotional disturbance.

(3) The technical and most restricted sense: an account of the fundamentally real, so far as from its consideration laws and truths may be derived, applying to all facts and phenomena: practically equivalent to METAPHYSICS (q.v.).

(4) A theory of truth, reality, or experience, taken as an organized whole, and so giving rise to general principles which unite the various branches or parts of experience into a coherent unity. As such, it is not so much any one discipline or science, as it is the system and animating spirit of all. Thus Kant, with apparent tautology but real discrimination, speaks of philosophy as the sum of the philosophic disciplines.

In all these various senses, certain common implications appear: (*a*) Totality: philosophy is conceived as a comprehensive view, as dealing (objectively) with the whole or universe, and accordingly as (subjectively) requiring to be pursued in a catholic, impartial spirit. It is thus marked off from what we term the special sciences, which limit their view to some one specific set of facts. Even when, as in (1) above, it is used in reference to a very limited sphere, it yet implies a certain totality within that sphere. (*b*) Generality: just because the view is of a whole, it manifests itself in universals, in principles; it deals with explanations, not with a mere summary, inventory, description, or narration. (*c*) Application: the general truths do not remain inert or sterile, but are carried over to illuminate and make reasonable the relevant details. While this application may primarily be to fact simply as observed or known, it yet extends, ultimately and derivatively, to conduct. The term implies the difference between wisdom and information or learning. The world, or particular subject, getting a certain organization, the acts and habits that have to do with it inevitably assume a corresponding arrangement. While some deprecate this ethical connotation as an intrusion into what should be a purely objective attitude of science, it is too deeply embedded to be exorcized. Hence the narrow meaning (3) has never become fixed, nor made its way into everyday usage. As A. Seth remarks (art. "Philosophy," *Encyc. Brit.*, xviii. 806): "It will not be easy to infuse into so abstract and bloodless a term as 'metaphysics' the fuller life (and especially the inclusion of ethical considerations) suggested by the more concrete term philosophy."

Gathering these various elements together, philosophy may be defined as the theory of a subject-matter, taken as a whole or organized unity; containing principles which bind together a variety of particular truths and facts, and requiring a certain harmony of theory and practice. Since all subordinate and derived subjects are, by the nature of the case, only wholes by courtesy or in a relative sense, the conception forces us back to *the* unity, Experience—to the universe or whatever is taken as a systematic whole.

If anyone complain that we have not here, after all, a clear-cut, well-limited definition of philosophy, the reply is that a certain vagueness, born of the very generality of the idea, is embodied in the conception itself; and that to eliminate this, by holding the term down to just this or that meaning, is to show oneself not so much a philosopher as an adherent of some philosophic sect. In other words, philosophy expresses a certain attitude, purpose, and temper of conjoined intellect and will rather than a discipline whose exact boundaries and contents can be neatly marked off.

The same indefiniteness of outline shows itself when we attempt to divide philosophy into its component parts, or sub-sciences. Various writers have regarded as desirable a regularly recognized subdivision which should be observed by various schools; but this wish, up to the present, is certainly not realized. The need for organization is felt in very different places at different times, and thus very diverse distributions of emphasis arise; e.g. with the early Greeks it was the world of nature which needed to be presented as a totality, hence the tendency of cosmology to be the supreme science; in mediaeval times, it was upon religious experiences that the stress of need fell, and so theology was dominant; with the rise of modern science, it is the methods of discovering truth that need organization, hence the dominance of epistemology, and so on. Now according as one discipline or another is regarded as central, various schemes of arranging the others are set forth.

Moreover, instead of having a formal subdivision, into

which materials fall, as matter of fact it is the interpretation of the material which controls the forms. One example will serve: What is the place of aesthetics as a philosophic discipline? Cannot those who differ in principles yet agree upon assigning a certain uniform position to this discipline, to which shall be referred all relevant material? No. The history of thought reveals that, at one period, sense, feeling, and imagination are all regarded as imperfect or confused thought, and hence aesthetics appears as a contributory, and probably minor, part of a dominant intellectual science; at another period the manifestation of truth in the realm of sensuous feeling is one of the coordinate spheres of the exhibition of the absolute, the other spheres being its appearance in the realm of intellect (logic), and in that of will (ethics). Or again, a certain equilibrium of sense and intellect is regarded as the highest ideal; this balance is supposed to be found in beauty, and aesthetics is virtually, at least (as in some aspects of Schelling's thought), the supreme and normative discipline; or ethics is made subordinate to aesthetics, as with Herbart. The various placings of psychology would indicate even more radical divergencies.

It is because the classification and arrangement of philosophic problems is really dependent upon the value and meaning attached to the material concepts of philosophy, that the history of philosophy is now regarded as the best introduction to philosophic study; and the so-called introductions have mainly a pedagogic value, as introducing students in an orderly way to the problems which have arisen historically. Accordingly, further account of these subdivisions is reserved for the historical sketch below.

A schematic classification of problems in philosophy may, however, be made by classifying the various historic philosophies in accordance with the questions that have preoccupied them, and the points upon which they have insisted in their solutions. Thus philosophic schools are classified: (1) According to the number of fundamental principles recognized, as MONISM, DUALISM, PLURALISM. (2) According to the sort of value attached to the fundamental principle chosen as basis of organization, as MATERIALISM, SPIRITUALISM, and PHENOMENALISM. (3) According to the organ or instrument of knowledge most emphasized, as RATIONALISM and SENSATIONALISM; or as INTUITIONALISM, INTELLECTUALISM, EMPIRICISM, and MYSTICISM. (4) According to the method pursued: (*a*) as regards its examination of its own procedure, philosophy is subdivided into DOGMATISM, SCEPTICISM, and CRITICISM; (*b*) as regards the relation of method to results reached, into AGNOSTICISM and GNOSTICISM, or into TRANSCENDENTALISM, POSITIVISM, SOLIPSISM, and NIHILISM. (5) According to the relationship assumed between subject and object in knowing, as REALISM (with its various subdivisions, naïve, natural, transcendental, hypothetic, reasoned, transfigured, etc.) and IDEALISM (subjective, objective, or absolute).

But since, of course, all actual systems are determined by complex cross-references, any such scheme is extremely formal, save as we keep in mind the influence which, say, the theory of the organ of knowledge has upon the theory of the relationship of subject and object, and upon the conception of the nature or quality of the object. Thus idealism tends to become identified with spiritualism, and often with rationalism or intuitionalism. Dogmatic materialism is replaced by a (relatively) critical MECHANISM, which substitutes the causally connected system of facts and events for the substance, Matter, and so tends towards Positivism or even Phenomenalism. Spiritualism may be dualistic, or even pluralistic as well as monistic; it may run into HYLOZOISM, which is quasi-materialistic, or into PANPSYCHISM; or it may mean just IMMATERIALISM, the denial of the substantial reality of matter, which in turn is identical, from certain points of view, with subjective idealism. If in Monism the theological problem sets the dominant interest, we get PANTHEISM (or even, under certain historic conditions, as with Xenophanes, MONOTHEISM); if the question of relation of mind and body, PARALLELISM; if the problem of reconciling subject and object in such a way as to account for the possibility of knowledge, absolute IDEALISM. It is these interrelations which one informed by the history of philosophy keeps in mind, and thereby avoids a rigid use of any of the terms; while the immature mind ignores them and thus indulges in wholesale proof or refutation of an -ism, refuting, say, Monism as a pantheistic or religious system, but ignoring its bearing as a theory of relation of subject and object in knowledge, and so on. See the topics cited in small capitals.

The traditional ascription of the origin of the term to Pythagoras (as by Cicero and the ancients generally) is probably unfounded. Plato clearly uses the term, first to discriminate the (Socratic) love of truth from the (Sophistic) assertion of it. Man is neither wholly wise ($\sigma o \phi \acute{o} s$) nor wholly ignorant ($\acute{a} \mu a \theta \acute{\eta} s$), but stands between (*Phaedrus*, 278; *Symposium*, 212; *Lysis*, 218). In this general sense, science, or even any special science, as geometry, is philosophy; morality and art are also forms of it, since the love of beauty and that of virtuous character are stages in the ascent towards complete truth. But it finds its most perfect expression in the knowing which is directed towards true and essential being, as distinct from the (probable) knowledge or opinion which terminates with the sensible and the changing (*Rep.*, v. 477 and 480, vi. 484). Since this knowledge of essential being is dependent upon a particular method, philosophy in its most special sense is dialectic. (For the early history of the use of the term, with bibliographical references, see Ueberweg, *Hist. of Philos.*, i. § 1. For Plato, see Erdmann, *Hist. of Philos.*, 1. 102–4.) But just because the supremely real is the Good, and because true knowing is true virtue, philosophy gets also with Plato an intensely ethical sense; it is the guide to conduct. Thus, indeed, dialectic (the undivided source of logic and metaphysic), ontology, and ethic are all one in the Platonic system, while physics is immediately derivative, since the world of nature is determined by ends, and finally by the Good.

If we do not find formal subdivisions, it is precisely because the material context of the Platonic thought demands a synthetic identification, which to modern analytic tendencies easily seems to be mere confusion. The method of ascending from the world of appearance to the world of being, and the corresponding descent, is not a merely subjective nor even merely logical process; it is paralleled by the relations of subordination and participation which exist objectively in the ideas, among themselves, and in relation

to the world of change. Hence there is a refusal to separate
logic and ontology; not merely their confusion. If physics
is more definitely marked off, it is just because the world of
change with which the earlier physicists had exclusively
occupied themselves (see NATURE) is distinguished from
the world of being; yet since it depends upon it, and since
again the essential being is also the Good, the physics of
Plato must be, so to speak, just an applied ontology and
ethics. Subsequent Greek thought hardly did more than make
explicit the distinctions involved in Plato, but often carrying
the discriminations necessary for this explicit formulation
into separations—the exact character of which depended
upon the material context of their own view of the world.
Aristotle gives logic that ambiguous position which it retained so long. On one hand, it seems to be propaedeutic
and instrumental only; a setting in order of the means by
which we most surely attain reality, rather than, as with
Plato, also an account of the truth itself; truth is agreement
with being, rather than the being itself, and thus Aristotle
dismisses dialectic as equivalent to empty and formal, almost verbal, thinking apart from subject-matter; treating it
as Plato treated sophistic. But he cannot so far escape the
Greek realistic absorption of subject and object into each
other, as to regard thinking as merely subjective, and so in
his ontology (called by him first philosophy, and by his followers metaphysic), or account of reality in its comprehensive and fundamental nature, the chief distinctions of
thought reappear as distinctions of being: the difference of
subject and predicate in judgment as distinction of substance, or essence, and quality and accident in being—so
that from one point of view Aristotle's logic is still thoroughly objective (see Adamson, art. "Logic" in *Encyc. Brit.*,
xiv. 792–4). Leaving the exact position of logic unsettled,
the other divisions are fairly clear, though not by any means
so fixed as they are frequently represented. After his first
philosophy or metaphysic comes physics, which treats respectively of the heavens; of meteorology, or the region between earth and heavens; of the history of animals; of
biology (within which is included psychology): these (probably with mathematics in his original conception) make up

theoretic philosophy. Practical philosophy has two sub-divisions, ethics and poetics, corresponding to the distinction of doing and making, or of action and production (πράττειν and ποιεῖν, *actio* and *factio*), since in one the motive, dis-position, and mental habit is the essential thing; in the other, the result, the "work of art." Ethics, in turn, deals both with the individual as such, although conditioned by organized social life—ethics in the narrower sense; and with the conditioning organization—politics. Here again an am-biguity similar to that found in the relation of logic to meta-physic affects subsequent thought; on the one hand, the state seems to be the presupposition and the completion of the individual moral life, and thus politics is the wider science; and again it appears as an adjunct or instrument, sometimes a more or less external one, of the individual life —the theoretic virtues, which belong to the individual, and transcend the state, being placed higher than the practical ones.

The distinctions of ontology or metaphysic, of theoretic and practical philosophy, and the subdivision of the former into logic and physics were easily drawn by the successors of Plato and Aristotle, and became its formal or conventional divisions. But, none the less, certain tendencies were at work which, underneath this formal arrangement, profoundly dis-turbed its equilibrium. Aristotle had expressly identified the supreme reality with God, and thus first philosophy is also theology. With the Neo-Platonists the implied religious factor comes to complete recognition, and since God as Pure Being is above thought and knowledge (see NEO-PLATONISM), a certain mystic condition of ecstasy becomes the means and sign of unity with him, and philosophy, as theory of the means of attaining this mystic unity, tends to become THEOSOPHY (q.v.). On the other hand, much of the definite content of previous philosophy is formulated for the pur-poses of the schools, and so leads to a variety of special disciplines; particular branches of science (astronomy, mathematics, etc.) and of culture (grammar and rhetoric) are set off by themselves. This tendency reaches a culmina-tion in Cassiodorus (c. 487–c. 583 A.D.) and Isidorus (560–636 A.D.), who distinguish, and put in encyclopedic form, the trivium, the three arts: grammar, dialectic, and rhetoric, summed up as logica; and the quadrivium, the four disciplines: arithmetic, economics, music, and astronomy—called collectively at first mathematics, and later physics. The writings of Isidorus, particularly, were the encyclopedia of the Middle Ages, and these classifications had great influence.

Another motive was the tendency, in which Stoics, Epicureans, and Sceptics all agreed, to make the practical of more importance than the theoretical, reversing Plato and Aristotle. With the Stoics, philosophy thus becomes the art of virtue; with the Epicureans, the art of living happily. Logic, in particular, takes a distinctly formal position; while physics, with the Epicureans at least, gets an almost negative value, being just the knowledge of nature which will enable one to avoid the burdens of superstition. A notable exception, however, is Lucretius, who, though animated by the same motive, yet develops the atomic theory in such a way as really to make physics the normative centre of philosophy.

All of these motives finally met and combined in the ethico-religious spirit of Christianity, resulting in the conception which identified theology and philosophy. Since theology was conceived at first wholly as a positive or revealed matter, this meant, for a time, the virtual abrogation of philosophy; but as soon as the need was felt of presenting even the purely positive and supernatural content of theology in a reasoned form, philosophy began to revive, although having no independent place. When the need was deeply felt of exhibiting the various church authorities in harmony with themselves and one another, and still more when the need was to show that there is no contradiction between faith and reason, philosophy became, though still in theological form, supreme. In the latter period, Aristotelianism was revived as furnishing the method and leading ideas of philosophic reason, and naturally his classification of philosophic sciences was more or less followed. There are, however, these differences: (1) Logic is clearly regarded as merely formal and propaedeutic; (2) ontology and metaphysic are identified with theology in a more thorough-going way than with Aristotle, and especially, of course, with the doctrines of the Church, particularly that of the Trinity; (3) the positive scientific content of physics is virtually lost, what remains being a philosophy of the creation of nature; (4) ethics is also, of course, submerged in religion, and becomes the theory of the Fall, or of sin and redemption. In view of later psychological developments, it is, moreover, interesting to note that, in spite of the disregard of psychology as a distinct discipline, when any ground for the classification is given, it is a psychological one. Thus with Gilbert of Poitiers (d. 1154) theology corresponds to *intellectus*, while physics is based upon *ratio*. Albertus exhibits the first systematic result of the revival of Aristotelianism, and the need of giving Christianity a reasonable statement over against the Aristotelianism of the Mohammedans, and against the heretics in the Church. Theoretical philosophy is (a) metaphysics, which is identified with theology, because (objectively) it deals with the divine, and because (subjectively) it is possible only through divine illumination, not through natural unaided reason; (b) mathematics; (c) physics. Psychologically, these correspond to the intelligible, the imaginable, and the sensible spheres. Practical philosophy is (a) monastics (that is, dealing with the individual in himself, the nearest approach to ancient ethics); (b) economics (the individual as member of a family); and (c) politics (the individual as a citizen). In spite of the nominal identification of theology and philosophy, Albert, however, makes little attempt to connect the peculiar content of Christian theology with metaphysic, and indeed often emphasizes the distinction between the theological and the philosophical (Aristotelian) view, since the former has a purely practical aim, salvation. Thomas Aquinas, the greatest of the schoolmen, makes the connection explicit. Salvation is the same as knowledge of the truth. The same God, or Truth, is thus the object of both theology and philosophy.

Nominalism, while not explicitly denying or even interfering with the classic and current distinctions, was yet bringing new elements into philosophy which tended towards a reconstruction. Its theory of universals, etc., tended to submerge logic (such as was not merely verbal) in psychology, and its emphasis upon will tended also in the same direction; while its distinction between philosophy and theology (the doctrine of the twofold character of truth), limiting the latter to positive faith or dogma, even when conceived in a thoroughly pious way, yet tended to give philosophy greater freedom and a basis for adequate attention to empirical facts.

With the Renaissance, philosophy regains its independence, and new points of view arise. Three tendencies are especially important as affecting both the definition of philosophy and its subdivisions. (1) Nature becomes an object of free inquiry, involving observation, experiment, and reflection unhindered by either the principles of Aristotle or the dogmas of the Church. Hence (*a*) while logic is, with the scholastics, regarded as purely formal (and consequently condemned as of little or no account), a new logic grows up—an account of thought as an instrument or mode of reaching truth. The so-called empiricists, as Bacon and Hobbes, are as much devoted to problems of method as are the rationalists, Descartes and Spinoza. (*b*) The world of material objects is regarded by many as the object of the most certain and also the most useful knowledge. Bacon tends strongly in this direction—though making provision still for metaphysics and final causes—while Hobbes is explicit and militant in identifying philosophy with the science of "bodies." And, upon the continent, Descartes, Spinoza, and Leibnitz are all profoundly influenced by concepts resulting from the growth of science; and all feel profoundly the need of a philosophy which will take account of and explain the physical world, newly revealed. (2) Psychology gets a more and more important place. Ancient psychology was distributed through three other disciplines, hardly having any existence of its own. It was partly contained in metaphysical logic, as a theory of the various forms and stages of truth; partly contained (and this is true from Plato, Aristotle, the Stoics and Epicureans, through St. Augustine) in ethics, as an analysis of will, its relation to desire, intellect, etc.; and partly contained in physics, as Plato derives the individual soul from the world-soul, and Aristotle treats human psychology as the highest part of his biology or theory of life. But the religious tendency of Protestantism; the new political conditions magnifying the individual; the ethics that grew from these tendencies and from the decline of the influence of dogmatic theology; and finally the tendency of all parties to find in an examination of conscious processes the justification, as well as the origin, of method —all conspired to give psychology a central position. And if we are accustomed to associate this tendency more with the names of Locke, Berkeley, Hume, Reid, Hamilton, and Mill, yet it is certainly a characteristic feature of the thought of Descartes, Leibnitz, Kant, Hegel, and Herbart as well. (3) The development, in connection with both the newer logic (or method) and psychology, of interest in the problem of the nature and possibility and implications of valid knowledge (EPISTEMOLOGY, q.v., Erkenntnisstheorie). While Kant first makes this explicitly the basis of all philosophy, occupying the central position of metaphysics with Aristotle, and theology with the scholastics, yet the conception all but breaks through from the time of Hobbes and Descartes.

Two further tendencies remain to note. (i) In the 18th century, through the influence of the ENLIGHTENMENT (q.v.), philosophy came to be regarded as practical wisdom, as knowledge of the world, arranged in some system (though the system was generally but eclecticism) with reference to its bearing upon life (Weltweisheit). While it may be difficult to point out the specific influence of this conception upon technical philosophy, yet it has been absorbed into modern culture (making up, indeed, a large part of the content of the term culture) in thorough-going fashion. (ii) In the present century, historical method has had so profound an influence upon philosophic thought, that it is not yet possible to comprehend it, or to state its limits. The prevalence of the method is seen in the tendency to take a dynamic view—to consider objects not as given or fixed, but with reference to a process. In view of this, fixed distinctions and classifications in philosophy tend to be obliterated; we get rather moments, stages of development, etc., a tendency obvious in Hegel, when he ranks under philosophy of spirit ethics, philosophy of state and history, aesthetics, and the philosophy of religion, as well as anthropology and psychology. For while the series is, of course, in no sense a historical one, it yet would be an incomprehensible jumble if presented in an age not saturated with the historical sense. It appears equally in Spencer when the successive portions of his system are presented as biology, psychology, and sociology. Hence the logic of history tends to replace a purely analytic logic, in setting forth the various spheres which fall within the scope of philosophy and their relations to one another: distinctions based upon positions occupied in a series of stages of development are substituted for those depending upon peculiar values presented in a static whole.

Many still make a radical distinction between questions of genesis, dealing with *how* things came to be, and questions of analysis, dealing with *what* they are, and refer the former, historical question to science, and the latter, analytic one to philosophy; yet it may be asked whether this distinction is not itself a survival of an age which had not the historical point of view; and whether genesis is anything but controlled, orderly, and complete analysis. Cf. ORIGIN *versus* NATURE.

At all events, it is the uncertainty as to the classification of psychology (whether as a special positive science, or a discipline in which logic, aesthetics, and ethics all have their roots), and uncertainty as to the exact value to be assigned to historical development—in its widest sense—that make the subdivisions of philosophy now offered by different writers so diverse, and that tend to reduce them (in default of any standard of certainty) to conveniencies of exposition. Cf., besides the topics mentioned, HISTORY OF PHILOSOPHY, EPISTEMOLOGY, METAPHYSICS, ORIENTAL PHILOSOPHY, and PATRISTIC PHILOSOPHY.

PHORONOMY [Gr. φόρος, spatial change (a term used technically by Aristotle), + νόμος, law]: Ger. *Phoronomie*; Fr. *phoronomie*; Ital. *foronomia*. A technical term in Kant's *Philosophy of Nature*. It means the theory of motion, so far as deducible from *a priori* conceptions, not from empirical observations.

Since space is an *a priori* form of perception, and quantity is an *a priori* function of conception, a pure, rational construction of motion is possible so far as motion can be

regarded as a spatial-quantitative fact—namely, as regards
(1) direction and (2) velocity. PERMANENCE (q.v.) is the
schema of substance as used in constructing phenomena,
and is strictly correlative to the idea of change. But change
as schematized is motion, which is thus capable of an *a priori*
treatment, so far as its concrete presentation or quality can
be abstracted from. When this is done, quantity of motion
remains (Kant, *Met. Anf. d. Naturwiss.*).

PLENUM [Lat. *plenus*, full]: Ger. *kontinuierliche Rau-
merfüllung*; Fr. *(le) plein*; Ital. *(il) pieno*. The existence of
matter in every portion of space; matter (or its energy) filling
space in such a way as to exclude the possibility of any void
or VACUUM (q.v.).

PLEROMA [Gr. πλήρωμα, fullness]: Ger. *Pleroma*; Fr.
plérôme; Ital. *pleroma*. A term used by GNOSTICS (q.v.) to
designate the spiritual world intermediate between God and
man. It is filled through and through with divine energy,
and thus opposed to κένωμα, the spatial void.

It is a matter of dispute as to how the Gnostic use is
derived from St. Paul's use of the term (Eph. i. 23, iii. 19,
and iv. 13; Col. i. 18, 19, ii. 9), and how far St. Paul himself
used the term in its philosophic connotation.

Literature: Teichmüller, *Gesch. d. Begriffe*; Matter,
Hist. du Gnosticisme; Mansel, *Gnostic Heresies*, 51–5, 178,
179 f.

PLEXUS [Lat. *plexus*, woven]: Ger. *Plexus*; Fr. *plexus*;
Ital. *plesso*. An interconnected whole where each part is so
dependent upon every other part that no adequate account
of one constituent can be given apart from its associates.

It is differentiated from the terms SYSTEM and ORGAN-
ISM (q.v.) in denoting *de facto* rather than ideal or teleological connection. It connotes more internal dependence,
however, than does the term aggregate.

PLURALISM [Lat. *plures*, several, many]: Ger. *Pluralis-
mus*; Fr. *pluralisme*; Ital. *pluralismo*. The theory that reality
consists in a plurality or multiplicity of distinct beings.

It may be materialistic, as with the ATOMISTS; hylozoistic, as with Empedocles; or spiritualistic, as with Leibnitz. Or, again, it may be conceived as indifferent, as the unknowable reals of Herbart which produce the phenomena both of consciousness and of matter. While opposed to monism as a theory of the essential and ultimate unity of all being, it may agree with it in opposition to a dualistic theory of the opposition of subject and object. The chief difficulties with the system are (*a*) in the idea of God (as with Leibnitz it seems to be both the highest of the monads, and the system of monads as such), and (*b*) in the ideas and facts of relationship, order, law, or harmony: if this harmony exists, we seem to have not a sheer plurality, but already an organized system; if it does not we have only chaos, no universe; and (*c*) in the idea of interaction. This, however, may be regarded only as a special çase of (*b*).

It need hardly be mentioned that we have here to do with one of the most serious problems of philosophy; one which was among the earliest to attract attention, and about which the conflict is most stubborn. The needs which pluralism endeavors chiefly to serve are (1) the possibility of real change, or an objectively valid dynamic view, since monism seems to make change a mere incident in the totality of being, or even a partly illusory phenomenon (Heraclitus and Hegel, however, seem to be dynamic monists in asserting the one reality to be essentially process); (2) the possibility of real variety, particularly in the differences of persons, as monism appears to lend itself to a pantheistic view, regarding all distinctions as simply limitations of the one being; (3) the possibility of freedom, as a self-initiating and moving power inherent in every real *qua* real.

The term pluralism is very recent in English (it is used as early as Wolff in German). Kant uses the term as opposed to egoism and solipsism—the tendency to regard self as only one among many (*Anthropology*). Bowne uses the term incidentally in *Philos. of Theism*, 57; James has probably done more than anyone else to give it currency, in his *Will to Believe* (see Preface in particular); and Howison employs it to denote the substantially distinct existence of free ethical personalities (*Limits of Evolution*, and in Royce's *Conception of God*, xiv).

PLURALITY [Lat. *pluralis*, numerous]: Ger. *Vielheit, Mehrheit*; Fr. *multiplicité, pluralité*; Ital. *pluralità*. More than oneness. See MANIFOLD, MULTIPLICITY, and (especially) UNITY and PLURALITY. Cf. also NUMBER.

According to Eucken (*Philosophische Terminologie*, 63), Scotus Erigena was the first to use *pluralitas* as a technical philosophical term.

PNEUMA [Gr. πνεῦμα, air, breath, spirit]. The vital soul or animating spirit.

It can be defined, however, only with reference to its historical use. Few terms, indeed, embody within themselves a more interesting combination of various sources and motives than does this one. The three chief elements in it are derived from Greek philosophy, from Greek medical science, and from Hebrew religion. The air was conceived as active (the wind) in Greek thought, and as a source of life in plants, animals, and men. Anaximenes, because of its restless, apparently self-caused, activity and its obvious connection (in breathing) with life, identified air with the soul of the universe and of the individual. While subsequent philosophy limited its scope and value, pneuma was universally accepted as a fact, and as something in man which mediated between his life and the larger world, and also between his strictly physiological functions and his higher spiritual nature. Through its relation to warmth (the living body is always warm and always inhaling air) it is the force which organizes the matter of the body, permeating, because of its fineness and activity, all parts. The Greek physicians accepted this doctrine and elaborated it. Praxagoras discovered the distinction between veins and arteries, and regarded the latter as carrying air (since they are empty in a dead person), the former blood; the circulation of this air stands in close relation to health and sickness. His successors regarded this circulation as most important in travelling between the heart as vital centre and brain as centre of thought, and hence as in some sense a connecting link of the physical and psychical.

Meanwhile, the later Peripatetics had taken up the tale and made the pneuma the physiological basis of all psychical activities. The Stoics made the conception (again as with

Anaximenes) a cosmic one—it is the objective union of the spiritual and material, God and the world. Earth and water are only condensed air (pneuma), and the psychical is but the highly refined residuum. Meantime Hebrew thought had also conceived the soul as primarily a form of "air," and made no difference between it, the wind, and respiration. But since it is regarded (in the Old Testament) as breathed into man by God, it loses its materialistic connotations; it is regarded as something coming into the body from without, instead of being its immanent function; and as the Spirit, itself immaterial, which rules matter. Philo attempted to unite the Greek and Hebrew conceptions, making the pneuma a mediating principle between God (Spirit) and the world (Matter). In the New Testament, it is Spirit *par excellence*, not simply in the psychological sense, but in the ethical—in the sense we associate with the term "spiritual," largely, indeed, just because that word was chosen to translate pneuma. Man consists, as with the Greeks, of body, soul, and spirit (pneuma), but spirit is elevated above the soul, not subordinated to it. The concept thus entered radically into the whole mediaeval and modern conception of spirit, and of soul and mind, and was certainly one of the chief factors in developing the concept of soul as a substantial, although wholly immaterial, entity. On the physical side, the doctrine passed over into the theory of animal spirits, and thus played, with Descartes, the same function of connecting soul and body that it had exercised with the Greeks. See Siebeck, *Gesch. d. Psychol.*, ii. Part II. chap. i.

PNEUMATOLOGY [Gr. πνεῦμα, spirit, + λόγος, theory, doctrine]: Ger. *Pneumatologie*; Fr. *pneumatologie*; Ital. *pneumatologia*. Literally, the doctrine of spirits, God, angels, and man. See PNEUMA. But, as a matter of fact, the term was chiefly used as the theory of spirits intermediate between God and man, angels and demons, i.e. good and bad. The term was largely appropriated by astrology and magic, though theology continued to use it in its proper sense. In the 17th century it had some vogue (largely in the form pneumatics) as the equivalent of what is now termed psychology. See Franck's *Dict. des Sci. philos.*, sub verbo.

POSIT [Lat. *ponere*, to put, place, lay down]: Ger. *Setzen, gesetzt* (posited), *Position* (a positing); Fr. *poser, affirmer*; Ital. *porre, affermare*. To affirm immediately, that is, not as a result of inference; to assert as given fact; to present as unquestioned existence, not depending on any prior process. Cf. IMMEDIACY (psychical, and logical).

The term had originally, in the main, a logical significance, meaning any premise so far as asserted without reference either to previous argument or to the concessions of a real or supposed opponent. In the post-Kantian movement, however, the term assumed a more metaphysical meaning, in harmony with the general tendency to give an objective rendering to the logical, or to hold that thought has a material and not merely a formal bearing. This tendency is most marked in Fichte. In following the effort, initiated by Descartes, to get something beyond all doubt, absolutely certain in itself, and hence a first principle in itself, he started from assertion as the principle of all judgment, and found as a condition of all judgment whatever, the ultimate and irreducible self-assertion of the Ego—its self-positing. "The Ego posits originally and simply its own being" (*Werke*, i. 98; see Adamson, *Fichte*, 153–63; Everett, *Fichte's Science of Knowledge*, 71). This act is at the same time a fact; the self-activity of the Ego is its existence. Further metaphysic consists in developing the system of positings implied in and derived from this original positing. Positing is, so to speak, the fundamental category—that in which the logical and ontological are one, in which thought (the activity of Ego) gets objective value.

Hegel, on the contrary, in accordance with his uniform tendency to do away with the merely or purely immediate, reduces "positing" to a lower level. It is the UNDERSTANDING (q.v.) which posits; that is to say, positing is dogmatic, unquestioned assertion, which, however valuable and necessary for practical purposes (to get a firm and definite basis from which to proceed), is really a process of reflection. Thus it turns out to be really a supposition involving a presupposition (Voraussetzen). The search for this presupposition is therefore the real "positing," since it alone determines what the true being is (Hegel, *Werke*, iv. chap. i). Or, put more simply, it is only as a working datum—a starting-point—that we find anything prior to reflection, and thus can distinguish that which is immediately given from that which is thought. The process of reflection, while apparently merely about the given reality, in the end always decides for us what that reality is, so that the original "fact" is displaced or transformed, instead of remaining as it was plus a number of new traits externally added to it by reflection. Thus the genuine process of positing is one of determining or defining through the whole system of thought. Cf. HEGEL's TERMINOLOGY, V, f.

In English the terms posit and pose are rarely used, save to translate the German Setzen; since, however, we use the terms suppose and presuppose freely and in nontechnical ways, it is a matter of regret that we have not, like the Greek (thesis and hypothesis) and the German (Setzung, Voraussetzung, Position), the correlates pose and position.

POSITIVE [Lat. *positum*, from *ponere*, to place]: Ger. *positiv*; Fr. *positif*; Ital. *positivo*. (1) Logical: as applied to judgments, affirmative or asserting, opposed to negative or denying. Applied to terms, referring to a quality which is inherent, while a negative term connotes absence or limitation.

(2) Social and practical: that which depends upon will or convention instead of upon the forces of nature irrespective of human intervention; e.g. positive law, rights, religion, morality, etc. It is opposed to NATURAL (q.v.).

(3) Philosophical: that which depends upon observation of phenomena, or facts in space and time, not upon a thought process: the scientifically verifiable. Opposed to the speculative. See POSITIVISM. According to Comte, mankind passes through the theological and metaphysical stages in arriving finally at the positive.

POSITIVISM: Ger. *Positivismus*; Fr. *positivisme*; Ital. *positivismo*. (1) The assertion of what is instituted in any sphere, as distinct from what is natural; revealed religion, for example. This use is rare.

(2) DOGMATISM (q.v.); assurance in holding or asserting philosophic tenets; the antithesis to scepticism, nihilism,
negativism. This is also rare.

(3) The name applied by Comte to his own philosophy,
and characterizing, negatively, its freedom from all speculative elements; and, affirmatively, its basis in the methods
and results of the hierarchy of positive sciences; i.e. mathematics, astronomy, physics, chemistry, biology, and sociology. It is allied to AGNOSTICISM (q.v., also UNKNOWABLE)
in its denial of the possibility of knowledge of reality in
itself, whether of mind, matter, force; it is allied to PHE-
NOMENALISM (q.v.) in its denial of capacity to know either
efficient or final causation, or anything except the relations
of coexistence and sequence in which sensible phenomena
present themselves. It differs, however, in insisting upon (a)
the possibility and necessity of a relative synthesis or organization of the data of all the sciences; (b) the value of science
for prevision and practical control; and (c) its availability,
when thus organized and applied, for moral guidance and
spiritual support and consolation. See RELIGION OF HUMAN-
ITY.

(4) The term is used more loosely to denote any
philosophy which agrees with that of Comte in limiting
philosophy to the data and methods of the natural sciences
—opposition to the *a priori*, and to speculation by any method
peculiar to metaphysics. In this sense Locke and Hume were
positivists: Hume, indeed, quite explicitly so in limiting
the method of philosophizing to the results of observation,
and stopping whenever going further means confused and
uncertain speculation about hypothetical causes (*Treat.*, i.
§ 4). Mill and Spencer are called positivists, though thoroughly opposed to Comte in many respects. George Eliot is a
positivist in a somewhat more strictly Comtian sense. Cf.
NATURALISM.

Literature: Comte, *Positive Philos.*; *Positive Polity* (sy-
nopsized in English by Harriet Martineau and George Henry
Lewes); J. S. Mill, *Auguste Comte and Positivism*; Spencer,
Genesis of Science; *Classification of the Sciences*; Huxley,
Scientific Aspects of Positivism; Fiske, *Outlines of Cosmic
Philos.*; E. Caird, *Social Philos. of Comte*; *Encyc. Brit.*, art. on

Comte; Laas, *Idealismus und Positivismus* (1879–84); H. Gruber, *A. Comte* (1889). On Comte's Social Philosophy see Barth, *Geschichtsphilos. als Soziol.*, i. (J.D.–K.G.–J.M.B.)

POSSIBILITY, IMPOSSIBILITY, and POSSIBLE [Lat. *possibile*, from *posse*, may, can, be able; equivalent to the Gr. δυνατόν]: Ger. *Möglichkeit, Unmöglichkeit, möglich*; Fr. *possibilité, impossibilité, possible*; Ital. *possibilità, impossibilità, possibile*. The term is used to express a variety of meanings which, although distinct in themselves, yet flow readily into one another. These meanings may best be grouped according as they have (1) an ontological objective value, or a logical subjective value; and (2) according as they are used antithetically to actuality or necessity. The antithetical point of view is the most convenient from which to begin.

Possibility may mean that something is (1) not actual, or (2) that, while it possesses actual existence, that existence lacks causal or rational necessity.

(1) As opposed to the actual, the phrase has again a double meaning. (*a*) Taken objectively, it may mean something as yet undeveloped, since not presenting itself in actually objectified form, but capable of doing so at some future time, when all the conditions of its realization occur: latent, potential being. This implies capacity for realization; and, if this capacity be taken in an active sense, connotes some inherent tendency to actuality, which if not thwarted leads to final completeness of being. This involves the active sense of POTENTIALITY (q.v.), of FORCE (q.v.), etc. It is close to the literal sense of the term (posse, *can* be). This is the dominating sense in Greek philosophy, being connected with Aristotle's teleological theory of development. See NATURE, and POWER (δύναμις and ἐντελέχεια). (*b*) Taken logically, it denotes that there is some ground for asserting actuality, but not sufficient to justify a positive statement: *may*, as distinct from *can*, be. Thus, possibly it will rain tomorrow. It has to do with degrees of certainty in judging. See PROBABILITY.

(2) As opposed to the necessary, the term has also a double sense. (*a*) It may mean chance, contingency, as an objective fact. CHANCE (q.v.), again, has a double meaning:

(i) something not derivable or explainable causally by reference to antecedent facts. There are those who assert the reality of such chance (see TYCHISM). On this view there are many *possibilities* in store in the future which no amount of knowledge would enable us to foresee or forestall. Indeterministic theories of the will assert possibilities of this sort also. (ii) Chance may mean that which, while necessary causally, is not necessary teleologically: the unplanned, the fatalistic. From this point of view the "possible" is that which unexpectedly prevents the carrying-out of a purpose or intention. It leads up to the logical sense (*b*), according to which the possible, as opposed to the necessary, is anything whose existence cannot be derived from reason: that, the existence of which, rationally speaking, might be otherwise. It is opposed to mathematical or metaphysical necessity, where existence cannot be otherwise than as it is. In this sense the objective actual may be only (logically) possible: the present rain-storm is actual, but since it does not follow from a necessity of thought, but only from empirical antecedents, it is not necessary, and hence just a contingent possibility. This distinction goes back also to Aristotle, being found in his logical writings, as the possible, as potential meaning, is found in his metaphysical. It has played a large part in modern RATIONALISM (q.v.), especially in the philosophy of Leibnitz, being identical with his distinction of "truths of reason" and "truths of fact." In the sphere of mathematics, logic, and metaphysics there is no possibility in the strict sense; all that exists exists of necessity. In the physical and practical spheres which deal with the space and time world the notion of possibility has full sway. Everything is possible which does not contradict the laws of reason; that which is inconceivable, which violates the law of reason, is impossible. The impossible is the self-contradictory. Kant's criticism of rational conceivability as a criterion of truth, to the effect that it is only formal, resting upon the principle of identity and contradiction, and when applied to existence must be supplemented by appeal to sense, made Leibnitz's distinctions of hardly more than historic interest.

The problems regarding the possible as a category of philosophy may be summed up as follows: Does it have any objective existence, or is it simply an expression of a certain logical attitude? If the former, is the objective possibility a necessary phase of a process of development, which will unfold itself into actuality; or does it express a particular fact, the reality of chance? If of logical significance only, does it flow from the distinction between *a priori* reason and *a posteriori* experience; or does it express a certain combination of ignorance and assurance in relation to facts, so that *real* possibilities would also be experienced facts?

PRE-ESTABLISHED HARMONY: Ger. *prästabilirte Harmonie*; Fr. *harmonie préétablie*; Ital. *armonia prestabilita*. The name given by Leibnitz to his theory (1) of the relation of the monads to one another; (2) of spirit to matter, of the soul to the body. The last is the commoner use, but is, relatively speaking, superficial.

The problem of the influence of mind upon body had been brought to the front by Descartes (see OCCASIONALISM). Leibnitz holds that there is no actual influence exercised by one of them upon the other, nor does God interfere to produce change in one upon occasion of change in the other. But he has eternally harmonized the two so that changes in one synchronize with, and represent, changes in the other. Leibnitz uses frequently the comparison of two clocks which keep perfect time. The vulgar view would assume that some influence passed from one to the other; Occasionalism, that an outsider changes one when the other changes; this theory, that they were originally so perfectly harmonized that no departure of one from the other can take place. In its wider philosophic sense, pre-established harmony means that while each monad acts out its own nature undisturbed by any other, yet each is so constituted as to reflect, mirror, or represent, "from its own point of view," the entire universe. The active or developed side of each monad is spirit; its passive or undeveloped side is matter. The active gives the law to the passive, i.e. defines its end or idea. Hence the universal harmony of mind and matter, thought and extension — Leibnitz's dynamic interpretation of Spinoza's parallelism of the two attributes. Cf. the standard works on the history of philosophy.

PRESENTATIONISM: Ger. *Präsentationismus*; Fr. *présentationisme*; Ital. *presentazionismo* (suggested—E.M.). (1) Used by Hamilton for presentative, as opposed to representative, theories of knowledge. Cf. NATURAL REALISM. (J.M.B.)

(2) Used by recent writers as equivalent to phenomenalism: the theory that the only knowable reality is found in what is presented as conscious content to the knower.

PRIMARY (1), PRIMITIVE (2), PRIMORDIAL (3) [Lat. *primus*, first, + *ordo*, rank]: Ger. (1) *erst, ursprünglich*, (2) *primitiv*, (3) *ursprünglich*; Fr. (1) *primaire*, (2) *primitif*, (3) *primordial*; Ital. (1) *primario*, (2) *primitivo*, (3) *primordiale* (the distinctions are not exact in any of the languages). These terms all relate to value or to elements, and characterize their original, underived character. The two meanings of early in time and first in rank are generally more or less blended. The idea of first in rank, because first in time and so fundamental, is uppermost in primary; it is used to emphasize what is not secondary or subsidiary in importance—as primary truths. Primitive refers rather to time, and may be used as a depreciatory term, connoting the undeveloped and crude character of what comes first. Primordial has an elemental significance; it denotes the original factors or forces out of which later development has proceeded. Among the Neo-Platonists it referred especially to the germinal, vital power of the original constituents. Cf. ORIGINAL (1).

PRIMUM MOBILE [Lat.]. In the Aristotelian system, the physical system which is next to God, the unmoved mover. Cf. MOTION.

Motion is a sign of change and so of imperfection; but the first mover as next in rank to God has a movement which continually returns into itself, and thus affords a symbol of permanence. Its movement is circular and recurrent. Thus the diurnal revolution of the heavens was accounted for. The idea was taken up and developed in the Ptolemaic system, the primum mobile being the tenth and uttermost concentric sphere, which in its daily revolution takes all the fixed stars with it.

PRINCIPLE [Lat. *principium,* commencement, beginning: trans. of Gr. ἀρχή, beginning, authority]: Ger. *Princip;* Fr. *principe;* Ital. *principio.* As the etymology suggests, the term principle has (or had) a double sense: chronological and normative (for a similar connection see PRIMARY). Literally, it means the first in time. But this may be taken as expressing the fundamental absolute reality, from which everything else is derived, and with reference to which all else is secondary and subsidiary. The chronological sense has almost disappeared in modern use, so that principle has come to mean the logical, or metaphysical, basis or ground of other truths. (1) Logically, the principle is a proposition upon which conclusions depend for their validity, and which, if conceded, establishes their truth: opposed to consequence.

(2) Scientifically, it is the law through which a diversity of facts, otherwise unrelated and unexplained, are classified and interpreted: opposed to datum, brute fact, or "mere" fact.

(3) Practically or morally, it is the law which controls the factors of conduct: opposed to pleasure or interest as the immediate, or individual, spring of action.

(4) Metaphysically, it is that which determines orders of fact or truth; which possesses superior and primary reality. While in the three previous senses the term principle has a regulative or normative sense, metaphysically this meaning is combined with the older sense of constitutive objective reality. The metaphysical principle includes the three notions of element, cause, and regulating law.

Greek philosophy began with the search after the principle in the literal sense: that original reality (*a*) from which other things are derived, and (*b*) out of which they consist. In the sense (*a*) it was implicitly or explicitly dynamic, a force, a causal power; in the sense (*b*) it was static, an element of subsistence. The first meaning led up to Aristotle's form (εἶδος) as a principle; the second to his matter (ὕλη). Modern thought, with its clearer distinction of subject and object, has tended to differentiate the notions of element, cause, force, and law, with the results stated above. The term "first principles" is used technically to express primary intuitions, truths to which assent must be given without any further reason or ground.

PROPERTY [Lat. *proprium*, one's own, belonging to; trans. of Gr. ἕξις, a technical term of the Stoics, also of Gr. ἴδιον]: Ger. *Eigenschaft*; Fr. *propriété*; Ital. *proprietà, qualità*. (1) One of the logical PREDICABLES (q.v.); that one of the five ways in which the predicate may be related to the subject (the others being genus, species, difference, and accident), which signifies that the predicate has inherent connection with the subject.

(2) Hence, in the ontological sense, any quality or attribute which flows necessarily from the nature of the thing possessing it—thus distinct from accident, which may or may not belong to a thing. Cf. SUBSTANCE.

PSYCHOLOGISM [Gr. ψυχή, soul, + λόγος, science]: Ger. *Psychologismus*; Fr. *psychologisme*; Ital. *psicologismo*. (1) The theory that "the soul can think without any real object, or with an object furnished by itself . . . that man is both intelligent and intelligible in himself, suffices for his own intelligence, without any dependence on any objective reality" (Brownson, *Works*, ii. 482). Cf. ONTOLOGISM.

(2) The doctrine of Fries and Beneke (see the histories of Falckenberg and Windelband), which translates the critical examination of reason (of Kant) into terms of empirical psychology.

PURE (in philosophy) [Lat. *purus*, clean]: Ger. *rein*; Fr. *pur*; Ital. *puro*. Free from all admixture with extraneous, foreign, or irrelevant matter; expressing the intrinsic essence or end, and containing nothing else; containing no reference to application or use, as pure mathematics. As a technical term, it translates Kant's "rein" as applied to reason, ego, concept, etc., denoting entire absence of any empirical element or factor arising from experience; equivalent to *a priori*.

Spatial determinations, like geometrical extension and figure, for example, belong to the pure form of perception, being distinguished from hardness, color, etc., which belong to sensation. Kant probably borrowed this use of the term from Wolff (see Wolff's *Vern. Ged.*, § 282). He was followed in it by Fichte, Schelling, and Hegel.

QUIETISM [Lat. *quies*, rest]: Ger. *Quietismus*; Fr. *quiétisme*; Ital. *quietismo*. A form of MYSTICISM (q.v.) which lays emphasis upon the passive and receptive attitude of the human spirit in relation to the influx of the divine Spirit, and making little or nothing of activity in religious matters, whether ceremonial or moral activity, and everything of contemplation.

It made the Sabbath a symbol of rest in God. Its aim was the absorption of the practical personality in God. Its chief representatives are Angelus Silesius and Molinos. The influence of the latter, a Spanish priest, was considerable in the Roman Catholic Church. Cf. PATRISTIC PHILOSOPHY, ad fin., also ST. THOMAS (philosophy of). Fénelon represented it until it was condemned by the pope under the influence of Bossuet. Madame Guyon is its chief literary representative. It is somewhat akin to PIETISM (q.v.) and to the religious philosophy of the Friends.

RATIONALISM [Lat. *rationalis*, from *ratio*, reason]: Ger. *Rationalismus*; Fr. *rationalisme*; Ital. *razionalismo*. (1) The theory that everything in religion is to be rationally explained or else rejected. The application of ordinary logical standards and methods to dogma. Opposed particularly to supernaturalism. As Lecky (*Hist. of Rationalism*, i. 16) says, it signifies not "any class of definite doctrines . . . but rather a certain cast of thought or bias of reasoning . . . which leads man on all occasions to subordinate dogmatic theology to the dictates of reason and of conscience." In this sense it finds its best expression in the ENLIGHTENMENT (q.v.) of the 18th century.

(2) The theory that reason is an independent source of knowledge, distinct from sense-perception and having a higher authority. Opposed to SENSATIONALISM (q.v.). See REASON; and cf. INTELLECTUALISM, INTUITION, NOUS, and UNDERSTANDING.

(3) The theory that, in philosophy, certain elementary concepts are to be sought, and that all the remaining content of philosophy is to be derived, in a deductive way, from these fundamental notions. Opposed to EMPIRICISM (q.v.). In this sense it is used particularly of the method first explicitly

stated by Descartes, developed by Spinoza and Leibnitz, formulated in detail by Wolff, and finally refuted by Kant.

The three senses are historically connected. The 18th century rationalism in morals and theology is derived from the insistence by Descartes upon method, and upon clearness and distinctness as criteria of truth. It is combined, however, with an empiricism which descends from Locke. The use of rational conceptions as the source from which other ideas are to be deductively derived is, of course, impossible unless there is some faculty through which these ideas are made known, as innate or *a priori* ideas, or through intuition, and so the second and third senses run together. None the less, rationalism in the second sense applies to a particular part of the *content* of philosophic doctrine, while in the third it expresses the *method* taken to be final in philosophy. The sketch that follows is confined to the third sense.

Descartes, seeking a criterion of certainty, hit upon the undoubted existence of inner experience, and of certain ideas there found, which are *clear*, i.e. intuitively present and manifest, and *distinct*, precisely determined in themselves and in relation to other ideas. From these, by a mathematical method, various other truths may be derived; and with the system of such truths, original and derived, certain truth or science ends. The Port Royal *Logic* and the logical treatises of Geulincx attempted to expound the method with greater explicitness; but Spinoza completes it, first, by arranging the Cartesian philosophy, *de more geometrico*, and then by presenting his own philosophy in the *Ethica* as a series of axioms, definitions, propositions, etc. Leibnitz took up the idea with his usual energy and systematizing power, and advanced the idea of a universal logic and language which should be to philosophy what his calculus was to physics. He analyzes all the conceptions involved more definitely; brings out the *a priori* character, the necessity and universality of all the primary notions; sets up as their criterion the principle of contradiction or impossibility of the opposite; and carries further the criterion of distinctness, making it to be that which is distinguished in itself from all other notions, and of "adequate"—that which is clear down to its last constituent element and their relations to one another. Wolff systematized these conceptions of Leibnitz and combined them with an academic exposition of all the branches of philosophy.

Kant, awakened from his "dogmatic slumber" in the rationalistic school by his acquaintance with Hume's sceptical attack upon causality and the principle of necessary connection, finally turns against rationalism as a method. He shows (*a*) that its identification with mathematical method is false, since the latter proceeds not by *analysis* of concepts, but by *construction* of space and time elements; (*b*) that from concepts only that can be deduced which has been previously put in them, and that hence the method is tautological or "analytic" merely; (*c*) that to be a source of new truth, or synthetic, rational concepts must be applied to material of sense, gained in experience; (*d*) that when they are used as if they were themselves synthetic, certain fundamental antinomies, or mutually self-contradictory propositions, arise. Kant still endeavors to combine the truth of rationalism with that of empiricism; these necessary concepts *exist* independently of experience, but are *valid* only when used in reference to experience. Although the rationalistic method is still incidentally used (even by those who claim to belong to the school of "experience," as by Spencer in his UNIVERSAL POSTULATE, q.v.), Kant gave it its deathblow as *the* method of philosophy. Hegel revived rationalism in a transformed sense, not applying to one factor or phase of knowledge, opposed to experience, but the construction of experience itself as a system of reason.

REALISM: Ger. *Realismus*; Fr. *réalisme*; Ital. *realismo*. The term has two important meanings in philosophy, wholly distinct from each other. (1) In one, and the older sense, it is a logical-metaphysical theory, having to do with the reality of universals in themselves, and their relation to individuals. Its classic expression is that universals are real *ante res* (in God's mind), *in rebus* (in nature), and *post res* (in their historical apprehension by human minds). However, it has even more extreme forms.

(2) In the more modern and epistemological-meta-

physical theory, it is the doctrine that reality exists apart from its presentation to, or conception by, consciousness; or that if, as matter of fact, it has no separate existence to the divine consciousness, it is not in virtue of anything appertaining to consciousness as such.

It is opposed to IDEALISM (q.v. for history of this meaning). Historically, it has been found in many forms and under many names. See NATURAL REALISM. Kant terms his philosophy *empirical realism*, meaning that it holds to an existence of things in space independent of our particular states of consciousness, opposing it to *transcendental realism*, which asserts that time and space are something in themselves independent of our sensibility (*Crit. of Pure Reason*, 320–6, Müller's trans.). Spencer calls his philosophy *transfigured realism*, which means that "*some* objective existence, manifested under *some* conditions," separate from and independent of subjective existence, is the final necessity of thought, and yet that the perceptions and objects in consciousness are not the reality, and do not resemble, but only symbolize it. At the same time he marks this off from "hypothetical realism," because that only asserts the existence of this real as an inference, not as a "fact" (*Psychol.*, ii. chap. xix). Lewes calls his theory *reasoned realism*, which he distinguishes not only from crude or natural realism, but also from the transfigured. It asserts that the reality of an external existence, a not-self, is given in feeling, and indissolubly woven into consciousness. Here realism seems to mean not externality to consciousness, but externality to the subject, or ego, in consciousness (*Problems of Life and Mind*, 176–95). See also REAL IDEALISM (or Ideal Realism).

We shall now take up realism in the first sense. In one aspect the problem goes back to Socrates, who asserted that the object of knowledge (and hence the true, the certain, the real) was the universal, endeavoring in this way to overcome the subjectivism of the Sophists. In Plato, the universals appear as the ideas and the true or absolute beings; and an exposition of the method of arriving at them, of their nature and interrelations, and their connection with the various forms of reality and experience constitutes the chief object of his philosophy. It was long fashionable to regard him as an extreme realist in the mediaeval sense, that is, as asserting the subsistence of universals by themselves, independent of any relation to individuals—*ante res*. Aristotle is largely responsible for this interpretation, since he continually polemicizes against the Platonic separation of the ideas; he is the authority with the Scholastics. But, in the first place, the ultimate reality with Aristotle, the pure form, has the same transcendence which he attributes to the Platonic idea, so far as existence is concerned. It is, at bottom, the lack of *dynamic* connection with the world which Aristotle, whether rightly or wrongly, criticizes in Plato—a lack which he attempts to fill by his theory of the form as the end, which matter as the potential always attempts to realize, and hence moves towards. But, in the second place, and more significantly, the whole mediaeval and modern conception of realism is foreign to the interests of Greek philosophy, both Platonic and Aristotelian. Plato and Aristotle are interested in showing that the real is universal, and under what conditions it becomes or is individual; but the interest in the obverse question, the reality of the universal and of the individual, is one which depends upon the whole intervening period, indicating indeed that the starting-point has been reversed. It could not arise until the psychological movement had gone far enough to correlate the universal and subjective thought.

This is not to say, of course, that mediaeval thought did not naturally and inevitably identify its own problems with those of Greek thought, and even cast them in the terms of that thought. Neo-Platonism, with its express derivation of the hierarchy of successive forms of thought and being from the more universal as the more real, was the immediate cause of this identification, so that realism is the first to make its appearance, which it does in full-fledged form in Scotus Erigena (q.v., and also Scholasticism). It is a matter of moment that realism is the doctrine of those who are especially interested in philosophic content, while nominalism appears, at first, rather as a merely formal and logical doctrine. As such, it is a passage in the translation by Boethius of Porphyry's introduction to the *Categories* of Aristotle which started the discussion—a treatise, it must be remembered, which at this period was known only quite apart from the metaphysics and physics of Aristotle. The passage raised the problem of genera and species, (1) as to whether they subsist in themselves or only in the mind; (2) whether, if subsistent, they are corporeal or incorporeal; and (3) whether separated from sensible things, or placed in them. Roscelin appears as an extreme nominalist, holding that the universals are only abstractions from particular things (are *post res*), and in themselves are only words (*voces*) or names (*nomina*). William of Champeaux asserted realism in its most extreme form. Only genera are substances; individuals are only their attributes; manhood is essential, Socrates accidental. Moreover, *every* universal is real; whiteness would be real even if there were no white thing. These extreme views obviously demanded some attempt at mediation. This was supplied by Abélard. He held that a universal, even as a name, is yet more than a name; it is a predicate, or *sermo*. This is reached only by conception, which, comparing individual things, reaches that which "naturally" is a predicate. So far Abélard would be classed as a conceptualist. But he goes on to develop the idea of a *natural* predicate. Since universals are the instruments of all knowledge, there must be something in the nature of things which is their basis; namely, *similarity* in the things themselves. Moreover, this similarity is due to the fact that the universals are the modes or archetypes in God's mind, according to which he creates particular things—a view emphasized also by Bernard of Chartres and by Gilbert of Poitiers. The latter, however, leans more to realism in holding that while these concepts or forms of the divine mind become *universals* only in things, they are really in things (*in re*), and not merely factors of likeness to be apprehended (collected) in turn by the human mind. Here the discussion practically rests for the time; justice seems to be done to all the elements involved, and the doctrine being accepted by Alexander, and by Thomists and Scotists alike, in the second period of *scholasticism* the discussion passes into the background.

It did not wholly rest, however; those who continued the tradition of the merely formal logic, occupying themselves with *propositions* rather than with *judgments*, continued the old nominalistic terminology. What was termed "modern logic," depending upon some Byzantine compendiums, was developed. It involved the theory of the syllogism, in its different figures, in relation to component propositions, and the elements of these propositions—very much, indeed, what passes in the logic of the syllogism today. This was elaborated by Peter of Spain. According to it the predicate (which of course is the universal) is only a sign. With Peter and his school the doctrine remained a harmless detail of formal logic. But William of Occam develops it and combines it with a metaphysical theory of the nature of (distinct) individuals, which had come to the front. Realism, even in its moderate forms, seemed to find the essential reality in the generic, if not in or before things literally, at least as "thoughts" in the mind of God. As long as the object of chief interest was the universe as a whole, and the Church and state as wholes, the doctrine naturally commended itself. But with the growth of consciousness of particular individuality (*haecceitas, this* special uniquely distinguished individual) the doctrine presented grave difficulties. It seemed to lead to a most thorough-going predeterminism, according to which everything in or about the individual is eternally foreordained in the thought of God. Duns Scotus had insisted upon the primal character of individuality (*haecceitas*), but had still regarded it as form, as the generic substantialized. But William of Occam recognized that this view still left the individual in an ambiguous position; logically, at least, the individual still appears as subordinate to the universal. Hence with him nominalism is not, as with the earlier writers, a merely negative assertion of the verbal or conceptual character of ideas; it is the positive assertion that specific individualities, differentiated in themselves, are the real; and that universals are discursively gathered from our original intuitive knowledge of these individuals. (In this direct apprehension, William includes both sensation, knowledge of our own internal states—more certain than sense-knowledge —and the intellectual intuition of the essence of the soul.) Just because Occam's theory was congruent with the rising practical individualism of the day (in politics and religion), because it agreed with the rising physical science—emphasizing the knowledge of particular phenomena instead of abstract and occult essences—and because it fell in with the growing psychological tendency to study the natural history of knowledge, and not simply its logical forms, nominalism became as triumphant at this period as realism had been at the earlier.

With the breaking up of mediaevalism, the discussion passed over into psychology. The interest was in abstract and general ideas, or abstraction and generalization, rather than in universals as such. Accordingly, our statement ends here—save to remark that, since modern science deals so evidently with universals, with laws, the problem of whether or no any objective reality is to be conceded to these universals, and if so, in what way, is coming to the front again in modern logic; and thus in so far the old discussion is again raised. In accordance with the spirit of an early remark, we may note from another point of view the difference of the ancient from the mediaeval realism. The ancient deals with the universal as the *essence*, the constitutive factor, whether before or in individuals; the mediaeval deals with it as the *generic*. Hence to an ancient to have identified the universal with a mere concept would have been impossible, save to assert absolute scepticism; with the moderns it was a natural outlet. With recent thought, the universal becomes law, or method. Cf. LATIN AND SCHOLASTIC TERMINOLOGY.

Literature, to (1): Prantl, *Gesch. d. Logik*, is the authority for the details of practically all writers. Cf. the titles cited under SCHOLASTICISM. The following are important: John of Salisbury, *Metalogicus*, ii. chap. xvii ff. (gives a summary of views of previous writers, all the more valuable because he confesses himself unable to take any position); Barach, *Zur Gesch. d. Nominalismus vor Rocellin*; Löwe, *Der Kampf zwischen Nominalismus u. Realismus*; Exner, *Nominalismus u. Realismus*; Köhler, *Realismus u. Nominalismus*.

REALS: Ger. *Realen*; Fr. *réels*, (*les*) *êtres*; Ital. *reali*. A term used by Herbart to name the (pluralistic) ultimate beings.

Each is a monad, and absolute in itself. A plurality of

qualities in a being means a relative element. Hence each real is perfectly simple in quality. This quality is undefinable. These reals act upon one another by way of disturbance, and react to disturbance in the way of self-preservation. Presentations (Vorstellungen) are self-preservative reactions on the part of that real called mind.

REIFY (-FICATION) [Lat. *res*, thing, + *facere*, to make]: not in use in the other languages. To change a mental attitude or abstraction into a supposed real thing; to attribute objective substantiality to an idea. It is the practical equivalent to hypostatize; see HYPOSTASIS.

RELATION [Lat. *re + latus*, p.p. of *ferre*, to bear]: Ger. *Beziehung, Verbindung, Verknüpfung, Verhältniss*; Fr. *relation, rapport*; Ital. *relazione, rapporto*. See RELATION (consciousness of).

More specifically, (1) Practical. The bearing or influence of one thing upon another—the way one thing "has to do" with another; for example, the testimony of A has relation to the guilt of B; the discovery of a new fact has relation to the truth of some theory.

(2) Logical. The mutual dependence of two or more subjects upon a common principle, fact, or truth, of such a kind that any assertion regarding one modifies the meaning of the other. Accordingly the predicate is true or false of one taken not independently or in isolation, but only in reference, regard, or respect to the other.

Examples: the relation of father and son, buyer and seller, of parasite and host. Many qualities may presumably be predicated of A which have no bearing upon what is asserted or believed of B, but in so far as A stands in relation to B (as father to son, seller to buyer, etc.), this indifference ceases, giving way to complete (logical) reciprocity. This does not mean that A and B are the common subjects of the same predicate, or are taken conjunctively or collectively. On the contrary, they may be affected by quite different, even opposite, predicates; or the predicate of A may be clearly asserted, and that of B remain quite undetermined. It means only that every assertion regarding A carries with it some further assertion regarding B; and, conversely, that any assertion regarding A is possible only because of some qualification of B. Every predicate of either term both depends upon and influences the other. This is possible, however, only if there is some further predicate which is common to both A and B, and which affords the basis or foundation of the relation in which they further stand to each other—the relationship proper. This relationship is commonly also called the relation; and theories as to its nature bring us to the third type of meaning.

(3) Metaphysical. How can a belief or judgment regarding one fact affect the content of our judgment or belief of another disparate fact? What is the guarantee of the assumption of validity attaching to such a transfer? This is the question of the ontological or real worth of the logical use of the relation. The problem widens its significance tremendously when it is seen that all judgment and inference presuppose just such extension. It is not merely a matter of the possibility of judgment with reference to such obvious correlates as father and son; science rests on the postulate of some sort of relation between any given fact and some other fact a relation which is the real, even if concealed, foundation of any scientific statement about either one taken separately. Thus the question of the truth conveying power of logical procedure is bound up with the question of the nature of relations. Various types of answer are afforded to the question.

(i) It is asserted that relations have no objective existence or counterpart. Relations are a purely mental product, stating something which emerges when facts having really nothing to do with one another are held before the same mental view, or are compared. This theory is of course the analogue of the older nominalism and conceptualism, the modern relation being the equivalent of the mediaeval universal. A relation is like a rhetorical simile. To compare a star and a tear institutes a relation between them *ad hoc* for the mind that compares; beyond that, nil. The same sort of thing (and no more) is true of a relation of cause and effect. Only sceptical philosophers have, however, carried the theory to this logical result. Most of the empiricists (who are characterized by their adherence to this view) assume without questioning that they have a right to the relation of resemblance; many fall back upon succession in time and coexistence in space, and (possibly) uniformity in the repetition of these successions and coexistences—an admission which the rationalists have seized upon to the undoing of this subjective notion of relations.

(ii) Another view, the popular survival of the realism of the Middle Ages, reinforced by pre-evolutionary zoology and botany, is that different things form natural classes, families, or kinds, and that it is in virtue of membership in the same sort or genus that things stand related to one another. The εἶδος, the form or species, is thus the ontological counterpart of the logical relation. As long as this view prevailed, the term relation was comparatively little used; universal doing service on the ontological side, and predication on the logical. With the growth of nominalism; with the scientific tendency to replace genera by laws; with the development of the view (3, i), making relations the products not the bases of classification, and classification a subjective instrument, another *fundamentum relationis* had to be found.

We have (iii) the tendency to view relation as equivalent with *law*. This is favored by the common tendency to confuse law and force; the relation of gravitation, the law of gravitation, the force of gravitation, are to many minds practically synonymous. Or, if the matter be pressed somewhat further, it would probably be admitted that while the relation is a way of viewing things, and hence intellectual only, the related things are somehow "connected" by a law which gives authority to the relation. It is clear, however, that this is a purely popular solution, evading the issue by circular reasoning.

(iv) Modern idealistic metaphysic has recognized with (3, i) that relations are connected with the process of judgment, but has attempted to invest relations with validity by regarding the world as the content of a single, permanent judgment, and hence made up of a system of relations. To try to follow the course of this argument would almost be to write the history of metaphysical logic since the time of Kant; but the following points may be briefly indicated. The notion of a hierarchy of forms, genera, species, etc., is wholly given up; it is recognized that the problem is in reality that of the possibility of a valid judgment. All real judgment is synthetic—that is, involves the carrying over of a predicate of one subject to affect the predicate of another subject numerically distinct. Any other form of proposition is tautological, and hence no judgment at all. Judgment as such is therefore bound up essentially, and not merely by occasion, with the question of the reality of relations. This positive conclusion is reinforced by noting that the denial of reality to the relations instituted in judgment leads to complete scepticism, and destroys the whole fabric of science; and by noting that even the more thorough-going empiricists (or non-relationists) are obliged to assume the relation of resemblance or similarity in order to give mental viewing together, or comparison, any basis. Summarizing, we may say that, according to this theory, a relation is a permanent and necessary mode of judgment by which objects, and the world as *the* object, of knowledge are constituted.

(v) This view has to contend with three inherent difficulties:—

(a) In emphasizing relational knowledge, it appears to make discursive or reflective thought the type of all thought, and to have no place for intuitive consciousness or immediate identification of subject and object.

(b) It emphasizes the intellectualistic view of the universal, reducing feeling and will to forms of cognitive judgment.

(c) It presupposes qualities, or an unrelated manifold of some sort upon which the relating activity is exercised. Hegel accordingly gave relations a central position in the logic of reflective cognition, and consequently in the world of appearance and essence, but regarded this realm as intermediate between a sphere of immediate perceptive recognition and a region of rational intuition apprehending self-related wholes. Of Hegel it must be said that he never made clear just the connection between the self-related whole and the self-contradictory scheme of relations which it includes and supersedes. As Green (*Prolegomena to Ethics*) gives the most consistent modern rendering of Kant, so Bradley, in his

Appearance and Reality, follows Hegel most successfully in pointing out the phenomenal character of any system of relations, and the necessity of a more immediate and harmonious whole in which relations as such cease.

(vi) There is a growing tendency to recur to the simple, practical statement of relation as the "having to do" of one thing with another in the way of effecting some result in which one is interested, and to classify and generalize this point of view into a systematic philosophy. See PRAGMATIC.

According to both (iv) and (v), relations are reducible to the identity-in-difference function of judgment (the disagreement between them being as to the absolute or merely phenomenal significance of judgment), and are the various modes in which this function progressively manifests itself. According to the view now stated, they are reducible to different forms of the means-and-end function—that is, while they develop out of judgment, judgment itself is an attempt to state experience with reference to discovering valuable ends and appropriate means of realizing them. The "relations" are thus objective definitions of the various influences which things have upon one another *practically*, that is, in the way of helping or hindering the attainment of aims, or in suggesting desirable modifications of these aims. The ultimate worth of this objective or intellectual statement of practical bearings is itself practical—that is, it facilitates the harmony and expansion of experience. By bringing to clear consciousness what the obstacles are, where they lie, and where favoring influences are found, it is itself an organic member of the practical process of setting up and effecting ends. The "relation" is thus a statement of how to employ one part or phase of experience in regard to another.

It is a matter of method of action, not of structure of existence, physical or metaphysical.

Historical. As will be obvious from the preceding statements, the essential philosophical problem involved in the discussion of "relation" is the connection between the logical process of knowledge (and knowledge is knowledge only in so far as it is logical) and the ontological order of reality. It thus occupies the same position in modern thought as was held by the mediaeval genus and species as the successor of the Platonic ἰδέα and the Aristotelian εἶδος. Locke was chiefly instrumental in effecting the transition. He defined knowledge as "nothing but the perception of the connection of and agreement or disagreement of and repugnance of our ideas" (*Essay*, Bk. IV. chap. i). Nominally, he does not define this agreement or disagreement as relation; but he expressly says that relation is one form of knowledge, and that of the three forms, two, viz. identity and coexistence, are only peculiar forms of relation. The fourth kind, "knowledge of real existence," brings us to such propositions as God is, and the existence of things. The former depends upon the relation of causation, and the latter upon some assurance or belief regarding the relation of immediate sensation to some object to which it corresponds, for practical purposes at least. Hence relation is, directly or indirectly, the central thing in knowledge. Berkeley only needed to make explicit this fact to make it evident that since one of the terms could not by any possibility be an idea, it was perfectly meaningless. Thus the problem of "knowledge of real existence" became a problem of some valid sort of relationship between our "ideas" or experiences, not of an "idea" to something beyond all experience. Hume made explicit this problem, expressly sought for any relationship which could assure valid reference of the terms of experience to one another, and distinctly criticized all candidates that offered themselves. He showed that the worth, for cognitive purposes, of all relations came back to that of causality. He followed out the logic of Locke's statement that relation is the result of comparison, of a mental operation (Locke's *Essay*, Bk. II. chap. xxv. § 1), to prove that in itself every distinct idea is a *separate* existence, and to show that causality (or any relation) cannot affect reality itself, and hence must have a purely subjective origin— which he found in the power of imagination to glide easily from one idea to another frequently associated with it (see Bk. I, Part III, of *Treatise upon Human Nature*). It is well known how this scepticism "awakened" Kant to a reconsideration of relations and their place in knowledge, and led him to redefine judgment as a necessary synthesis of sensations through concepts of the understanding, instead of as their casual association. The relations termed CATEGORIES (q.v.) by Kant and his successors are then the necessary, universal, and hence *a priori* (inherent in thought itself) functions of judgment in construing a world of experience (see the transcendental analytic in Kant's *Critique of Pure Reason*). The stone which Hume rejected became the cornerstone of modern epistemological idealism. Kant derived his table of twelve categories from a mere inventory of the forms of judgment recognized in formal logic. His successors took the idea of their being necessary modes of thought more seriously, and endeavored to show how thought inevitably shows itself in such and such a system of relations. Fichte's *Wissenschaftslehre* and Hegel's *Logik* are the results. After Hegel's time the current divided into two streams: one the logical proper, attempting a more empirical and detached investigation of all the various relations or categories employed in judgment, e.g. number, quality, thing and attribute, etc., and the other the metaphysical, concerning itself with the objective validity of relation and hence of thought.

Literature: as will be inferred from this summary sketch, the discussion of relation is rather to be gathered in the whole drift of any modern writing upon metaphysics, than located in any one passage; but the following additional references may be of some value: Hamilton, *Lects. on Met.*, ii. 535–8; *Discussions*, 603–8; Reid, on *Intellectual Powers*, Essay VI. chap. i; Mill, *Logic*, Bk. I. chap. ii. § 7, and chap. iii. §§ 10 and 11; Lotze, *Logic*, § 337–8; *Metaphysic*, § 80–4; Green, *Prolegomena to Ethics*, Bk. I, and the whole course of his criticism of Locke, Berkeley, and Hume (*Works*, i); Bradley, *Appearance and Reality*, Bk. I, especially chap. iii; Bosanquet, *Knowledge and Reality*. Discussion upon the psychology of relations is inadequate. The following may be noted: Spencer, *Princ. of Psychol.*, § 65; James, *Psychology*, i. chap. ix (especially 243–71) and ii. 663–75; Stout, *Analytic Psychol.*, Bk. I. chap. iii; Lotze, *Metaphysic*, Bk. III. chap. iii. The general tenor of the more recent discussion from the psychological side is distinctly "pragmatic" in its direction—to find the reality of relation in the inherent "motor" tendency of any experience, and not in the structure of the sensation, in its casual associations, or in any separate "relating" function. Cf. James, *Will to Believe*, especially the Essay on The Sentiment of Rationality.

SAME (the) and (the) OTHER: Ger. (*das*) *Gleiche und* (*das*) *Andere*; Fr. (*le*) *même et* (*le*) *différent*; Ital. (*il*) *medesimo e* (*l'*)*altro*. These terms, with sameness and otherness, are correlates which have their technical meaning as translations of certain terms in the Platonic philosophy— being otherwise equivalent to the terms IDENTITY and DIFFERENCE, PERMANENCE and CHANGE (q.v.). Plato used the term ταὐτότης (ταὐτόν) for sameness.

Self-sameness is the characteristic sign of the Idea, the essential Being; while the material, having movement as its defining feature, is in continual change or process, a fact which is expressed by calling it the Other (τὸ ἕτερον = θάτερον). The *Sophist* (254–60) aims to show that logically the Same and the Other require each other; and thus to refute the Eleatic conception of pure Being. According to *Timaeus* (35–8, and 44), God made the soul (the World soul primarily) by taking the Same (which is indivisible and unchangeable) and mixing it with the Other (which is divisible and has to do with material things), and then mixing them both with existence. This mixture was then subdivided according to complicated mathematical principles; the various proportions and positions of the Same and the Other account for the peculiarities of the universe (e.g. the uniformity of the stellar heavens, and the regular irregularity of the planetary), and also for the possibilities of true knowledge and of certain belief. This identification of the logical principles of identity and difference with the cosmic principles of permanence and change, reinforced by mathematic speculation upon the ONE AND THE MANY (q.v.), had great influence upon the later Neo-Platonic theories of the constitution of the world. Hegel revived the conception of the Other (das Andere) as expressing the Non-Being, involved in every Somewhat (Etwas) or defined Being (Dasein), constituting its finitude and its intrinsic tendency to change (Veränderung). Thus nature is the other of spirit, and as such is otherness in itself and to itself, and thus a world of space and time (Hegel, *Werke*, iii. 115–8).

SCEPTICISM [Gr. σκέψις, doubt, hesitation, from σκέπτεσθαι, to look at carefully, to scrutinize]: Ger. *Skepticismus*; Fr. *scepticisme*; Ital. *scetticismo*. (1) The theory that positive and certain truth is not attainable by the human intellect; or (2) the theory that it is necessary to doubt before reaching truth.

As scepticism denotes a certain mental attitude or temper, or method of attacking philosophical problems, the purely formal definition is worth even less than are most terms which characterize philosophical systems. It varies from dogmatic assertion of unbelief, uncertainty, and the impossibility of attaining truth, to the most nicely balanced doubt which will not even assert that all is doubtful, into thorough-going subjection of all philosophical concepts to disbelief until rational grounds can be found for them. In this last sense it is opposed to dogmatism, rather than to theories of the impossibility of true knowledge. In this sense scepticism has been at least an implicit factor in all independent philosophy; it has been asserted by some (Descartes) to be the necessary preliminary to all philosophic belief, and by others (Hegel) to be a necessary moment in the complete self-evolution of every philosophic idea and system.

Very different motives have also contributed to the development of the sceptical attitude. There is (1) the strictly *philosophical*. This is generally evoked as reaction from highly dogmatic systems; and it endeavors, by criticizing their premises and methods, to show their entire untenability. This *motif* is reinforced, as a rule, by the fact that different dogmatic systems hold quite contrary views, and the arguments of one may be turned against those of another until they mutually demolish one another. Thus the opposition of the schools of Heraclitus and Parmenides was a great factor in calling out the scepticism of the SOPHISTS (q.v.). Moreover, the rapid appearance of diverse and incompatible systems produces a psychological condition of unrest and satiety of system which is highly favorable to scepticism.

(2) The *ethical*. A dogmatic system of thought tends to develop an over-positive and strenuous disposition in action, a temper which insists upon carrying its universals into all the details of conduct, and of imposing them upon others. It is the basis of political and theological exclusiveness and persecution. This is met by pointing out the fallibility and relativity of all such principles, leading to the consequent

position that "probability is the guide of life." Hence the
necessity of tempering even the most general principles in
action by adaptation to circumstances, a moral opportunism;
and as regards the conduct of others, of pursuing a policy of
toleration. This motive, while not often explicitly stated, has
perhaps been the animating spark of the most influential
scepticism. It is certainly the chief motive of the scepticism
of the middle Academy. It influenced also the school of
sceptics headed by Pyrrho, but was overshadowed in him by
another ethical motive—that imperturbability (complete
balance, to give a somewhat too positive interpretation) is
attainable only as the outcome of complete doubt, and this
is the pre-condition of complete and undisturbed happiness.
Cf. SCHOOLS OF GREECE, and PYRRHONISM.

(3) The *religious*. To do away with the capacity of
reason for attaining substantial spiritual truth has been a
favorite way of proving the necessity of a revelation of such
truth, and establishing the incapacity of reason to impeach
this truth when revealed. This motive influenced the Latin
fathers of the Church, was active in mediaeval thought, the
nominalistic theory of twofold truth (see SCHOLASTICISM)
being only the explicit statement of what after all was a
logical presupposition of the orthodox philosophy. Its most
celebrated modern adherent is Pascal; but the point of view
appears in another form in Mansel's *Limits of Religious
Thought*, and, combined with other *motifs*, is contained in
Balfour's *Foundations of Belief*.

(4) The *culture point of view*. This is generally united
with the first and second tendencies, and arises from the feeling that dogmatism of thought is not compatible with wide
learning and with the polite and urbane temper. It made
itself felt in the Academics, particularly in Cicero. Montaigne
is its consistent and delightful representative in modern
thought; Hume is touched by it; while secondary philosophic
writers, like Matthew Arnold, are quite sure to be permeated
with it.

The arguments adduced in ancient thought for scepticism may be summed up as follows: (1) The relativity of
the senses: in man and animals; in different men; in the
same man in different conditions; among the different senses

at the same time. (2) The relativity of objects: dependent upon the medium; upon position and distance; and manifest in their constant change and dissolution. (3) The relativity of belief and opinion: customs, manners, fundamental moral and religious beliefs differ radically in different peoples. (4) The reasoning process itself is intrinsically inadequate, because all demonstration depends on prior assumptions or premises, and so on *ad infinitum*—the exact converse of the reasoning which made Aristotle assume ultimate unproved or self-evident premises—the axioms. The writings of Sextus Empiricus (about 200 A.D.) were a summary of all ancient arguments, and exercised great influence upon thought after the revival of learning.

Modern scepticism, as in Hume, draws freely upon the ancient arguments, and yet has a distinct coloring of its own. It consists largely in turning the senses and reason, as the two supposed sources of knowledge, against each other, as with Hume; and attempts by an analysis of the process and elements of (supposed) knowledge as such, rather than by accumulating particulars, to show its inherent incapacity to reach valid conclusions. It has thus been an indispensable factor in the evolution of the modern theory of knowledge. Indeed, the chief difference appears just here. Ancient scepticism acted simply as a check, or as resource to minds that could not accept the dogmatic systems. It reacted *from* them, but not *into* them; they continued practically unaffected, save in details. Modern scepticism has been an integral factor in constituting not merely the form, but the content of modern thought. In this general sense, at least, Kant's assertion that CRITICISM (q.v.) unites dogmatism and scepticism, and Hegel's contention that sceptical doubt is an immanent factor in all philosophizing, must be accepted.

Literature: Seth, art. "Scepticism," *Encyc. Brit.* (9th ed.), xxi. 395–401; Zimmermann, *Darstellung d. Pyrrhonischen Philos.*; Sepp, *Pyrrhonische Studien*; MacColl, *Greek Sceptics from Pyrrho to Sextus*; Brochard, *Les Sceptiques grecs*; Tafel, *Gesch. u. Krit. des Skepticismus u. Irrationalismus*; Saisset, *Le Scepticisme*; Zeller, *Stoics, Epicureans, and Sceptics*; Stäudlin, *Gesch. u. Geist des Skepticismus*; Owen, *Evenings with the Sceptics*.

SCHEMA [Gr. σχῆμα, a diagram]: Ger. *Schema*; Fr. *schème*; Ital. *schema*. (1) The product, in the Kantian philosophy, of the exercise of the transcendental imagination in giving generality to sense and particularity to thought. See SCHEMATISM.

(2) A mode of construction; a formula for synthesis which as formula or method is general, but as embodied or acted upon is particular. Thus the triangle, or circle, to the geometer, is schematic. An image which illustrates a method of space construction (Kant, *Krit. d. reinen Vernunft*, 126–30 of Müller's translation).

The schema of quantity is number; of a reality is the continuous and uniform production of degrees of sensation; of substance is permanence in time; of causality, succession of manifold in time so far as subject to rule; of reciprocity, coexistence of the manifold in time so far as subject to rule. Democritus used the term schemata, σχήματα, to denote the characteristic forms of his atoms. It was also employed to designate the figures of the Aristotelian syllogism.

SCHEMATISM: Ger. *Schematismus*; Fr. *schématisme*; Ital. *schematismo*. The theory, in the Kantian analysis of knowledge, of the use of the transcendental imagination as mediating between sense and understanding.

Kant pushed his dualism between sense and understanding, or more strictly between the matter of intuition and the concepts or functions of discursive thought, to such an extreme as to require a connecting bit. The former is immediately given, or received, in sensibility; it constitutes the material of knowledge, is manifold, and in itself is blind and unordered. The latter has only mediate reference, is an active and unifying process, and in itself is empty, i.e. is lacking in objective content and validity. Kant seems to have thought at first that the *a priori* forms of perception, space, and time would suffice to order the otherwise chaotic material of sense. At least, they are treated in the *aesthetic* as given and complete in themselves. But in the *analytic* it became apparent that space and time forms themselves had to be construed by means of the synthetic functions of thought. It also became obvious that the concepts needed to be imaged in order to exist even as definite subjective thoughts, to say nothing of acquiring valid objective reference. Hence the need of a go-between to overcome the heterogeneity of the two factors in all knowledge, a go-between, moreover, which is necessary even for the formally distinct existence of each factor. This was found in the pure or transcendental imagination which constructs the pure logical concepts in relation to the function which they perform in ordering time elements (the moment, duration, and succession). Time is like thought, as *a priori*; like sensibility as a manifold; and thus it possesses characteristics which render it homogeneous with both, and which fit it for occupying an intermediate position. Thus the schematism of the pure understanding "treats of the sensuous conditions under which alone pure concepts of the understanding can be used" (Kant, *Crit. of Pure Reason*, Pt. II. Bk. II. chap. i; see 119–24 of Müller's translation).

SCHOLASTICISM (the Schoolmen) [Lat. *scholasticus*, trans. of Gr. σχολαστικός, from σχολάζειν, to lecture, to be master of a school]: Ger. *Scholastik, scholastische Philosophie*; Fr. *philosophie scolastique*, or simply *scolastique*; Ital. *(la) scolastica*. (1) The name of the period of mediaeval thought in which philosophy was pursued under the domination of theology, having for its aim the exposition of Christian dogma in its relations to reason. See HISTORY OF PHILOSOPHY, and LATIN AND SCHOLASTIC TERMINOLOGY.

(2) Any mode of thought characterized by excessive refinement and subtlety; the making of formal distinctions without end and without special point.

Scholasticism is distinguished, on one hand, from Arabian philosophy (see, however, lower down) carried on outside the pale of the Church; and from MYSTICISM (q.v.), which is found within the Church paralleling Scholasticism. The latter emphasizes logical and formal processes; as the former, feeling and inner experience. Charlemagne founded schools of learning all over France, which was, thereafter, the special home of learning and of science. The teachers were termed *doctores scholastici* (Ueberweg, *Hist. of Philos.*, i, according to whom the use of the term may be traced back to Theophrastus), while the wandering scholar-teachers from the mission schools of the Church were termed *scholastici* (Erdmann, *Hist. of Philos.*, i. 288). They were ecclesiastics, so it is not a matter of surprise that they philosophize wholly in the interests of the Church. The language is Latin. The method is comment upon and exposition of selected passages of Scripture and the early logicians, and finally of the Church fathers and Aristotle. They combined with their strictly philosophic pursuits all the science and culture of their age (in the *Trivium* and *Quadrivium*). Cf. PATRISTIC PHILOSOPHY.

The schools were founded in the 8th century, but it is not till the 9th that specifically philosophic thought appears. While in one sense scholasticism still continues as the official teaching of the Roman Catholic Church, its dominance and its independent career ceased with the Renaissance and the 15th century. The intervening five centuries are conveniently divided into three sub-periods: (1) the formation of scholasticism, formulation of its problems; (2) its systematization; (3) its decline. The three periods may also be characterized by their reference to antiquity. The first was based upon fragments of Aristotle's logical writings and Neo-Platonic commentaries; the second is due to systematic acquaintance with Aristotle; the third to the humanistic revival of all ancient learning, which, even when honoring Aristotle, gave him a freer interpretation.

I. In the first period, Scotus Erigena is in many respects nearer to the mystics than to the scholastics proper, and is pantheistic in his theology. He is influenced chiefly by the Neo-Platonists rather than by Aristotle. But in two respects he is extremely important for scholasticism in the narrower sense. (*a*) He asserts the essential identity of the content of faith and reason, and in the most immediate way. Any dictum of authority is reasonable, and every rational principle may be considered as dogma; true religion *is* true philosophy, and vice versa. The problem thus raised of the relation between the two is of determining importance for the entire period. (*b*) He assumes a complete parallelism of the hierarchy of being on one side, and thought on the other, proceeding from the most universal to the most particular; the former comprehends and produces the latter. Creation is equivalent to the logical unfolding or making explicit of the supreme universal, from God down, in a graded scale of beings, to the individual things of sense—the lowest form of reality. This might be termed the deductive process. On the other hand is the eternal return to God—i.e. the logical inclusion of the particulars again in the universal, the inductive movement. This involves, as applied to man, the theory of redemption, immortality, etc. Now the significance of this is not only in its frankly stated REALISM (q.v., 1), but in the use of this realism to state and explain the fundamental doctrines of the Church—those of creation, the Trinity, sin, and redemption.

In this connection the discussion becomes one of tremendous import—of the relation of God as the universal to the individual, to man. When separated from this relationship, the whole realistic-nominalistic discussion degenerates into formal subtleties and refinements. It is Anselm who carries out in a systematic and reflective way the philosophical statement of all the dogmas of the Church, and who sees in realism the only justification of the supreme authority of God, of the doctrine of the Trinity, and asserts that nominalism is only the deification of sensible things. It also leads him to the ONTOLOGICAL ARGUMENT (q.v.). Roscelin, as a nominalist, had shown that its effect on theology is to substitute a doctrine of tritheism for the Trinity, while Berengar had used it to attack the doctrine of transubstantiation. Thus the doctrine was brought under the ban of the Church. But the statement of realism as a theory of the divine nature and of creation revealed the essential difficulties in it. Admitting that the universals are the real in the mind of God, and the archetypes of all created things, the problem arises as to just how these are related to the things of the sensible world. The doctrine easily lent itself to a pantheistic interpretation or absorption of individuals in God. This tendency was evident in William of Champeaux and also in Bernard of Chartres. It also led to the conclusion that since the class as substance is in all the individuals it includes (these being indeed only its accidents), one and the same substance must have mutually contradictory attributes. Hence Abélard attempts a mediation of these extreme views in a realistically tempered conceptualism. This theory was long completely victorious, and put to rest this strife, appearing satisfactory both theologically and logically.

But as to the other problem raised by Erigena, Abélard leaned decidedly to the side of reason; he attributes to it a decisive, not merely a formalizing power, and criticizes the fathers freely, bringing out their contradictions not to show how they may be nullified, but in order that reason may get at the truth of the matter—the *real* content of faith. So far as the logical movement is concerned, we find it after this time carried on in a highly rationalistic theology, as in Gilbert of Poitiers, and in the development of that system of argumentative distinctions which is still to some minds the chief characteristic of scholasticism. This brought out a reaction—a condemnation of all dialectic; and the assertion of the content of faith as supreme above all reason, as in Hugo, and still more the VICTORINES (q.v.)—following a more or less mystic path and occupied mainly with the anthropology of the inner religious life. John of Salisbury reacts in another direction, and occupies himself with a psychological examination of the questions which, on their logical side, had gone to seed in empty formalism—questions of the relation of sensation, perception, and understanding in arriving at concepts, and the psychical relations of faith, opinion, and knowledge; and also with scholarly synopses of previous thought.

II. The second period is not only richer in content, but much clearer in its main features. The struggle with oriental Mohammedanism and the outcome of the crusades resulted in opening Europe not only to Arabian philosophy with its interpretation of Aristotle, but also to Arabian and Jewish science, much wider and more exact than was occidental, and systematized, after the Aristotelian fashion, by relation to metaphysical principles. The period commences accordingly in the 13th century; and while in the early part of this century the writings of Aristotle are condemned by the Church, in the next century Aristotle stands on practically the same level with Augustine, the greatest of the fathers, and is officially declared to be the forerunner of Christ in natural matters, as John the Baptist was in matters of grace, and is known, briefly, as *The* philosopher. The writings of Aristotle were made known in their completeness; not simply the logical treatises—in fragmentary form at best. The scholastic method gets shape, consisting first in the breaking up of the text discussed into a number of propositions; secondly, questions are raised, and the variety of possible answers set forth; thirdly, arguments, *pro* and *con*, are adduced in a syllogistic chain, leading to a conclusion. The logical distinguishing or dialectic, so developed in the previous period, and yet having little or no aim outside itself, now becomes a useful instrument, and is handled with great power, being reinforced by the more substantial parts of the Aristotelian logic. When we apply this apparatus, both of the substance—metaphysics, physics, psychology, and ethics —and form—the modified logic, or dialectic of thought—to the service of the doctrines of the Church (themselves the richest summary in existence of spiritual and ethical experience), we have the scholastic philosophy of this period, of which Windelband (*Hist. of Philos.*, 311) says it was "an adjustment and arrangement of world-moving thoughts upon the largest and most imposing scale history has known."

Alexander of Hales, Albertus Magnus, and St. Thomas Aquinas are the greatest of many names here. The first develops the method in a practical way, as a help to the orderly exposition and demonstration of dogma; the second develops it in a theoretical way, and as applied to the entire philosophy of Aristotle as well as to the dogma of the Church; while the third makes an organic fusion of the two factors, and thus brings the movement to its culmination. As to the content of their philosophy, it must be borne in mind that Arabian Aristotelianism was conceived in a Neo-Platonic sense. It was pantheistic in tendency, denying the transcendence of the absolute reason or God; holding to the eternity of matter, "creation" being the realization of potentiality, not a distinct act of effecting the world out of nothing; and denying the individual immortality of the soul. Hence Albertus and St. Thomas must, while adhering to Aristotle, justify the doctrines of the transcendent and creating God and the immortal individuality of the soul, as distinct from its realistic absorption in deity. Cf. ST. THOMAS (philosophy of).

The Aristotelianism of these men produced a reaction, of which Duns Scotus is the leader: Bonaventura and Eckhart are classed among the mystics. Their controversy concerned three points in particular: (1) the relation of faith to reason; (2) the relation of intellect and will; (3) the nature of individuality.

(1) In spite of (or, better, because of) the conviction of Albertus and St. Thomas as to the relation of Aristotle to Church dogma, they are compelled to set aside certain doctrines as simply the products of revelation, utterly inaccessible to the natural mind—it being clear that Aristotle had not taught the doctrine of the Trinity or the Incarnation, etc. (In this period, as in the earlier one, it was the mystics who, drawing on Neo-Platonism, attempted a speculative construction of these doctrines.) They are above reason, but not contrary to it. The natural light can lead to certain truths, the content of natural religion and morality, but above this is supernatural religious and ethical truth, which is "of grace," not of nature, and is revealed, not discovered. This, the so-called doctrine of the *twofold truth*, is the basis of the teachings of Albert and St. Thomas. But having gone so far, it is difficult not to go further; and here is the rift in the lute which finally destroys the unity of scholasticism. Duns Scotus (generally regarded as the most acute philosophical mind of the period) held that theology was only a practical matter, aiming at salvation from sin, having to do with the will, not the intellect, while philosophy is pure theory. Each is right in its own sphere. The doctrine was conceived in good faith in order to give to dogma a claim untouched by reason; for Scotus was acute enough to see that if reason can assist or confirm theology, it can also attack or criticize it. But its actual effect was in the other direction. Reason was given greater scope and stringency; all sorts of propositions, theologically heretical, were proved, with the pious clause (sometimes in good faith, sometimes not) that though this was so according to reason, the opposite was true according to faith.

(2) The same insistence upon the practical side is found in the psychology and ethics of Scotus. While St. Thomas followed the Greek position which uniformly made knowl-

edge, contemplation, identity of subject and object in rational intuition, higher than the will, Scotus followed Latin thought, which had found its religious expression in St. Augustine. The will, according to the Thomists, is determined by the good, which is discerned, both in general and in particular cases, by the reason (see PERSEITY); moreover, reason has an objective metaphysical significance, an intrinsic relation to truth. But Scotus gives a psychological, or historical, account of knowledge; it is a natural process, and hence, if the will is dependent upon it, it in turn is really determined by nature with its necessity. Hence the will, as self-included power of choice, is really fundamental. God is free, because of the radical primacy of the will. He created the world out of his sheer will, not in conformity to prescriptions of reason—a position which, of course, dovetailed excellently into the separation of theology from philosophy. Moreover, salvation is not the eternal vision or contemplation of God, but a state of will—love—superior to contemplation.

(3) The emphasis upon reason tends to leave the individual in a precarious condition, for it is connected with the Greek realism, the assertion of the higher reality of universals. While Aristotle had held to God as a transcendent individual, as pure form, Averroës had insisted that there is no form without matter, and thus developed a pantheistic theory. St. Thomas here, as in his theory of the sphere of grace and of nature, attempted to establish an equilibrium. In the immaterial world, pure and *subsistent* forms are real and active without any attachment to matter; while in the material, forms are realized only in matter (are *inherent*). Now man belongs to both worlds: as rational soul, he is the lowest of pure immaterial forms; as animal soul (having body), he is the highest of the other type. And in man both of these are bound together into a single unity—the only form which is both subsistent and inherent. But St. Thomas had also to deal with differences of personality—the so-called *principium individuationis*. God is absolute genus and individual at the same time, and uniquely so. Each angel is relative genus and individual in one. But different human individualities have but one genus. Their differentiation is due to the determination of matter, to distinctions of time

and place; hence they are substantialized only through their relations to definite bodies. Against this view, which seemed to them to deny spiritual and ethical individuality, the Scotists protested. According to them, the individual soul, *qua* individual or differentiated, is a self-subsistent reality, and is not a mere determination of a genus (see REALISM, I).

III. There are both intrinsic and, relatively speaking, extrinsic reasons for the break-up of scholasticism. Intrinsically, in Thomism it reached its culmination. After reason and faith had each received its exact position, and reason had been used wherever possible to demonstrate faith, and when this was not possible, to show that, at least, the dogma was not contrary to reason, the scheme was virtually complete. To develop it was to transform it. And the Scotist teachings threatened in a more active way the unity of the system. This happened not only by emphasizing the rights of reason within the theoretical world, but by its assertion of the reality of the individual soul, which easily developed—as in William of Occam—into extreme nominalism, the doctrine that only individuals are anywhere real. Moreover, this led to empiricism, for while the universal can be apprehended in thought, the individual (as even Scotus had taught) must be met with in experience to be known. Moreover, Scotism had everywhere a more psychological coloring than Thomism, and by furthering reflection in empirical psychology, went far to usher in a new way of thinking. The external causes (stimulated, however, by these intrinsic ones) were HUMANISM (q.v.), the revival of learning, and the newly awakened interest in nature, with its daughter, mathematical and physical science. The latter finds its forerunner in Roger Bacon and its expression in Copernicus and Galileo. With them, the natural world of the scholastics, so intimately bound up with their metaphysics and theology, is destroyed, and a new order of conception ushered in.

Literature: of the histories of philosophy, Erdmann is unusually full in this period; and Windelband (who has been largely followed) is noteworthy in his seizing upon main problems and streams amid all the diversity of writings—a thing more difficult in Scholasticism than elsewhere. Prantl's *Gesch. d. Logik* is the authority on the logical side. The art.

"Scholasticism" in the *Encyc. Brit.* is an excellent summary. As general histories, we have Hauréau, *Hist. de la philos. scol.*; Kaulich, *Gesch. d. skol. Philos.*; and Stöckl, *Gesch. d. Philos. d. Mittelalters.* See also ST. THOMAS (philosophy of).

SCHOPENHAUERISM (or -eanism): Ger. *die Schopenhauer'sche Philosophie*; Fr. *Schopenhauerisme*; Ital. *Schopenhauerismo.* (1) The philosophy of Schopenhauer. (2) VOLUNTARISM (q.v.).

SCOTISM: Ger. *Scotismus*; Fr. *Scotisme*; Ital. *Scotismo.* The philosophic system and tendencies of Johannes Duns Scotus; opposed to Thomism, the system of ST. THOMAS (q.v., philosophy of). It is characterized by its tendency to separate philosophy from theology (see TWOFOLD TRUTH); its indeterminism, and emphasis upon will (see VOLUNTARISM); and by a movement in the direction of nominalism, although Scotus himself remained a realist. See TERMINISM, OCCAMISM, and REALISM (1).

SEMINAL REASONS [Lat. *rationes seminales*, trans. of Gr. λόγος σπερματικός]. The forces, lodged in matter, by which natural effects result; active powers of nature, like heat and cold.

It is in virtue of them that the indefinite series of changes take place; they are, after being implanted in nature by God in the original act of creation, the causes of all subsequent combination and differentiation. They find their highest form of expression in the sex-process. As intermediary in the process of natural change and evolution, they are the media by which a universal is differentiated into individuals; these, however, in their specific nature, remain true to their genus. A scholastic term and concept. Cf. Harper, *The Philos. of the School,* ii. 731–32, iii. 412–13. See LOGOS, and REALISM.

The theory of λόγος σπερματικός found its way into Augustine under the form of the *ratio seminalis*; it was then taken up into the theory of creation by St. Thomas Aquinas, from whom the definition given is derived. The immediate creation had its cause in God, and had accordingly imparted to it the power of continuing the process of creation into the multiplicity of orders, genera, and species (and in the sex-processes) of individuals. See references to St. Thomas in the passages of Harper referred to.

SENSATIONALISM [Lat. *sensus*, a sense]: Ger. *Sensualismus*; Fr. *sensationisme* (*sensualisme* is often used, as is its English equivalent—J.M.B.); Ital. *sensismo*. The theory that all knowledge originates in sensations; that all cognitions, even reflective ideas and so-called intuitions, can be traced back to elementary sensations.

Historically, it is generally combined with ASSOCIATIONALISM (q.v.). In an ethical sense (for which, however, in English the term sensualism is more often used) it means that all moral values, or goods, are ultimately reducible to states of feeling which, psychologically, determine the will: Epicureanism.

In the first place it is a theory of the *origin* of knowledge, yet since questions arise (*a*) as to whether truth and certainty exist beyond sensation (in the derived forms), or are restricted to sensation, and (*b*) whether any truth can be found in purely immediate sensation, it comes to be also a theory regarding the validity of knowledge-forms, and as such is often used as synonymous with EMPIRICISM (q.v.).

Some of the Sophists (Protagoras, in particular, to all appearance) applied the conception of Heraclitus, that all is becoming, in such a way as to give validity, on the side of the knowing process, only to that which is in itself changing and partakes of motion, viz. sense. (But this may be merely the Platonic interpretation in *Theaetetus*.) Aristippus, the founder of the Cyrenaic school, taught most definitely that our knowledge is restricted to sensations. The Stoics asserted the idea of the origin of knowledge in sensations, but not its restriction to them. With them originated the famous simile that the soul is at first a blank tablet (see TABULA RASA) on which the outer world imprints its signs (Windelband, *Hist. of Philos.*, 203).

While the Stoics gave validity to the general ideas which result from perceptions, especially to those ideas which develop in all men alike, the Epicureans held that certainty is found conjoined with the necessity and clearness with which sensations force themselves upon us.

Some of the Latin fathers adopted this sensationalism as

a basis for dogmatic orthodoxy. Since the soul in itself is limited to sensations, it cannot acquire the idea of God, salvation, or immortality. Hence the need of revelation to make known and valid these ideas. The Neo-Platonic and Scholastic philosophy universally admits a rational knowledge over and above sensation (in some Nominalists, however, the individual or real appears to have been identified with the individual presented to sense; but this doctrine left next to no impress). Hobbes is the founder of modern sensationalism, which he conjoined to his theory of moving body as the seat and the source of all sensation. Locke holds to reflection, besides sensation; the former gives us knowledge of our own or inner powers, like memory, judging, etc.; but sensation is the sole source of knowledge of the external world. In three ways Locke's sensationalism was highly influential in settling the problems of later epistemology. (*a*) He taught the doctrine of "simple ideas," or elementary sensations. While he himself attributed positive value to relations, and to general ideas (at least in mathematics), his standpoint raised the question of the possibility and value of relations, and led Hume to his scepticism—to his substitution of the subjective principle of habit for the objective principle of causality. (*b*) He assumed (after the manner of Hobbes, but with less emphasis upon motion) atoms as the real ground and cause of sensations; but was logical enough to see that if our knowledge is limited to sensation, their existence can be asserted only hypothetically—though it was rather substance or substrate (whose relationship to physical atoms he seems never to have fairly faced) the existence of which is inferential, as the *unknown* cause. Hence the problem of reconciling physical science and sensationalism. (*c*) He defined knowledge as agreement (relationship) of ideas, and yet, in places, limited *certain* knowledge to the immediately experienced sensation. Hence the problem of knowledge as judgment, and the relation of this to sensation. While the French school, through the influence of Voltaire and Condillac, translated Locke's wavering sensationalism into a thorough-going system, and made it the fashionable philosophy of the ENLIGHTENMENT (q.v.), it is Hume who, realizing the epistemological and metaphysical consequences of it, continues the main line of thought. Kant, stirred directly by Hume, revises the empiricism of one period of his thought, gives up his naïve assumption that the object as such can be given in sense, and reduces sense to one coordinate factor in knowledge, that which gives it matter, which, however, is chaotic and disconnected till acted upon by the forms of sense and the categories of the understanding. While it is perhaps too much to say that, since his time, sensationalism is a historic anachronism (since, for example, Spencer holds it and even tries to combine it with the results of physical science), yet it is certain that he weakened greatly the conception of the origin of knowledge through atomic, disconnected sensations; and, for the most part, 19th-century sensationalism is simply a popular survival of the philosophy of the Enlightenment.

SENSUALISM (in ethics). The popular use of the term is to denote a low or depraved form of moral theory, according to which indulgence in the more gross forms of pleasure is made the chief end of life.

SINGULARISM: Ger. *Singularismus*; Fr. *singularisme* (suggested); Ital. *singolarismo* (suggested). A term used (cf. Külpe, *Introd. to Philos.*, § 14) to characterize philosophic schools "explaining or deducing all the phenomena of the universe from one principle"; opposed to pluralism. See MONISM.

SPECULATION [Lat. *speculari*, to view, contemplate]: Ger. *Spekulation*; Fr. *spéculation*; Ital. *speculazione*. (1) Meditation or reflection of the mind upon itself, or upon spiritual things.

The Greek θεωρία meant direct intuition (Schauen) of transcendent, which is not discursive; thus opposed to dialectic. (J.D.–K.G.)

(2) A form of theorizing which goes beyond verifiable observation and reflection, characterized by loose and venturesome hypotheses (popular use).

(3) The conclusion and completion of the movement of thought which apprehends the unity of categories in and

through their opposition. It has this last and technical sense in the Hegelian philosophy. The understanding lays down propositions in an uncritical and dogmatic form; unaware of any relation between its propositions, it asserts each as ultimate in its isolation. The negative reason, or dialectic, reveals the essential self-contradiction and self-transcendence, the fluidity of all these fixed concepts. When made ultimate it leads to scepticism; but when used as a factor in developing a more comprehensive point of view and a conception from and within which both the previous isolated notions and their opposition can be explained, it passes into speculative reason. This, like the understanding, is positive, but it is a positive which manifests itself through a process of development, instead of being assumed as fixed (Hegel, *Logic*, § 82). See UNDERSTANDING, and REASON. Cf. Eisler, *Wörterb. d. philos. Begriffe*, "Speculation," for citations, meanings (1) and (3).

STATUE OF CONDILLAC. Condillac, in his *Traité des Sensations* (1754), popularized Locke's theory of the origin of knowledge from "sensation," eliminating Locke's "reflection." In illustration of the process, he employed the fiction of a statue, at first without mind, which receives the gift of the senses one after the other, beginning with smell; and attempted to show how the mere presence of these sensations would generate all mental processes and products. The presence of the sensation equals perception; the stronger one gives attention; recurrence of a former one, memory; the practically simultaneous presence of an old and new one, judgment (comparison), etc.; while the sense of touch carries with it the consciousness of objectivity. This allegory of the statue became a favorite literary device of the sensationalists.

SUBJECT (-IVE) [Lat. *sub*, under, below, + *iacĕre*, to throw]: Ger. *Subjekt, subjektiv*; Fr. *sujet, subjectif*; Ital. *soggetto, soggettivo*. (1) The material or content of a thought or discourse, as distinct from that with which the thought is concerned; or OBJECT (q.v.), subject-matter.

(2) Hence, the substantive, the real.

(3) That which is the source and centre of the process of thought, or, more widely, of all psychical processes — the self, ego, mind. In this latter connection *subjective* assumes two meanings: (*a*) that which is concerned with, or arises from, mental operations, as distinguished from the objective as appertaining to the external and material world; (*b*) that which is *merely* mental; the illusory; that which lacks validity; that which is not universal, but confined to some one individual, and to him because of something accidental in his make-up.

In aesthetics, subjective and objective are often opposed to one another as designating two types of criticism: the former, that into which the personality of the author enters; the latter, impersonal, impartial, and more or less cold.

The term begins with a logical sense in Aristotle, which, however, as is usual in Greek thought, has an ontological meaning as well. Logically, it is the subject of a proposition, or of a discourse, that of which something is asserted, ὑποκείμενον. But Plato had distinguished between ὄνομα as subject and ῥῆμα as predicate, the ὄνομα being the noun or substantive, the constant as against the changing verb, which thus connotes οὐσία, essence (*Theaet.*, 206, and *Crat.*, 399). Aristotle even more explicitly identifies the subject with the substrate, the SUBSTANCE (q.v.) — which, indeed, is only the Latin translation of his ὑποκείμενον. This, as indeterminate subject, is ὕλη, matter; but as determinate, it is specific individual being, genera being only secondary subjects. It can be subject only, never predicate (see Prantl, *Gesch. d. Logik*, i. 217 ff.; Ueberweg, *Logic*, 143–4; Trendelenburg, *Hist. Beitr.*, i. 13–34, and 54–6). According to the Stoics (Prantl, *Gesch. d. Logik*, i. 428–32; Trendelenburg, *Hist. Beitr.*, 221), the subject is one of the four fundamental categories, and designates being without quality, and, therefore, the ultimate subject of all judgment; the unqualified — the pure universal. As such it is the receptacle in which the formative or seminal reason works.

Here we have a complete fusion of the logical and ontological senses. Apuleius and Capella (Prantl, *Gesch. d. Logik*, i. 581, 676) used the terms *subdita* and *subjectiva* as technical terms for the subject of a proposition or judgment; while Boethius for the first time (so Prantl, *Gesch. d. Logik*, i. 696) makes use of the terms *subjectivum* and *praedicatum*. In this form the term passed into scholastic thought. As might be expected, we owe to a nominalist, Occam, the first exposition of the ambiguity of the term, and the distinction of its real form and its logical sense (*ad existentiam, ad praedicationem*, Prantl, *Gesch. d. Logik*, iii. 368). It is to Scotus that we owe the distinction of subjective and objective in the sense which persisted practically till the time of Baumgarten and Kant.

Scotus identified the two terms with the familiar distinction of Arabian thought of "first and second intentions"; subjective designating the first intention, concrete substantiality, and objective the second intention, or this thing as constituted through a mental operation (Prantl, *Gesch. d. Logik*, iii. 208; also the Index, for other similar uses of the term objective).

Gerson anticipated the modern use of the term, using the phrase "objectum vel substratum," and speaks of an objective reason, "ratio objectalis," which mediates real being in knowledge, "having two aspects, as it were, an external and an internal" (Prantl, *Gesch. d. Logik*, iv. 145). Descartes is true to the scholastic use, objective with him meaning always present to thought (existing *idealiter in intellectu*), and subjective that which is really in the things themselves (*formaliter in se ipsis*; *Medit.*, iii). Eucken (*The Fundamental Concepts of Modern Philosophic Thought*) gives instances of the use of the term in the 18th century prior to Kant. The reversal of meanings in Kant is not hard to understand. The proposition "I think" has transcendental value: that is to say, it is the function of the self-identity of thought, which, lying at the basis of the categories, is the fundamental *a priori* condition of all knowledge and experience. It cannot be regarded, however, as a thing, as substance, i.e. as soul. "By this *I* or *he* or *it*, that is, the thing which thinks, nothing is represented beyond a transcendental subject of thoughts = *x*, which is known only through the thoughts that are its predicates" (*Critique of Pure Reason*, 301, Müller's trans.). It is, then, just the absolute subject of all judgments; a significance which clearly enough connects the term with the

Aristotelian and logical meaning. But the activity of this function, through the forms of sense and categories of understanding, is necessary to the constitution of objects in experience (of the empirical as distinct from the transcendent object or thing-in-itself); thus, epistemologically considered, if not ontologically, the pure "I think" or subject has positive significance and value. Thus Kant says: "If we drop our subject, or the subjective form of our senses, all qualities, all relations of objects in time and space, nay, space and time themselves, would vanish" (*Critique of Pure Reason*, 37). Thus, all the part played by mental activity in constituting empirical objects is repeatedly termed "subjective." A double sense is clearly contained here: on one side, this subjective is set over against the objective, when things-in-themselves— reality in its intrinsic nature—are in mind; it is the source of the phenomenal, of that which has not unconditioned validity—tending towards the sceptical and illusory sense of the term. But, on the other hand, it is constitutive of objects as experienced, and therefore has complete (empirical) objectivity; indeed, because of its universal and necessary character, it is more "objective" than any law or object found in experience itself.

Kant's successors, by abolishing the thing-in-itself, endeavored to do away with this ambiguity. They endeavored to give the pure "I think," or unity of thought, a completely objective sense; Kant himself having, indeed, admitted the possibility of the transcendental object being at the same time the subject of thinking (*Critique of Pure Reason*, 311). The subject thus becomes the activity which appears equally in mental processes and in the world of experienced objects. It differs from the soul-substance against which Kant had made his polemic, in being essentially activity rather than substrate, and hence by being considered in its functions in the structure of the world of knowledge, morals, and art, rather than in its isolated subsistence; and as transcending the historical, or empirical, individual mind. Such is its use in Fichte; and Hegel fixed the distinction in a classic way in the introduction to his *Phänomenologie* (*Werke*, 14) by saying the truth, the absolute, was to be apprehended as subject, not as substance. But this technical sense easily passed over into a loose, popular one, in which subject meant mind, soul, though with more psychological implication and with more reference (often very vague, however) to the part played by mind in the process of knowledge. Sir William Hamilton was chiefly influential in making the Kantian distinction of subjective and objective at home in English speech, Cousin and the other followers of German thought, in France. When members of quite the opposite schools, such as Spencer and Comte, adopted the terms, they were thoroughly naturalized, and are now in such general use as practically to have displaced the older senses.

Literature: Eucken, *Fundamental Concepts of Modern Philosophic Thought*, chap. i; and *Gesch. d. philos. Terminologie*, 203–4; Franck's *Dict. des Sci. philos.*, iv. 468–71; Hamilton, ed. of Reid, 97, 221, 806–9; *Discussions on Philos.*, 5, 605; *Metaphysics*, i. 157–62.

SUBJECTIVISM [for deriv. see SUBJECT]: Ger. *Subjektivismus*; Fr. *subjectivisme*; Ital. *soggettivismo*. (1) The theory which denies the possibility of objective knowledge, which limits the mind to consciousness of its own states; as such, equivalent to subjective idealism.

(2) Any theory which attaches great importance to the part played by the subjective factor in constituting experience; e.g. Kantianism in its doctrine of the subjective origin of the forms of perception (space and time) and the categories of conception.

(3) The theory, in ethics, which conceives the aim of morality to be the attainment of states of feeling, pleasure or happiness (Külpe, *Intro. to Philos.*, secs. 14, 30). Cf. OBJECTIVISM.

Subjectivistic products of all sorts (no less than the producers) are said to have "subjectivity."

SUBSTANCE [Lat. *sub*, under, + *stare*, to stand]: Ger. *Substanz*; Fr. *substance*; Ital. *sostanza*. (1) Essence: the important characteristic or constitutive elements in any subject.

(2) Any individual real thing; an entity.

(3) The generalized reality which is manifested in a variety of particular things.

(4) The reality which underlies the properties in any

thing, whether mental or material; unknown, while they are known; substrate. The properties have an ambiguous reference: on the one hand, they are supposed to inhere in the substance; on the other, they are simply the impressions which the unknown substance makes upon our senses; they stand, therefore, with one leg in the object and another in the subject.

SUBJECT (q.v.) and ESSENCE (q.v.) in the early history of the term substance largely divide its meaning between them. Aristotle had used the term οὐσία in ways which certainly appear incompatible. On the one hand, it is the concrete, individual thing; it is asserted that it is not possible for it to be the universal—this when he is opposing Platonism. On the other hand, he declares that all science and knowledge are of the universal. Again, it is the mixture, or concrete, of matter and form, the universal realized through being merged in the particular. And again, the substrate or subject (ὑποκείμενον) is sometimes defined as pure indeterminate matter. If it is too much to say that the scholastics rolled these meanings into one, they certainly confused substance as individual thing with essence as the real being, or form, found in particular things, and thus prepared the way for the triple modern sense. (1, above) As essence it is the universal and determining real—Descartes and Spinoza—the substantial, as distinct from the attributive or accidental. (4, above) As that which underlies particular things and qualities, it indeed exists, but is unknown; it is simply that which serves as a background and cause, utterly inaccessible in its real nature—Locke and the popular philosophy derived from him—akin to Kant's thing-in-itself. (2, above) Any individual thing or object, having its highest philosophical expression in Leibnitz's monadism. Berkeley acutely sees that Locke's substance is only an abstract idea, and as such, according to his nominalism, meaningless, and so abolishes the substance, matter. Hume repeats the operation upon mind as substance. Kant gives a new meaning to it—that which persists in quantity through a series of temporal changes. See PERMANENCE.

SUBSTANTIALITY THEORY OR SUBSTANTIALISM [for deriv. see SUBSTANCE]: Ger. *Substantialitätstheorie*,

Substantialismus; Fr. *substantialisme*; Ital. *sustanzialismo*. (1) In general, the theory that there are real substances, or distinct entities, underlying phenomenal facts or events.

(2) Its more definite meanings depend upon, and vary with, that which it is opposed to.

(1) As opposed to phenomenalism, it asserts that substances "mind" and "matter" exist, and are known to exist with as much certainty as are particular physical and psychical facts.

Hamilton says: "Philosophers, as they affirm or deny the authority of consciousness in guaranteeing a substratum or substance to the manifestations of the ego and non-ego, are divided into Realists or Substantialists and into Nihilists or Non-Substantialists" (*Lect. on Metaphys.*, i. 294). In a somewhat more limited sense, the term is used to denote the belief of those who hold to a separate self or soul distinct from the phenomena of consciousness, as over against that view which regards the soul as simply the sum-total of conscious activities or modes, the latter school being called "Actualists" (so Hibben, *Problems of Philos.*, 79), and the theory "Actuality Theory" (cf. Eisler, *Wörterb. d. philos. Begriffe*, "Actualitätstheorie," for numerous citations).

(2) As opposed to the dynamic theory of matter, substantialism holds that matter cannot be resolved into "centres of force," or modes of energy, but that mass is a necessary and irreducible concept, over and above that of motion, in considering the physical constitution of the universe.

SUI GENERIS [Lat.]. Of its own peculiar kind, singular, unique.

A phrase used to designate an individual which is the only representative or specimen of its kind, and so identical with the genus, so far as denotation is concerned.

SUMMISTS [Lat. *summa*, collection, sum]: Ger. *Summisten*; Fr. *sommistes*; Ital. *sommisti*. A name applied in SCHOLASTICISM (q.v.) to the successors of Hugo. Their chief aim was to systematize the writings of the great teachers of the Church, and present them as a consistent whole. They thus commence, although only in a formal way, the movement towards the presentation of the content of faith in its unity with reason.

Besides Hugo, Sully, Peter of Lombard, and Alanus are the chief representatives of the school. The name is derived from the fact that Hugo wrote a work entitled *Summa Sententiarum*. See Erdmann, *Hist. of Philos.*, ii. 331–47.

SYNCRETISM [Gr. σύν + κρητίζειν, probably to combine or unite]: Ger. *Synkretismus*; Fr. *syncrétisme*; Ital. *sincretismo*. The attempt to select and combine various elements from a number of philosophic systems without much regard to the intrinsic value of what is selected, or to the logical method of the combination; about the same as eclecticism, but used, upon the whole, in a somewhat more disparaging sense.

SYSTEM [Gr. σύν + στῆναι, to be set up, to stand up]: Ger. *System*; Fr. *système*; Ital. *sistema*. The term system is employed to designate a whole from the standpoint of the methodic connection and arrangement of its constituent members.

It differs from such terms as aggregate, collection, and inventory, in expressly connoting the orderly inherent bonds which bind together, from the standpoint of rational apprehension and explanation, the parts of the whole. It differs from such terms as organism, totality, and whole, in expressly connoting that it is from the standpoint of *thought*, of mental *method*, that the parts are interdependent. It differs, however, from "classification" in implying that the mental method has been successfully applied to, and as it were worked over into, the facts; it does not remain outside of them as a merely mental scheme. A system arises whenever a particular plan, a working hypothesis, or scientific method has been so consistently, extensively, and deductively applied to the interpretation and arrangement of a body of facts as to give them internal intellectual coherence and unity, and obvious external detachment or distinction from other facts. This meaning will be found to apply to such apparently diverse uses as the solar system, the post-office system, the system of Platonic philosophy, the system of

Shakespearean dramas. The term is more nearly allied to "organization" than to any of its congeners, all of which agree with it in connoting some kind of whole made up of parts. Cf. AGGREGATE, CLASSIFICATION, COLLECTIVE, ORGANISM, UNIT, and WHOLE AND PARTS.

TABULA RASA [Lat. *tabula*, tablet, *rasa*, empty]: used also in the other languages. The waxed tablet used by the Romans for writing purposes; used metaphorically to characterize the soul prior to sense-experience; employed to denote the theory of the empiricists, according to which all knowledge is imprinted by objects on a passive blank mind.

Plato used the metaphor of a waxed tablet, κήρινον ἐκμαγεῖον (*Theaet.*, 191), in discussing images of memory. Aristotle (*De Anima*, iii. 4) used a metaphor of a piece of writing paper to express the relation of potential to actual reason. This was erroneously used (as by Leibnitz) to make him the author of the *tabula rasa* theory. This was really first stated by the Stoics. Descartes used the phrase, but only ironically and incidentally. Leibnitz, in criticizing Locke's *Essay upon Human Understanding*, uses the phrase continually and technically, and from him it gained general currency as a summary view of the empirical theory (*New Essays*, Introduction). Locke himself does not use the phrase, though he speaks of the mind as a piece of white paper (*Essay upon Human Understanding*, Bk. II. chap. i. § 2), and employs constantly the metaphor of "imprinting" sensations upon the mind.

THOMISM: Ger. *Lehre des Thomas von Aquino*; Fr. *le Thomisme*; Ital. *il Tomismo*.

The Thomists were originally called Albertists, after the teacher of St. Thomas, ALBERTUS MAGNUS (q.v.). At first the Dominican Order took St. Thomas for their official philosopher. It was opposed by the Franciscan, which followed Alexander and Bonaventura. As the Nominalists were opposed to Thomism, and as the former came under the ban of the Church, there was a growing tendency for Thomism to become more and more the orthodox philosophy of the Church. It has received a notable revival in our own generation from the peculiar interest taken in it by Pope Leo XIII.

TRANSCENDENT (-AL): Ger. *transzendent* (*-al*); Fr. *transcendant* (*-al*); Ital. *trascendente* (*-ale*). (1) In scholastic thought, transcendent and transcendental were equivalent, and were applied to terms or notions higher than the CATEGORIES (q.v.) of Aristotle, and comprehending the latter. (The conception of the secondary character of the categories is due to Neo-Platonism.) Such concepts are *ens, unum, verum, bonum,* and afterwards *res* and *aliquid.*

(2) Kant distinguishes between transcendent and transcendental (though he is not always true to his formal definition). *Transcendent* applies to whatever lies beyond the realm of experience and of knowledge; the transcendent use of concepts is the illegitimate extension of concepts, valid within experience, to what is beyond experience—as the use of the concept of causality with reference to God. This term accordingly has a bad sense. *Transcendental,* on the contrary, is used in a good sense. It is applied to the *a priori* and necessary factors in experience; it accordingly does not go beyond experience, but beyond the empirically given factors of experience.

(3) Transcendent is opposed to immanent. See TRANSCENDENCE (in theology). (This is a connecting link with sense (2). Kant opposes the immanent use of his transcendental principles, remaining within the limits of experience, to the transcendent which goes beyond.) It is particularly used in religious philosophy as defining the relation of God to the world; the transcendent theory (first clearly formulated by Aristotle) holding to the existence of God external to the universe, the immanent theory holding to the presence of God in the world (cf. PANTHEISM). See Eucken, *Fundamental Concepts,* 92–4; Vaihinger, *Commentar zu Kant,* i. 83–4, 467–76.

According to Prantl (*Gesch. d. Logik,* iii. 245), we owe to a pseudo-Thomas the term *transcendentia* to express the four highest concepts, and also the addition of the two new ones (*res* and *aliquid*), probably under Arabian influence. According to Prantl still further, St. Thomas Aquinas was influenced by the mystic *De Causis,* of Arabian origin, which attempted a Neo-Platonic derivation of the universals. St. Thomas avoided its pantheistic character, however, by giving them a theological cast—*ens* belongs to essence as such, *unum* to the Father, *verum* to the Son, and *bonum* to the Holy Spirit (*Gesch. d. Logik*, iii. 8–9, 114). Before this time the phrase "transcendental terms" was used of the letters in the syllogistic figures, as signifying "nothing and everything," and as being "without matter."

TRANSCENDENTALISM: Ger. *Transzendentalismus*; Fr. *transcendantalisme*; Ital. *trascendentalismo*. (1) The philosophy of the TRANSCENDENTAL (q.v., 2) in the Kantian sense. An explanation of the possibility of an *a priori* knowledge of objects, together with a systematic inventory of the concepts which may thus be applied, and of the principles which result from their application under proper conditions.

(2) Kant's successors attempted (through the elimination or transformation of the Kantian thing-in-itself) to unify the ultimate subject and object of knowledge, and thereby to give complete and not merely phenomenal value to the concepts of absolute or pure thought. This did away with the Kantian distinction of transcendent and transcendental; and transcendentalism comes to mean any theory asserting the dependence of the world upon the activity of reason, provided a systematic attempt is made (as in Fichte's *Wissenschaftslehre* and Hegel's *Logik*) to give a methodic development of reason into the particular categories that constitute the world of experience.

(3) In a loose sense, any philosophy which emphasizes the intuitive, spiritual, and supersensuous; any mode of thought which is aggressively non-empirical or anti-empirical. Thus we hear of the transcendentalism of Emerson, etc.

TRANSIENT [Lat. *trans* + *ire*, to go]: Ger. *transgredient*; Fr. (2) *transitif*; Ital. (2) *transeunte*. (1) Transient, in its earlier use, is the equivalent of the post-Kantian term TRANSCENDENT (q.v.), as opposed to immanent.

(2) As applied to activity or causes, see reference under TRANSEUNT.

Aristotle distinguished πράττειν (doing) from ποιεῖν (making), the former denoting an activity expended upon itself, the latter upon bringing into effect some modification of an external existence. Conduct fell into the former sphere, art into the latter. The scholastics regularly distinguished between *causa* or *actio transiens* and *causa* or *actio immanens*. Thus St. Thomas Aquinas says *actio* is twofold; *transiens*, which goes forth into external material (to heat, to dry), and that which remains in the agent, as thinking, feeling, willing. See Eucken, *Grundbegriffe der Gegenwart*, 292 and note.

TYCHISM [Gr. τύχη, chance]: not in use in the other languages. A term introduced by C. S. Peirce to denote the theories which give to chance an objective existence in the universe, instead of regarding it as due to our lack of knowledge; a theory which gives both chance and necessity share in the process of evolution.

"The mere proposition that absolute chance . . . is operative in the cosmos may receive the name of *tychism*." Evolution by fortuitous variation he calls tychasm, and the theory that regards this as of principal importance tychasticism (*Monist,* iii. 188). The term appears to be first used (*Monist,* ii. 533) as follows: "I endeavored to show what ideas ought to form the warp of a system of philosophy, and particularly emphasised that of absolute chance. In the number for April, 1892, I argued further in favor of that way of thinking, which it will be convenient to christen *tychism* (from τύχη, chance)."

UBICATION [Lat. *ubicatio*, from *ubi*, where]: Ger. and Fr. the same; Ital. *ubicazione*. A term of scholastic philosophy to express the placing of an entity.

It includes minds in its reference as well as bodies; in the former sense it signifies the point where mind is regarded as acting on body. See Harper, *The Metaphysics of the School*, 413–4.

UNDERSTANDING AND REASON: Ger. *Verstand und Vernunft*; Fr. *entendement et raison*; Ital. *intendimento e ragione*. This pair of correlative terms is used to distinguish two forms of knowledge, one of which, UNDERSTANDING (q.v.), is discursive, and hence based on premises and hypotheses themselves not subjected to reflection, while the other, REASON (q.v.) apprehends in one immediate act the whole system, both premise and inference, and thus has complete or unconditioned validity.

Accordingly, to those who hold to this distinction, the understanding is the instrument of scientific knowledge, the reason the instrument of philosophic. The need of the distinction was felt as early as Plato. He defines the comprehensive and self-sufficing knowledge as νόησις (see NOUS); the conditional as διάνοια—reflective, "knowing through" another, and hence mediate (ἐπιστήμη is used differently, sometimes as including both; sometimes as reflective or mediate; sometimes as original and intuitive). Aristotle uses the term νόησις in the same sense, with a more technical consideration of the axiomatic or self-evident. For mediate knowledge which yet arrives at certainty (as distinct from that of mere probability, δόξα, OPINION, q.v.), he uses the term τέχνη (this is empirical knowledge, plus a knowledge of its reason or ground. As pointed out by Erdmann, *Hist. of Philos.*, i. 134, the use of this term meaning also "art," as against the διάνοια of Plato, is due to the fact that mathematics is its type to Plato, while to Aristotle it is trained skill, like that of the physician. It is experience rationalized).

The Neo-Platonic thinkers, here as elsewhere, multiply distinctions; but, in essence, they are true to Plato. Scholasticism keeps the ideas, and derives its terms from Boethius (Eucken, *Philos. Terminol.*, 59). *Intellectus* is synonymous with *noesis*, and *ratio* with reflective knowledge. (Hence the ambiguity of "reason" in English: meaning often reason*ing*, or reflective thought, and less often intuitive and certain knowledge; *raison* in French is so filled with the concept of logical process that it is hardly fit at all to translate the German Vernunft.) But the significance of the modern distinction is due to Kant. The understanding is thought working according to the schematized categories, and so having validity in relation to experience; reason is thought working without reference to the application of concepts to the material of sense, hence soaring into the supersensuous, and so, while giving us certain ideals of a regulative value, sharing no positive (or constitutive) worth. Coleridge made much of the distinction in English, but without any regard to Kant's careful and critical limitations. Hegel developed the ideas so that reason should express a knowledge which is immediate in certainty and grasp, but the result of the development of the understanding to its full implications (*Lesser Logic*, chap. vi). See SPECULATION. He seems to follow Nicholas of Cusa, who defines understanding as distinguishing and name-giving, separating opposites according to the principle of contradiction, and reason as that which recognizes the compatibility of opposites.

UNIFICATION OF KNOWLEDGE: not in use in other languages. A phrase used by Herbert Spencer to define philosophy. He distinguishes three stages of knowledge. The first is ordinary unscientific knowledge, in which each fact stands detached and unconnected. It is ununified. Science generalizes related truths of various departments, but does not attempt to bring these generalizations into a single whole. It is partially unified knowledge. "The truth of philosophy bears the same relation to the highest scientific truths that each of these bears to lower scientific truths. . . . It is completely-unified knowledge." That is, it takes the generalizations of, say, physics, psychology, and sociology, and reduces them to special cases of a still more general law. In Spencer's theory this highest generalization, through which knowledge is completely unified, is that of evolution and dissolution considered as the formula of the redistribution of matter and motion, and derived from the persistence of force (*First Princ.*, Pt. II. chap. i; see also Guthrie, *On Spencer's Unification of Knowledge*).

UNITARIANISM [Lat. *unus*, one]: Ger. *Unitarianismus*; Fr. *unitarianisme*; Ital. *unitarianismo*. A term used by Sir William Hamilton alone (*Lects. on Met.*, i. 295) as equivalent to monism. One who denies dualism in favor of either mind or matter as the sole reality is a unitarian.

UNITY (and PLURALITY) [Lat. *unitas*, oneness]: Ger. *Einheit* (and *Mehrheit*); Fr. *unité* (and *pluralité*); Ital. *unità* (and *pluralità*). Formally, unity means whatever exists, or is considered, as a single, indivisible reality, and by whose repetition composite beings, or through whose agency derived beings, exist.

Aesthetic unity: singleness or congruousness of effect immediately produced through sensuous presentation.

Formal and *material unity*: scholastic terms, derived from Aristotle. Material unity is that which pertains to an individual as such, and which cannot be abstracted even in thought from the individual; the material unity of Socrates is just that which constitutes him Socrates. Formal unity is that which pertains to an individual in such a way as to be distinguishable from his individuality; the humanity of Socrates can be conceived apart from Socrates, and as such constitutes a formal unity. Cf. IDENTITY (formal, and material).

Functional unity: a unity which consists not in the composition of elements or parts of structure as such, but in the conspiring or working together of these various parts—a unity of value effected—also termed teleological unity. The term ideal unity properly has the same meaning.

Logical unity: that which is constituted by the mutual support given to one another by the various terms and propositions of reasoning in the process of establishing a conclusion.

Metaphysical unity: that whose identity is inherent, having within itself a principle of being or action which makes it essentially distinct from all other beings.

Moral unity: that which is produced by a variety of factors cooperating intentionally, and under the control of some consciously regulating principle, to bring about a particular result; in this sense the state, as well as the person may be a moral unity.

Numerical unity: that the identity of which is external, rather than intrinsic; whatever is sufficiently marked off or separate from other things to be counted as one; also termed physical or mechanical unity. Cf. NUMBER (different topics).

Organic unity: a unity which is constituted in and through diversity, since it requires a manifold of parts or members which are mutually dependent upon one another; opposed to a mechanical unity or unity of an aggregate in which every part is so homogeneous with the other parts and with the whole as to be capable of being itself a unity, which in quality (though not in quantity) is regarded as the same as the original unit. Cf. ORGANISM.

The Kantian philosophy also supplies a number of technical distinctions (see KANTIAN TERMINOLOGY,—especially the synthetic or transcendental unity of apperception—and above).

We owe most of the main distinctions to Aristotle, who differentiated absolute and relative unity; the former being continuous and indivisible within itself, the latter complex and diversified, as of an orchestra. Unity proper he subdivided into four forms: first, that of continuity, not due to contact; second, natural unity of form and figure—that is, original, not due to violence or external force; third, individual, that which is numerically distinct; fourth, unity of the universal, that constituted by thought as present in a variety of objects—practically equivalent to the formal unity of the Scholastics.

But the philosophic interest of the idea of unity cannot be gathered from any cluster of formal definitions or distinctions. It attaches to the content of the idea. All philosophy is a search for unity, or, if this cannot be found, for unities; and it is the nature and quality ascribed to unity or unities, together with the reasons given for selecting it as such, that constitute the true philosophic history of the term. See MONISM, MONADS, PLURALISM, ONE AND MANY.

Moreover, *unum* was with the Scholastics one of the three ultimate predicates of being, and it was an axiom of philosophy that every real being is unity, and every true (not artificial) unity is being. Hence the standard and definition of unity and substance are the same. See SUBSTANCE, and TRANSCENDENT. The whole question of the philosophic ground of mathematics (on the side of arithmetic and algebra) is connected with the question of unity.

UNIVERSAL (and UNIVERSALITY) [Lat. *universalis*, pertaining to all]: Ger. *allgemein*; Fr. *universel*; Ital. *universale*. (1) This word was used in the Middle Ages where we should now use the word GENERAL (q.v.). Another synonym was praedicabile: "Praedicabile est quod aptum natum est praedicari de pluribus," says Petrus Hispanus. Albertus Magnus says, "Universale est quod cum sit in uno aptum natum est esse in pluribus." Burgersdicius, literally translating from Aristotle, says, "Universale (τὸ καθ ὅλου) appello, quod de pluribus suapte natura praedicari aptum est," i.e. ὃ ἐπὶ πλειόνων πέφυκε κατηγορεῖσθαι. When the Scholastics talk of universals, they merely mean general terms (which are said to be *simple universals*), with the exception here following.

(2) The five terms of second intention, or more accurately the five classes of predicates, *genus, species, difference, property, accident*, were in the Middle Ages (as they still are) called "the predicables." But since predicable also means fit to be a predicate, in which sense it is almost an exact synonym of universal in the first sense, the five predicables came to be often referred to as "the universals."

(3) Predicated, or asserted, in a proposition *de omni*; said to be true, without exception, whatever there may be of which the subject term is predicable. See QUANTITY (in logic). . . . (C. S. P.)

(4) The logical use (3) passes easily into the metaphysical. Provided the common attribute is regarded as important or essential, provided it is regarded as constituting a "natural" genus or class, it expresses the *essence* of the thing under consideration—its permanent and abiding reality as distinct from transitory accidents. But since this essence is also what is *common* to a number of individuals, the class itself taken as an objective whole is regarded as a universal. When a predicate of this sort is applied to a subject, it expresses not merely an empirical, but a necessary, application to the whole of the subject-matter; the relationship ceases to be simply a quantitative one, and becomes qualitative or essential; e.g. "All swans are white" would be a quantitative universal judgment, and so empirical. But "all events must have a cause" is a qualitative universal—it is the "essence" of an event to be caused. Now mediaeval thought was thus led to identify the universalia or generic notions with essences and with classes. Thus arose the discussion regarding the relation of universals to individual things (see REALISM, I). Cf. ABSTRACT IDEAS.

(5) Aristotle had illustrated the common as the basis of a "natural" class, by the common strain in various members of a family—those of common descent. This aspect of the term tends to identify the universal not merely with the static qualities or essence, but with the productive force— the generic is the generative—by which numerically distinct individuals are really connected with one another. This meaning presents a picture of what is meant by the objective reality of a universal. With modern science and the growth of the conception of force, causation, and the tendency to define (as in geometry) by reference to mode of production, this dynamic sense got the upper hand of the static. It is used in this sense in the school of Hegel to mean the general which, as function or activity, exists only in the specific differences to which it determines itself.

UNIVERSAL POSTULATE: no foreign equivalents in use. The term is used as a technical one by Spencer, to denote the "inconceivableness of the negative" of any proposition as the supreme test of the necessary coexistence of a given subject and predicate. It has psychological necessity— the necessity of thinking the proposition in such and such a way; and also logical—the reason for holding it valid. This criterion is in effect nothing but the criterion of RATIONALISM (q.v.) as stated by Leibnitz—the impossibility of the opposite. As such, it was shown by Kant to be applicable only to "analytic judgments." Cf. TESTS OF TRUTH.

UNIVERSE [Lat. *unus*, one, + *vertere*, to turn]: Ger. *Weltall, All*; Fr. *univers*; Ital. *universo*. The term is often used as synonymous with WORLD (q.v.), but is distinguished from it by the idea of completeness, all-inclusiveness.

So the German Weltall is distinguished from Welt. It, rather than world, is the equivalent of the Latin MUNDUS (q.v.). It is sometimes restricted to the entire created system, but is also used, like the Greek one-and-all (ἕν καὶ τὸ πᾶν), to include God as well. In this last sense it is equivalent to nature as used by Spinoza. It is also used in logic to denote the subject or topic taken as a whole—the UNIVERSE (q.v.) of discourse.

UNKNOWABLE (the) [Lat. *in + gnoscere*, to know]: Ger. *das Unerkennbare*; Fr. *l'inconnaissable, ce qu'on ne peut connaître*; Ital. *l'inconoscibile*. That which is not and cannot be known; that whose nature is such as to transcend or defy apprehension by any of the processes by which mind apprehends its objects.   (J.D.—J.M.B.)

The existence of something unknowable is postulated from two different standpoints, one of which (roughly speaking) is that of ancient, the other that of modern thought. In the ancient view it is the essential nature and dignity of being which renders it unknowable; mind and knowledge are derivatives from the absolute reality which accordingly remains ineffably above them. Indeed, this absolute reality is the source of being which it also transcends. It is above distinctions of being and non-being as well as of knowledge and ignorance. This is the attitude of the Neo-Platonists. In modern thought the assumption of the existence of the unknowable is a consequence of the limitations of the faculty of knowledge. Kant, with his thing-in-itself contrasted with the phenomenon; Spencer, with his absolute contrasted with the related; and v. Hartmann, with his identification of the absolute with the unconscious, are the typical representatives of modern conceptions of the unknowable. Such theories differ from those of the agnostics and positivists in that the assertion of the absolute reality as unknowable is an integral part of the system, while in agnosticism and positivism it is a matter of pure indifference whether there be such hyperphenomenal existences or not. They differ from phenomenalism in that the latter positively deny any such unknowable entity behind the knowable congeries of facts and series of events.

UNTHINKABLE (the) [for derivation see THOUGHT]: Ger. (*das*) *Undenkbare*; Fr. (*l'*)*inconcevable*, (*l'*)*impensable*; Ital. (*l'*)*impensabile*. As a technical term the word grows out of Sir William Hamilton's philosophy of the conditioned, especially as developed by Mansel, and borrowed by Herbert Spencer. According to his theory to think is to relate, or to condition. Hence anything which is absolute, or infinite, or unconditioned is, of necessity, unthinkable. It is inconceivable, and hence can be neither affirmed nor denied (Hamilton, *Discussions*, 13–16).

VACUUM [Lat. *vacuus*, empty]: Ger. (*das*) *Leere*; Fr. (*le*) *vide*; Ital. (*il*) *vacuo*, (*il*) *vuoto*. The condition of empty space; space unfilled by matter. Cf. PLENUM, and SPACE.

The concepts of the full (plenum) and the empty (vacuum or void) originated very early in the cosmology of Pre-Socratic philosophy. The Pythagoreans had asserted the existence of empty space beyond the confines of the world (Zeller, *Pre-Socratic Philos.*, i. 408–69, Eng. trans.). This was necessary in order that there might be movement, since to make room for bodies in motion something would have to be pushed outside the world; it was also necessary to account for the possibility of condensation and rarefaction; also to divide things (even numbers) from one another (i.e. if everything was a plenum there would be of necessity complete homogeneity and no distinction). At the same time, in accordance with the highly realistic character of Pre-Socratic philosophy, empty space was identified with air. Parmenides easily recognizes that air is, and, since it is Being, cannot be regarded as NON-BEING (q.v.), which the void would be. Hence everything is full, and accordingly one and homogeneous and at rest—thus admitting that the Pythagorean assertion of the void as necessary for motion and for distinction and plurality is valid (Zeller, *Pre-Socratic Philos.*, i. 506, 633–6). The Atomists accordingly take up the opposite pole of the argument, and in asserting the multiplicity of distinct and moving atoms, assert also the existence of an empty space (τὸ κενόν) which separates them and in which they can move about (Zeller, *Pre-Socratic Philos.*, ii. 210–20). Empedocles, on the contrary, denied the existence of a vacuum, but supposed that the qualitatively different elements had pores in them, so that the elements are able to mix with one another indefinitely and thus produce the appearance of change and of indefinite variety. Anaxagoras attempts by a more thorough-going qualitative mixture of beings to deny the void and yet uphold change and distinction. Plato arrives at the abstract generalization of pure or empty space, which is Non-being, and as the void, the all-receptive ($\pi\alpha\nu\delta\epsilon\chi\acute{\epsilon}s$) background of the creative energy, which, through being first distinguished into geometrical figures, becomes the framework of the physical world (Zeller, *Plato*, 305–7, Eng. trans.). In the existent physical world there is no void, for the spherical limit of the universe, being continuous, holds all within pressed together (*Timaeus*, 58–60), so that as to nature Plato agrees with Empedocles and Anaxagoras, while returning to the Pythagoreans to get a metaphysical empty space. (This conception of it as correlative to geometry, and thus the mean term between the physical and mathematical, was largely influential in displacing the physico-metaphysical conception of the vacuum by the mathematico-metaphysical conception of pure SPACE, q.v.) Aristotle undertakes an explicit and extensive refutation of the atomic theory of the vacuum: according to him space is the limit of the including body with reference to the included; and hence, of course, where there is no body there can be no space. Specially ingenious is his statement (against the Atomists) that not the plenum but the void is incompatible with motion. The void would be absolutely homogeneous in all directions, without distinctions of place, and there would be in it, therefore, nothing which could give a body any definite movement (which implies place) and nothing to bring a body ever to rest (Zeller, *Gesch. d. griech. Philos.*, ii. 399–401). Strato agreed with Aristotle in his polemic against the Atomists, but still asserted the void as necessary to account for certain phenomena of light and heat. Outside the world, however, there is no empty space. The Stoics reversed this position. Space within the world is simply the limits of bodies, or the distance between the limits of a body; but beyond the world there exists an absolutely empty and infinite space. After this time, the conception is best treated in connection with that of space, save to remark that Descartes, by identifying matter with extension, reduced the conception of the vacuum to a self-contradictory absurdity. In general, it may be remarked that the conflict regarding plenum and void is part of the larger conflict between a mathematical-logical construction of nature which tends to identify space with the ultimate basis of the material (as Plato and Descartes), and a mechanico-physical one, like Atomism; or, logically, it has to do with the relation of the discrete and continuous; metaphysically, with the question of the finite and infinite.

WORLD [AS. *wer*, man, + *eald*, akin to old, the age of a man, generation]: Ger. *Welt*; Fr. *monde*; Ital. *mondo*. Any sphere or domain of existence, or even of subjective experience, regarded as a relatively self-included whole.

When used without qualification it generally means the physical realm, nature, especially that part which is nearest man—the earth or globe. It is extended, however, to include the whole universe taken as an object; and, when used with qualifying terms, to mean any object or system of objects as material of inquiry, discussion, or reflection; as the world of nature and man, world of art, of spirit: a realm or sphere, whether physical or intellectual, constituting, for the purpose in hand, a single unified content. See COSMOS, MUNDUS, NATURE, and UNIVERSE (2).

The Child and the Curriculum

Profound differences in theory are never gratuitous or invented. They grow out of conflicting elements in a genuine problem—a problem which is genuine just because the elements, taken as they stand, are conflicting. Any significant problem involves conditions that for the moment contradict each other. Solution comes only by getting away from the meaning of terms that is already fixed upon and coming to see the conditions from another point of view, and hence in a fresh light. But this reconstruction means travail of thought. Easier than thinking with surrender of already formed ideas and detachment from facts already learned, is just to stick by what is already said, looking about for something with which to buttress it against attack.

Thus sects arise; schools of opinion. Each selects that set of conditions that appeal to it; and then erects them into a complete and independent truth, instead of treating them as a factor in a problem, needing adjustment.

The fundamental factors in the educative process are an immature, undeveloped being; and certain social aims, meanings, values incarnate in the matured experience of the adult. The educative process is the due interaction of these forces. Such a conception of each in relation to the other as facilitates completest and freest interaction is the essence of educational theory.

But here comes the effort of thought. It is easier to see the conditions in their separateness, to insist upon one at the expense of the other, to make antagonists of them, than to discover a reality to which each belongs. The easy thing is to seize upon something in the nature of the child, or upon something in the developed consciousness of the adult, and insist upon *that* as the key to the whole problem. When this happens a really serious practical problem—that of inter-action—is transformed into an unreal, and hence insoluble, theoretic problem. Instead of seeing the educative steadily and as a whole, we see conflicting terms. We get the case of the child *vs.* the curriculum; of the individual nature *vs.* social culture. Below all other divisions in pedagogic opinion lies this opposition.

The child lives in a somewhat narrow world of personal contacts. Things hardly come within his experience unless they touch, intimately and obviously, his own well-being, or that of his family and friends. His world is a world of persons with their personal interests, rather than a realm of facts and laws. Not truth, in the sense of conformity to external fact, but affection and sympathy, is its keynote. As against this, the course of study met in the school presents material stretching back indefinitely in time, and extending outward indefinitely into space. The child is taken out of his familiar physical environment, hardly more than a square mile or so in area, into the wide world—yes, and even to the bounds of the solar system. His little span of personal memory and tradition is overlaid with the long centuries of the history of all peoples.

Again, the child's life is an integral, a total one. He passes quickly and readily from one topic to another, as from one spot to another, but is not conscious of transition or break. There is no conscious isolation, hardly conscious distinction. The things that occupy him are held together by the unity of the personal and social interests which his life carries along. Whatever is uppermost in his mind constitutes to him, for the time being, the whole universe. That universe is fluid and fluent; its contents dissolve and re-form with amazing rapidity. But, after all, it is the child's own world. It has the unity and completeness of his own life. He goes to school, and various studies divide and fractionize the world for him. Geography selects, it abstracts and analyzes one set of facts, and from one particular point of view. Arithmetic is another division, grammar another department, and so on indefinitely.

Again, in school each of these subjects is classified. Facts are torn away from their original place in experience and rearranged with reference to some general principle. Classification is not a matter of child experience; things do not come to the individual pigeon-holed. The vital ties of affection, the connecting bonds of activity, hold together the variety of his personal experiences. The adult mind is so familiar with the notion of logically ordered facts that it does not recognize—it cannot realize—the amount of separating and reformulating which the facts of direct experience have to undergo before they can appear as a "study," or branch of learning. A principle, for the intellect, has had to be distinguished and defined; facts have had to be interpreted in relation to this principle, not as they are in themselves. They have had to be regathered about a new centre which is wholly abstract and ideal. All this means a development of a special intellectual interest. It means ability to view facts impartially and objectively; that is, without reference to their place and meaning in one's own experience. It means capacity to analyze and to synthesize. It means highly matured intellectual habits and the command of a definite technique and apparatus of scientific inquiry. The studies as classified are the product, in a word, of the science of the ages, not of the experience of the child.

These apparent deviations and differences between child and curriculum might be almost indefinitely widened. But we have here sufficiently fundamental divergences: first, the narrow but personal world of the child against the impersonal but infinitely extended world of space and time; second, the unity, the single whole-heartedness of the child's life, and the specializations and divisions of the curriculum; third, an abstract principle of logical classification and arrangement, and the practical and emotional bonds of child life.

From these elements of conflict grow up different educational sects. One school fixes its attention upon the importance of the subject-matter of the curriculum as compared with the contents of the child's own experience. It is as if they said: Is life petty, narrow, and crude? Then studies reveal the great, wide universe with all its fullness and complexity of meaning. Is the life of the child egoistic, self-centered, impulsive? Then in these studies is found an objective universe of truth, law, and order. Is his experience confused, vague, uncertain, at the mercy of the moment's caprice and circumstance? Then studies introduce a world arranged on the basis of eternal and general truth; a world where all is measured and defined. Hence the moral: ignore and minimize the child's individual peculiarities, whims, and experiences. They are what we need to get away from. They are to be obscured or eliminated. As educators our work is precisely to substitute for these superficial and casual affairs stable and well-ordered realities; and these are found in studies and lessons.

Subdivide each topic into studies; each study into lessons; each lesson into specific facts and formulae. Let the child proceed step by step to master each one of these separate parts, and at last he will have covered the entire ground. The road which looks so long when viewed in its entirety, is easily traveled, considered as a series of particular steps. Thus emphasis is put upon the logical subdivisions and consecutions of the subject-matter. Problems of instruction are problems of procuring texts giving logical parts and sequences, and of presenting these portions in class in a similar definite and graded way. Subject-matter furnishes the end, and it determines method. The child is simply the immature being who is to be matured; he is the superficial being who is to be deepened; his is narrow experience which is to be widened. It is his to receive, to accept. His part is fulfilled when he is ductile and docile.

Not so, says the other sect. The child is the starting-point, the centre, and the end. His development, his growth, is the ideal. It alone furnishes the standard. To the growth of the child all studies are subservient; they are instruments valued as they serve the needs of growth. Personality, character, is more than subject-matter. Not knowledge or information, but self-realization, is the goal. To possess all the world of knowledge and lose one's own self is as awful a fate in education as in religion. Moreover, subject-matter never can be got into the child from without. Learning is active. It involves reaching out of the mind. It involves organic assimilation starting from within. Literally, we must take our stand with the child and our departure from him. It is he and not the subject-matter which determines both quality and quantity of learning.

The only significant method is the method of the mind as it reaches out and assimilates. Subject-matter is but spiritual food, possible nutritive material. It cannot digest itself; it cannot of its own accord turn into bone and muscle and blood. The source of whatever is dead, mechanical, and formal in schools is found precisely in the subordination of the life and experience of the child to the curriculum. It is because of this that "study" has become a synonym for what is irksome, and a lesson identical with a task.

This fundamental opposition of child and curriculum set up by these two modes of doctrine can be duplicated in a series of other terms. "Discipline" is the watchword of those who magnify the course of study; "interest" that of those who blazon "The Child" upon their banner. The standpoint of the former is logical; that of the latter psychological. The first emphasizes the necessity of adequate training and scholarship on the part of the teacher; the latter that of need of sympathy with the child, and knowledge of his natural instincts. "Guidance and control" are the catchwords of one school; "freedom and initiative" of the other. Law is asserted here; spontaneity proclaimed there. The old, the conservation of what has been achieved in the pain and toil of the ages, is dear to the one; the new, change, progress, wins the affection of the other. Inertness and routine, chaos and anarchism, are accusations bandied back and forth. Neglect of the sacred authority of duty is charged by one side, only to be met by counter-charges of suppression of individuality through tyrannical despotism.

Such oppositions are rarely carried to their logical conclusion. Common sense recoils at the extreme character of these results. They are left to theorists, while common sense vibrates back and forward in a maze of inconsistent compromise. The need of getting theory and practical common sense into closer connection suggests a return to our original thesis: that we have here conditions which are necessarily related to each other in the educative process, since this is precisely one of interaction and adjustment.

What, then, is the problem? It is just to get rid of the prejudicial notion that there is some gap in kind (as distinct from degree) between the child's experience and the various forms of subject-matter that make up the course of study. From the side of the child, it is a question of seeing how his experience already contains within itself elements—facts and truths—of just the same sort as those entering into the formulated study; and, what is of more importance, of how it contains within itself the attitudes, the motives, and the interests which have operated in developing and organizing the subject-matter to the plane which it now occupies. From the side of the studies, it is a question of interpreting them as outgrowths of forces operating in the child's life, and of discovering the steps that intervene between the child's present experience and their richer maturity.

Abandon the notion of subject-matter as something fixed and ready-made in itself, outside the child's experience; cease thinking of the child's experience as also something hard and fast; see it as something fluent, embryonic, vital; and we realize that the child and the curriculum are simply two limits which define a single process. Just as two points define a straight line, so the present standpoint of the child and the facts and truths of studies define instruction. It is continuous reconstruction, moving from the child's present experience out into that represented by the organized bodies of truth that we call studies.

On the face of it, the various studies, arithmetic, geography, language, botany, etc., are themselves experience— they are that of the race. They embody the cumulative outcome of the efforts, the strivings, and successes of the human race generation after generation. They present this, not as a mere accumulation, not as a miscellaneous heap of separate bits of experience, but in some organized and systematized way—that is, as reflectively formulated.

Hence, the facts and truths that enter into the child's present experience, and those contained in the subject-matter of studies, are the initial and final terms of one reality. To oppose one to the other is to oppose the infancy and maturity of the same growing life; it is to set the moving tendency and the final result of the same process over against each other; it is to hold that the nature and the destiny of the child war with each other.

If such be the case, the problem of the relation of the

child and the curriculum presents itself in this guise: Of what use, educationally speaking, is it to be able to see the end in the beginning? How does it assist us in dealing with the early stages of growth to be able to anticipate its later phases? The studies, as we have agreed, represent the possibilities of development inherent in the child's immediate crude experience. But, after all, they are not parts of that present and immediate life. Why, then, or how, make account of them?

Asking such a question suggests its own answer. To see the outcome is to know in what direction the present experience is moving, provided it move normally and soundly. The far-away point, which is of no significance to us simply as far away, becomes of huge importance the moment we take it as defining a present direction of movement. Taken in this way it is no remote and distant result to be achieved, but a guiding method in dealing with the present. The systematized and defined experience of the adult mind, in other words, is of value to us in interpreting the child's life as it immediately shows itself, and in passing on to guidance or direction.

Let us look for a moment at these two ideas: interpretation and guidance. The child's present experience is in no way self-explanatory. It is not final, but transitional. It is nothing complete in itself, but just a sign or index of certain growth-tendencies. As long as we confine our gaze to what the child here and now puts forth, we are confused and misled. We cannot read its meaning. Extreme depreciations of the child morally and intellectually, and sentimental idealizations of him, have their root in a common fallacy. Both spring from taking stages of a growth or movement as something cut off and fixed. The first fails to see the promise contained in feelings and deeds which, taken by themselves, are unpromising and repellant; the second fails to see that even the most pleasing and beautiful exhibitions are but signs, and that they begin to spoil and rot the moment they are treated as achievements.

What we need is something which will enable us to interpret, to appraise, the elements in the child's present puttings forth and fallings away, his exhibitions of power and weakness, in the light of some larger growth-process in which they have their place. Only in this way can we discriminate. If we isolate the child's present inclinations, purposes, and experiences from the place they occupy and the part they have to perform in a developing experience, all stand upon the same level; all alike are equally good and equally bad. But in the movement of life different elements stand upon different planes of value. Some of the child's deeds are symptoms of a waning tendency; they are survivals in functioning of an organ which has done its part and is passing out of vital use. To give positive attention to such qualities is to arrest development upon a lower level. It is systematically to maintain a rudimentary phase of growth. Other activities are signs of a culminating power and interest; to them applies the maxim of striking while the iron is hot. As regards them, it is perhaps a matter of now or never. Selected, utilized, emphasized, they may mark a turning-point for good in the child's whole career; neglected, an opportunity goes, never to be recalled. Other acts and feelings are prophetic; they represent the dawning of flickering light that will shine steadily only in the far future. As regards them there is little at present to do but give them fair and full chance, waiting for the future for definite direction.

Just as, upon the whole, it was the weakness of the "old education" that it made invidious comparisons between the immaturity of the child and the maturity of the adult, regarding the former as something to be got away from as soon as possible and as much as possible; so it is the danger of the "new education" that it regard the child's present powers and interests as something finally significant in themselves. In truth, his learnings and achievements are fluid and moving. They change from day to day and from hour to hour.

It will do harm if child-study leave in the popular mind the impression that a child of a given age has a positive equipment of purposes and interests to be cultivated just as they stand. Interests in reality are but attitudes toward possible experiences; they are not achievements; their worth is in the leverage they afford, not in the accomplishment they represent. To take the phenomena presented at a given age as in any way self-explanatory or self-contained is inevitably to result in indulgence and spoiling. Any power, whether of child or adult, is indulged when it is taken on its given and present level in consciousness. Its genuine meaning is in the propulsion it affords toward a higher level. It is just something to do with. Appealing to the interest upon the present plane means excitation; it means playing with a power so as continually to stir it up without directing it toward definite achievement. Continuous initiation, continuous starting of activities that do not arrive, is, for all practical purposes, as bad as the continual repression of initiative in conformity with supposed interests of some more perfect thought or will. It is as if the child were forever tasting and never eating; always having his palate tickled upon the emotional side, but never getting the organic satisfaction that comes only with digestion of food and transformation of it into working power.

As against such a view, the subject-matter of science and history and art serves to reveal the real child to us. We do not know the meaning either of his tendencies or of his performances excepting as we take them as germinating seed, or opening bud, of some fruit to be borne. The whole world of visual nature is all too small an answer to the problem of the meaning of the child's instinct for light and form. The entire science of physics is none too much to interpret adequately to us what is involved in some simple demand of the child for explanation of some casual change that has attracted his attention. The art of Rafael or of Corot is none too much to enable us to value the impulses stirring in the child when he draws and daubs.

So much for the use of the subject-matter in interpretation. Its further employment in direction or guidance is but an expansion of the same thought. To interpret the fact is to see it in its vital movement, to see it in its relation to growth. But to view it as a part of a normal growth is to secure the basis for guiding it. Guidance is not external imposition. *It is freeing the life-process for its own most adequate fulfillment.* What was said about disregard of the child's present experience because of its remoteness from mature experience; and of the sentimental idealization of

the child's naïve caprices and performances, may be repeated here with slightly altered phrase. There are those who
see no alternative between forcing the child from without, or
leaving him entirely alone. Seeing no alternative, some
choose one mode, some another. Both fall into the same
fundamental error. Both fail to see that development is a
definite process, having its own law which can be fulfilled
only when adequate and normal conditions are provided.
Really to interpret the child's present crude impulses in
counting, measuring, and arranging things in rhythmic
series, involves mathematical scholarship—a knowledge of
the mathematical formulae and relations which have, in the
history of the race, grown out of just such crude beginnings.
To see the whole history of development which intervenes between these two terms is simply to see what step the child
needs to take just here and now; to what use he needs to put
his blind impulse in order that it may get clarity and gain
force.

     If, once more, the "old education" tended to ignore the
dynamic quality, the developing force inherent in the child's
present experience, and therefore to assume that direction
and control were just matters of arbitrarily putting the child
in a given path and compelling him to walk there, the "new
education" is in danger of taking the idea of development in
altogether too formal and empty a way. The child is expected to "develop" this or that fact or truth out of his own
mind. He is told to think things out, or work things out for
himself, without being supplied any of the environing conditions which are requisite to start and guide thought.
Nothing can be developed from nothing; nothing but the
crude can be developed out of the crude—and this is what
surely happens when we throw the child back upon his
achieved self as a finality, and invite him to spin new truths
of nature or of conduct out of that. It is certainly as futile
to expect a child to evolve a universe out of his own mere
mind as it is for a philosopher to attempt that task. Development does not mean just getting something out of the
mind. It is a development of experience and into experience
that is really wanted. And this is impossible save as just
that educative medium is provided which will enable the

powers and interests that have been selected as valuable to function. They must operate, and how they operate will depend almost entirely upon the stimuli which surround them, and the material upon which they exercise themselves. The problem of direction is thus the problem of selecting appropriate stimuli for instincts and impulses which it is desired to employ in the gaining of new experience. What new experiences are desirable, and thus what stimuli are needed, it is impossible to tell except as there is some comprehension of the development which is aimed at; except, in a word, as the adult knowledge is drawn upon as revealing the possible career open to the child.

It may be of use to distinguish and to relate to each other the logical and the psychological aspects of experience —the former standing for subject-matter in itself, the latter for it in relation to the child. A psychological statement of experience follows its actual growth; it is historic; it notes steps actually taken, the uncertain and tortuous, as well as the efficient and successful. The logical point of view, on the other hand, assumes that the development has reached a certain positive stage of fulfillment. It neglects the process and considers the outcome. It summarizes and arranges, and thus separates the achieved results from the actual steps by which they were forthcoming in the first instance. We may compare the difference between the logical and the psychological to the difference between the notes which an explorer makes in a new country, blazing a trail and finding his way along as best he may, and the finished map that is constructed after the country has been thoroughly explored. The two are mutually dependent. Without the more or less accidental and devious paths traced by the explorer there would be no facts which could be utilized in the making of the complete and related chart. But no one would get the benefit of the explorer's trip if it was not compared and checked up with similar wanderings undertaken by others; unless the new geographical facts learned, the streams crossed, the mountains climbed, etc., were viewed, not as mere incidents in the journey of the particular traveler, but (quite apart from the individual explorer's life) in relation to other similar facts already known. The map orders in-

dividual experiences, connecting them with one another irrespective of the local and temporal circumstances and
accidents of their original discovery.

Of what use is this formulated statement of experience?
Of what use is the map?

Well, we may first tell what the map is not. The map is
not a substitute for a personal experience. The map does not
take the place of an actual journey. The logically formulated
material of a science or branch of learning, of a study, is no
substitute for the having of individual experiences. The
mathematical formula for a falling body does not take the
place of personal contact and immediate individual experience with the falling thing. But the map, a summary, an
arranged and orderly view of previous experiences, serves as
a guide to future experience; it gives direction; it facilitates
control; it economizes effort, preventing useless wandering,
and pointing out the paths which lead most quickly and most
certainly to a desired result. Through the map every new
traveler may get for his own journey the benefits of the
results of others' explorations without the waste of energy
and loss of time involved in their wanderings—wanderings
which he himself would be obliged to repeat were it not for
just the assistance of the objective and generalized record
of their performances. That which we call a science or study
puts the net product of past experience in the form which
makes it most available for the future. It represents a capitalization which may at once be turned to interest. It economizes the workings of the mind in every way. Memory is
less taxed because the facts are grouped together about some
common principle, instead of being connected solely with
the varying incidents of their original discovery. Observation
is assisted; we know what to look for and where to look. It is
the difference between looking for a needle in a haystack,
and searching for a given paper in a well-arranged cabinet.
Reasoning is directed, because there is a certain general
path or line laid out along which ideas naturally march, instead of moving from one chance association to another.

There is, then, nothing final about a logical rendering
of experience. Its value is not contained in itself; its significance is that of standpoint, outlook, method. It intervenes

between the more casual, tentative, and round-about experiences of the past, and more controlled and orderly experiences of the future. It gives past experience in that net form which renders it most available and most significant, most fecund for future experience. The abstractions, generalizations, and classifications which it introduces all have prospective meaning.

The formulated result is then not to be opposed to the process of growth. The logical is not set over against the psychological. The surveyed and arranged result occupies a critical position in the process of growth. It marks a turning-point. It shows how we may get the benefit of past effort in controlling future endeavor. In the largest sense the logical standpoint is itself psychological; it has its meaning as a point in the development of experience, and its justification is in its functioning in the future growth which it insures.

Hence the need of reinstating into experience the sub ject-matter of the studies, or branches of learning. It must be restored to the experience from which it has been abstracted. It needs to be *psychologized*; turned over, translated into the immediate and individual experiencing within which it has its origin and significance.

Every study or subject thus has two aspects: one for the scientist as a scientist; the other for the teacher as a teacher. These two aspects are in no sense opposed or conflicting. But neither are they immediately identical. For the scientist, the subject-matter represents simply a given body of truth to be employed in locating new problems, instituting new researches, and carrying them through to a verified outcome. To him the subject-matter of the science is self-contained. He refers various portions of it to each other; he connects new facts with it. He is not, as a scientist, called upon to travel outside its particular bounds; if he does, it is only to get more facts of the same general sort. The problem of the teacher is a different one. As a teacher he is not concerned with adding new facts to the science he teaches; in propounding new hypotheses or in verifying them. He is concerned with the subject-matter of the science as *representing a given stage and phase of the development of experience*. His problem is that of inducing a vital and personal experiencing. Hence, what concerns him, as teacher, is the ways in which that subject may become a part of experience; what there is in the child's present that is usable with reference to it; how such elements are to be used; how his own knowledge of the subject-matter may assist in interpreting the child's needs and doings, and determine the medium in which the child should be placed in order that his growth may be properly directed. He is concerned, not with the subject-matter as such, but with the subject-matter as a related factor in a total and growing experience. Thus to see it is to psychologize it.

It is the failure to keep in mind the double aspect of subject-matter which causes the curriculum and child to be set over against each other as described in our early pages. The subject-matter, just as it is for the scientist, has no direct relationship to the child's present experience. It stands outside of it. The danger here is not a merely theoretical one. We are practically threatened on all sides. Text-book and teacher vie with each other in presenting to the child the subject-matter as it stands to the specialist. Such modification and revision as it undergoes are a mere elimination of certain scientific difficulties, and the general reduction to a lower intellectual level. The material is not translated into life-terms, but is directly offered as a substitute for, or an external annex to, the child's present life.

Three typical evils result: In the first place, the lack of any organic connection with what the child has already seen and felt and loved makes the material purely formal and symbolic. There is a sense in which it is impossible to value too highly the formal and the symbolic. The genuine form, the real symbol, serve as methods in the holding and discovery of truth. They are tools by which the individual pushes out most surely and widely into unexplored areas. They are means by which he brings to bear whatever of reality he has succeeded in gaining in past searchings. But this happens only when the symbol really symbolizes— when it stands for and sums up in shorthand actual experiences which the individual has already gone through. A symbol which is induced from without, which has not been led up to in preliminary activities, is, as we say, a *bare* or *mere* symbol; it is dead and barren. Now, any fact, whether of arithmetic, or geography, or grammar, which is not led up to and into out of something which has previously occupied a significant position in the child's life for its own sake, is forced into this position. It is not a reality, but just the sign of a reality which *might* be experienced if certain conditions were fulfilled. But the abrupt presentation of the fact as something known by others, and requiring only to be studied and learned by the child, rules out such conditions of fulfillment. It condemns the fact to be a hieroglyph: it would mean something if one only had the key. The clue being lacking, it remains an idle curiosity, to fret and obstruct the mind, a dead weight to burden it.

The second evil in this external presentation is lack of motivation. There are not only no facts or truths which have been previously felt as such with which to appropriate and assimilate the new, but there is no craving, no need, no demand. When the subject-matter has been psychologized, that is, viewed as an outgrowth of present tendencies and activities, it is easy to locate in the present some obstacle, intellectual, practical, or ethical, which can be handled more adequately if the truth in question be mastered. This need supplies motive for the learning. An end which is the child's own carries him on to possess the means of its accomplishment. But when material is directly supplied in the form of a lesson to be learned as a lesson, the connecting links of need and aim are conspicuous for their absence. What we mean by the mechanical and dead in instruction is a result of this lack of motivation. The organic and vital mean interaction—they mean play of mental demand and material supply.

The third evil is that even the most scientific matter, arranged in most logical fashion, loses this quality, when presented in external, ready-made fashion, by the time it gets to the child. It has to undergo some modification in order to shut out some phases too hard to grasp, and to reduce some of the attendant difficulties. What happens? Those things which are most significant to the scientific man, and most valuable in the logic of actual inquiry and classification, drop out. The really thought-provoking character is obscured, and the organizing function disappears. Or, as we commonly say, the child's reasoning powers, the faculty of abstraction and generalization, are not adequately developed. So the subject-matter is evacuated of its logical value, and, though it is what it is only from the logical standpoint, is presented as stuff only for "memory." This is the contradiction: the child gets the advantage neither of the adult logical formulation, nor of his own native competencies of apprehension and response. Hence the logic of the child is hampered and mortified, and we are almost fortunate if he does not get actual non-science, flat and commonplace residua of what was gaining scientific vitality a generation or two ago— degenerate reminiscence of what someone else once formulated on the basis of the experience that some further person had, once upon a time, experienced.

The train of evils does not cease. It is all too common for opposed erroneous theories to play straight into each other's hands. Psychological considerations may be slurred or shoved one side; they cannot be crowded out. Put out of the door, they come back through the window. Somehow and somewhere motive must be appealed to, connection must be established between the mind and its material. There is no question of getting along without this bond of connection; the only question is whether it be such as grows out of the material itself in relation to the mind, or be imported and hitched on from some outside source. If the subject-matter of the lessons be such as to have an appropriate place within the expanding consciousness of the child, if it grows out of his own past doings, thinkings, and sufferings, and grows into application in further achievements and receptivities, then no device or trick of method has to be resorted to in order to enlist "interest." The psychologized *is* of interest— that is, it is placed in the whole of conscious life so that it shares the worth of that life. But the externally presented material, that, conceived and generated in standpoints and attitudes remote from the child, and developed in motives alien to him, has no such place of its own. Hence the recourse to adventitious leverage to push it in, to factitious drill to drive it in, to artificial bribe to lure it in.

Three aspects of this recourse to outside ways for giving

the subject-matter some psychological meaning may be worth mentioning. Familiarity breeds contempt, but it also breeds something like affection. We get used to the chains we wear, and we miss them when removed. 'Tis an old story that through custom we finally embrace what at first wore a hideous mien. Unpleasant, because meaningless, activities may get agreeable if long enough persisted in. *It is possible for the mind to develop interest in a routine or mechanical procedure, if conditions are continually supplied which demand that mode of operation and preclude any other sort.* I frequently hear dulling devices and empty exercises defended and extolled because "the children take such an 'interest' in them." Yes, that is the worst of it; the mind, shut out from worthy employ and missing the taste of adequate performance, comes down to the level of that which is left to it to know and do, and perforce takes an interest in a cabined and cramped experience. To find satisfaction in its own exercise is the normal law of mind, and if large and meaningful business for the mind be denied, it tries to content itself with the formal movements that remain to it—and too often succeeds, save in those cases of more intense activity which cannot accommodate themselves, and that make up the unruly and *declassé* of our school product. An interest in the formal apprehension of symbols and in their memorized reproduction becomes in many pupils a substitute for the original and vital interest in reality; and all because, the subject-matter of the course of study being out of relation to the concrete mind of the individual, some substitute bond to hold it in some kind of working relation to the mind must be discovered and elaborated.

The second substitute for living motivation in the subject-matter is that of contrast-effects; the material of the lesson is rendered interesting, if not in itself, at least in contrast with some alternative experience. To learn the lesson is more interesting than to take a scolding, be held up to general ridicule, stay after school, receive degradingly low marks, or fail to be promoted. And very much of what goes by the name of "discipline," and prides itself upon opposing the doctrines of a soft pedagogy and upon upholding the banner of effort and duty, is nothing more or less than just this appeal to "interest" in its obverse aspect—to fear, to dislike of various kinds of physical, social, and personal pain. The subject-matter does not appeal; it cannot appeal; it lacks origin and bearing in a growing experience. So the appeal is to the thousand and one outside and irrelevant agencies which may serve to throw, by sheer rebuff and rebound, the mind back upon the material from which it is constantly wandering.

Human nature being what it is, however, it tends to seek its motivation in the agreeable rather than in the disagreeable, in direct pleasure rather than in alternative pain. And so has come up the modern theory and practice of the "interesting," in the false sense of that term. The material is still left; so far as its own characteristics are concerned, just material externally selected and formulated. It is still just so much geography and arithmetic and grammar study; not so much potentiality of child-experience with regard to language, earth, and numbered and measured reality. Hence the difficulty of bringing the mind to bear upon it; hence its repulsiveness; the tendency for attention to wander; for other acts and images to crowd in and expel the lesson. The legitimate way out is to transform the material; to psychologize it—that is, once more, to take it and to develop it within the range and scope of the child's life. But it is easier and simpler to leave it as it is, and then by trick of method to *arouse* interest, to *make* it *interesting*; to cover it with sugar-coating; to conceal its barrenness by intermediate and unrelated material; and finally, as it were, to get the child to swallow and digest the unpalatable morsel while he is enjoying tasting something quite different. But alas for the analogy! Mental assimilation is a matter of consciousness; and if the attention has not been playing upon the actual material, that has not been apprehended, nor worked into faculty.

How, then, stands the case of Child *vs.* Curriculum? What shall the verdict be? The radical fallacy in the original pleadings with which we set out is the supposition that we have no choice save either to leave the child to his own unguided spontaneity or to inspire direction upon him from without. Action is response; it is adaptation, adjustment.

There is no such thing as sheer self-activity possible — because all activity takes place in a medium, in a situation, and with reference to its conditions. But, again, no such thing as imposition of truth from without, as insertion of truth from without, is possible. All depends upon the activity which the mind itself undergoes in responding to what is presented from without. Now, the value of the formulated wealth of knowledge that makes up the course of study is that it may enable the educator *to determine the environment of the child*, and thus by indirection to direct. Its primary value, its primary indication, is for the teacher, not for the child. It says to the teacher: Such and such are the capacities, the fulfillments, in truth and beauty and behavior, open to these children. Now see to it that day by day the conditions are such that *their own activities* move inevitably in this direction, toward such culmination of themselves. Let the child's nature fulfill its own destiny, revealed to you in whatever of science and art and industry the world now holds as its own.

The case is of Child. It is his present powers which are to assert themselves; his present capacities which are to be exercised; his present attitudes which are to be realized. But save as the teacher knows, knows wisely and thoroughly, the race experience which is embodied in that thing we call the Curriculum, the teacher knows neither what the present power, capacity, or attitude is, nor yet how it is to be asserted, exercised, and realized.

Studies in Logical Theory

Preface

This volume presents some results of the work done in the matter of logical theory in the Department of Philosophy of the University of Chicago in the first decade of its existence. The eleven Studies are the work of eight different hands, all, with the exception of the editor, having at some period held Fellowships in this University, Dr. Heidel in Greek, the others in Philosophy. Their names and present pursuits are indicated in the Table of Contents. The editor has occasionally, though rarely, added a footnote or phrase which might serve to connect one Study more closely with another. The pages in the discussion of Hypothesis, on Mill and Whewell, are by him.* With these exceptions, each writer is individually and completely responsible for his own Study.

The various Studies present, the editor believes, about the relative amount of agreement and disagreement that is natural in view of the conditions of their origin. The various writers have been in contact with one another in Seminars and lecture courses in pursuit of the same topics, and have had to do with shaping one another's views. There are several others, not represented in this volume, who have also participated in the evolution of the point of view herein set forth, and to whom the writers acknowledge their indebtedness. The disagreements proceed from the diversity of interests with which the different writers approach the logical topic; and from the fact that the point of view in question is still (happily) developing and showing no signs of becoming a closed system.

If the Studies themselves do not give a fair notion of the nature and degree of the harmony in the different writers' methods, a preface is not likely to succeed in so doing. A few words may be in place, however, about a matter re-

* See pp. 368–75, this volume.

peatedly touched upon, but nowhere consecutively elaborated—the more ultimate philosophical bearing of what is
set forth. All agree, the editor takes the liberty of saying,
that judgment is the central function of knowing, and hence
affords the central problem of logic; that since the act of
knowing is intimately and indissolubly connected with the
like yet diverse functions of affection, appreciation, and
practice, it only distorts results reached to treat knowing as
a self-enclosed and self-explanatory whole—hence the intimate connections of logical theory with functional psychology; that since knowledge appears as a function within
experience, and yet passes judgment upon both the processes
and contents of other functions, its work and aim must be
distinctively reconstructive or transformatory; that since
Reality must be defined in terms of experience, judgment
appears accordingly as the medium through which the consciously effected evolution of Reality goes on; that there is
no reasonable standard of truth (or of success of the knowing function) in general, except upon the postulate that
Reality is thus dynamic or self-evolving, and, in particular,
except through reference to the specific offices which knowing is called upon to perform in readjusting and expanding
the means and ends of life. And all agree that this conception
gives the only promising basis upon which the working
methods of science, and the proper demands of the moral
life, may cooperate. All this, doubtless, does not take us very
far on the road to detailed conclusions, but it is better, perhaps, to get started in the right direction than to be so
definite as to erect a dead-wall in the way of farther movement of thought.

In general, the obligations in logical matters of the
writers are roughly commensurate with the direction of their
criticisms. Upon the whole, most is due to those whose views
are most sharply opposed. To Mill, Lotze, Bosanquet, and
Bradley the writers then owe special indebtedness. The
editor acknowledges personal indebtedness to his present colleagues, particularly to Mr. George H. Mead, in the Faculty
of Philosophy, and to a former colleague, Dr. Alfred H. Lloyd,
of the University of Michigan. For both inspiration and the
forging of the tools with which the writers have worked

there is a pre-eminent obligation on the part of all of us to William James, of Harvard University, who, we hope, will accept this acknowledgment and this book as unworthy tokens of a regard and an admiration that are coequal.

No one doubts that thought, at least reflective, as distinct from what is sometimes called constitutive, thought, is
derivative and secondary. It comes after something and out
of something, and for the sake of something. No one doubts
that the thinking of everyday practical life and of science is
of this reflective type. We think about; we reflect over. If
we ask what it is which is primary and radical to thought;
if we ask what is the final objective for the sake of which
thought intervenes; if we ask in what sense we are to understand thought as a derived procedure, we are plunging
ourselves into the very heart of the logical problem: the relation of thought to its empirical antecedents and to its consequent, truth, and the relation of truth to reality.

Yet from the naïve point of view no difficulty attaches
to these questions. The antecedents of thought are our universe of life and love; of appreciation and struggle. We think
about anything and everything: snow on the ground; the
alternating clanks and thuds that rise from below; the relation of the Monroe Doctrine to the embroglio in Venezuela;
the relation of art to industry; the poetic quality of a painting
by Botticelli; the battle of Marathon; the economic interpretation of history; the proper definition of cause; the best
method of reducing expenses; whether and how to renew the
ties of a broken friendship; the interpretation of an equation
in hydrodynamics, etc.

Through the madness of this miscellaneous citation
there appears so much of method: anything—event, act,

[First published as "Thought and Its Subject-Matter: The General Problem of Logical Theory," in *Studies in Logical Theory*,
by John Dewey, with the cooperation of Members and Fellows of
the Department of Philosophy. University of Chicago, The Decennial Publications, Second Series, Vol. XI (Chicago: University of
Chicago Press, 1903). Revised and reprinted in *Essays in Experimental Logic* (Chicago: University of Chicago Press, 1916).]

value, ideal, person, or place—may be an object of thought. Reflection busies itself alike with physical nature, the record of social achievement, and the endeavors of social aspiration. It is with reference to *such* affairs that thought is derivative; it is with reference to them that it intervenes or mediates. Taking some part of the universe of action, of affection, of social construction, under its special charge, and having busied itself therewith sufficiently to meet the special difficulty presented, thought releases that topic and enters into further more direct experience.

Sticking for a moment to this naïve standpoint, we recognize a certain rhythm of direct practice and derived theory; of primary construction and of secondary criticism; of living appreciation and of abstract description; of active endeavor and of pale reflection. We find that every more direct primary attitude passes upon occasion into its secondary deliberative and discursive counterpart. We find that when the latter has done its work it passes away and passes on. From the naïve standpoint such rhythm is taken as a matter of course. There is no attempt either to state the nature of the occasion which demands the thinking attitude, or to formulate a theory of the standard by which is judged its success. No general theory is propounded as to the exact relationship between thinking and what antecedes and succeeds it. Much less do we ask how empirical circumstances can generate rationality of thought; nor how it is possible for reflection to lay claim to power of determining truth and thereby of constructing further reality.

If we were to ask the thinking of naïve life to present, with a minimum of theoretical elaboration, its conception of its own practice, we should get an answer running not unlike this: Thinking is a kind of activity which we perform at specific need, just as at other need we engage in other sorts of activity: as converse with a friend; draw a plan for a house; take a walk; eat a dinner; purchase a suit of clothes, etc. In general, its material is anything in the wide universe which seems to be relevant to this need—anything which may serve as a resource in defining the difficulty or in suggesting modes of dealing effectively with it. The measure of its success, the standard of its validity, is precisely the degree in which the thinking actually disposes of the difficulty and allows us to proceed with more direct modes of experiencing, that are forthwith possessed of more assured and deepened value.

If we inquire why the naïve attitude does not go on to elaborate these implications of its own practice into a systematic theory, the answer, on its own basis, is obvious. Thought arises in response to its own occasion. And this occasion is so exacting that there is time, as there is need, only to do the thinking which is needed in that occasion—not to reflect upon the thinking itself. Reflection follows so naturally upon its appropriate cue, its issue is so obvious, so practical, the entire relationship is so organic, that once grant the position that thought arises in reaction to specific demand, and there is not the particular type of thinking called logical theory because there is not the practical demand for reflection of that sort. Our attention is taken up with particular questions and specific answers. What we have to reckon with is not the problem of, How can I think *überhaupt?* but, How shall I think right *here and now?* Not what is the test of thought at large, but what validates and confirms *this* thought?

In conformity with this view, it follows that a generic account of our thinking behavior, the generic account termed logical theory, arises at historic periods in which the situation has lost the organic character above described. The general theory of reflection, as over against its concrete exercise, appears when occasions for reflection are so overwhelming and so mutually conflicting that specific adequate response in thought is blocked. Again, it shows itself when practical affairs are so multifarious, complicated, and remote from control that thinking is held off from successful passage into them.

Anyhow (sticking to the naïve standpoint), it is true that the stimulus to that particular form of reflective thinking termed logical theory is found when circumstances require the act of thinking and nevertheless impede clear and coherent thinking in detail; or when they occasion thought and then prevent the results of thinking from exercising directive influence upon the immediate concerns of life.

Under these conditions we get such questions as the following: What is the relation of rational thought to crude or unreflective experience? What is the relation of thought to reality? What is the barrier which prevents reason from complete penetration into the world of truth? What is it that makes us live alternately in a concrete world of experience in which thought as such finds not satisfaction, and in a world of ordered thought which is yet only abstract and ideal?

It is not my intention here to pursue the line of historical inquiry thus suggested. Indeed, the point would not be mentioned did it not serve to fix attention upon the nature of the logical problem.

It is in dealing with this latter type of question that logical theory has taken a turn which separates it widely from the theoretical implications of practical deliberation and of scientific research. The two latter, however much they differ from each other in detail, agree in a fundamental principle. They both assume that every reflective problem and operation arises with reference to some *specific* situation, and has to subserve a *specific* purpose dependent upon its own occasion. They assume and observe distinct limits—limits from which and to which. There is the limit of origin in the needs of the particular situation which evokes reflection. There is the limit of terminus in successful dealing with the particular problem presented—or in retiring, baffled, to take up some other question. The query that at once faces us regarding the nature of logical theory is whether reflection upon reflection shall recognize these limits, endeavoring to formulate them more exactly and to define their relationships to each other more adequately; or shall it abolish limits, do away with the matter of specific conditions and specific aims of thought, and discuss thought and its relation to empirical antecedents and rational consequents (truth) at large?

At first blush, it might seem as if the very nature of logical theory as generalization of the reflective process must of necessity disregard the matter of particular conditions and particular results as irrelevant. How, the implication runs, could reflection become generalized save by elimination of

details as irrelevant? Such a conception in fixing the central
problem of logic fixes once for all its future career and
material. The essential business of logic is henceforth to
discuss the relation of thought as such to reality as such. It
may, indeed, involve much psychological material, particularly in the discussion of the processes which antecede thinking and which call it out. It may involve much discussion of
the concrete methods of investigation and verification employed in the various sciences. It may busily concern itself
with the differentiation of various types and forms of
thought—different modes of conceiving, various conforma-
tions of judgment, various types of inferential reasoning. But
it concerns itself with any and all of these three fields, not
on their own account or as ultimate, but as subsidiary to the
main problem: the relation of thought as such, or at large,
to reality as such, or at large. Some of the detailed considerations referred to may throw light upon the terms under
which thought transacts its business with reality; upon, say,
certain peculiar limitations it has to submit to as best it may.
Other considerations throw light upon the ways in which
thought gets at reality. Still other considerations throw light
upon the forms which thought assumes in attacking and
apprehending reality. But in the end all this is incidental. In
the end the one problem holds: How do the specifications of
thought as such hold good of reality as such? In fine, logic is
supposed to grow out of the epistemological inquiry and to
lead up to its solution.

From this point of view various aspects of logical theory
are well stated by an author whom later on we shall consider
in some detail. Lotze[1] refers to "universal forms and principles of thought which hold good everywhere both in judging
of reality and in weighing possibility, *irrespective of any difference in the objects.*" This defines the business of *pure*
logic. This is clearly the question of thought as such—of
thought at large or in general. Then we have the question of
"how far the most complete structure of thought . . . can
claim to be an adequate account of that which we seem
compelled to assume as the object and occasion of our ideas."

---

1. *Logic* (translation, Oxford, 1888), I, 10, 11. Italics mine.

This is clearly the question of the relation of thought at large to reality at large. It is epistemology. Then comes "applied logic," having to do with the actual employment of concrete forms of thought with reference to investigation of specific topics and subjects. This "applied" logic would, if the standpoint of practical deliberation and of scientific research were adopted, be the sole genuine logic. But the existence of thought *in itself* having been agreed upon, we have in this "applied" logic only an incidental inquiry of how the particular resistances and oppositions which "pure" thought meets from particular matters may best be discounted. It is concerned with methods of investigation which obviate defects in the relationship of thought at large to reality at large, as these present themselves under the limitations of human experience. It deals merely with hindrances, and with devices for overcoming them; it is directed by considerations of utility. When we reflect that this field includes the entire procedure of practical deliberation and of concrete scientific research, we begin to realize something of the significance of the theory of logic which regards the limitations of specific origination and specific outcome as irrelevant to its main problem, which assumes an activity of thought "pure" or "in itself," that is, "irrespective of any difference in its objects."

This suggests, by contrast, the opposite mode of stating the problem of logical theory. Generalization of the nature of the reflective process certainly involves elimination of much of the specific material and contents of the thought-situations of daily life and of critical science. Quite compatible with this, however, is the notion that it seizes upon *certain* specific conditions and factors, and aims to bring them to clear consciousness—not to abolish them. While eliminating the particular material of particular practical and scientific pursuits, (1) it may strive to hit upon the common denominator in the various situations which are antecedent or primary to thought and which evoke it; (2) it may attempt to show how typical features in the specific antecedents of thought call out diverse typical modes of thought-reaction; (3) it may attempt to state the nature of the specific consequences in which thought fulfills its career.

(1) It does not eliminate dependence upon specific occasions as provocative of thought, but endeavors to define *what* in the various occasions renders them thought-provoking. The specific occasion is not eliminated, but insisted upon and brought into the foreground. Consequently, empirical considerations are not subsidiary incidents, but are of essential importance so far as they enable us to trace the generation of the thought-situation. (2) From this point of view the various types and modes of conceiving, judging, and inference are treated, not as qualifications of thought *per se* or at large, but of reflection engaged in its specific, most economic, effective response to its own particular occasion; they are adaptations for control of stimuli. The distinctions and classifications that have been accumulated in "formal" logic are relevant data; but they demand interpretation from the standpoint of use as organs of adjustment to material antecedents and stimuli. (3) Finally the question of validity, or ultimate objective of thought, is relevant; but relevant as a matter of the specific issue of the specific career of a thought-function. All the typical investigatory and verificatory procedures of the various sciences indicate the ways in which thought actually brings to successful fulfillment its dealing with various types of problems.

While the epistemological type of logic may, as we have seen, leave (under the name of applied logic) a subsidiary place open for the instrumental type, the type which deals with thinking as a specific procedure relative to a specific antecedent occasion and to a subsequent specific fulfillment is not able to reciprocate the favor. From its point of view, an attempt to discuss the antecedents, data, forms, and objectives of thought, apart from reference to particular position occupied, and particular part played in the growth of experience, is to reach results which are not so much either true or false as they are radically meaningless—because they are considered apart from limits. Its results are not only abstractions (for all theorizing ends in abstractions), but abstractions without possible reference or bearing. From this point of view, the taking of something (whether that something be a thinking activity, its empirical stimulus, or its objective goal), apart from the limits of a historic or de-

veloping situation, is the essence of *metaphysical* procedure—
in that sense of metaphysics which makes a gulf between it
and science.

As the reader has doubtless anticipated, it is the object
of this chapter to present the problem and industry of reflective thought from the standpoint of naïve experience,
using the term in a sense wide enough to cover both practical
procedure and concrete scientific research. I resume by saying that this point of view knows no fixed distinction between the empirical things and values of unreflective life
and the most abstract process of rational thought. It knows
no fixed gulf between the highest flight of theory and a control of the details of practical construction and behavior. It
passes, according to the occasion and opportunity of the
moment, from the attitude of loving and struggling and
doing to that of thinking and the reverse. Its contents or
material shift their values back and forth from technological
or utilitarian to aesthetic, ethical, or affectional. It utilizes
data of perception of meaning or of discursive ideation as
need calls, just as an inventor now utilizes heat, now mechanical strain, now electricity, according to the demands
set by his aim. Anything from past experience may be taken
which appears to be an element in either the statement or
the solution of the present problem. Thus we understand
the coexistence, without contradiction, of an indeterminate
possible field and a limited actual field. The undefined range
of possible materials becomes specific through reference to
an end.

In all this, there is no difference of kind between the
methods of science and those of the plain man. The difference
is the greater control by science of the statement of the
problem, and of the selection and use of relevant material,
both sensible and conceptual. The two are related to each
other just as the hit-or-miss, trial-and-error inventions of
uncivilized man stand to the deliberate and consecutively
persistent efforts of a modern inventor to produce a certain
complicated device for doing a comprehensive piece of work.
Neither the plain man nor the scientific inquirer is aware,
as he engages in his reflective activity, of any transition
from one sphere of existence to another. He knows no two

fixed worlds—reality on one side and mere subjective ideas on the other; he is aware of no gulf to cross. He assumes uninterrupted, free, and fluid passage from ordinary experience to abstract thinking, from thought to fact, from things to theories and back again. Observation passes into development of hypothesis; deductive methods pass into use in description of the particular; inference passes into action, all with no sense of difficulty save those found in the particular task in question. The fundamental assumption is *continuity*.

This does not mean that fact is confused with idea, or observed datum with voluntary hypothesis, theory with doing, any more than a traveler confuses land and water when he journeys from one to the other. It simply means that each is placed and used with reference to service rendered the other, and with reference to the future use of the other.

Only the epistemological spectator of traditional controversies is aware of the fact that the everyday man and the scientific man in this free and easy intercourse are rashly assuming the right to glide over a cleft in the very structure of reality. This fact raises a query not favorable to the epistemologist. Why is it that the scientific man, who is constantly plying his venturous traffic of exchange of facts for ideas, of theories for laws, of real things for hypotheses, should be so wholly unaware of the radical and generic (as distinct from specific) difficulty of the undertakings in which he is engaged? We thus come afresh to our inquiry: Does not the epistemological logician unwittingly transfer the specific difficulty which always faces the scientific man—the difficulty in detail of correct and adequate translation back and forth of *this* set of facts and *this* group of reflective considerations—into a totally different problem of the wholesale relation of thought at large to reality in general? If such be the case, it is clear that the very way in which the epistemological type of logic states the problem of thinking, in relation both to empirical antecedents and to objective truth, makes that problem insoluble. Working terms, terms which as working are flexible and historic, relative and methodological, are transformed into absolute, fixed, and predetermined properties of being.

We come a little closer to the problem when we recognize that every scientific inquiry passes historically through at least four stages. (*a*) The first of these stages is, if I may be allowed the bull, that in which scientific inquiry does not take place at all, because no problem or difficulty in the quality of the experience presents itself to provoke reflection. We have only to cast our eye back from the existing status of any science, or back from the status of any particular topic in any science, to discover a time when no reflective or critical thinking busied itself with the matter—when the facts and relations were taken for granted and thus were lost and absorbed in the net meaning which accrued from the experience. (*b*) After the dawning of the problem, there comes a period of occupation with relatively crude and unorganized facts—hunting for, locating, and collecting raw material. This is the empiric stage, which no existing science, however proud in its attained rationality, can disavow as its own progenitor. (*c*) Then there is also a speculative stage: a period of guessing, of making hypotheses, of framing ideas which later on are labeled and condemned as only ideas. There is a period of distinction-making and classification-making which later on is regarded as only mentally gymnastic in character. And no science, however proud in its present security of experimental assurance, can disavow a scholastic ancestor. (*d*) Finally, there comes a period of fruitful interaction between the mere ideas and the mere facts: a period when observation is determined by experimental conditions depending upon the use of certain guiding conceptions; when reflection is directed and checked at every point by the use of experimental data, and by the necessity of finding such a form for itself as will enable it to serve in a deduction leading to evolution of new meanings, and ultimately to experimental inquiry, which brings to light new facts. In the emerging of a more orderly and significant region of fact, and of a more coherent and self-luminous system of meaning, we have the natural limit of evolution of the logic of a given science.

But consider what has happened in this historic record. Unanalyzed experience has broken up into distinctions of facts and ideas; the factual side has been developed by indefinite and almost miscellaneous descriptions and cumulative listings; the conceptual side has been developed by unchecked and speculative elaboration of definitions, classifications, etc. Then there has been a relegation of accepted meanings to the limbo of mere ideas; there has been a passage of some of the accepted facts into the region of mere hypothesis and opinion. Conversely, there has been a continued issuing of ideas from the region of hypotheses and theories into that of facts, of accepted objective and meaningful objects. Out of a world of only *seeming* facts, and of only *doubtful* ideas, there emerges a world continually growing in definiteness, order, and luminosity.

This progress, verified in every record of science, is an absolute monstrosity from the standpoint of the epistemology which assumes a thought in general, on one side, and a reality in general, on the other. The reason that it does not present itself as such a monster and miracle to those actually concerned with it is because *continuity* of reference and of use controls all diversities in the modes of existence specified and the types of significance assigned. The distinction of meaning and fact is treated in the growth of a science, or of any particular scientific problem, as an *induced* and *intentional* practical division of labor; as assignments of relative position with reference to performance of a task; as deliberate distribution of forces at command for their more economic use. The absorption of bald fact and hypothetical idea into the formation of a single world of scientific apprehension and comprehension is but the successful achieving of the aim on account of which the distinctions in question were instituted.

Thus we come back to the problem of logical theory. To take the distinctions of thought and fact, etc., as ontological, as inherently fixed in the make-up of the structure of being, results in treating the actual technique of scientific inquiry and scientific control as a mere subsidiary topic—ultimately of only utilitarian worth. It also states the terms upon which thought and being transact business in a way so totally alien to concrete experience that it creates a problem which can be discussed only in terms of itself—not in terms of the conduct of life. As against this, the logic which aligns itself with the origin and employ of reflective thought in everyday life and critical science follows the natural history of thinking as a life-process having its own generating antecedents and stimuli, its own states and career, and its own specific objective or limit.

This point of view makes it possible for logical theory to come to terms with psychology. When logic is considered as having to do with the wholesale activity of thought *per se*, the question of the historic process by which this or that particular thought came to be, of how its object happens to present itself as sensory, or perceptual, or conceptual, is quite irrelevant. These things are mere temporal accidents. The psychologist (not lifting his gaze from the realm of the changeable) may find in them matters of interest. His whole industry is just with natural history— to trace events as they mutually excite and inhibit one another. But the logician, we are told, has a deeper problem and an outlook of more unbounded horizon. He deals with the question of the eternal nature of thought and its eternal validity in relation to an eternal reality. He is concerned, not with genesis, but with value, not with a historic cycle, but with absolute entities and relations.

Still the query haunts us: Is this so in truth? Or has the logician of a certain type arbitrarily made it so by taking his terms apart from reference to the specific occasions in which they arise and situations in which they function? If the latter, then the very denial of historic relationship, the denial of the significance of historic method, is indicative of the unreal character of his own abstraction. It means in effect that the affairs under consideration have been isolated from the conditions in which alone they have determinable meaning and assignable worth. It is astonishing that, in the face of the advance of the evolutionary method in natural science, any logician can persist in the assertion of a rigid difference between the problem of origin and of nature; between genesis and analysis; between history and validity. Such assertion simply reiterates as final a distinction which grew up and had meaning in pre-evolutionary science. It asserts, against the most marked advance which scientific method has yet made, a survival of a crude period of logical scientific procedure. We have no choice save either to conceive of

thinking as a response to a specific stimulus, or else to regard
it as something "in itself," having just in and of itself certain
traits, elements, and laws. If we give up the last view, we
must take the former. In this case it will still possess distinctive traits, but they will be traits of a specific response to a
specific stimulus.

The significance of the evolutionary method in biology
and social history is that every distinct organ, structure, or
formation, every grouping of cells or elements, is to be
treated as an instrument of adjustment or adaptation to a
particular environing situation. Its meaning, its character,
its force, is known when, and only when, it is considered as
an arrangement for meeting the conditions involved in some
specific situation. This analysis is carried out by tracing successive stages of development—by endeavoring to locate the
particular situation in which each structure has its origin,
and by tracing the successive modifications through which,
in response to changing media, it has reached its present
conformation.[2] To persist in condemning natural history
from the standpoint of what natural history meant before it identified itself with an evolutionary process is not so
much to exclude the natural-history standpoint from philosophic consideration as it is to evince ignorance of what it
signifies.

Psychology as the natural history of the various attitudes and structures through which experiencing passes,
as an account of the conditions under which this or that
attitude emerges, and of the way in which it influences, by
stimulation or inhibition, production of other states or con-
formations of reflection, is indispensable to logical evaluation, the moment we treat logical theory as an account of
thinking as a response to its own generating conditions, and
consequently judge its validity by reference to its efficiency
in meeting its problems. The historical point of view describes the sequence; the normative follows the history to its
conclusion, and then turns back and judges each historical
step by viewing it in reference to its own outcome.

In the course of changing experience we keep our

2. See *Philosophical Review*, Vol. XI, pp. 117–20 [*Middle Works of
John Dewey*, 2:13–16].

balance in moving from situations of an affectional quality to those which are practical or appreciative or reflective, because we bear constantly in mind the context in which any particular distinction presents itself. As we submit each characteristic function and situation of experience to our gaze, we find it has a dual aspect. Wherever there is striving there are obstacles; wherever there is affection there are persons who are attached; wherever there is doing there is accomplishment; wherever there is appreciation there is value; wherever there is thinking there is material-in-question. We keep our footing as we move from one attitude to another, from one characteristic quality to another, because of the position occupied in the whole movement by the particular function in which we are engaged.

The distinction *between* each attitude and function and its predecessor and successor is serial, dynamic, operative. The distinctions *within* any given operation or function are structural, contemporaneous, and distributive. Thinking follows, we will say, striving, and doing follows thinking. Each in the fulfillment of its own function inevitably calls out its successor. But coincident, simultaneous, and correspondent *within* doing is the distinction of doer and of deed; *within* the function of thought, of thinking and material thought upon; within the function of striving, of obstacle and aim, of means and end. We keep our paths straight because we do not confuse the sequential and functional relationship of types of experience with the contemporaneous and structural distinctions of elements within a given function. In the seeming maze of endless confusion and unlimited shiftings, we find our way by the means of the stimulations and checks occurring within the process in which we are actually engaged. Operating within empirical situations we do not contrast or confuse a condition which is an element in the formation of one operation with the status which is one of the distributive terms of another function. When we ignore these specific empirical clues and limitations, we have at once an insoluble, because meaningless, problem upon our hands.

Now the epistemological logician deliberately shuts himself off from those cues and checks upon which the plain man instinctively relies, and which the scientific man deliberately searches for and adopts as constituting his technique. Consequently he is likely to set the attitude which has place and significance only in one of the serial functional situations of experience, over against the active attitude which describes part of the structural constitution of another situation; or with equal lack of justification to assimilate materials characteristic of different stages to one another. He sets the agent, as he is found in the intimacy of love or appreciation, over against the externality of the fact, as that is defined within the reflective process. He takes the material which thought selects as its problematic data as identical with the significant content which results from successful pursuit of inquiry; and this in turn he regards as the material which was presented before thinking began, whose peculiarities were the means of awakening thought. He identifies the final deposit of the thought-function with its own generating antecedent, and then disposes of the resulting surd by reference to some metaphysical consideration, which remains when logical inquiry, when science (as interpreted by him), has done its work. He does this, not because he prefers confusion to order, or error to truth, but simply because, when the chain of historic sequence is cut, the vessel of thought is afloat to veer upon a sea without soundings or moorings. There are but two alternatives: either there is an object "in itself" of mind "in itself," or else there are a series of situations where elements vary with the varying functions to which they belong. If the latter, the only way in which the characteristic terms of situations can be defined is by discriminating the functions to which they belong. And the epistemological logician, in choosing to take his question as one of thought which has its own form just as "thought," apart from the limits of the special work it has to do, has deprived himself of these supports and stays.

The problem of logic has a more general and a more specific phase. In its generic form, it deals with this question: How does one type of functional situation and attitude in experience pass out of and into another; for example, the technological or utilitarian into the aesthetic, the aesthetic into the religious, the religious into the scientific, and this into the socio-ethical and so on? The more specific question is: How does the particular functional situation termed the reflective behave? How shall we describe it? What in detail are its diverse contemporaneous distinctions, or divisions of labor, its correspondent *statuses*; in what specific ways do these operate with reference to each other so as to effect the specific aim which is proposed by the needs of the affair?

This chapter may be brought to conclusion by reference to the more ultimate value of the logic of experience, of logic taken in its wider sense; that is, as an account of the sequence of the various typical functions or situations of experience in their determining relations to one another. Philosophy, defined as such a logic, makes no pretense to be an account of a closed and finished universe. Its business is not to secure or guarantee any particular reality or value. *Per contra*, it gets the significance of a method. The right relationship and adjustment of the various typical phases of experience to one another is a problem felt in every department of life. Intellectual rectification and control of these adjustments cannot fail to reflect itself in an added clearness and security on the practical side. It may be that general logic cannot become an instrument in the immediate direction of the activities of science or art or industry; but it is of value in criticizing and organizing tools of immediate research. It also has direct significance in the valuation for social or life-purposes of results achieved in particular branches. Much of the immediate business of life is badly done because we do not know the genesis and outcome of the work that occupies us. The manner and degree of appropriation of the goods achieved in various departments of social interest and vocation are partial and faulty because we are not clear as to the due rights and responsibilities of one function of experience in reference to others.

The value of research for social progress; the bearing of psychology upon educational procedure; the mutual relations of fine and industrial art; the question of the extent and nature of specialization in science in comparison with the claims of applied science; the adjustment of religious aspirations to scientific statements; the justification of a refined culture for a few in face of economic insufficiency for the mass, the relation of organization to individuality—such are a few of the many social questions whose answer depends upon the possession and use of a general logic of experience as a method of inquiry and interpretation. I do not say that headway cannot be made in such questions apart from the method indicated: a logic of experience. But unless we have a critical and assured view of the juncture in which and with reference to which a given attitude or interest arises, unless we know the service it is thereby called upon to perform and hence the organs or methods by which it best functions in that service, our progress is impeded and irregular. We take a part for a whole, a means for an end; or we attack wholesale some interest because it interferes with the deified sway of the one we have selected as ultimate. A clear and comprehensive consensus of social conviction, and a consequent concentrated and economical direction of effort, are assured only as there is some way of locating the position and rôle of each typical interest and occupation. The domain of opinion is one of conflict; its rule is arbitrary and costly. Only intellectual method affords a substitute for opinion. A general logic of experience alone can do for social qualities and aims what the natural sciences after centuries of struggle are doing for activity in the physical realm.

This does not mean that systems of philosophy which have attempted to state the nature of thought and of reality at large, apart from limits of particular situations in the movement of experience, have been worthless—though it does mean that their industry has been somewhat misapplied. The unfolding of metaphysical theory has made large contributions to positive evaluations of the typical situations and relationships of experience—even when its conscious intention has been quite otherwise. Every system of philosophy is itself a mode of reflection; consequently (if our main contention be true), it too has been evoked out of specific social antecedents, and has had its use as a response to them. It has effected something in modifying the situation within which it found its origin. It may not have solved the problem which it consciously put itself; in many cases we may freely admit that the question put has been found afterward to be so wrongly put as to be insoluble. Yet exactly the same thing is true, in precisely the same sense, in the history of science. For this reason, if for no other, it is impossible for the scientific man to cast the first stone at the philosopher.

The progress of science in any branch continually brings with it a realization that problems in their previous form of statement are insoluble because put in terms of unreal conditions; because the real conditions have been mixed up with mental artifacts or misconstructions. Every science is continually learning that its supposed solutions are only apparent, because the "solution" solves, not the actual problem, but one which has been made up. But the very putting of the question, the very giving of the wrong answer, induces modification of existing intellectual habits, standpoints, and aims. Wrestling with the problem, there is evolution of new technique to control inquiry, there is search for new facts, institution of new types of experimentation; there is gain in the methodic control of experience. And all this is progress. It is only the worn-out cynic, the devitalized sensualist, and the fanatical dogmatist who interpret the continuous change of science as proving that, since each successive statement is wrong, the whole record is error and folly; and that the present truth is only the error not yet found out. Such draw the moral of caring naught for all these things, or of flying to some external authority which will deliver once for all the fixed and unchangeable truth. But historic philosophy even in its aberrant forms has proved a factor in the valuation of experience; it has brought problems to light, it has provoked intellectual conflicts without which values are only nominal; even through its would-be absolutistic isolations, it has secured recognition of mutual dependencies and reciprocal reinforcements. Yet if it can define its work more clearly, it can concentrate its energy upon its own characteristic problem: the genesis and functioning in experience of various typical interests and occupations with reference to one another.

2. THE ANTECEDENTS AND STIMULI OF THINKING

We have discriminated logic in its wider sense—concerned with the sequence of characteristic functions and attitudes in experience—from logic in its stricter meaning, concerned with the function of reflective thought. We must avoid yielding to the temptation of identifying logic with either of these to the exclusion of the other; or of supposing that it is possible to isolate one finally from the other. The more detailed treatment of the organs and methods of reflection cannot be carried on with security save as we have a correct idea of the position of reflection amid the typical functions of experience. Yet it is impossible to determine this larger placing, save as we have a defined and analytic, as distinct from a merely vague and gross, view of what we mean by reflection—what is its actual constitution. It is necessary to work back and forth between the larger and the narrower fields, transforming every increment upon one side into a method of work upon the other, and thereby testing it. The evident confusion of existing logical theory, its uncertainty as to its own bounds and limits, its tendency to oscillate from larger questions of the meaning of judgment and the validity of inference over to details of scientific technique, and to translate distinctions of formal logic into acts in an investigatory or verificatory process, are indications of the need of this double movement.

In the next three chapters it is proposed to take up some of the considerations that lie on the borderland between the larger and the narrower conceptions of logical theory. I shall discuss the *locus* of the function of thought in experience so far as such *locus* enables us to characterize some of the most fundamental distinctions, or divisions of labor,

[First published as "Thought and Its Subject-Matter: The Antecedent Conditions and Cues of the Thought-Function," in *Studies in Logical Theory*. Revised and reprinted in *Essays in Experimental Logic*.]

within the reflective process. In taking up the problem of the subject-matter of thought, I shall try to make clear that it assumes three quite distinct forms according to the epochal moment reached in control of experience. I shall attempt to show that we must consider subject-matter from the standpoint, first, of the *antecedents* or conditions that evoke thought; secondly, of the *datum* or *immediate material* presented to thought; and, thirdly, of the *proper objective* of thought. Of these three distinctions the first, that of antecedent and stimulus, clearly refers to the situation that is immediately prior to the thought-function as such. The second, that of datum or immediately given matter, refers to a distinction which is made within the thought-process as a part of and for the sake of its own *modus operandi*. It is a status in the scheme of thinking. The third, that of content or object, refers to the progress actually made in any thought-function; material which is organized by inquiry so far as inquiry has fulfilled its purpose. This chapter will get at the matter of preliminary conditions of thought indirectly rather than directly, by indicating the contradictory positions into which one of the most vigorous and acute of modern logicians, Lotze, has been forced through failing to define logical distinctions in terms of the history of readjustment and control of things in experience, and being thereby compelled to interpret certain notions as absolute instead of as historic and methodological.

Before passing directly to the exposition and criticism of Lotze, it will be well, however, to take the matter in a somewhat freer way. We cannot approach logical inquiry in a wholly direct and uncompromised manner. Of necessity we bring to it certain distinctions—distinctions partly the outcome of concrete experience; partly due to the logical theory which has got embodied in ordinary language and in current intellectual habits; partly results of deliberate scientific and philosophic inquiry. These more or less ready-made results are resources; they are the only weapons with which we can attack the new problem. Yet they are full of unexamined assumptions; they commit us to all sorts of logically predetermined conclusions. In one sense our study of the new subject-matter, let us say logical theory, is in truth only a

review, a re-testing and criticizing of the intellectual standpoints and methods which we bring with us to the study.

Nowadays everyone comes with certain distinctions
already made between the subjective and the objective, between the physical and the mental, between the intellectual
and the factual. (1) We have learned to regard the region of
emotional disturbance, of uncertainty and aspiration, as belonging peculiarly to ourselves; we have learned to set over
against this the world of observation and of valid thought as
something unaffected by our moods, hopes, fears, and
opinions. (2) We have also come to distinguish between what
is immediately present in our experience and the past and
the future; we contrast the realms of memory and anticipation with that of sense-perception; more generally we contrast the given with the inferential. (3) We are confirmed in
a habit of distinguishing between what we call actual fact
and our mental attitude toward that fact—the attitude of
surmise or wonder or reflective investigation. While one of
the aims of logical theory is precisely to make us critically
conscious of the significance and bearing of these various
distinctions, to change them from ready-made assumptions
into controlled conceptions, our mental habits are so set
that they tend to have their own way with us; we read into
logical theory conceptions that were formed before we had
even dreamed of the logical undertaking which after all has
for its business to assign to the terms in question their
proper meaning. Our conclusions are thus controlled by the
very notions which need criticism and revision.

We find in Lotze an unusually explicit inventory of
these various preliminary distinctions, and an unusually
serious effort to deal with the problems which arise from
introducing them into the structure of logical theory. (1)
He expressly separates the matter of logical worth from that
of psychological genesis. He consequently abstracts the subject-matter of logic as such wholly from the question of
historic *locus* and *situs*. (2) He agrees with common sense
in holding that logical thought is reflective and thus presupposes a given material. He occupies himself with the nature
of the antecedent conditions. (3) He wrestles with the problem of how a material formed prior to thought and irrespec-

tive of it can yet afford stuff upon which thought may exercise itself. (4) He expressly raises the question of how thought working independently and from without upon a foreign material can shape the latter into results which are valid—that is, objective.

If this discussion is successful; if Lotze can provide the intermediaries which span the gulf between the exercise of logical functions by thought upon a material wholly external to it; if he can show that the question of the origin of subject-matter of thought and of thought-activity is irrelevant to the question of its meaning and validity, we shall have to surrender the position already taken. But if we find that Lotze's elaborations only elaborate the fundamental difficulty, presenting it now in this light and now in that, but always presenting the problem as if it were its own solution, we shall be confirmed in our idea of the need of considering logical questions from a different point of view. If we find that, whatever his formal treatment, he always, as matter of fact, falls back upon some organized situation or function as the source of both the material and the process of inquiry, we shall have in so far an elucidation and even a corroboration of our theory.

We begin with the question of the material antecedents of thought—antecedents which condition reflection, and which call it out as reaction or response, by giving its cue. Lotze differs from many logicians of the same type in furnishing an explicit account of these antecedents.

1. The ultimate material antecedents of thought are found in impressions which are due to external objects as stimuli. Taken in themselves, these impressions are mere psychical states or events. They exist in us side by side, or one after the other, according as the objects which excite them operate simultaneously or successively. The occurrence of these various psychical states is not, however, entirely dependent upon the presence of the exciting thing. After a state has once been excited, it gets the power of reawakening other states which have accompanied it or followed it. The associative mechanism of revival plays a part. If we had a complete knowledge of both the stimulating object and its effects, and of the details of the associative mechanism, we

should be able from given data to predict the whole course of any given train or current of ideas (for the impressions as conjoined simultaneously or successively become ideas and a current of ideas).

Taken in itself, a sensation or impression is nothing but a "state of our consciousness, a mood of ourselves." Any given current of ideas is a necessary sequence of existences (just as necessary as any succession of material events), happening in some particular sensitive soul or organism. "Just because, under their respective conditions, every such series of ideas hangs together by the same necessity and law as every other, there would be no ground for making any such distinction of value as that between truth and untruth, thus placing one group in opposition to all the others."[1]

2. Thus far, as the last quotation clearly indicates, there is no question of reflective thought, and hence no question of logical theory. But further examination reveals a peculiar property of the current of ideas. Some ideas are merely coincident, while others may be termed coherent. That is to say, the exciting causes of some of our simultaneous and successive ideas really belong together; while in other cases they simply happen to act at the same time, without there being a real connection between them. By the associative mechanism, however, both the coherent and the merely coincident combinations recur. The first type of recurrence supplies positive material for knowledge; the second gives occasion for error.

3. It is a peculiar mixture of the coincident and the coherent which sets the peculiar problem of reflective thought. The business of thought is to recover and confirm the coherent, the really connected, adding to its reinstatement an accessory justifying notion of the real ground of coherence, while it eliminates the coincident as such. While the mere current of ideas is something which just happens within us, the process of elimination and of confirmation by means of statement of real ground and basis of connection is an activity which mind as such exercises. This distinction

1. Lotze, *Logic* (translation, Oxford, 1888), I, 2. For the preceding exposition see I, 1, 2, 13, 14, 37, 38; also *Mikrokosmus*, Bk. V, Ch. 4.

marks off thought as activity from any psychical event and from the associative mechanism as mere happenings. One is concerned with mere *de facto* coexistences and sequences; the other with the cognitive *worth* of these combinations.[2]

Consideration of the peculiar work of thought in going over, sorting out, and determining various ideas according to a standard of value will occupy us in our next chapter. Here we are concerned with the material antecedents of thought as they are described by Lotze. At first glance, he seems to propound a satisfactory theory. He avoids the extravagancies of transcendental logic, which assumes that all the matter of experience is determined from the very start by rational thought; and he also avoids the pitfall of purely empirical logic, which makes no distinction between the mere occurrence and association of ideas and the real worth and validity of the various conjunctions thus produced. He allows unreflective experience, defined in terms of sensations and their combinations, to provide material conditions for thinking, while he reserves for thought a distinctive work and dignity of its own. Sense-experience furnishes the antecedents; thought has to introduce and develop systematic connection—rationality.

A further analysis of Lotze's treatment may, however, lead us to believe that his statement is riddled through and through with inconsistencies and self-contradictions; that, indeed, any one part of it can be maintained only by the denial of some other portion.

1. The impression is the ultimate antecedent in its purest or crudest form (according to the angle from which one views it). It is that which has never felt, for good or for bad, the influence of thought. Combined into ideas, these impressions stimulate or arouse the activities of thought, which are forthwith directed upon them. As the recipient of the activity which they have excited and brought to bear upon themselves, they furnish also the material content of thought —its actual stuff. As Lotze says over and over again: "It is the relations themselves already subsisting between impressions, when we become conscious of them, by which the

action of thought which is never anything but reaction, is attracted; and this action consists merely in interpreting relations which we find existing between our passive impressions into aspects of the matter of impressions."[3] And again: "Thought can make no difference where it finds none already in the matter of the impressions."[4] And again: "The possibility and the success of thought's procedure depends upon this original constitution and organisation of the whole world of ideas, a constitution which, though not necessary in thought, is all the more necessary to make thinking possible."[5]

The impressions and ideas thus play a versatile rôle; they now assume the part of ultimate antecedents and provocative conditions; of crude material; and somehow, when arranged, of content for thought. This very versatility awakens suspicion.

While the impression is merely subjective and a bare state of our own consciousness, yet it is determined, both as to its existence and as to its relation to other similar existences, by external objects as stimuli, if not as causes. It is also determined by a psychical mechanism so thoroughly objective or regular in its workings as to give the same necessary character to the current of ideas that is possessed by any physical sequence. Thus that which is "nothing but a state of our consciousness" turns out straightway to be a specifically determined objective fact in a system of facts.

That this absolute transformation is a contradiction is no clearer than that just such a contradiction is indispensable to Lotze. If impressions were nothing but states of consciousness, moods of ourselves, bare psychical existences, it is sure enough that we should never even know them to be such, to say nothing of conserving them as adequate conditions and material for thought. It is only by treating them as real facts in a real world, and only by carrying over into them, in some assumed and unexplained way, the capacity of representing the cosmic facts which cause them, that impressions or ideas come in any sense within the scope of

3. Lotze, *Logic* (translation, Oxford, 1888), I, 25.
4. *Logic*, I, 36.
5. *Logic*, I, 36.

thought. But if the antecedents are really impressions-in-their-objective-setting, then Lotze's whole way of distinguishing thought-worth from *mere* existence or event without objective significance must be radically modified.

The implication that impressions have actually a quality or meaning of their own becomes explicit when we refer to Lotze's theory that the immediate antecedent of thought is found in the *matter* of ideas. When thought is said to "take cognizance of *relations* which its own activity does not originate, but which have been prepared for it by the unconscious mechanism of the psychic states,"[6] the attribution of objective content, of reference and meaning to ideas, is unambiguous. The idea forms a most convenient halfway house for Lotze. On one hand, as absolutely prior to thought, as material antecedent condition, it is merely psychical, bald subjective event. But as subject-matter for thought, as antecedent which affords stuff for thought's exercise, it characteristically qualifies content.

Although we have been told that the impression is a mere receptive irritation without participation of mental activity, we are not surprised, in view of this capacity of ideas, to learn that the mind actually has a determining share in both the reception of stimuli and in their further associative combinations. The subject always enters into the presentation of any mental object, even the sensational, to say nothing of the perceptional and the imaged. The perception of a given state of things is possible only on the assumption that "the perceiving subject is at once enabled and compelled by its own nature to combine the excitations which reach it from objects into those forms which it is to perceive in the objects, and which it supposes itself simply to *receive* from them."[7]

It is only by continual transition from impression and ideas as mental states and events to ideas as logical *objects or contents*, that Lotze bridges the gulf from bare exciting antecedent to concrete material conditions of thought. This contradiction, again, is necessary to Lotze's standpoint. To set out frankly with objects as antecedents would demand

6. *Mikrokosmus*, Bk. V, Ch. 4.
7. *Logic*, II, 235; see the whole discussion, Secs. 325–27.

reconsideration of the whole viewpoint, which supposes that the difference between the logical and its antecedent is a matter of the difference between *worth* and mere *existence* or *occurrence*. It would indicate that since meaning or value is already there, the task of thought must be that of the transformation or *reconstruction of meaning* through an intermediary process. On the other hand, to stick by the standpoint of *mere* existence is not to get anything which can be called even antecedent of thought.

2. Why is there a task of transformation? Consideration of the material in its function of evoking thought, giving it its cue, will serve to complete the picture of the contradiction and of the real facts. It is the conflict between ideas as merely coincident and ideas as coherent which constitutes the need that provokes the response of thought. Here Lotze vibrates between (*a*) considering both coincidence and coherence as psychical events; (*b*) considering coincidence as purely psychical a'nd coherence as at least quasi-logical, and (*c*) making them both determinations within the sphere of reflective thought. In strict accordance with his own premises, coincidence and coherence ought both to be mere peculiarities of the current of ideas as events within ourselves. But so taken the distinction becomes absolutely meaningless. Events do not cohere; at the most certain sets of them happen more or less frequently than other sets; the only intelligible difference is one of frequency of coincidence. And even this attributes to an event the supernatural trait of reappearing after it has disappeared. Even coincidence has to be defined in terms of relation of the *objects* which are supposed to excite the psychical events that happen together.

As recent psychological discussion has made clear enough, it is the matter, meaning, or content, of ideas that is associated, not the ideas as states or existences. Take such an idea as sun-revolving-about-earth. We may *say* it means the conjunction of various sense-impressions, but it is connection, or mutual reference, of *attributes* that we have in mind in the assertion. It is absolutely certain that our psychical image of the sun is not psychically engaged in revolving about our psychical image of the earth. It would be amusing if such were the case; theatres and all dramatic representations would be at a discount. But in truth, sun-revolving-about-earth is a single meaning or intellectual object; it is a unified subject-matter within which certain distinctions of reference appear. It is concerned with what we intend when we think earth and sun, and think them in their relation to each other. It is a rule, specification, or direction of how to think when we have occasion to think a certain subject-matter. To treat this mutual reference as if it were simply a case of conjunction of mental events produced by psycho-physical irritation and association is a profound case of the psychological fallacy. We may, indeed, analyze an experience involving belief in an object of a certain kind and find that it had its origin in certain conditions of the sensitive organism, in certain peculiarities of perception and of association, and hence conclude that the belief involved in it was not justified by the facts themselves. But the significance of the belief in sun-revolving-about-earth by those who held it, consisted precisely in the fact that it was taken not as a mere association of feelings, but as a definite portion of the whole structure of objective experience, guaranteed by other parts of the fabric, and lending its support and giving its tone to them. It was to them part of the experienced frame of things—of the real world.

Put the other way, if such an instance meant a mere conjunction of psychical states, there would be in it absolutely nothing to evoke thought. Each idea as event, as Lotze himself points out (*Logic*, I, 2), may be regarded as adequately and necessarily determined to the place it occupies. There is absolutely no question on the side of events of mere coincidence *versus* genuine connection. As event, it is there and it belongs there. We cannot treat something as at once a bare fact of existence and a problematic subject-matter of logical inquiry. To take the reflective point of view is to consider the matter in a totally new light; as Lotze says, it is to raise the question of rightful claims to a position or relation.

The point becomes clearer when we contrast coincidence with connection. To consider coincidence as simply psychical, and coherence as at least quasi-logical, is to put the two on such different bases that no question of contrasting them can arise. The coincidence which precedes a valid or grounded coherence (the conjunction which as coexistence of objects and sequence of acts is perfectly adequate) never is, as antecedent, the coincidence which is set over against coherence. The side-by-sideness of books on my bookshelf, the succession of noises that rise through my window, do not trouble me logically. They do not appear as errors or even as problems. One coexistence is just as good as any other until some new point of view, or new end, presents itself. If it is a question of the convenience of arrangement of books, then the value of their present collocation becomes a problem. Then I contrast their present state as bare conjunction over against another scheme as one which is coherent. If I regard the sequence of noises as a case of articulate speech, their order becomes important—it is a problem to be determined. The inquiry whether a given combination presents apparent or real connection, shows that reflective inquiry is already going on. Does this phase of the moon really mean rain, or does it just happen that the rain-storm comes when the moon has reached this phase? To ask such questions shows that a certain portion of the universe of objective experience is subjected to critical analysis for purposes of definitive restatement. The tendency to regard some combination as mere coincidence is absolutely a *part* of the movement of mind in its search for the real connection.

If coexistence as such is to be set against coherence as such, as the non-logical against the logical, then, since our whole spatial universe is one of collocation, and since thought in this universe can never get farther than substituting one collocation for another, the whole realm of space-experience is condemned off-hand and in perpetuity to anti-rationality. But, in truth, coincidence as over against coherence, conjunction as over against connection, is just *suspected* coherence, one which is under the fire of active inquiry. The distinction is one which arises only within the logical or reflective function.

3. This brings us explicitly to the fact that there is neither coincidence nor coherence in terms of the elements or meanings contained in any couple or pair of ideas taken by itself. It is only when they are co-factors in a situation or

function which includes more than either the "coincident" or the "coherent" and more than the arithmetical sum of the two, that thought's activity can be evoked. Lotze is continually in this dilemma: Thought either shapes its own material or else just accepts it. In the first case (since Lotze cannot rid himself of the presumption that thought must have a fixed ready-made antecedent) its activity can only alter this stuff and thus lead the mind farther away from reality. But if thought just accepts its material, how can there be any distinctive aim or activity of thought at all? As we have seen, Lotze endeavors to escape this dilemma by supposing that, while thought receives its material yet checks it up, it eliminates certain portions of it and reinstates others, plus the stamp and seal of its own validity.

Lotze objects most strenuously to the Kantian notion that thought awaits its subject-matter with certain ready-made modes of apprehension. This notion would raise the insoluble question of how thought contrives to bring the matter of each impression under that particular form which is appropriate to it (*Logic*, I, 24). But he has not avoided the difficulty. How does thought know which of the combinations are merely coincident and which are merely coherent? How does it know which to eliminate as irrelevant and which to confirm as grounded? Either this evaluation is an imposition of its own, or else gets its cue and clue from the subject-matter. Now, if the coincident and the coherent taken in and of themselves are competent to give this direction, they are already labeled. The further work of thought is one of supererogation. It has at most barely to note and seal the material combinations that are already there. Such a view clearly renders thought's work as unnecessary in form as it is futile in force.

But there is no alternative except to recognize that an entire situation or environment, within which exist both that which is afterward found to be mere coincidence and that found to be real connection, actually provokes thought. It is only as an experience previously accepted comes up in its wholeness against another one equally integral; and only as some larger experience dawns which requires each as a part of itself and yet within which the required factors show

themselves mutually incompatible, that thought arises. It is
not bare coincidence, or bare connection, or bare addition of
one to the other, that excites thought. The stimulus is a
situation which is organized or constituted as a whole, and
yet which is falling to pieces in its parts—a situation which
is in conflict within itself—that arouses the search to find
what really goes together and a correspondent effort to shut
out what only seemingly goes together. And real coherence
means precisely capacity to exist within the comprehending
whole. To read back into the preliminary situation those distinctions of mere conjunction of material and of valid coherence which get existence, to say nothing of fixation, only
within the process of inquiry is a fallacy.

We must not leave this phase of the discussion, however, until it is quite clear that our objection is not to Lotze's
position that reflective thought arises from an antecedent
which is not reflectional in character; nor yet to his idea that
this antecedent has a certain structure and content of its
own setting the peculiar problem of thought, giving the
cue to its specific activities and determining its object. On
the contrary, it is this latter point upon which we would
insist; so as (by insisting) to point out, negatively, that this
view is absolutely inconsistent with Lotze's theory that
psychical impressions and ideas are the true antecedents of
thought; and, positively, to show that it is the *situation as a
whole*, and not any one isolated part of it, or distinction
within it, that calls forth and directs thinking. We must be-
ware the fallacy of assuming that some one element in the
prior situation in isolation or detachment induces the reflection which in reality comes forth only from the whole dis-
turbed situation. On the negative side, characterizations of
impression and idea are distinctions which arise only within
reflection upon that situation which is the genuine antecedent of thought. Positively, it is the whole dynamic experience with its qualitative and pervasive continuity, and
its inner active distraction, its elements at odds with each
other, in tension against each other, each contending for
its proper placing and relationship, which generates the
thought-situation.

From this point of view, at this period of development,

the distinctions of objective and subjective have a characteristic meaning. The antecedent, to repeat, is a situation in
which the various factors are actively incompatible with
each other, and yet in and through the striving tend to a re-
formation of the whole and to a restatement of the parts.
This situation as such is clearly "objective." It is there; it is
there as a whole; the various parts are there; and their active
incompatibility with one another is there. Nothing is con-
veyed at this point by asserting that any particular part of
the situation is illusory or subjective, or mere appearance; or
that any other is truly real. The experience exists as one of
vital and active confusion and conflict among its elements.
The conflict is not only objective in a *de facto* sense (that
is, really existent), but is objective in a logical sense as
well; it is just this conflict which effects a transition into
the thought-situation—this, in turn, being only a constant
movement toward a defined equilibrium. The conflict has
objective worth because it is the antecedent condition and
cue of thought. Deny an organization of things within which
competing incompatible tendencies appear and thinking becomes merely "mental."

Every reflective attitude and function, whether of naïve
life, deliberate invention, or controlled scientific research,
has risen through the medium of some such total objective
situation. The abstract logician may tell us that sensations
or impressions, or associated ideas, or bare physical things,
or conventional symbols, are antecedent conditions. But
such statements cannot be verified by reference to a single
instance of thought in connection with actual practice or
actual scientific research. Of course, by extreme mediation
symbols may become conditions of evoking thought. They
get to be objects in an active experience. But they are stimuli
to thinking only in case their manipulation to form a new
whole occasions resistance, and thus reciprocal tension.
Symbols and their definitions develop to a point where dealing with them becomes itself an experience, having its own
identity; just as the handling of commercial commodities, or
arrangement of parts of an invention, is a specific experience.

There is always as antecedent to thought an experience

of subject-matter of the physical or social world, or the previously organized intellectual world, whose parts are actively at war with each other—so much so that they threaten to disrupt the situation, which accordingly for its own maintenance requires deliberate redefinition and re-relation of its tensional parts. This redefining and re-relating is the constructive process termed thinking: the reconstructive situation, with its parts in tension and in such movement toward each other as tends to a unified arrangement of things, is the thought-situation.

This at once suggests the subjective phase. The situation, the experience as such, is objective. There is an experience of the confused and conflicting tendencies. But just *what in particular* is objective, just *what* form the situation shall take as an organized harmonious whole, is unknown; that is the problem. It is the uncertainty as to the *what* of the experience together with the certainty *that* there is such an experience, that evokes the thought-function. Viewed from this standpoint of uncertainty, the situation as a whole is subjective. No particular content or reference can be asserted off-hand. Definite assertion is expressly reserved —it is to be the outcome of the procedure of reflective inquiry now undertaken. This holding off of contents from definitely asserted position, this viewing them as candidates for reform, is what we mean at this stage of the natural history of thought by the subjective.

We have followed Lotze through his tortuous course of inconsistencies. It is better, perhaps, to run the risk of vain repetition than that of leaving the impression that these are *mere* dialectical contradictions. It is an idle task to expose contradictions unless we realize them in relation to the fundamental assumption which breeds them. Lotze is bound to differentiate thought from its antecedents. He is intent upon doing this, however, through a preconception that marks off the thought-situation radically from its predecessor, through a difference that is complete, fixed, and absolute, or at large. It is a total contrast of thought as such to something else as such that he requires, not a contrast within experience of one temporal phase of a process, one period of a rhythm, from others.

This complete and rigid difference Lotze finds in the difference between an experience which is *mere existence* or occurrence, and one which has to do with worth, truth, right relationship. Now things have connection, organization, value or force, practical and aesthetic meaning, on their own account. The same is true of deeds, affections, etc. Only states of feelings, bare impressions, etc., seem to fulfill the prerequisite of being given as existence, and yet without qualification as to worth, etc. Then the current of ideas offers itself, a ready-made stream of events, of existences, which can be characterized as wholly innocent of reflective determination, and as the natural predecessor of thought.

But this stream of existences is no sooner regarded than its total incapacity to officiate as material condition and cue of thought appears. It is about as relevant to thinking as are changes that may be happening on the other side of the moon. So, one by one, the whole series of determinations of force and worth already traced are introduced *into* the very make-up, the inner structure, of what was to be *mere* existence: viz., (1) things of whose spatial and temporal relations the mere impressions are somehow *representative*; (2) *meaning*—the idea as significant, possessed of quality, and not a mere event; (3) distinguished traits of coincidence and coherence within the stream. All these features are explicitly asserted, as we have seen; underlying and running through them all is the recognition of the supreme value of a situation which has been organized as a whole, yet is now conflicting in its inner constitution.

These contradictions all arise in the attempt to put thought's work, as concerned with objective validity, over against experience as a mere antecedent happening, or occurrence. This contrast arises because of the attempt to consider thought as an independent somewhat in general which nevertheless, in *our* experience, is dependent upon a raw material of mere impressions given to it. Hence the sole radical avoidance of the contradictions can be secured only when thinking is seen to be a specific event in the movement of experienced things, having its own specific occasion or demand, and its own specific place.

The nature of the organization and force that the antecedent conditions of the thought-function possess is too large a question here to enter upon in detail. Lotze himself suggests the answer. He speaks of the current of ideas, just as a current, supplying us with the "mass of well-grounded information which *regulates daily life*" (*Logic*, I, 4). It gives rise to "useful combinations," "correct expectations," "seasonable reactions" (*Logic*, I, 7). He speaks of it, indeed, as if it were just the ordinary world of naïve experience, the so-called empirical world, as distinct from the world as critically revised and rationalized in scientific and philosophic inquiry. The contradiction between this interpretation and that of a mere stream of psychical impressions is only another instance of the difficulty already discussed. But the phraseology suggests the real state of things. The unreflective world is a world of practical things; of ends and means, of their effective adaptations; of control and regulation of conduct in view of results. The world of uncritical experience also is a world of social aims and means, involving at every turn the goods and objects of affection and attachment, of competition and cooperation. It has incorporate also in its own being the surprise of aesthetic values—the sudden joy of light, the gracious wonder of tone and form.

I do not mean that this holds in gross of the unreflective world of experience over against the critical thought-situation—such a contrast implies the very wholesale, at large, consideration of thought which I am striving to avoid. Doubtless many and many an act of thought has intervened in effecting the organization of our commonest practical-affectional-aesthetic environment. I only mean to indicate that thought does take place *in* such a world; not *after* a world of bare existences; and that while the more systematic reflection we call organized science, may, in some fair sense, be said to come *after*, it comes after affectional, artistic, and technological interests which have found realization.

Having entered so far upon a suggestion which cannot be followed out, I venture one other digression. The notion that value or significance as distinct from mere existentiality is the product of thought or reason, and that the source of Lotze's contradictions lies in the effort to find *any* situation prior or antecedent to thought, is a familiar one—it is even possible that my criticisms of Lotze have been interpreted by some readers in this sense.[8] This is the position frequently called neo-Hegelian (though, I think, with questionable accuracy), and has been developed by many writers in criticizing Kant. This position and that taken in this chapter do indeed agree in certain general regards. They are at one in denial of the factuality and the possibility of developing fruitful reflection out of antecedent bare existence or mere events. They unite in denying that there is or can be any such thing as *mere* existence—phenomenon unqualified as respects organization and force, whether such phenomenon be psychic or cosmic. They agree that reflective thought grows organically out of an experience which is already organized, and that it functions within such an organism. But they part company when a fundamental question is raised: Is all organized meaning the work of thought? Does it therefore follow that the organization out of which reflective thought grows is the work of thought of some other type of Pure Thought, Creative or Constitutive Thought, Intuitive Reason, etc.? I shall indicate briefly the reasons for divergence at this point.

To cover all the practical-social-aesthetic objects involved, the term "thought" has to be so stretched that the situation might as well be called by any other name that describes a typical form of experience. More specifically, when the difference is minimized between the organized and arranged scheme out of which reflective inquiry proceeds, and reflective inquiry itself (and there can be no other reason for insisting that the antecedent of reflective thought is itself somehow thought), exactly the same type of problem recurs

8. We have a most acute and valuable criticism of Lotze from this point of view in Professor Henry Jones, *Philosophy of Lotze*, 1895. My specific criticisms agree in the main with his, and I am glad to acknowledge my indebtedness. But I cannot agree in the belief that the business of thought is to qualify reality as such; its occupation appears to me to be determining the reconstruction of some aspect or portion of reality, and to fall within the course of reality itself; being, indeed, the characteristic medium of its activity. And I cannot agree that reality as such, with increasing fullness of knowledge, presents itself as a thought-system, though, as just indicated, I have no doubt that practical existence presents itself in its temporal course as thought-specifications, just as it does as affectional and aesthetic and the rest of them.

which presents itself when the distinction is exaggerated into one between bare existences and rational coherent meanings.

For the more one insists that the antecedent situation is constituted by thought, the more one has to wonder why another type of thought is required; what need arouses it, and how it is possible for it to improve upon the work of previous constitutive thought. This difficulty at once forces idealists from a logic of experience as it is concretely experienced into a metaphysic of a purely hypothetical experience. Constitutive thought precedes *our* conscious thought-operations; hence it must be the working of some absolute universal thought which, unconsciously to our reflection, builds up an organized world. But this recourse only deepens the difficulty. How does it happen that the absolute constitutive and intuitive Thought does such a poor and bungling job that it requires a finite discursive activity to patch up its products? Here more metaphysic is called for: The Absolute Reason is now supposed to work under limiting conditions of finitude, of a sensitive and temporal organism. The antecedents of reflective thought are not, therefore, determinations of thought pure and undefiled, but of what thought can do when it stoops to assume the yoke of change and of feeling. I pass by the metaphysical problem left unsolved by this flight: Why and how should a perfect, absolute, complete, finished thought find it necessary to submit to alien, disturbing, and corrupting conditions in order, in the end, to recover through reflective thought in a partial, piecemeal, wholly inadequate way what it possessed at the outset in a much more satisfactory way?

I confine myself to the logical difficulty. How can thought relate itself to the fragmentary sensations, impressions, feelings, which, in their contrast with and disparity from the workings of constitutive thought, mark it off from the latter; and which in their connection with its products give the cue to reflective thinking? *Here we have again exactly the problem with which Lotze has been wrestling:* we have the same insoluble question of the reference of thought-activity to a wholly indeterminate unrationalized, independent, prior existence. The absolute idealist who takes up the problem at this point will find himself forced into the same continuous seesaw, the same scheme of alternate rude robbery and gratuitous gift, that Lotze engaged in. The simple fact is that here *is* just where Lotze began; he saw that previous transcendental logicians had left untouched the specific question of relation of *our* supposedly finite, reflective thought to its own antecedents, and he set out to make good the defect. If reflective thought is required because constitutive thought works under externally limiting conditions of sense, then we have some elements which are, after all, mere existences, events, etc. Or, if they have organization from some other source than thought, and induce reflective thought not as bare impressions, etc., but through their place in some whole, then we have admitted the possibility of organization in experience, apart from Reason, and the ground for assuming Pure Constitutive Thought is abandoned.

The contradiction appears equally when viewed from the side of thought-activity and its characteristic forms. All our knowledge, after all, of thought as constitutive is gained by consideration of the operations of reflective thought. The perfect system of thought is so perfect that it is a luminous, harmonious whole, without definite parts or distinctions— or, if there are such, it is only reflection that brings them out. The categories and methods of constitutive thought itself must therefore be characterized in terms of the *modus operandi* of reflective thought. Yet the latter takes place just because of the peculiar problem of the peculiar conditions under which it arises. Its work is progressive, reformatory, reconstructive, synthetic, in the terminology made familiar by Kant. We are not only *not* justified, accordingly, in transferring its determinations over to "constitutive" thought, but are prohibited from attempting any such transfer. To identify logical processes, states, devices, results which are conditioned upon the primary fact of resistance to thought as constitutive with the structure of constitutive thought is as complete an instance of the fallacy of recourse from one genus to another as could well be found. Constitutive and reflective thought are, first, defined in terms of their dissimilarity and even opposition, and then without more ado the forms of the description of the latter are carried over bodily to the former!

This is not a merely controversial criticism. It points positively toward the fundamental thesis of these chapters: All the distinctions discovered within thinking, of conception as over against sense-perception, of various modes and forms of judgment, of inference in its vast diversity of operation—all these distinctions come within the thought-situation as growing out of a characteristic antecedent typical formation of experience; and have for their purpose the solution of the peculiar problem with respect to which the thought-function is generated or evolved: the restoration of a deliberately integrated experience from the inherent conflict into which it has fallen.

The failure of transcendental logic has the same origin as the failure of the empiristic (whether taken pure or in the mixed form in which Lotze presents it). It makes into absolute and fixed distinctions of existence and meaning, and of one kind of meaning and another kind, things which are historic or temporal in their origin and their significance. It views thought as attempting to represent or state reality once for all, instead of trying to determine some phases or contents of it with reference to their more effective and significant employ—instead of as reconstructive. The rock against which every such logic splits is that either existence already has the statement which thought is endeavoring to give it, or else it has not. In the former case, thought is futilely reiterative; in the latter, it is falsificatory.

The significance of Lotze for critical purposes is that his peculiar effort to combine a transcendental view of thought (*i.e.*, of Thought as active in forms of its own, pure in and of themselves) with certain obvious facts of the dependence of our thought upon specific empirical antecedents, brings to light fundamental defects in both the empiristic and the transcendental logics. We discover a common failure in both: the failure to view logical terms and distinctions with respect to their necessary function in the redintegration of experience.

3. DATA AND MEANINGS

We have reached the point of conflict in the matters of an experience. It is *in* this conflict and because of it that the matters, or significant quales, stand out *as* matters. As long as the sun revolves about earth without question, this "content" is not in any way abstracted. Its distinction from the form or mode of experience as its matter is the work of reflection. The same conflict makes other experiences assume discriminated objectification; they, too, cease to be ways of living, and become distinct objects of observation and consideration. The movements of planets, eclipses, etc., are cases in point.[1] The maintenance of a unified experience has become a problem, an end, for it is no longer secure. But this involves such restatement of the conflicting elements as will enable them to take a place somewhere in the world of the new experience; they must be disposed of somehow, and they can be disposed of finally only as they are provided for. That is, they cannot be simply denied or excluded or eliminated; they must be taken into the fold. But such introduc-

---

1. This is but to say that the presentation of objects as specifically different things in experience is the work of reflection, and that the discrimination of something experienced from modes of experiencing is also the work of reflection. The latter statement is, of course, but a particular case of the first; for an act of experiencing is one object, among others, which may be discriminated out of the original experience. When so discriminated, it has exactly the same existential status as any other discriminated object; seeing and thing seen stand on the same level of existentiality. But primary experience is innocent of the discrimination of the *what* experienced and the *how*, or mode, of experiencing. We are not in it aware of the seeing, nor yet of objects *as* something seen. Any experience in all of its non-reflective phases is innocent of any discrimination of subject and object. It involves within itself what may be reflectively discriminated into objects located outside the organism and objects referred to the organism. (Note added in revision.)

[First published as "Thought and Its Subject-Matter: The Datum of Thinking," in *Studies in Logical Theory*. Revised and reprinted in *Essays in Experimental Logic*.]

tion clearly demands more or less modification or transformation on their part. The thought-situation is the deliberate maintenance of an organization in experience, with a critical consideration of the claims of the various conflicting contents to a place, and a final assignment of position.

The conflicting situation inevitably polarizes or dichotomizes itself. There is somewhat which is untouched in the contention of incompatibles. There is something which remains secure, unquestioned. On the other hand, there are elements which are doubtful and precarious. This gives the framework of the general distribution of the field into "facts," the given, the presented, the Datum; and ideas, the *Quaesitum,* the conceived, the Inferential.

a) There is always something unquestioned in any problematic situation at any stage of its process,[2] even if it be only the fact of conflict or tension. For this is never *mere* tension at large. It is thoroughly qualified, or characteristically toned and colored, by the particular elements which are in strife. Hence it is *this* conflict, unique and irreplaceable. That it comes now means precisely that it has never come before; that it is now passed in review and some sort of a settlement reached, means that just *this* conflict will never recur. In a word, the conflict is immediately of just this and no other sort, and this immediately given quality is an irreducible datum. *It* is fact, even if all else be *doubtful.* As it is subjected to examination, it loses vagueness and assumes more definite form.

Only in very extreme cases, however, does the assured, unquestioned element reduce to terms as low as we have here imagined. Certain things come to stand forth as facts, no matter what else may be doubted. There are certain *apparent* diurnal changes of the sun; there is a certain annual course or track. There are certain nocturnal changes in the planets, and certain seasonal rhythmic paths. The significance of these may be doubted: Do they *mean* real change

2. Of course, this very element may be the precarious, the ideal, and possibly fanciful of some other situation. But it is to change the historic into the absolute to conclude that therefore everything is uncertain, all at once, or as such. This gives metaphysical scepticism as distinct from the working scepticism which is an inherent factor in all reflection and scientific inquiry.

in the sun or in the earth? But change, and change of a certain definite and numerically determinate character is there. It is clear that such out-standing facts (ex-istences) constitute the data, the given or presented, in the thought-function.

b) It is obvious that this is only one correspondent, or status, in the total situation. With the consciousness of *this* as certain, as given to be reckoned with, goes the consciousness of uncertainty as to *what it means*—of how it is to be understood or interpreted, that is, of its reference and connection. The facts *qua* presentations or existences are sure; *qua* meanings (position and relationship in an experience yet to be secured) they are doubtful. Yet doubt does not preclude memory or anticipation. Indeed, it is possible only through them. The memory of past experience makes sun-revolving-about-earth an object of attentive regard. The recollection of certain other experiences suggests the idea of earth-rotating-daily-on-axis and revolving-annually-about-sun. These contents are as much present as is the observation of change, but as respects connection they are only possibilities. Accordingly, they are categorized or disposed of as ideas, meanings, thoughts, ways of conceiving, comprehending, interpreting facts.

Correspondence of reference here is as obvious as correlation of existence. In the logical process, the datum is not just external existence, and the idea mere psychical existence. Both are modes of existence—one of *given* existence, the other of *possible*, of inferred existence. And if the latter is regarded, from the standpoint of the unified experience aimed at, as having only *possible* existence, the datum also is regarded as incomplete and unassured. Or, as we commonly put it, while the ideas are impressions, suggestions, guesses, theories, estimates, etc., facts are crude, raw, unorganized, brute. They lack relationship, that is, assured place; they are deficient as to continuity. Mere change of relative position of sun, which is absolutely unquestioned as datum, is a sheer abstraction from the standpoint either of the organized experience left behind, or of the reorganized experience which is the end—the objective. It is impossible as a persistent object. In other words, datum and ideatum are divisions of labor, cooperative instrumentalities, for economical dealing with the problem of the maintenance of the integrity of experience.

Once more, and briefly, both datum and ideatum may (and positively, veritably, do) break up, each for itself, into physical and mental. In so far as the conviction gains ground that the earth revolves about the sun, the old fact is broken up into a new cosmic existence, and a new psychological condition—the recognition of a process in virtue of which movements of smaller bodies in relation to very remote larger bodies are interpreted in a reverse sense. We do not just eliminate the source of error in the old content. We reinterpret it as valid in its own place, viz., a case of the psychology of perception, although invalid as a matter of cosmic structure. Until we have detected the source of error as itself a perfectly genuine existence, we are not, scientifically, satisfied. If we decide that the snake is but a hallucination, our reflection is not, in purport, complete until we have found some fact just as existential as the snake would have been had it been there, which accounts for the hallucination. We never stop, except temporarily, with a reference to the mind or knower as source of an error. We hunt for a specific existence. In other words, with increasing accuracy of determination of the given, there comes a distinction, for methodological purposes, between the *quality* or matter of the sense-experience and its *form*—the sense-perceiving, as itself a psychological fact, having its own place and laws or relations. Moreover, the old experience, that of sun-revolving, abides. But it is regarded as belonging to "me"—to this experiencing individual, rather than to the cosmic world.

Here, then, *within* the growth of the thought-situation and as a part of the process of determining *specific* truth under *specific* conditions, we get for the first time the clue to that distinction with which, as ready-made and prior to all thinking, Lotze started out, namely, the separation of the matter of impression from impression as a personal event. The separation which, taken at large, engenders an insoluble problem, appears within a particular reflective inquiry, as an inevitable differentiation of a scheme of existence.

The same sort of thing occurs on the side of thought, or meaning. The meaning or idea which is growing in acceptance, which is gaining ground as meaning-of-datum, gets logical or intellectual or objective force; that which is losing standing, which is increasingly doubtful, gets qualified as just a notion, a fancy, a prejudice, misconception—or finally just an error, a mental slip.

Evaluated as fanciful in *validity* it becomes a mere fancy in its existence.[3] It is not eliminated, but receives a new reference or meaning. Thus the distinction between subjectivity and objectivity is not one between meaning as such and datum as such. It is a specification that emerges, correspondently, in *both* datum and ideatum. That which is left behind in the evolution of accepted meaning is still characterized as real, but real now in relation only to a way of experiencing—to a peculiarity of the organism. That which is moved toward is regarded as real in a cosmic or extra-organic sense.

1. *The data of thought.*—When we turn to Lotze, we find that he makes a clear distinction between the presented material of thought, its datum, and the typical characteristic modes of thinking in virtue of which the datum gets organization or system. It is interesting to note also that he states the datum in terms different from those in which the antecedents of thought are defined. From the point of view of the data or material upon which ideas exercise themselves, it is not coincidence, collocation, or succession that counts, but gradation of degrees in a scale. It is not things in spatial or temporal arrangement that are emphasized, but qualities as mutually distinguished, yet resembling and classed. There is no inherent inconceivability in the idea that every impression should be as incomparably different from every other as sweet is from warm. But by a remarkable circumstance such is not the case. We have series, and networks of series. We have diversity of a common—diverse colors, sounds, smells, tastes, etc. In other words, the data are sense-qualities

3. But this is a slow progress within reflection. Plato, who was influential in bringing this general distinction to consciousness, still thought and wrote as if "image" were itself a queer sort of objective existence; it was only gradually that it was disposed of as a phase of personal experiencing.

which, fortunately for thought, are given arranged, as shades, degrees, variations, or qualities of somewhat that is identical.[4]

All this is given, presented, to our ideational activities. Even the universal, the common color which runs through the various qualities of blue, green, white, etc., is not a product of thought, but something which thought finds already in existence. It conditions comparison and reciprocal distinction. Particularly all mathematical determinations, whether of counting (number), degree (more or less), and quantity (greatness and smallness), come back to this peculiarity of the datum. Here Lotze dwells at considerable length upon the fact that the very possibility, as well as the success, of thought is due to this peculiar universalization or *prima facie* ordering with which its material is given to it. Such pre-established fitness in the meeting of two things that have nothing to do with each other is certainly cause enough for wonder and congratulation.

It should not be difficult to see why Lotze uses different categories in describing the material of thought from those employed in describing its antecedent conditions, even though, according to him, the two are absolutely the same.[5]

4. *Logic*, I, 28–34.
5. It is interesting to see how explicitly Lotze is compelled finally to differentiate two aspects in the antecedents of thoughts, one of which is necessary in order that there may be anything to call out thought (a lack, or problem); the other in order that when thought is evoked it may find data at hand—that is, material in shape to receive and respond to its exercise. "The manifold matter of ideas is brought before us, not only in the *systematic order of its qualitative relationships*, but in the rich *variety of local and temporal combinations*. . . . The *combinations of heterogeneous ideas* . . . form the *problems*, in connexion with which the efforts of thought to reduce coexistence to coherence will *subsequently* be made. The *homogeneous or similar* ideas, on the other hand, give occasion to separate, to connect, and to count their repetitions" (*Logic*, I, 33, 34; italics mine). Without the heterogeneous variety of the local and temporal juxtapositions there would be nothing to excite thought. Without the systematic arrangement of quality there would be nothing to meet thought and reward it for its efforts. The homogeneity of qualitative relationships, *in the pre-thought material*, gives the tools or instruments by which thought is enabled successfully to tackle the heterogeneity of collocations and conjunctions also found in the same material! One would suppose that when Lotze reached this point he might have been led to suspect that in his remarkable adjustment of thought-stimuli, thought-material, and thought-

He has different *functions* in mind. In one case, the material must be characterized as evoking, as incentive, as stimulus —from this point of view the peculiar feature of spatial and temporal arrangement in contrast with coherence or connection is emphasized. But in the other case the material must be characterized as affording stuff, actual subject-matter. Data are not only what is given *to* thought, but they are also the food, the raw material, *of* thought. They must be described as, on the one hand, wholly outside of thought. This clearly puts them into the region of sense-perception. They are matters of *sensation* given free from all inferring, judging, relating influence. Sensation is just what is *not* called up in memory or in anticipated projection—it is the immediate, the irreducible. On the other hand, sensory-*matter* is qualitative, and quales are made up on a common basis. They are degrees or grades of a common quality. Thus they have a certain ready-made setting of mutual distinction and reference which is already almost, if not quite, the effect of comparing, of relating, effects which are the express traits of thinking.

It is easy to interpret this miraculous gift of grace in the light of what has been said. The data are in truth precisely that which is selected and set aside *as* present, as immediate. Thus they are *given* to *further* thought. But the selection has occurred in view of the need for thought; it is a listing of the capital in the way of the undisturbed, the undiscussed, which thought can count upon in this particular problem. Hence it is not strange that it has a peculiar fitness of adaptation for thought's further work. Having been selected with precisely that end in view, the wonder would be if it were not so fitted. A man may coin counterfeit money for use upon others, but hardly with the intent of passing it off upon himself.

Our only difficulty here is that the mind flies away from the logical interpretation of sense-datum to a ready-made notion of it brought over from abstract psychological inquiry. The belief in isolated sensory quales which are some-

tools to one another, he must after all be dealing, not with something prior to the thought-function, but with the necessary structures and tools of the thought-situation.

how forced upon us, and forced upon us at large, and thus
conditioning thought wholly *ab extra*, instead of determining it as instrumentalities or elements selected from experienced things for that very purpose, is too fixed. Sensory
qualities *are* forced upon us, but *not* at large. The sensory
data of experience always come *in a context*; they always
appear as variations in a continuum. Even the thunder which
breaks in upon me (to take the extreme of apparent dis-
continuity and irrelevancy) disturbs me because it is taken
as thunder: as a part of the same space-world as that in
which my chair and room and house are located; and it is
taken as an influence which interrupts and disturbs, *because*
it is part of a common world of causes and effects. The
solution of continuity is itself practical or teleological, and
thus presupposes and affects continuity of purpose, occupations, and means in a life-process. It is not metaphysics, it is
biology which enforces the idea that actual sensation is not
only determined as an event in a world of events,[6] but is an
occurrence occurring at a certain period in the control and
use of stimuli.[7]

2. *Forms of thinking data.*—As sensory datum is material set for work of thought, so the ideational forms with
which thought does its work are apt and prompt to meet
the needs of the material. The "accessory"[8] notion of ground
of coherence turns out, in truth, not to be a formal, or external, addition to the data, but a requalification of them.
Thought is accessory as accomplice, not as addendum.
"Thought" is to eliminate mere coincidence, and to assert
grounded coherence. Lotze makes it clear that he does not at
bottom conceive of "thought" as an activity "in itself" imposing a form of coherence; but that the organizing work of
"thought" is only the progressive realization of an inherent
unity, or system, in the material experienced. The specific
modes in which thought brings its "accessory" power to

6. *Supra,* pp. 322–23.
7. For the identity of sensory experience with the point of greatest
   strain and stress in conflicting or tensional experience, see "The
   Reflex Arc Concept in Psychology," *Psychological Review,* Vol.
   III, p. 57 [*Early Works of John Dewey,* 5:96–109].
8. For the "accessory" character of thought, see *Logic,* I, 7, 25–27,
   61, etc.

bear—names, conception, judgment, and inference—are successive stages in the adequate organization of the matter which comes to us first as data; they are successive stages of the effort to overcome the original defects of the data. Conception starts from the universal (the common element) of sense. Yet (and this is the significant point) it does not simply abstract this common element, and consciously generalize it over against its own differences. Such a "universal" is *not* coherence, just because it does not *include* and dominate the temporal and local heterogeneity. The *true* concept (see *Logic*, I, 38) is a system of attributes, held together on the basis of some ground, or determining, dominating principle— a ground which so controls all its own instances as to make them into an inwardly connected whole, and which so specifies its own limits as to be exclusive of all else. If we abstract color as the common element of various colors, the result is not a scientific idea or concept. Discovery of a process of light-waves whose various rates constitute the various colors of the spectrum gives the concept. And when we get such a concept, the former mere temporal abruptness of color experiences gives way to ordered parts of a color system. The logical product—the concept, in other words— is not a formal seal or stamp; it is a thorough-going connection of data in a dynamic continuity of existence.

The form or mode of thought which marks the continued transformation of the data and the idea in reference to each other is judgment. Judgment makes explicit the assumption of a principle which determines connection within an individualized whole. It definitely states red as *this* case or instance of the law or process of color, and thus further overcomes the defect in *subject-matter* or data still left by conception.[9] Now judgment logically terminates in disjunction.

9. Bosanquet (*Logic*, I, 30–34) and Jones (*Philosophy of Lotze*, 1895, Ch. 4) have called attention to a curious inconsistency in Lotze's treatment of judgment. On one hand, the statement is as given above. Judgment grows out of conception in making explicit the determining relation of universal to its own particular, implied in conception. But, on the other hand, judgment grows not out of conception at all, but out of the question of determining connection in change. Lotze's nominal reason for this latter view is that the conceptual world is purely static; since the actual world is one of change, we need to pass upon what really goes together (is causal) in the change as distinct from

It gives a universal which may determine any one of a number of alternative defined particulars, but which is arbitrary as to *what* one is selected. Systematic *inference* brings to light the material conditions under which the law, or dominating universal, applies to this, rather than that alternative particular, and so completes the ideal organization of the subject-matter. If this act were complete, we should finally have present to us a whole on which we should know the determining and effective or authorizing elements, and the order of development or hierarchy of dependence, in which others follow from them.[10]

In this account by Lotze of the operations of the forms of thought, there is clearly put before us the picture of a

---

such as are merely coincident. But, as Jones clearly shows, it is also connected with the fact that, while Lotze nominally asserts that judgment grows out of conception, he treats conception as the result of judgment since the first view makes judgment a mere explication of the content of an idea, and hence merely expository or analytic (in the Kantian sense) and so of more than doubtful applicability to reality. The affair is too large to discuss here, and I will content myself with referring to the oscillation between conflicting contents, and gradation of sensory qualities already discussed (p. 342, note). It is judgment which grows out of the former, because judgment is the whole situation as such; conception is referable to the latter because it *is* one abstraction within the whole (the solution of possible meanings of the data) just as the datum is another. In truth, since the sensory datum is not absolute, but comes in a historical context, the qualities apprehended as constituting the datum simply define the locus of conflict in the entire situation. They are attributives of the contents-in-tension of the colliding things, not calm untroubled ultimates. On pp. 33 and 34 of Vol. I, Lotze recognizes (as we have just seen) that, as matter of fact, it is both sensory qualities in their systematic grading, or quantitative determinations (see *Logic*, I, 34, for the recognition of the necessary place of the quantitative in the true concept), *and* the "rich variety of local and temporal combinations," that provoke thought and supply it with material. But, as usual, he treats this simply as a historical accident, not as furnishing the key to the whole matter. In fine, while the heterogeneous collocations and successions constitute the problematic element that stimulates thought, quantitative determination of the sensory quality furnishes one of the two chief means through which thought deals with the problem. It is a reduction of the original colliding contents to a form in which the effort at redintegration gets maximum efficiency. The concept, as ideal meaning, is of course the other partner to the transaction. It is getting the various possible meanings-of-the-data into such shape as to make them most useful in construing the data. The bearing of this upon the subject and predicate of judgment cannot be discussed here.

10. See *Logic*, I, 38, 59, 61, 105, 129, 197, for Lotze's treatment of these distinctions.

continuous correlative determination of datum on one side and of idea or meaning on the other, till experience is again integral, data being thoroughly defined and connected, and ideas being the relevant meanings of subject-matter. That we have here in outline a description of what actually occurs there can be no doubt. But there is as little doubt that the description is thoroughly inconsistent with Lotze's supposition that the material or data of thought is precisely the same as the antecedent of thought; or that ideas, conceptions, are purely mental somewhats extraneously brought to bear, as the sole essential characteristics of thought, upon a material provided ready-made. It means but one thing: The maintenance of unity and wholeness in experience through conflicting contents occurs by means of a strictly correspondent setting apart of facts to be accurately described and properly related, and meanings to be adequately construed and properly referred. The datum is given *in* the thought-situation, and *to* further qualification of ideas or meanings. But even in this aspect it presents a problem. To find out *what is* given is an inquiry which taxes reflection to the uttermost. Every important advance in scientific method means better agencies, more skilled technique for simply detaching and describing what is barely there, or given. To be able to find out what can safely be taken as *there*, as given in any particular inquiry, and hence be taken as material for orderly and verifiable inference, for fruitful hypothesis-making, for entertaining of explanatory and interpretative ideas, is one phase of the effort of systematic scientific inquiry. It marks its inductive phase. To take what is discovered to be reliable evidence within a more complex *situation* as if it were given absolutely and in isolation, or apart from a particular historic situs and context, is the fallacy of empiricism as a logical theory. To regard the thought-forms of conception, judgment, and inference as qualifications of "pure thought, apart from any difference in objects," instead of as successive dispositions in the progressive organization of the material (or objects), is the fallacy of rationalism. Lotze, like Kant, attempts to combine the two, thinking thereby to correct each by the other.

Lotze recognizes the futility of thought if the sense-data

as data are final, if they alone are real, the truly existent, self-justificatory and valid. He sees that, if the empiricist were right in his assumption as to the real worth of the given data, thinking would be a ridiculous pretender, either toilfully and poorly doing over again what needs no doing, or making a willful departure from truth. He realizes that thought is evoked because it is needed, and that it has a work to do which is not merely formal, but which effects a modification of the subject-matter of experience. Consequently he assumes a thought-in-itself, with certain forms and modes of action of its own, a realm of meaning possessed of a directive and normative worth of its own—the root-fallacy of rationalism. His attempted compromise between the two turns out to be based on the assumption of the indefensible ideas of both—the notion of an independent matter given to thought, on one side, and of an independent worth or force of thought-forms, on the other.

This pointing out of inconsistencies becomes stale and unprofitable save as we bring them back into connection with their root-origin—the erection of distinctions that are genetic and historic, and working or instrumental divisions of labor, into rigid and ready-made structural differences of reality. Lotze clearly recognizes that thought's nature is dependent upon its aim, its aim upon its problem, and this upon the situation in which it finds its incentive and excuse. Its work is cut out for it. It does not what it would, but what it must. As Lotze puts it, "Logic has to do with thought, not as it would be under hypothetical conditions, but as it is" (*Logic*, I, 33), and this statement is made in explicit combination with statements to the effect that the peculiarity of the material of thought conditions its activity. Similarly he says, in a passage already referred to: "The possibility and the success of thought's production in general depends upon this original constitution and organisation of the whole world of ideas, a constitution which, though not necessary in thought, is all the more necessary to make thought possible."[11]

As we have seen, the essential nature of conception, judgment, and inference is dependent upon peculiarities of

11. *Logic*, I, 36; see also II, 290, 291.

the propounded material, they being forms dependent for their significance upon the stage of organization in which they begin.

From this only one conclusion is possible. If thought's nature is dependent upon its actual conditions and circumstances, the primary logical problem is to study thought-in-its-conditioning; it is to detect the crisis within which thought and its subject-matter present themselves in their mutual distinction and cross-reference. But Lotze is so thoroughly committed to a ready-made antecedent of some sort, that this genetic consideration is of no account to him. The historic method is a mere matter of psychology, and has no logical worth (*Logic*, I, 2). We must presuppose a psychological mechanism and psychological material, but logic is concerned not with origin or history, but with authority, worth, value (*Logic*, I, 10). Again: "Logic is not concerned with the manner in which the elements utilised by thought come into existence, but their value *after* they have somehow come into existence, for the carrying out of intellectual operations" (*Logic*, I, 34). And finally: "I have maintained throughout my work that Logic cannot derive any serious advantage from a discussion of *the conditions under which thought as a psychological process comes about.* The significance of logical forms . . . is to be found in the utterances of thought, the laws which it imposes, after or during the act of thinking, not in the conditions which lie back of any which produce thought."[12]

Lotze, in truth, represents a halting-stage in the evolution of logical theory. He is too far along to be contented with the reiteration of the purely formal distinctions of a merely formal thought-by-itself. He recognizes that thought as formal is the form of some matter, and has its worth only as organizing that matter to meet the ideal demands of reason; and that "reason" is in truth only an adequate systematization of the matter or content. Consequently he has to open the door to admit "psychical processes" which furnish

---

12. *Logic*, II, 246; the same is reiterated in II, 250, where the question of origin is referred to as a corruption in logic. Certain psychical acts are necessary as "conditions and occasions" of logical operations, but the "deep gulf between psychical mechanism and thought remains unfilled."

this material. Having let in the material, he is bound to shut the door again in the face of the processes from which the material proceeded—to dismiss them as impertinent intruders. If thought gets its data in such a surreptitious manner, there is no occasion for wonder that the legitimacy of its dealings with the material remains an open question. Logical theory, like every branch of the philosophic disciplines, waits upon a surrender of the obstinate conviction that, while the work and aim of thought is conditioned by the material supplied to it, yet the *worth* of its performances is something to be passed upon in complete abstraction from conditions of origin and development.

4. THE OBJECTS OF THOUGHT

In the foregoing discussion, particularly in the last chapter, we were repeatedly led to recognize that thought has its own distinctive objects. At times Lotze gives way to the tendency to define thought entirely in terms of modes and forms of activity which are exercised by it upon a strictly foreign material. But two motives continually push him in the other direction. (1) Thought has a distinctive work to do, one which involves a qualitative transformation of (at least) the *relationships* of the presented matter; as fast as it accomplishes this work, the subject-matter becomes somehow thought's subject-matter. As we have just seen, the data are progressively organized to meet thought's ideal of a complete whole, with its members interconnected according to a determining principle. Such progressive organization throws backward doubt upon the assumption of the original total irrelevancy of the data and thought-forms to each other. (2) A like motive operates from the side of the subject-matter. As merely foreign and external, it is too heterogeneous to lend itself to thought's exercise and influence. The idea, as we saw in the first chapter, is the convenient medium through which Lotze passes from the purely heterogeneous psychical impression or event, which is totally irrelevant to thought's purpose and working, over to a state of affairs which can reward thought. Idea as meaning forms the bridge over from the brute factuality of the psychical impression to the coherent value of thought's own content.

We have, in this chapter, to consider the question of the idea or content of thought from two points of view: first, the *possibility* of such a content—its consistency with Lotze's

[First published as "Thought and Its Subject-Matter: The Content and Object of Thought," in *Studies in Logical Theory.* Revised and reprinted in *Essays in Experimental Logic.*]

fundamental premises; secondly, its *objective* character—its validity and test.

I. The question of the possibility of a specific content of thought is the question of the nature of the idea as meaning. *Meaning* is the characteristic object of thought. We have thus far left unquestioned Lotze's continual assumption of meaning as a sort of thought-unit; the building-stone of thought's construction. In his treatment of meaning, Lotze's contradictions regarding the antecedents, data, and content of thought reach their full conclusion. He expressly makes meaning to be the product of thought's activity and also the unreflective material out of which thought's operations grow.

This contradiction has been worked out in accurate and complete detail by Professor Jones.[1] He summarizes it as follows (pp. 98–99): "No other way was left to him [Lotze] except this of first attributing all to sense and afterwards attributing all to thought, and, finally of attributing it to thought only because it was already in its material. This *see-saw* is essential to his theory; the elements of knowledge as he describes them can subsist only by the alternate robbery of each other." We have already seen how strenuously Lotze insists upon the fact that the given subject-matter of thought is to be regarded wholly as the work of a physical mechanism, "without any action of thought."[2] But Lotze also states that if the products of the psychical mechanism "are to admit of combination in the definite form of a *thought*, they each require some previous shaping to make them into logical building-stones and to convert them from *impressions* into *ideas*. Nothing is really more familiar to us than this first operation of thought; the only reason why we usually overlook it is that in the language which we inherit, it is already carried out, and it seems, therefore, to belong to the self-evident presuppositions of thought, *not to its own specific work*."[3] And again (*Logic*, I, 23), judgments "can consist of nothing but combinations of ideas which are no longer mere

1. *Philosophy of Lotze*, Ch. 3, "Thought and the Preliminary Process of Experience."
2. *Logic*, I, 38.
3. *Logic*, I, 13; last italics mine.

impressions: every such idea must have undergone at least the simple formation mentioned above." Such ideas are, Lotze goes on to urge, already rudimentary concepts—that is to say, logical determinations.

The obviousness of the logical contradiction of attributing to a preliminary specific work of thought exactly the condition of affairs which is elsewhere explicitly attributed to a psychical mechanism prior to any thought-activity, should not blind us to its import and relative necessity. The impression, it will be recalled, is a mere state of our own consciousness—a mood of ourselves. As such it has simply *de facto* relations as an event to other similar events. But reflective thought is concerned with the relationship of a content or matter to other contents. Hence the impression must have a matter before it can come at all within the sphere of thought's exercise. How shall it secure this? Why, by a preliminary activity of thought which objectifies the impression. Blue as a mere sensuous irritation or feeling is given a quality, the meaning "blue"—blueness; the sense-impression is objectified; it is presented "no longer as a condition which we undergo, but as a something which has its being and its meaning in itself, and which continues to be what it is, and to mean what it means whether we are conscious of it or not. It is easy to see here the *necessary beginning of that activity which we above appropriated to thought as such*: it has not yet got so far as converting coexistence into coherence. It has first to perform the previous task of investing each single impression with an independent validity, without which the later opposition of their real coherence to mere coexistence could not be made in any intelligible sense."[4]

This objectification, which converts a sensitive state into a sensible matter to which the sensitive state is referred, also gives this matter "position," a certain typical character. It is not objectified in a merely general way, but is given a specific sort of objectivity. Of these sorts of objectivity there are three mentioned: that of a substantive content; that of an attached dependent content; that of an active relationship

4. *Logic*, I, 14; italics mine.

connecting the various contents with each other. In short, we have the types of meaning embodied in language in the form of nouns, adjectives, and verbs. It is through this preliminary formative activity of thought that reflective or *logical* thought has presented to it a world of meanings ranged in an order of relative independence and dependence, and arranged as elements in a complex of meanings whose various constituent parts mutually influence one another's meanings.[5]

As usual, Lotze mediates the contradiction between material constituted *by* thought and the same material just presented *to* thought, by a further position so disparate to each that, taken in connection with each by turns, it seems to bridge the gulf. After describing the prior constitutive work of thought as above, he goes on to discuss a *second* phase of thought which is intermediary between this and the third phase, viz., reflective thought proper. This second activity is that of arranging experienced quales in series and groups, thus ascribing a sort of universal or common somewhat to various instances (as already described; see pp. 342–43). On one hand, it is clearly stated that this second phase of thought's activity is in reality the *same* as the first phase: since all objectification involves positing, since positing involves distinction of one matter from others, and since this involves placing it in a series or group in which each is measurably marked off, as to the degree and nature of its diversity, from every other. We are told that we are only considering "a really inseparable operation" of thought from two different sides: first, as to the effect which objectifying thought has upon the matter as set over against the feeling *subject*; secondly, the effect which this objectification has upon the matter in relation to *other matters*.[6] Afterward, however, these two operations are declared to be radically different in type and nature. The first is determinant and formative; it gives ideas "the shape without which the logical spirit could not accept them." In a way it dictates "its own laws to its object-matter."[7] The second activity of thought is

5. See *Logic*, I, 16–20. On p. 22 this work is declared to be not only the first, but the most indispensable of all thought's operations.
6. *Logic*, I, 26.
7. *Logic*, I, 35.

rather passive and receptive. It simply recognizes what is already there. "Thought can make no difference where it finds none already in the matter of impressions."[8] "The first universal, as we saw, can only be experienced in immediate sensation. It is no product of thought, but something that thought finds already in existence."[9]

The obviousness of this further contradiction is paralleled only by its inevitableness. Thought is in the air, is arbitrary and wild in dealing with meanings, unless it gets its start and cue from actual experience. Hence the necessity of insisting upon thought's activity as just recognizing the contents already given. But, on the other hand, prior to the work of thought there is to Lotze no content or meaning. It requires a work of thought to detach anything from the flux of sense-irritations and invest it with a meaning of its own. This dilemma is inevitable to any writer who declines to consider as correlative the nature of thought-activity and thought-content from the standpoint of their generating conditions in the movement of experience. Viewed from such a standpoint the principle of solution is clear enough. As we have already seen (pp. 327–28), the internal dissension of an experience leads to detaching certain factors previously integrated in the concrete experience as aspects of its own qualitative coloring, and to relegating them, for the time being (pending integration into further immediate qualities of a reconstituted experience), into a world of bare meanings, a sphere qualified as ideal throughout. These meanings then become the tools of thought in interpreting the data, just as the sense-qualities which define the presented situation are the immediate matter for thought. The two *as*

8. *Logic*, I, 36; see the strong statements already quoted, pp. 321–22. What if this canon were applied in the first act of thought referred to above: the original objectification which transforms the mere state into an abiding quality or meaning? Suppose, that is, it were said that the first objectifying act cannot make a substantial (or attached) quale out of a mere state of feeling; it must *find* the distinction it makes there already! It is clear we should at once get a *regressus ad infinitum*. We here find Lotze face-to-face with this fundamental dilemma: thought either arbitrarily forces in its own distinctions, or else just repeats what is already there—is either falsifying or futile. This same contradiction, so far as it affects the impression, has already been discussed. See p. 323.

9. *Logic*, I, 31.

mutually referred are content. That is, the datum and the meaning as reciprocally qualified by each other constitute the objective of thought.

To reach this unification is thought's objective or goal. Every successive cross-section of reflective inquiry presents what may be taken for granted as the outcome of previous thinking, and as the determinant of further reflective procedure. Taken as defining the point reached in the thought-function and serving as constituent unit in further thought, it is content or logical object. Lotze's instinct is sure in identifying and setting over against each other the material given to thought and the content which is thought's own "building-stone." His contradictions arise simply from the fact that his absolute, non-historic method does not permit him to interpret this joint identity and distinction in a working, and hence relative, sense.

II. The question of how the existence of meanings, or thought-contents, is to be understood merges imperceptibly into the question of the real objectivity or validity of such contents. The difficulty for Lotze is the now familiar one: So far as his logic compels him to insist that these meanings are the possession and product of thought (since thought is an independent activity), the ideas are merely ideas; there is no test of objectivity beyond the thoroughly unsatisfactory and formal one of their own mutual consistency. In reaction from this Lotze is thrown back upon the idea of these contents as the original matter given in the impressions themselves. Here there seems to be an objective or external test by which the reality of thought's operations may be tried; a given idea is verified or found false according to its measure of correspondence with the matter of experience as such. But now we are no better off. The original independence and heterogeneity of impressions and of thought is so great that there is no way to compare the results of the latter with the former. We cannot compare or contrast distinctions of worth with bare differences of factual existence (*Logic*, I, 2). The standard or test of objectivity is so thoroughly external that by original definition it is wholly outside the realm of thought. How can thought compare meanings with existences?

Or again, the given material of experience apart from thought is precisely the relatively chaotic and unorganized; it even reduces itself to a mere sequence of psychical events. What sense is there in directing us to compare the highest results of scientific inquiry with the bare sequence of our own states of feeling; or even with the original data whose fragmentary and uncertain character was the exact motive for entering upon scientific inquiry? How can the former in any sense give a check or test of the value of the latter? This is professedly to test the validity of a system of meanings by comparison with that whose defects call forth the construction of the system of meanings.

Our subsequent inquiry simply consists in tracing some of the phases of the characteristic seesaw from one to the other of the two horns of the now familiar dilemma: either thought is separate from the matter of experience, and then its validity is wholly its own private business; or else the objective results of thought are already in the antecedent material, and then thought is either unnecessary, or else has no way of checking its own performances.

1. Lotze assumes, as we have seen, a certain independent validity in each meaning or qualified content, taken in and of itself. "Blue" has a certain meaning, in and of itself; it is an *object* for consciousness as such, not merely its state or mood. After the original sense-irritation through which it was mediated has entirely disappeared it persists as a valid meaning. Moreover, it is an object or content of thought for others as well. Thus it has a double mark of validity: in the comparison of one part of my own experience with another, and in the comparison of my experience as a whole with that of others. Here we have a sort of validity which does not raise at all the question of *metaphysical* reality (*Logic*, I, 14, 15). Lotze thus seems to have escaped from the necessity of employing as check or test for the validity of ideas any reference to a real outside the sphere of thought itself. Such terms as "conjunction," "franchise," "constitution," "algebraic zero," etc., claim to possess objective validity. Yet none of these professes to refer to a reality beyond thought. Generalizing this point of view, validity or objectivity of meaning means simply that

which is "identical for all consciousness" (*Logic*, I, 3); "it is quite indifferent whether certain parts of the world of thought indicate something which has besides an independent reality outside of thinking minds, or whether all that it contains exists only in the thoughts of those who think it, but with equal validity for them all" (*Logic*, I, 16).

So far it seems clear sailing. Difficulties, however, show themselves, the moment we inquire what is meant by a self-identical content for all thought. Is this to be taken in a static or in a dynamic way? That is to say: Does it express the fact that a given content or meaning is *de facto* presented to the consciousness of all alike? Does this coequal presence guarantee an objectivity? Or does validity attach to a given meaning or content in the sense that it directs and controls the further exercise of thinking, and thus the formation of further *new* objects of knowledge?

The former interpretation is alone consistent with Lotze's notion that the independent idea as such is invested with a certain validity or objectivity. It alone is consistent with his assertion that concepts precede judgments. It alone, that is to say, is consistent with the notion that reflective thinking has a sphere of ideas or meanings supplied to it at the outset. But it is impossible to entertain this belief. The stimulus which, according to Lotze, goads thought on from ideas or concepts to judgments and inferences, is in truth simply the lack of validity, of objectivity in its original independent meanings or contents. A meaning as independent is precisely that which is not invested with validity, but which is a mere idea, a "notion," a fancy, at best a surmise which may turn out to be valid (and of course this indicates possible reference); a standpoint to have its value determined by its further active use. "Blue" as a mere detached floating meaning, an idea at large, would not gain in validity simply by being entertained continuously in a given consciousness, or by being made at one and the same time the persistent object of attentive regard by all human consciousnesses. If this were all that were required, the chimera, the centaur, or any other subjective construction, could easily gain validity. "Christian Science" has made just this notion the basis of its philosophy.

The simple fact is that in such illustrations as "blue," "franchise," "conjunction," Lotze instinctively takes cases which are not mere independent and detached meanings, but which involve reference to a *region* of experience, to a region of mutually determining social activities. The conception that reference to a *social* activity does not involve the same sort of reference of a meaning beyond itself that is found in physical matters, and hence may be taken quite innocent and free of the problem of reference to existence beyond meaning, is one of the strangest that has ever found lodgment in human thinking. Either both physical and social reference or neither, is logical; if neither, then it is because the meaning functions, as it originates, in a specific situation which carries with it its own tests (see pp. 311–12). Lotze's conception is made possible only by unconsciously substituting the idea of an object as a content of thought for a large number of persons (or a *de facto* somewhat for every consciousness), for the genuine definition of object as a *determinant* in a scheme of activity. The former is consistent with Lotze's conception of thought, but wholly indeterminate as to validity or intent. The latter is the test used experimentally in all concrete thinking, but involves a radical transformation of all Lotze's assumptions. A given idea of the conjunction of the franchise, or of blue, is valid, not because everybody happens to entertain it, but because it expresses the factor of control or direction in a given movement of experience. The test of validity of idea[10] is its functional or instrumental use in effecting the transition from a relatively conflicting experience to a relatively integrated one. If Lotze's view were correct, "blue" valid once would be valid always— even when red or green were actually called for to fulfill specific conditions. This is to say validity really refers to rightfulness or adequacy of performance in an asserting of connection—not to a meaning as contemplated in detachment.

If we refer again to the fact that the genuine antecedent

10. As we have already seen, the concept, the meaning as such, is always a factor or status in a reflective situation; it is always a predicate of judgment, in use in interpreting and developing the logical subject, or datum of perception.

of thought is a situation which is disorganized in its structural elements, we can easily understand how certain contents may be detached and *held* apart as meanings or references, actual or possible. We can understand how such
detached contents may be of use in effecting a review of the
entire experience, and as affording standpoints and methods
of a reconstruction which will maintain the integrity of
behavior. We can understand how validity of meaning is
measured by reference to something which is not mere meaning; by reference to something which lies beyond it as such—
viz., the reconstitution of an experience into which it enters
as method of control. That paradox of ordinary experience
and of scientific inquiry by which objectivity is given alike
to matter of perception and to conceived relations—to facts
and to laws—affords no peculiar difficulty because the test
of objectivity is everywhere the same: anything is objective
in so far as, through the medium of conflict, it controls the
movement of experience in its reconstructive transition.
There is not first an object, whether of sense-perception or
of conception, which afterward somehow exercises this controlling influence; but the objective is *any* existence exercising the function of control. It may only control the act of
inquiry; it may only set on foot doubt, but this is direction
of subsequent experience, and, in so far, is a token of objectivity. It has to be reckoned with.

So much for the thought-content or meaning as having
a validity of its own. It does not have it as isolated or given
or static; it has it in its dynamic reference, its use in determining further movement of experience. In other words, the
"meaning," having been selected and made up with reference
to performing a certain office in the evolution of a unified
experience, can be tested in no other way than by discovering
whether it does what it was intended to do and what it pur-
ports to do.[11]

11. Royce, in his *World and Individual*, I, Chs. 6 and 7, has criti-
     cized the conception of meaning as valid, but in a way which
     implies that there is a difference between validity and reality, in
     the sense that the meaning or content of the valid idea becomes
     real only when it is experienced in direct *feeling*. The foregoing
     implies, of course, a difference between validity and reality, but
     finds the test of validity in exercise of the function of direction
     or control to which the idea makes pretension or claim. The

2. Lotze has to wrestle with this question of validity in a further respect: What constitutes the objectivity of thinking as a total attitude, activity, or function? According to his own statement, the meanings or valid ideas are after all only building-stones for logical thought. Validity is thus not a property of them in their independent existences, but of their mutual reference to each other. Thinking is the process of instituting these mutual references; of building up the various scattered and independent building-stones into the coherent system of thought. What is the validity of the various forms of thinking which find expression in the various types of judgment and in the various forms of inference? Categorical, hypothetical, disjunctive judgment; inference by induction, by analogy, by mathematical equation; classification, theory of explanation—all these are processes of reflection by which connection in an organized whole is given to the fragmentary meanings with which thought sets out. What shall we say of the validity of such processes?

On one point Lotze is quite clear. These various logical acts do not really enter into the constitution of the valid world. The logical forms as such are maintained *only* in the process of thinking. The world of valid truth does not undergo a series of contortions and evolutions, paralleling in any way the successive steps and missteps, the succession of tentative trials, withdrawals, and retracings, which mark the course of our own thinking.[12]

Lotze is explicit upon the point that only the thought-content in which the process of thinking issues has objective validity; the act of thinking is "purely and simply an inner movement of our own minds, made necessary to us by reason of the constitution of our nature and of our place in the world" (*Logic*, II, 279).

---

same point of view would profoundly modify Royce's interpretation of what he terms "inner" and "outer" meaning. See Moore, *University of Chicago Decennial Publications*, III, on "Existence, Meaning, and Reality."

12. *Logic*, II, 257, 265, and in general Bk. III, Ch. 4. It is significant that thought itself, appearing as an act of thinking over against its own content, is here treated as psychical rather than as logical. Consequently, as we see in the text, it gives him one more difficulty to wrestle with: how a process which is *ex officio* purely psychical and subjective can yet yield results which are valid, in a logical, to say nothing of an ontological, sense.

Here the problem of validity presents itself as the problem of the relation of the act of thinking to its own product. In his solution Lotze uses two metaphors: one derived from building operations, the other from traveling. The construction of a building requires of necessity certain tools and extraneous constructions, stagings, scaffoldings, etc., which are necessary to effect the final construction, but which do not enter into the building as such. The activity has an instrumental, though not a constitutive, value as regards its product. Similarly, in order to get a view from the top of a mountain—this view being the objective—the traveler has to go through preliminary movements along devious courses. These again are antecedent prerequisites, but do not constitute a portion of the attained view.

The problem of thought as activity, as distinct from thought as content, opens up altogether too large a question to receive complete consideration at this point. Fortunately, however, the previous discussion enables us to narrow the point which is in issue just here. The question is whether the activity of thought is to be regarded as an independent function supervening entirely from without upon antecedents, and directed from without upon data, or whether it marks the phase of the transformation which the course of experience (whether practical, or artistic, or socially affectional or whatever) undergoes for the sake of its deliberate control. If it be the latter, a thoroughly intelligent sense can be given to the proposition that the activity of thinking is instrumental, and that its worth is found, not in its own successive states as such, but in the result in which it comes to conclusion. But the conception of thinking as an independent activity somehow occurring after an independent antecedent, playing upon an independent subject-matter, and finally effecting an independent result, presents us with just one miracle the more.

I do not question the strictly instrumental character of thinking. The problem lies not here, but in the interpretation of the nature of the instrument. The difficulty with Lotze's position is that it forces us into the assumption of a means and an end which are simply and only external to each other, and yet necessarily dependent upon each other—a position which, whenever found, is thoroughly self-contradictory. Lotze vibrates between the notion of thought as a tool in the external sense, a mere scaffolding to a finished building in which it has no part nor lot, and the notion of thought as an immanent tool, as a scaffolding which is an integral part of the very operation of building, and which is set up for the sake of the building-activity which is carried on effectively only with and through a scaffolding. Only in the former case can the scaffolding be considered as a *mere* tool. In the latter case the external scaffolding is *not* the instrumentality; the actual tool is the *action* of erecting the building, and this action involves the scaffolding as a constituent part of itself. The work of building is not set over against the completed building as mere means to an end; it *is* the end taken in process or historically, longitudinally, temporally viewed. The scaffolding, moreover, is not an external means to the process of erecting, but an organic member of it. It is no mere accident of language that "building" has a double sense—meaning at once the process and the finished product. The outcome of thought is the thinking activity carried on to its own completion; the activity, on the other hand, *is* the outcome taken anywhere short of its own realization, and thereby still going on.

The only consideration which prevents easy and immediate acceptance of this view is the notion of thinking as something purely formal. It is strange that the empiricist does not see that his insistence upon a matter accidentally given to thought only strengthens the hands of the rationalist with his claim of thinking as an independent activity, separate from the actual make-up of the affairs of experience. Thinking as a merely formal activity exercised upon certain sensations or images or objects sets forth an absolutely meaningless proposition. The psychological identification of thinking with the process of association is much nearer the truth. It is, indeed, on the way to the truth. We need only to recognize that association is of matters or meanings, not of ideas as existences or events; and that the type of association we call thinking differs from casual fancy and revery by control in reference to an end, to apprehend how completely thinking is a reconstructive movement of actual contents of experience in relation to each other.

There is no miracle in the fact that tool and material

are adapted to each other in the process of reaching a valid conclusion. Were they external in origin to each other and to the result, the whole affair would, indeed, present an insoluble problem—so insoluble that, if this were the true condition of affairs, we never should even know that there was a problem. But, in truth, both material and tool have been secured and determined with reference to economy and efficiency in effecting the end desired—the maintenance of a harmonious experience. The builder has discovered that his building means building tools, and also building material. Each has been slowly evolved with reference to its fit employ in the entire function; and this evolution has been checked at every point by reference to its own correspondent. The carpenter has not thought at large on his building and then constructed tools at large, but has thought of his building in terms of the material which enters into it, and through that medium has come to the consideration of the tools which are helpful.

This is not a formal question, but one of the place and relations of the matters actually entering into experience. And they in turn determine the taking up of just those mental attitudes, and the employing of just those intellectual operations which most effectively handle and organize the material. Thinking is adaptation *to* an end *through* the adjustment of particular objective contents.

The thinker, like the carpenter, is at once stimulated and checked in every stage of his procedure by the particular situation which confronts him. A person is at the stage of wanting a new house: well then, his materials are available resources, the price of labor, the cost of building, the state and needs of his family, profession, etc.; his tools are paper and pencil and compass, or possibly the bank as a credit instrumentality, etc. Again, the work is beginning. The foundations are laid. This in turn determines its own specific materials and tools. Again, the building is almost ready for occupancy. The concrete process is that of taking away the scaffolding, clearing up the grounds, furnishing and decorating rooms, etc. This specific operation again determines its own fit or relevant materials and tools. It defines the time and mode and manner of beginning and ceasing to use them.

Logical theory will get along as well as does the practice of knowing when it sticks close by and observes the directions and checks inherent in each successive phase of the evolution of the cycle of experience. The problem in general of validity of the thinking process as distinct from the validity of this or that process arises only when thinking is isolated from its historic position and its material context (see *ante*, p. 311).

3. But Lotze is not yet done with the problem of validity, even from his own standpoint. The ground shifts again under his feet. It is no longer a question of the validity of the idea or meaning with which thought is supposed to set out; it is no longer a question of the validity of the process of thinking in reference to its own product; it is the question of the validity of the product. Supposing, after all, that the final meaning, or logical idea, is thoroughly coherent and organized; supposing it is an object for all consciousness as such. Once more arises the question: What is the validity of even the most coherent and complete idea?—a question which arises and will not down. We may reconstruct the notion of the chimera until it ceases to be an independent idea and becomes a part of the system of Greek mythology. Has it gained in validity in ceasing to be an independent myth, in becoming an element in systematized myth? Myth it was and myth it remains. Mythology does not get validity by growing bigger. How do we know the same is not the case with the ideas which are the product of our most deliberate and extended scientific inquiry? The reference again to the content as the self-identical object of all consciousness proves nothing; the subject-matter of a hallucination does not gain validity in proportion to its social contagiousness.

According to Lotze, the final product is, after all, still thought. Now, Lotze is committed once for all to the notion that thought, in any form, is directed by and at an outside reality. The ghost haunts him to the last. How, after all, does even the ideally perfect valid thought apply or refer to reality? Its genuine subject is still beyond itself. At the last Lotze can dispose of this question only by regarding it as a metaphysical, not a logical, problem (*Logic*, II, 281, 282). In other words, *logically* speaking, we are at the end just exactly where we were at the beginning—in the sphere of ideas, and of ideas only, plus a consciousness of the necessity of referring these ideas to a reality which is beyond them, which is utterly inaccessible to them, which is out of reach of any influence which they may exercise, and which transcends any possible comparison with their results. "It is vain," says Lotze, "to shrink from acknowledging the circle here involved. . . . All we know of the external world depends upon the ideas of it which are within us" (*Logic*, II, 185). "It is then this varied world of ideas within us which forms the sole material directly given to us" (*Logic*, II, 186). As it is the only material given to us, so it is the only material with which thought can end. To talk about knowing the external world through ideas which are merely within us is to talk of an inherent self-contradiction. There is no common ground in which the external world and our ideas can meet. In other words, the original separation between an independent thought-material and an independent thought-function and purpose lands us inevitably in the metaphysics of subjective idealism, plus a belief in an unknown reality beyond, which although unknowable is yet taken as the ultimate test of the value of our ideas. At the end, after all our maneuvering we are where we began:—with two separate disparates, one of meaning, but no existence, the other of existence, but no meaning.

The other aspect of Lotze's contradiction which completes the circle is clear when we refer to his original propositions, and recall that at the outset he was compelled to regard the origination and conjunctions of the impressions, the elements of ideas, as themselves the effects exercised by a world of things already in existence (see p. 334). He sets up an independent world of thought, and yet has to confess that both at its origin and at its termination it points with absolute necessity to a world beyond itself. Only the stubborn refusal to take this initial and terminal reference of thought beyond itself as having a *historic* or temporal meaning, indicating a particular place of generation and a particular point of fulfillment, compels Lotze to give such objective references a transcendental turn.

When Lotze goes on to say (*Logic*, II, 191) that the

measure of truth of particular parts of experience is found in asking whether, when judged by thought, they are in harmony with other parts of experience; when he goes on to say that there is no sense in trying to compare the entire world of ideas with a reality which is non-existent (excepting as it itself should become an idea), he lands where he might better have frankly commenced.[13] He saves himself from utter scepticism only by claiming that the explicit assumption of scepticism—the need of agreement of a ready-made idea as such with an extraneous ready-made material as such—is meaningless. He defines correctly the work of thought as consisting in harmonizing the various portions of experience with each other. In this case the test of thought is the harmony or unity of experience actually effected. The test of validity of thought is beyond thought, just as at the other limit thought originates out of a situation which is not dependent upon thought. Interpret this before and beyond in a historic sense, as an affair of the place occupied and rôle played by thinking as a function in experience in relation to other non-intellectual experiences of things, and then the intermediate and instrumental character of thought, its dependence upon unreflective antecedents for its existence, and upon a consequent experience for its final test, becomes significant and necessary. Taken at large, apart from temporal development and control, it plunges us in the depths of a hopelessly complicated and self-revolving metaphysic.

13. Lotze even goes so far in this connection as to say that the antithesis between our ideas and the objects to which they are directed is itself a part of the world of ideas (*Logic*, II, 192). Barring the phrase "world of *ideas*" (as against world of continuous experience), he need only have commenced at this point to have traveled straight and arrived somewhere. But it is absolutely impossible to hold both this view and that of the original independent existence of something given to and in thought and an independent existence of a thought-activity, thought-forms, and thought-contents.

5. [ON MILL AND WHEWELL]

The subsequent history of logical theory in England* is conditioned upon its attempt to combine into one system the theories of empiristic logic with recognition of the procedure of experimental science. This attempt finds its culmination in the *Logic* of John Stuart Mill. Of his interest in and fidelity to the actual procedure of experimental science, as he saw it, there can be no doubt. Of his good faith in concluding his Introduction with the words following there can be no doubt: "I can conscientiously affirm that no one proposition laid down in this work has been adopted for the sake of establishing, or with any reference for its fitness in being employed in establishing, preconceived opinions in any department of knowledge or of inquiry on which the speculative world is still undecided." Yet Mill was equally attached to the belief that ultimate reality, as it is for the human mind, is given in sensations, independent of ideas; and that all valid ideas are combinations and convenient ways of using such given material. Mill's very sincerity made it impossible that this belief should not determine, at every point, his treatment of the thinking process and of its various instrumentalities.

In Bk. III, Ch. 14, Mill discusses the logic of explanation, and in discussing this topic naturally finds it necessary to consider the matter of the proper use of scientific hypotheses. This is conducted from the standpoint of their use as that is reflected in the technique of scientific discovery. In Bk. IV, Ch. 2, he discusses "Abstraction or the Formation of Conceptions"—a topic which obviously involves the forming of hypotheses. In this chapter, his consideration is conducted in terms, not of scientific procedure, but of general philosophical theory, and this point of view is emphasized by the fact that he is opposing a certain view of Dr. Whewell.

* After Bacon.

The contradiction between the statements in the two chapters will serve to bring out the two points already made, viz., the correspondent character of datum and hypothesis, and the origin of the latter in a problematic situation and its consequent use as an instrument of unification and solution. Mill first points out that hypotheses are invented to enable the deductive method to be applied earlier to phenomena; that it does this by suppressing the first of the three steps, induction, ratiocination, and verification. He states that:

> The process of tracing regularity in any complicated, and at first sight confused, set of appearances is necessarily tentative; we begin by making any supposition, even a false one, to see what consequences will follow from it; and by observing how these differ from the real phenomena, we learn what corrections to make in our assumption. . . . *Neither induction nor deduction would enable us to understand even the simplest phenomena,* if we did not often commence by anticipating the results; by making a provisional supposition, at first essentially conjectural, as to some of the very notions which constitute the final object of the inquiry.[1]

If in addition we recognize that, according to Mill, our direct experience of nature always presents us with a complicated and confused set of appearances, we shall be in no doubt as to the importance of ideas as anticipations of a possible experience not yet had. Thus he says:

> The order of nature, as perceived at a first glance, presents at every instant a chaos followed by another chaos. We must decompose each chaos into single facts. We must learn to see in the chaotic antecedent a multitude of distinct antecedents, in the chaotic consequent a multitude of distinct consequents.[2]

In the next section of the same chapter he goes on to state that, having discriminated the various antecedents and consequents, we then "are to inquire which is connected with which." This requires a still further resolution of the complex and of the confused. To effect this we must vary the circumstances; we must modify the experience as given with

1. Bk. III, Ch. 14, Sec. 5; italics mine. The latter part of the passage, beginning with the words "If we did not often commence," etc., is quoted by Mill from Comte. The words "neither induction nor deduction would enable us to understand even the simplest phenomena" are his own.
2. Bk. III, Ch. 7, Sec. 1.

reference to accomplishing our purpose. To accomplish this purpose we have recourse either to observation or to experiment: "We may either *find* an instance in nature *suited to our purposes*, or, by an artificial arrangement of circumstances, *make* one" (the italics in "suited to our purpose" are mine; the others are Mill's). He then goes on to say that there is no real logical distinction between observation and experimentation. The four methods of experimental inquiry are expressly discussed by Mill in terms of their worth in singling out and connecting the antecedents and consequents which actually belong together, from the chaos and confusion of direct experience.

We have only to take these statements in their logical connection with each other (and this connection runs through the entire treatment by Mill of scientific inquiry), to recognize the absolute necessity of hypothesis to undertaking any directed inquiry or scientific operation. Consequently we are not surprised at finding him saying that "the function of hypotheses is one which must be reckoned absolutely indispensable in science"; and again that "the hypothesis by suggesting observations and experiments puts us on the road to independent evidence."[3]

Since Mill's virtual retraction, from the theoretical point of view, of what is here said from the standpoint of scientific procedure, regarding the necessity of ideas is an accompaniment of his criticism of Whewell, it will put the discussion in better perspective if we turn first to Whewell's views.[4] The latter began by stating a distinction which easily might have been developed into a theory of the relation of fact and idea which is in line with that advanced in this chapter, and indeed in this volume as a whole. He questions (Ch. 2) the fixity of the distinction between theory and practice. He points out that what we term facts are in effect simply accepted inferences; and that what we call theories are describable as facts, in proportion as they become thoroughly established. A true theory is a fact. "All the great theories which have successively been established in the world are

3. Bk. III, Ch. 14, Secs. 4 and 5.
4. William Whewell, *The Philosophy of the Inductive Sciences*, London, 1840.

now thought of as facts." "The most recondite theories when firmly established are accepted as facts; the simplest facts seem to involve something of the nature of theory."

The conclusion is that the distinction is a historic one, depending upon the state of knowledge at the time, and upon the attitude of the individual. What is theory for one epoch, or for one inquirer in a given epoch, is fact for some other epoch, or even for some other more advanced inquirer in the same epoch. It is theory when the element of inference involved in judging any fact is consciously brought out; it is fact when the conditions are such that we have never been led to question the inference involved, or else, having questioned it, have so thoroughly examined into the inferential process that there is no need of holding it further before the mind, and it relapses into unconsciousness again. "If this greater or less consciousness of our own internal act be all that distinguishes fact from theory, we must allow that the distinction is still untenable" (untenable, that is to say, as a fixed separation). Again, "Fact and Theory have no essential difference except in the degree of their *certainty and familiarity*. Theory, when it becomes firmly established and steadily lodged in the mind becomes Fact" (p. 45; italics mine). And, of course, it is equally true that as fast as facts are suspected or doubted, certain aspects of them are transferred into the class of theories and even of mere opinions.

I say this conception might have been developed in a way entirely congruous with the position of this chapter. This would have happened if the final distinction between fact and idea had been formulated upon the basis simply of the points, "relative certainty and familiarity." From this point of view the distinction between fact and idea is one purely relative to the doubt-inquiry function. It has to do with the evolution of an experience as regards its conscious surety. It has its origin in problematic situations. Whatever appears to us as a problem appears as contrasted with a possible solution. Whatever objects of thought refer particularly to the problematic side are theories, ideas, hypotheses; whatever relates to the solution side is surety, unquestioned familiarity, fact. This point of view makes the

distinctions entirely relative to the exigencies of the process
of reflective transformation of experience.

Whewell, however, had no sooner started in this train of
thought than he turns his back upon it. In Ch. 3 he transforms what he had proclaimed to be a relative, historic, and
working distinction into a fixed and absolute one. He distinguishes between sensations and ideas, not upon a genetic
basis with reference to establishing the conditions of further
operation; but with reference to a fundamentally fixed line
of demarcation between what is passively *given* to the mind
and the *activity* put forth by the mind. Thus he reinstates in
its most generalized and fixed, and therefore most vicious,
form the separation which he has just rejected. Sensations
are a brute unchangeable element of fact which exists and
persists independent of ideas; an idea is a mode of mental
operation which occurs and recurs in an independent individuality of its own. If he had carried out the line of
thought with which he began, sensation as fact would have
been that residuum of familiarity and certainty which cannot
be eliminated, however much else of an experience is dis-
solved in the inner conflict. Idea as hypothesis or theory
would have been the corresponding element in experience
which is necessary to redintegrate this residuum into a coherent and significant experience.

But since Whewell did not follow out his own line of
thought, choosing rather to fall back on the Kantian antithesis of sense and thought, he had no sooner separated his
fact and idea, his given datum and his mental relation, than
he is compelled to get them together again. The idea becomes a "general relation which is imposed upon perception
by an act of the mind, and which is different from anything
which our senses directly offer to us" (p. 26). Such conceptions are necessary to connect the facts which we learn
from our senses into truths. "The ideal conception which the
mind itself supplies is superinduced upon the facts as they
are originally presented to observation. Before the inductive
truth is detected, the facts are there, but they are many and
unconnected. The conception which the discoverer applies
to them gives them connexion and unity" (p. 42). All induction, according to Whewell, thus depends upon super-

induction—imposition upon sensory data of certain ideas or general relations existing independently in the mind.[5]

We do not need to present again the objections already offered to this view: the impossibility of any orderly stimulation of ideas by facts, and the impossibility of any check in the imposition of idea upon fact. "Facts" and conception are so thoroughly separate and independent that any sensory datum is indifferently and equally related to any conceivable idea. There is no basis for "superinducing" one idea or hypothesis, rather than any other, upon any particular set of data.

In the chapter already referred to upon abstraction, or the formation of conceptions, Mill seizes upon this difficulty. Yet he and Whewell have one point in common: they both agree in the existence of a certain subject-matter which is given for logical purposes quite outside of the logical process itself. Mill agrees with Whewell in postulating a raw material of pure sensational data. In criticizing Whewell's theory of superinduction of idea upon fact, he is therefore led to the opposite assertion of the complete dependence of ideas as such upon the given facts as such—in other words, he is led to a reiteration of the fundamental Baconian empiricism; and thus to a virtual retraction of what he had asserted regarding the necessity of ideas to fruitful scientific inquiry, whether in the way of observation or experimentation. The following quotation gives a fair notion of the extent of Mill's retraction:

> The conceptions then which we employ for the colligation and methodization of facts, do not develop themselves from within, *but are impressed upon the mind from without*; they are never obtained otherwise than by way of comparison and abstraction, and, in the most important and most numerous cases, are evolved by abstraction *from the very phenomena which it is their office to colligate*.[6]

Even here Mill's sense for the positive side of scientific inquiry suffices to reveal to him that the "facts" are somehow inadequate and defective, and are in need of assistance from

5. The essential similarity between Whewell's view and that of Lotze, already discussed (see Ch. 3) is of course explainable on the basis of their common relationship to Kant.
6. Bk. IV, Ch. 2, Sec. 2; italics mine.

ideas—and yet the ideas which are to help out the facts are to be the impress of the unsure facts! The contradiction comes out very clearly when Mill says: "The really difficult cases are those in which the conception destined to create light and order out of darkness and confusion has to be sought for among the very phenomena which it afterwards serves to arrange."[7]

Of course, there is a sense in which Mill's view is very much nearer the truth than is Whewell's. Mill at least sees that "idea" must be relevant to the facts or data which it is to arrange, which are to have "light and order" introduced into them by means of the idea. He sees clearly enough that this is impossible save as the idea develops *within* the same experience in which the "dark and confused" facts are presented. He goes on to show correctly enough how conflicting data lead the mind to a "confused feeling of an analogy" between the data of the confused experience and of some other experience which is orderly (or already colligated and methodized); and how this vague feeling, through processes of further exploration and comparison of experiences, gets a clearer and more adequate form until we finally accept it. He shows how in this process we continually judge of the worth of the idea which is in process of formation, by reference to its appropriateness to *our purpose*. He goes so far as to say: "The question of appropriateness is relative to the *particular object we have in view*."[8] He sums up his discussion by stating: "We cannot frame good general conceptions beforehand. That the conception we have obtained is the one we want can only be known when we have *done the work for the sake of which we wanted it*."[9]

This all describes the actual state of the case, but it is consistent only with a logical theory which makes the distinction between fact and hypothesis instrumental in the transformation of experience from a confused into an organized form; not with Mill's notion that sensations are somehow finally and completely given as ultimate facts, and

7. *Logic*, Sec. 4.
8. *Logic*, Sec. 4; in Sec. 6 he states even more expressly that any conception is appropriate in the degree in which it "helps us towards what we wish to understand."
9. *Logic*, Sec. 6; italics mine.

that ideas are mere re-registrations of such facts. It is perfectly just to say that the hypothesis is impressed upon the mind (in the sense that any notion which occurs to the mind is impressed) *in the course* of an experience. It is well enough, if one define what he means, to say that the hypothesis is impressed (that is to say, occurs or is suggested) through the medium of given facts, or even of sensations. But it is equally true that the *facts* are presented and that *sensations* occur within the course of an experience which is larger than the bare facts, because involving the conflicts among them and the corresponding intention to treat them in some fashion which will secure a unified experience. Facts get power to suggest ideas to the mind—to "impress"—only through their position in an entire experience which is in process of disintegration and of reconstruction—their "fringe" or feeling of tendency is quite as factual as they are. The fact that "the conception we have obtained is the one we want can be known only when we have done the work for the sake of which we wanted it," is enough to show that it is not bare facts, but facts in relation to want and purpose and purpose in relation to facts, which originate the hypothesis.

Appendix

Appendix

WHAT OUR SCHOOLS OWE TO CHILD STUDY
by Theodore B. Noss*

In the study of the child, as in the study of nature, much
has been left to the last two decades to discover. We speak of
the present as an extraordinary era of invention and discovery. It may be that the greatest discovery of all is that
of the child. People will say, "We have had child study for
twenty years. What has it done for our schools?" The answer
is: It has done much to give us a new education. More particularly child study has contributed much to give elementary
schools (1) an improved curriculum; (2) a better method;
and, most of all, (3) a new goal.

The curriculum.—The employments of an up-to-date
primary school bear slight resemblance to those of a primary
school of thirty or forty years ago. The child then had little
to do and much to remember. Even yet it is painful to see
that in thousands of elementary schools the traditions of the
past enthrall the teacher. The children in less-favored locali-
ties still devote their time, not to doing what is interesting
and useful, but to memorizing what is for the most part dull
and useless. The secret of the best primary work of today is
that it is essentially doing something, instead of committing
something to memory. It has been truly said that "the strongest potential capacity in the child is capacity for action."

In the kindergarten, where the blight of custom is less
felt, and where there is a constant appeal to what is natural
and interesting, the principle of freedom and self-activity
dominates. So in the university and the technical schools
(which in some measure have caught the spirit of the
kindergarten), where there is a constant demand for what is
useful and vital, again the method of freedom and self-
activity dominates. It is only between these happy extremes

* Principal of the Southwestern State Normal School, Califor-
nia, Pa.

[First printed in *Proceedings and Addresses* of the National Educational Association, 1902, pp. 716–19.]

that the practices of the school still show in many places the stupid memory habit and the text-book disease of a past generation. And now, fortunately, we see that many of these schools are moving toward the light. Are we not indebted in a large measure to child study for this new view of education which adapts subject-matter and school employments to the real needs and interests of the pupil?

It is a matter of regret that more progress has not been made, that in so many schools there is still an adherence to old forms from which the soul of truth has departed. Lesson matter was formerly chosen because of the utilities of life; hence the prevailing notion of the paramount value of the three R's. Now we have no patience with such puerilities in education. The utility of the child himself as a personality to be developed is of such towering importance that nothing else is worthy to be compared with it.

Child study has given new emphasis to the old doctrine that the essential element in education is not knowledge, but training. Nothing can be truer in practical pedagogy than Solomon's dictum: "Train up a child in the way he should go, and when he is old he will not depart from it." Education consists chiefly in forming rather than informing the mind; the creating of interests, the formation of habits, rather than the storing of memory with conventional knowledge.

All great success in early training springs from intelligent and sympathetic interest in the child himself. Child study has come when most needed to direct the attention and interest of teachers to the paramount importance of the child himself in the process of education, and to emphasize the importance of beginnings. What is put into the first of life is put into the whole of it. The earliest efforts yield the best and the most fruit. To concentrate upon the early years is to seize the strategic point. Lose this and we lose the battle. The failure and waste of life in thousands of men and women thru neglect of early training is the saddest tragedy of modern life.

The method.—In education most depends, not upon what we study, but how, and with whom. The method of the teacher is always important. Here is the pearl of great price in the art of teaching. How is a method of teaching learned?

By a study of the subject-matter alone? No, but by a patient, loving study of the child.

Child study has taught us the value of motive in education. President Eliot recently said: "When you appeal to a child with motives he won't use when he is a man, you have not helped him much." "Motive," he adds, "makes all the difference between slavery and freedom, between misery and happiness." We sometimes hear the fear expressed that the new methods make education too easy. It is true that for the best results oft-repeated and severe exertion is necessary, but it is never necessary that this exertion be made without motive. Hard work is necessary, but should it ever be done without interest and a pleasurable sense of reward? "The time of interest is the time of opportunity." There can be no excuse for making things dull or difficult that may be made easy and attractive. The child must be dealt with sincerely, naturally. We do not expect success by finding the longest way instead of the shortest, the slowest instead of the quickest, the hardest instead of the easiest. The common-sense of the busy and prosperous life of the farm, the store, and the street is just what is needed in the schoolroom. Good teachers will soon cease to believe that some studies are good for discipline that are not good for anything else. The best discipline is and must be found in doing something worth doing, and doing it well. Life is a unity and is continuous from the cradle to the grave. The school is not to be viewed merely as a preparation for life, but as a very important part of it. Those interests should be begun, those methods started, those purposes planted that are to characterize the life thruout.

If this be true, how important it is that we scrutinize very carefully the usages, employments, and methods of the school, lest haply we find that we have wasted time and dissipated energy and acted very foolishly in dealing with children!

The end or goal.—It is now more evident than ever before that the true aim of education is not knowledge merely, or chiefly, but a many-sided development. Child study has helped us most by enhancing our value of the product of our work. This is nothing less than skill of hand and eye and tongue, a well-poised body, a well-rounded mind, a sympathetic and altruistic nature, strong and worthy interests, force of will, and power to do.

Knowledge is not the end. Tho the pupil have all knowledge, and have not interest and motive, it profits him nothing. To what, then, shall we appeal in education? To the needs of the individual child. There is but one rule that will never fail us, and that is, study and serve each child. Everything else must be secondary to this. School is but a contrivance to help the child. The rigidity of the curriculum and the school routine must yield somehow to the needs of the individual child, or it would in many cases be better to take the child out of school. By far the richest fruit of the whole child-study movement is the greatly increased interest in the child to be educated.

The Great Teacher said, "Consider the lilies of the field how they grow." In education we have at last happily reached the stage when many teachers really "consider" the child.

Child study seems destined, not to modify merely, but to revolutionize, our methods of discipline. The teacher who punishes the child in ignorance of physical infirmities and home deficiencies is inexcusable, and the teacher who does so with a knowledge of, but without allowance for, these things, is cruel and brutal. No hand is fit to touch young life in the schoolroom except the hand of skill and kindness. Almost as well employ an eighteen-year-old girl without special training to fill prescriptions in a drug store as to employ her without training or preparation to teach children. The demand should be instant, constant, persistent that only well-trained teachers shall be put in charge of schools. Child study has emphasized this demand as no other educational movement has done or could do.

In spite of all that child study has accomplished, a recent writer says: "There are some healthful signs that the child-study diversion which has been carried to such extremes has well-nigh run its course." In my judgment the most hopeful sign for the future of elementary education is that child study has only begun its course.

TEXTUAL APPARATUS
INDEX

TEXTUAL COMMENTARY

Both years covered by publications in this volume, 1902 and 1903, were spent by John Dewey at the University of Chicago, where his ten-year stay was drawing to a close. In spite of the difficulties arising from his assuming many new administrative duties in 1902,[1] it was an extremely productive year—even for the highly productive Dewey. Of the fifteen "items" that make up the present volume, only the *Studies in Logical Theory* was published in 1903; all the rest, including Dewey's 119 contributions to the *Dictionary of Philosophy and Psychology*, appeared in 1902.[2]

Eight of these 1902 articles were printed only once: "The Evolutionary Method as Applied to Morality"; the two reviews: of Witmer's *Analytical Psychology*, and of Royce's *The World and the Individual*; "Academic Freedom"; "In Remembrance: Francis W. Parker"; two with the same title, "The University of Chicago School of Education";[3] and the discussion of Moss's "What Our Schools Owe to Child Study." Two previously unpublished 1902 statements on coeducation are also included here. For these ten items, no problems of editorial treatment arise and the original appearance serves as copy-text. The remaining six parts of the present volume are discussed individually in the sections that follow.[4]

1. The difficulties and the duties are discussed in detail by Robert McCaul in his "Dewey and the University of Chicago," *School and Society* 89 (1961): 152–57, 179–83, 202–6.
2. "The Battle for Progress," *Journal of Education* 61 (1902): 249, has been listed among Dewey's publications for this year as an "abstract of an address"; it is an excerpt from "The Situation as Regards the Course of Study," *School Journal* 62 (1901): 421 [*The Middle Works of John Dewey, 1899–1924*, ed. Jo Ann Boydston, vol. 1, 1899–1901, *Essays, THE SCHOOL AND SOCIETY, and THE EDUCATIONAL SITUATION* (Carbondale: Southern Illinois University Press, 1975), pp. 260–61].
3. Dewey told Wilbur Jackman in a letter of 1 December 1902 that he had written the unsigned circular that appeared as a *Bulletin of Information*. John Dewey Papers, Special Collections, Morris Library, Southern Illinois University at Carbondale.
4. The editorial principles and procedures used in preparing volumes of *The Middle Works of John Dewey* are discussed fully

"Interpretation of Savage Mind"

First published in *Psychological Review* (9 [1902]: 217–30),[5] which serves as copy-text for the present version, this article was reprinted in 1909 by William Isaac Thomas in his *Sourcebook for Social Origins* (Chicago: University of Chicago Press, 1909), pp. 173–86, with Dewey's permission but apparently without his intervention. In 1931, the article was included with minimal revision in Dewey's collective volume *Philosophy and Civilization* (New York: Minton, Balch, 1931), pp. 173–87. These few substantive changes made by Dewey for that later publication appear in this volume in a List of 1931 Variants; they have not been incorporated into the critically edited text because Dewey made them during a period well after that covered by *The Middle Works*.

"The School as Social Centre"

Dewey's July 1902 address to the National Educational Association, "The School as Social Centre," first appeared in print in October in the *Elementary School Teacher* (3 [1902]: 73–86); the next month, it was published with revisions in the 1902 *Proceedings and Addresses* of the National Educational Association.

The *Elementary School Teacher*, founded in 1900 as the *Course of Study* by Francis W. Parker, had been—even with the change of title—in Dewey's words, a "quasi personal venture of Colonel Parker's, not an official University organ."[6] But upon Parker's death in March 1902, responsibility

---

by Fredson Bowers in *Middle Works* 1:347–60 (Carbondale: Southern Illinois University Press, 1976).

5. William James wrote Dewey just after publication of the article, "I cannot refrain from thanking you for a thing so 'concrete' and full of veracious psychological imagination. Also humane, and calculated to dampen the conceit of our all-destroying 'Civilization.' Pray keep up that line of study." Ralph Barton Perry, *The Thought and Character of William James* (Boston: Little, Brown, and Co., 1935), 2:520.

6. Letter to Frank A. Manny, 3 June 1902. Frank A. Manny Papers, Michigan Historical Collections, University of Michigan, Ann Arbor.

for the journal devolved upon the School of Education, of which Dewey became director in the summer of 1902. Although Dewey in the summer expressed doubts about the journal's viability, issues starting with October 1902 carried the notice, "Edited by the University of Chicago School of Education / John Dewey, Director / Ella F. Young, Managing Editor." Dewey's correspondence with Frank Manny indicates that Ella Flagg Young was, in fact, the editor and that Dewey's role was to search and solicit material for the magazine.[7]

After delivering his address in Minneapolis, Dewey returned to the University of Chicago for the rest of the month of July and then spent August and most of September at his summer home in Essex County, New York. It seems likely that printer's-copy for his article in the *Elementary School Teacher* was the typescript or manuscript he had used for his speech in Minneapolis. The *Elementary School Teacher* (EST) was published on the first day of each month except August and September. As the N.E.A. *Proceedings and Addresses* (PA) were published late in November, Dewey probably marked up a printed copy of the EST version with his revisions of the article to provide printer's-copy for PA. The first printing in EST has been used here as copy-text.

Between the EST and the PA texts, there are sixty-four variants in substantives and eighty-three in accidentals. The substantive variants, with one exception, clearly constitute Dewey's revisions of the material and have been incorporated into the edited text as his intended changes. Of the eighty-three accidental variants, eighteen PA readings appear in the present text as emendations, having been judged Dewey's own alterations that resulted directly from substantive changes or were made in close proximity to such changes. For example, commas are removed or added in connection with substantive changes at 83.12, 87.2–3, 88.32, 89.8, 91.18 (3); dashes are substituted for colons in revisions at 91.12, 91.13–14, and 93.10; a period is changed to a colon at 83.20 to introduce explanatory material and a colon is added as

7. See letters of 3 June 1902, 3 October 1902, and 20 October 1902. Manny Papers, Michigan Historical Collections.

part of a revision at 90.26; a second dash is added to mark a series at 81.15; a semicolon is changed to a comma at 83.18; a comma is taken out after an initial serial subject at 88.2; a new paragraph break is introduced at 90.21–22; and hyphens are added to "de-nationalized" at 85.25 and "dance-house" at 91.35–36.

[*In Memoriam: Colonel Francis Wayland Parker*]

Dewey's address at the memorial service for F. W. Parker was published in the *Elementary School Teacher* (2 [1902]: 704–8) from a stenographic report, probably typewritten. The printed version has served as copy-text for the critical text. The address was reprinted in *Characters and Events*, edited by Joseph Ratner (New York: Henry Holt and Co., 1929), 1: 95–99, with the title "Francis W. Parker," without Dewey's intervention.

Contributions to Dictionary of Philosophy and Psychology

The second volume of the massive *Dictionary*, "written by many hands and edited by James Mark Baldwin, with the co-operation and assistance of an international board of consulting editors," was published in 1902 (New York: Macmillan Co.). For this volume, as for Volume 1, published the year before, Dewey's name appeared both as "Consulting Editor" (for English) and as "Contributor" (Philosophy). But whereas Dewey had no independent contributions in the first volume, his signed mini-essays of varying length in Volume 2 totaled 119.[8]

8. One item, "History of Philosophy," in Volume 1 signed (J.R., J.D.) was omitted from the Dewey writings in Volume 1 of *The Middle Works* because it was written by Josiah Royce and approved by Dewey only as Consulting Editor. In the "Editor's Preface," James Mark Baldwin had explained (p. xii): "Another case is the signature by two persons with a comma—not a hyphen—between them: (A.B.C., X.Y.Z.). This indicates that the article was written by A.B.C. and accepted without alteration by X.Y.Z., who thus adds the weight of his authority to it." Simi-

Both volumes of the *Dictionary* were reprinted in 1925, with the title-page statement "New edition, with corrections." The type was not reset for that second printing and the "corrections" in the front-matter and Dewey contributions consisted of updating academic titles and locations, and of changing "to which" at 141.29 to "to that which." A comma after "Aristotle," dropped from the lower right corner of the page at 211.21 points to the use of the same plates, which is verified by identical anomalies in various pieces of type apparent in sight collation. It was not possible to compare copies on the Hinman Machine because bound volumes could not be obtained and Xerox copies (made from tightly-bound volumes) were not suitable for machining. Two sight collations of the Library of Congress copyright deposit copy (90555) against the Southern Illinois University Library volume (63418) reveal in the Dewey texts only the two differences mentioned. A facsimile reprint of the 1925 printing was published by Peter Smith in 1940.

Emendations made in the first-impression copy-text include the second-printing addition of "that" at 141.29; correction of the page number at 174.23, of the quotation at 180.6, and of "philosopic" at 198.36; capitalizing seven occurrences of "middle ages," at 146.37, 179.14, 186.38 39, 198.6, 226.9, 263.37, and 264.12; restoration of Dewey's typical spelling of "-ize" and "-or" words; and regularization of "&c." to "etc."

The Child and the Curriculum

Number 5 in Dewey's and Ella Flagg Young's series of Contributions to Education, this small book published in 1902

---

larly, in Volume 2 of the *Dictionary*, the article on "Mind" is not included in the Dewey corpus because it is signed (J.M.B., J.D.). Baldwin explained further that a hyphen between names signaled joint authorship, even though "in most cases this form of signature indicates that the article was originally written by A.B.C. . . . but has undergone more or less important modification to meet the criticisms or suggestions of X.Y.Z." In Volume 2 of the *Dictionary*, initials that appear with Dewey's, either as collaborators, or as writers of separate and related sections, are C.S.P. (Charles Sanders Peirce), J.M.B. (James Mark Baldwin), and K.G. (K. Groos, Basel University).

continues to be widely read and used, although when first published it was not reviewed by even one journal.

Twenty-five impressions, usually 1,000–2,000 copies, of *The Child and the Curriculum* were made from a single set of plates during Dewey's lifetime, producing a total of more than 27,000 books between 1902 and 1950. Machine collation of the copyright deposit copy (24726) of the first impression against the twenty-fifth impression (Northwestern University 803174) reveals only one change in the text itself —correction of "curirculum" at 290.35; however, a number of changes were made in the preliminary pages to change dates and listing of impressions, and both the running heads and page numbers were reset between the thirteenth and eighteenth impressions.

In 1956, the University of Chicago Press combined *The Child and the Curriculum* with *The School and Society* in its Phoenix Books series; the combined volume is available in paper, and the two books are also sold separately in hard cover. The Phoenix Books version is now in the eleventh impression of the third edition and has sold more than 260,000 copies in paper and cased volumes.

Studies in Logical Theory

Published in 1903, but culminating the work of many years,[9] the *Studies in Logical Theory* included four essays by Dewey, along with contributions of his colleagues and students in the Department of Philosophy edited by Dewey.[10]

9. Dewey wrote to William James in March 1903, "As for the standpoint [of the *Studies*],—we have all been at work at it for about twelve years." Perry, *Thought and Character of James*, 2:520. Many years later, Dewey identified the *Studies* as the first published writing to present the essentials of the philosophical view that he developed through the succeeding thirty-five years. "Experience, Knowledge, Value: A Rejoinder," in *The Philosophy of John Dewey*, ed. Paul Schilpp (Evanston: Northwestern University, 1939), p. 520.
10. Ten reviews of the first impression of the *Studies* appeared between 1904 and 1909: William James, *Psychological Bulletin* 1 (1904): 1–5, reprinted as an article "The Chicago School" in James's *Collected Essays and Reviews* (New York: Longmans, Green and Co., 1920); Ferdinand Canning Scott Schiller, *Mind*

Two other parts of the work written by Dewey—the Preface and a discussion on Mill and Whewell—are reprinted here for the first time outside the *Studies* volume.

In its first impression, *Studies in Logical Theory*, as Volume II of the Second Series of University of Chicago Decennial Publications, had 1,000 copies printed; in May 1909, a second printing of 517 copies was made from plates.[11] Machine collation of Dewey's contributions to the volume (pp. ix–xi, 1–85, 160–68) in the second impression[12] against the copyright deposit copy (A66023) of the first impression reveals no variants between them.

By 1914, sales of the *Studies* had dwindled to some fifty per year and the University of Chicago Press decided to make an abridged edition, using just the Dewey part, rather than reprint the entire book or let it go out of print. G. J. Laing of the Press wrote Dewey on 5 October 1915 that the Press believed "it would be better to reissue only those chapters which were written by yourself. These are the first four and make up a total of 85 pages. We should set them up again, using a page of the same size as that employed in your *School and Society*."[13]

n.s. 13 (1904): 100–106; *Monist* 14 (1904): 312; William Henry Sheldon, *Journal of Philosophy* 1 (1904): 100–105; Arthur Kenyon Rogers, *Dial* 36 (1904): 328–29; Charles Santiago Sanders Peirce, *Nation* 79 (1904): 219–20; Edwin Lee Norton, *Educational Review* 28 (1904): 310–13; Andrew Seth Pringle-Pattison, *Philosophical Review* 13 (1904): 666–77; Francis H. Bradley, "On Truth and Practice," *Mind* n.s. 13 (1904): 309n; Bertrand Russell, *Edinburgh Review* 209 (1909): 363–88.

The reviews were generally enthusiastic, with the earliest and most enthusiastic coming from William James, to whom the book was dedicated. James wrote, "Chicago has a School of Thought!—a school of thought which, it is safe to predict, will figure in literature as the School of Chicago for twenty-five years to come. Some universities have plenty of thought to show, but no school; others plenty of school, but no thought. . . . It . . . is certainly something of which Americans may be proud."

11. The second impression was reviewed by Bernard Bosanquet in *Mind* (20 [1911]: 435), who noted that "this volume is re-issued without change, and it is satisfactory evidence of the general interest in the advance of logical theory that a second impression should have been called for."

12. Dewey Center (a).

13. University of Chicago Press, Langley Office. Unless otherwise noted, all correspondence and records of the University of Chicago Press are from the Langley Office and are quoted with the permission of the Press.

Upon Dewey's suggestion that it would be "churlish" of
him to disassociate himself from the other contributors to
the work, the Press secured permission from all the others
for the proposed new edition. Dewey said to Laing that he
"should be glad of an opportunity to make some changes; if
you are going to reset anyway, this would not involve you in
any added expense, I take it."[14] Laing responded on 1 November 1915 that he was sending Dewey "a copy of the book
so that you can make such changes as you like on the
margin. As we shall reset the book . . . you may make additions also." In his first letter to Dewey proposing the new edition, Laing had also encouraged him to "make any additions
that seem desirable to you." Again in December, he wrote,
"Please do not hesitate to make additions if you care to do
so." Laing's encouragement led to unexpected results: in
January 1916, Dewey returned to Laing "corrected copy of
the four essays," saying, "if you wish to begin setting up for
galley proof at once you can do so," which Laing proceeded
to do despite Dewey's warning in the same letter that "the
copy sent is about *half* the whole book." By the end of February, the extent of Dewey's additions was embarrassingly
apparent. A memorandum to Newman Miller, Director of the
Press, from A. C. McFarland noted:

All of the copy of Dewey's "Logical Theory" is now in, and
we find that we have a much larger book than we planned on.
The original estimate of 224 pages was made on the supposition
that the four chapters of which he was the author in the old book
were to be used with corrections and some minor additions. We
now find that several chapters from other sources have been added
and that the book will now make about 450 pages. Before these
facts were learned the first lot of manuscript had been set up,
but I have stopped the work at that point.

Despite the doubling in size of the book, the page size was
not changed and apparently the first part, already in galleys,
was not reset; the proposed price was, however, increased
from $1.25 to $1.75 as the cost of printing, plating, and binding had increased from an estimated $650 to $1,135.

The newly expanded work was given a new title that
was a combination of suggestions by Newman Miller and

14. 11 October 1915.

Dewey. Miller wrote to Dewey in February 1916 to offer ideas for a "slightly altered title," because, he said, "We have always been under the impression that 'Studies in Logical Theory' made the book a bit formidable to certain constituencies." His suggestions were "Studies in Experimental Logic" or, what he thought might be even better, "Studies in Pragmatic Logic," "on account of the interest in pragmatism." Dewey responded that he thought "some change of title would be desirable in any case; to keep the old title with so much change of contents would be very confusing. I had thought of changing the word Studies to Essays. . . . Essays is perhaps less formidable, but I am not particular." On the face of that letter of 17 February 1916, "Essays in Experimental Logic" was penciled in at the Press and the new title established.

The University of Chicago Press made three printings from a single set of plates of *Essays in Experimental Logic*, in June 1916, May 1918, and October 1920. After sales of the book fell to fewer than seventy-five copies a year, the book was allowed to go out of print in December 1925. The Press still had the plates in its vault as late as 1940, but no further reprinting of the book occurred.

Machine collation of copies[15] of the second and third impressions of Dewey's four *Studies* articles in *Essays in Experimental Logic* (EE) against the copyright deposit copy (A433372) reveals that type was reset for the third impression without change once, probably to repair a plate, and at five places to improve or eliminate line-end hyphenation.

The present text has used the copyright deposit copy of Dewey's *Studies in Logical Theory* as copy-text, adopting as emendations the substantive changes judged to have been made by him in the copy sent by the University of Chicago Press to prepare printer's-copy for EE; in the section ["On Mill and Whewell"] that did not appear in EE, three editorial emendations were made.

In addition, a number of accidental readings have been emended in the four *Studies*, chiefly in connection with sub-

15. First impression, Dewey Center; second impression, University of Minnesota, 1329092; third impression, University of Chicago Press Collection of Record Copies.

stantive revisions but also when Dewey's intention to change the accidentals was clear. These kinds of intentional changes include restoring his usual spelling of "cannot," at 313.22, and of "criticizing" at 313.24 and 333.4–5; italicizing material at 337.4, 341.8, 352.5, 359.4, 359.18–19, 360.3, 360n.5, and 363.9; removing hyphens only in some words and not in others in a sentence, as at 307.21–22, 330.5, 341.6 (2), 342.5; and substituting parentheses or dashes for commas in long complex sentences, as at 304.38, 304.40, 308.34, 316.5, and 367.11.

TEXTUAL NOTES

16.30   quotations illustrate] When Dewey introduced the quoted material, he may have intended to use only one passage, failing later to correct his introductory statement, "The following quotation illustrates. . . ." As there are two widely separated quotations, which he himself recognized at 17.6, "The implication of the quotations . . . ," the first reference has been made to agree.

23.18   are] Apparently Dewey thought of the subject "certain conditions" as only one of the "facts described," but did not make the sentence structure reflect his intention.

81.38   goes on in] The word "on" in the copy-text, necessary for the sense of the sentence, was probably accidentally omitted in typesetting the revised version of the article.

89.27   the country] The omission of "the" in the revised impression appears to have been a compositorial error.

180.6   outness no power] Omission of the word "no" that appeared in the original quotation changes the basic definition of this entry, it has accordingly been restored.

319.18–19   as matter of fact] This typical expression of Dewey's was frequently altered by editors to the more common "as a matter of fact". The "a" was probably added editorially rather than by Dewey in preparing copy for the revised edition and it has therefore not been accepted as a revision here.

350.7–8   disciplines] Substitution of the word "disciples" in the revision must have been a typographical error overlooked in proofreading, not a change intended by Dewey.

358.3   besides] The final "s" in the original quotation was dropped, probably in typesetting, making it likely that this word would be read incorrectly as a preposition rather than as an adverb.

364.18   helpful.] The footnote omitted in revision for *Essays in Experimental Logic* was not keyed to a number in the text of the *Studies*. The footnote number has been added, as shown in the Emendations List, after the word "conflict" where it logically belongs.

LIST OF SYMBOLS

Page-line number at left is from present edition; all lines of print except running heads are counted.

The abbreviation *et seq.* following a page-line number means that all subsequent appearances of the reading in that section are identical with the one noted.

Reading before bracket is from present edition.

Square bracket signals end of reading from present edition, followed by the symbol identifying the first appearance of reading.

W means Works—the present edition—and is used for emendations made here for the first time.

The abbreviation [*om.*] means the reading before the bracket was omitted in the editions and impressions identified after the abbreviation; [*not present*] is used where appropriate to signal material not appearing in identified sources.

The abbreviation [*rom.*] means roman type and is used to signal the omission of italics.

Stet used with an edition or impression number indicates a substantive reading retained from an edition or impression subsequently revised; the rejected variant follows the semicolon.

The asterisk before an emendation page-line number indicates the reading is discussed in the Textual Notes.

The plus sign ⁺ means that the same reading appears in all collated printings and editions later than the one noted.

For emendations restricted to punctuation, the curved dash ∼ means the same word(s) as before the bracket, and the inferior caret ∧ indicates the absence of a punctuation mark.

EMENDATIONS LIST

All emendations in both substantives and accidentals introduced into the copy-texts are recorded in the list that follows, with the exception of certain regularizations described and listed at the end of this introductory explanation. The reading to the left of the square bracket is from the present edition. The bracket is followed by the abbreviation for the source of the emendation's first appearance and abbreviations for subsequent editions and printings collated that had the same reading. After the source abbreviations comes a semicolon, followed by the copy-text reading. Substantive variants in all texts collated are also recorded here; the list thus serves as a historical collation as well as a record of emendations.

Copy-texts for each item and abbreviations used in the list of emendations are identified at the beginning of that list; for items that had a single previous printing, no abbreviation for the copy-text appears in the list itself.

The following formal changes have been made throughout:

1. Book and journal titles are in upper and lower case italic type; articles and sections of books are in quotation marks. Book titles have been supplied and expanded where necessary.

2. Superior numbers have been assigned consecutively throughout an item to Dewey's footnotes; the asterisk is used only for editorial footnotes.

3. Single quotation marks have been changed to double when not inside quoted material; opening or closing quotation marks have been supplied where necessary.

The following spellings have been editorially regularized to the known Dewey usage appearing before the brackets:

although] altho 59.10
analyzes] analyses 217.34

anyone] any one 192.13, 204.36
centre] center 15.23, 49.31, 80.1, 80.4, 80.8, 80.9, 80.23, 84.3,
        84.13, 90.17, 90.21, 90.34, 91.3, 91.20, 92.9, 92.38,
        93.16, 93.17, 116.1, 275.11, 276.27; (-s) 11.29, 15.9,
        91.28, 124n.11
clues] clews 311.36
color] colour 215.35; (-ing) 163.3, 234.15, 243.24; (-less) 190.14
cooperation] coöperation 124.22, 125.6, 127n.11
coordinations] coördinations 42.12, 43.2
criticize] criticise 78.7; (-ing) 36.5, 373.18
demarcation] demarkation 372.10
emphasize] emphasise 102.4
endeavor] endeavour (-ed) 170.15, 230.10, 251.23–24, 251.24;
        (-ing) 219.34; (-s) 204.20, 218.19, 232.23
entrenched] intrenched 10.32
favor] favour 261.32; (-able) 232.33; (-ed) 226.23; (-ing) 228.28
favorite] favourite 179.25, 233.17, 248.31
fulfill] fulfil 291.17, 331.7, 359.31; (-ment) 159.23, 281.38,
        283.21, 287.10, 304.22–23, 304.28, 311.20, 366.38;
        (-ments) 291.13; (-s) 303.40
fullness] fulness 275.36, 333n.10
honor] honour (-ed) 164.7; (-ing) 237.24
meagreness] meagerness 89.5
modelling] modeling 75.28, 79.22, 92.16
mold] mould 121.28
monopolizing] monopolising 112.10
program] programme 77.29
sceptical] skeptical 36.29
scepticism] skepticism 57.12, 338n.5 (2), 367.8, 367.9
self-enclosed] self-inclosed 296.9
theatres] theaters 324.40
thorough] thoro (-ly) 59.14, 61.14–15; (thorough-going) 64.39
though] tho 103.10
through] thru 54.4, 56.5, 57.32, 63.40; (-out) 61.9
willful] wilful 348.6; (-ly) 30.9
zoology] zoölogy 41.9, 99.29, 226.9

The following instances of word-division and hyphenation have been editorially altered to the known Dewey forms
appearing before the brackets:

clay-modelling] clay modeling 75.28
coeducation] co-education 105.10, 105.13, 105.16, 105.17, 105.21,
        105.23, 105.25, 105.27, 105.30, 106.1, 106.7, 106.15,
        106.16, 107.24, 107.26; (-al) 105.20
co-instruction] coinstruction 115.6

common sense (n.)] common-sense 70.21, 277.30, 277.31, 277.33–
    34, 318.36
cooperate] co-operate 70.20–21, 296.26; (-ing) 72.30, 153.2,
    262.28; (-tion) 74.20, 75.16, 111.20–21, 332.20; (-tive)
    68.36, 340.1
coordinate] co-ordinate 148.25, 193.12, 247.4
elementary-school (adj.)] elementary school 75.20
face-to-face] face to face 57.35, 84.27, 355n.9
life-history] life history 27.24
public-school (adj.)] public school 97.6
reinforce] re-enforce, re-inforce 66.11; (-ed) 78.26
secondary-school (adj.)] secondary school 79.30
someone] some one 37.1
subject-matter] subject matter 46.18
today] to-day 6.30, 28.37, 29.7, 65.25, 149.21, 222.7
tomorrow] to-morrow 210.34
thorough-going] thoroughgoing 198.40, 201.29, 232.11, 246.37,
    267.37, 345.23

"The Evolutionary Method as Applied to Morality"

Copy-text is the only previous impression, *Philosophical
Review* 11 (1902): 107–24, 353–71.

9.39	unjustifiable] W; unjust-/fiable
16.28	process_∧] W; ∾,
16.28	viz.] W; ∼_∧
16.30	quotations Illustrate] W; quotation illustrates
16.31	∧We may "raise] W; "We may ∧raise
17.5	pp. 255–56] W; p. 255
23.18	are] W; is

"Interpretation of Savage Mind"

Copy-text is the first printing in *Psychological Review* 9
(1902): 217–30. The reprint in PC: *Philosophy and Civilization* (New York: Minton, Balch and Co., 1931), pp. 173–87
is noted as the first appearance of an emendation that would
have been made editorially.

40n.1	*Sociology*]	W;	*Ibid.*
40n.2	*Sociology*]	W;	*Ibid.*
40n.3	*Sociology*]	W;	*Ibid*

41.31   traits] W;   tracts
45n.2   Hodgkinson] W;   Hodinksson PC;   Hodginkson
50.26   ∧fights with "a maximum] W;   "fights with ∧a maxi-
           mum
50.27–28   maneuvering] PC;   manouvering
50n.1   Part Four] W;   Vol. IV.

"Academic Freedom"

Copy-text is the only previous impression, *Educational
Review* 23 (1902): 1–14.

60.22   propagate] W;   progagate

Bulletin of Information: *The University of Chicago School of Education*

Copy-text is the only previous impression as one of the
*Official Publications of the University of Chicago, Bulletin of
Information* 2 (Oct. 1902).

73.33   two,] W;   ∼∧
74.2   student's] W;   students
74.13–14   *Departments*] W;   *Department*
75.11   subject] W;   suhject
75.15   the School] W;   The School
75.17   two years' course] W;   Two Years' Course

"The School as Social Centre"

Copy-text is the first impression, "The School as Social
Center," in EST: *Elementary School Teacher* 3 (1902):
73–86. Emendations have been adopted from the revised new
printing in PA: *Proceedings and Addresses* of the National
Educational Association, 1902, pp. 373–83.

80.12   that occupy] PA;   occupy
81.2   has] PA;   have
81.5   on the principle of] PA;   through
81.15   etc.—] PA;   ∼;

81.30	education function] PA; function of education
81.31	in] PA; a
*81.38	goes on in] *stet* EST; goes in PA
83.12	citizenship$_\Lambda$] PA; ~,
83.13	what is the] PA; what the
83.13	school] PA; school is
83.18	ages,] PA; ~;
83.20	here:] PA; ~.
83.33	Constitution] W; constitution
84.10	efficacy] PA; efficiency
84.15	one another] PA; each other
84.17	of the circulation] PA; the circulation
84.36	peoples] PA; elements
84.37–38	instrumentalities of which . . . taken.] PA; instrumentalities which may be taken advantage of.
85.3	in] PA; by
85.14	different] PA; differing
85.25	de-nationalized] PA; denationalized
85.32–33	of the newly] PA; of newly
86.5	²the] PA; this
86.10	was] PA; is
86.21	ties themselves, as between] PA; ties between
86.22	wife] PA; wife themselves,
86.22	as in relation to] PA; as to their
86.26	away from it] PA; away
86.27–28	and of keeping them] PA; that kept men
86.29–30	which rested for their force upon] PA; whose force rested in
86.34	results which] PA; results
87.2–3	further$_\Lambda$] PA; farther,
87.18	When] PA; Where
87.20	was just] PA; was
87.21	the] PA; only the
87.25	just] PA; but
88.1	come] PA; comes
88.2	anatomy$_\Lambda$] PA; ~,
88.30–31	great motives for the flourishing] PA; chief reasons for the success
88.32	day$_\Lambda$] PA; ~,
88.32	is not only] PA; besides
88.33	but] PA; is
88.38	forms] PA; is
88.40	added] PA; has added
89.7	social] PA; the social
89.8	them,] PA; ~$_\Lambda$
89.9	engaging] PA; engaged
89.25	accurate the study, did] PA; accurate, does
*89.27	the country] *stet* EST; country PA

89.33   and so the] PA;   and where therefore the
89.39   history. Now,] PA;   history, and
90.13   one] PA;   him
90.21–22   centre. [¶] It] W;   center. [¶] It PA;   center. It
90.24   interpret] PA;   so interpret
90.26   engaged:] PA;   ~∧
90.26   that is, must] PA;   that it will
90.29   supply him compensation] PA;   compensate him
90.29   and] PA;   and of
90.32   such ways as] PA;   ways that
90.39   mixing people up] PA;   a mixing up of people
90.39   bringing] PA;   a bringing
91.4   is particularly] PA;   particularly is
91.8   And we] PA;   We
91.8   work] PA;   function
91.11–12   exchanged, not merely in] PA;   exchanged in
91.12   discussion—] PA;   ~,
91.13–14   prejudice—] PA;   ~;
91.14   in ways] PA;   it is much more a place
91.16   all] PA;   they
91.17   barriers] PA;   the barriers
91.18   caste,] PA;   ~∧
91.18   class,] PA;   ~∧
91.18   race,] PA;   ~∧
91.35–36   dance-house] PA;   ~∧~
92.2   recreation there is] PA;   recreation is
92.31   it as a natural] PA;   that it is quite as natural
92.32   part] PA;   a part
92.32–33   duty—quite . . . children—to provide] PA;   duty to
           provide
92.36   them.] PA;   them, as it is to give instructions to little
           children.
93.3   excepting] PA;   except
93.9   resources] PA;   sources
93.10   dispute—] PA;   ~:
93.12   fullness] PA;   fulness
93.16   demand] PA;   the demand

Discussion of "What Our Schools Owe to Child Study"

Copy-text is the only previous impression, in *Proceedings and Addresses* of the National Educational Association, 1902, pp. 719–20.

103.37   excrescences] W;   excresences

Memorandum to President Harper on Coeducation

Copy-text is the typewritten letter, Dewey to William Rainey Harper, 9 January 1902, Presidents' Papers, 1899–1925, Department of Special Collections, Joseph Regenstein Library, University of Chicago.

106.8	safeguard] W; safe guard
106.20	especially] W; especially
106.27	University] W; Unoversity
107.4	introducing] W; introduction
107.15	a.] W; ~/

Letter to A. K. Parker on Coeducation

Copy-text is the typewritten letter in Presidents' Papers, 1899–1925, Department of Special Collections, University of Chicago Library.

113.22	alone] W; alonr
113.31	University] W; university

Review of The World and the Individual, *Second Series*

Copy-text is *Philosophical Review* 11 (1902): 392–407.

122.13	deficiencies] W; deficences
124.9	we recognize] W; were cognize
126.7	processes] W; proccss
128.3	Absolute] W; absolute
129.7–8	pp. 315–16] W; p. 315
132.8	the] W; the the
133.16	443] W; 445
135.28	instant] W; incident

Contributions to Dictionary of Philosophy and Psychology

Copy-text is the first impression of the entries in *Dictionary of Philosophy and Psychology*, ed. James Mark Baldwin (New York: Macmillan Co., 1902), Vol. 2. One emendation has been adopted from the 1925 second printing, D².

141.29	to that which] D²; to which	
143.22	as (α)] W; (α) as	
145.12	*Antigone*] W; [*rom.*]	
146.37	Middle Ages] W; middle ages	
147.29	*Hist. of Philos.*] W; loc. cit.	
153.12	headquarters] W; head quarters	
154.37	Leontini] W; Leontium	
168.35	is such] W; as such	
174.23	30] W; 34	
179.14	Middle Ages] W; middle ages	
180.5	Hutchison] W; Hutchinson	
*180.6	outness—no power] W; outness, power	
181.15–16	*Panpsychismus*] W; *Pampsychismus*	
186.38–39	Middle Ages] W; middle ages	
187.2	1525] W; 1625	
187.2	(1484–1558)] W; (1558)	
197.39	(c. 487–c. A.D. 583)] W; (469–A.D. 508)	
198.6	Middle Ages] W; middle ages	
198.36	philosophic] W; philosopic	
203.9	*kontinuierliche*] W; *continuirliche*	
215.37	Wolff's] W; his	
216.10	Molinos] W; Molinox	
226.9	Middle Ages] W; middle ages	
240.7	*con*ₐ] W; ~.	
244.10	Johannes] W; Joannes	
247.5	gives it matter] W; gives its matter	
249.31	*Gesch. d. Logik*] W; op. cit.	
249.31–32	*Hist. Beitr.*] W; op. cit.	
250.1–2	*Gesch. d. Logik*] W; loc. cit.	
250.7	*Gesch. d. Logik*] W; loc. cit.	
250.15–16	*Gesch. d. Logik,*] W; [*not present*]	
250.22	*Gesch. d. Logik,*] W; [*not present*]	
251.10	*Critique of Pure Reason*] W; ibid.	
251.28	*Critique of Pure Reason*] W; ibid.	
256.25	*Essay upon Human Understanding*] W; loc. cit.	
257.1	*transzendent*] W; *transscendent*	
258.6	*Transzendentalismus*] W; *Transscendentalismus*	
259.19	*Monist,*] W; ibid.ₐ	
263.37	Middle Ages] W; middle ages	
264.12	Middle Ages] W; middle ages	
267.26	*Pre-Socratic Philos.*] W; op. cit.	
267.31	*Pre-Socratic Philos.*] W; op. cit.	

The Child and the Curriculum

Copy-text is the first impression (Chicago: University of Chicago Press, 1902).

290.35   curriculum] W;   curirculum

Studies in Logical Theory I
"The Relationship of Thought and Its
Subject-Matter"

Copy-text is the first impression, "Thought and Its Subject-Matter: The General Problem of Logical Theory," in *Studies in Logical Theory* (Chicago: University of Chicago Press, 1903), pp. 1–22. Emendations have been adopted from the revised new edition in *Essays in Experimental Logic* (Chicago: University of Chicago Press, 1916), pp. 75–102.

298.1–2   I. THE RELATIONSHIP OF THOUGHT AND ITS SUB-
            JECT MATTER] W;   II The Relationship of Thought
            and Its Subject-Matter EE;   I Thought and Its Subject-
            Matter: The General Problem of Logical Theory
298.27   hydrodynamics,] EE;   ~;
299.10   Into] EE;   upon
299.20   either to state] EE;   to state either
299.22   or] EE;   nor
299.36   clothes,] EE;   ~;
299.36   etc.] EE;   etc., etc.
301.14   question] EE;   questions
302.35–36   ∧of "how] W;   "of ∧how
303.38   out diverse] EE;   out to diverse
304.2   thought,] EE;   ~;
304.3   occasions renders] EE;   situations constitutes
304.5   Consequently,] EE;   ~∧
304.6   empirical] EE;   psychological
304.6–7   but are of] EE;   but of
304.8   From] EE;   So from
304.11   reflection] EE;   thought
304.18–19   but relevant] EE;   but is such
304.21   indicate] EE;   are inherently concerned as indicating
304.22   brings to] EE;   brings itself to its own
304.23   its] EE;   in

304.25   logic)$_\wedge$] EE;   ~),
304.28   fulfillment$_\wedge$] W;   fulfilment$_\wedge$ EE;   ~,
304.30–31   objectives] EE;   objective
304.33   experience,] EE;   ~$_\wedge$
304.38   something (whether] EE;   ~, ~
304.39   be a thinking] EE;   be thinking
304.39   stimulus] EE;   condition
304.40   goal)] EE;   ~$_\wedge$
305.2   that] EE;   the
305.6   from the] EE;   from this latter point of view. I recur
         again to the
305.10   empirical things and values] EE;   empirical values
305.12–13   and a control] EE;   and control
305.18   ethical] EE;   ethic
305.19   perception of meaning or] EE;   perception or
305.22   aim.] EE;   aim. From this point of view, more definite
         logical import is attached to our earlier statements (p.
         2) regarding the possibility of taking anything in the
         universe of experience as subject-matter of thought.
305.25   coexistence,] EE;   ~$_\wedge$
305.25   contradiction,] EE;   ~$_\wedge$
305.26   range] EE;   set
305.27   possible materials] EE;   means
305.31   by] EE;   in
305.33   and conceptual] EE;   or ideational
306.6   into] EE;   to
306.7–8   action, all with] EE;   action with
306.9   *continuity*.] EE;   *continuity* in and of experience.
306.15   the future] EE;   future
306.16–17   spectator . . . is] EE;   spectator is
306.30–31   reflective considerations] W;   reflective considera-
         tion EE;   ideas
306.32   to] EE;   with
306.37–38   relative and methodological,] EE;   relative,
306.39   properties] EE;   forms
307.5   presents] EE;   has presented
307.11   net meaning] EE;   value
307.14   hunting] EE;   the hunting
307.14   collecting raw] EE;   collecting of raw
307.20   distinction-making] EE;   distinction
307.21–22   mentally$_\wedge$gymnastic] EE;   ~-~
307.30   such a form] EE;   such form
307.30   serve in] EE;   serve as premise in
308.3   Then there] EE;   There
308.9   objects] EE;   contents
308.10   world] EE;   universe
308.17   because *continuity*] EE;   because there is a certain
         homogeneity or *continuity*

308.18   use controls] EE;   use which controls
308.18   in the] EE;   in both the
308.19   types] EE;   grades
308.19   significance] EE;   value
308.20   meaning] EE;   thought
308.22–23 assignments of relative] EE;   relative assignments of
308.25   absorption] EE;   interaction
308.26   formation] EE;   outcome
308.33   results in treating] EE;   is to treat
308.33   technique] EE;   development
308.34   topic—] EE;   ~∧
308.35   It also states] EE;   It is also to state
308.37   to concrete] EE;   to the use made of these distinctions
          in concrete
308.37   that it creates] EE;   as to create
308.39   life.] EE;   life—metaphysics again in the bad sense of
          that term.
308.39   logic] EE;   problem of a logic
309.1   critical] EE;   in critical
309.1   science follows] EE;   science, is to follow
309.6   psychology.] EE;   psychology.[1] . . . [1]See Angell, "The
          Relations of Structural and Functional Psychology to
          Philosophy," *The Decennial Publications of the Uni-
          versity of Chicago*, Vol. III (1903), Part II, pp. 61–6,
          70–72.
309.10   sensory] EE;   sensation
309.10   perceptual] EE;   perception
309.10   conceptual] EE;   conception
309.14   trace events] EE;   trace series of psychical events
309.20   entities] EE;   distinctions
309.23   so] EE;   thus
309.26   relationship,] EE;   ~∧
309.26   the denial] EE;   and
309.27   indicative of] EE;   indicative only of
309.37   asserts,] EE;   ~∧
309.39   made,] EE;   ~∧
310.4–6   former. In . . . stimulus.] EE;   former.
310.7   significance] EE;   entire significance
310.9   is] EE;   has
310.12   force] EE;   value
310.14   analysis] EE;   analysis of value
310.14   out] EE;   out in detail
310.28   attitude] EE;   state
310.30   reflection] EE;   consciousness
310.32   response] EE;   mode of adaptation
310.33   consequently judge] EE;   judge
310.35   history] EE;   sequence
310.37   outcome.] EE;   outcome.[1] . . . [1]See statements regard-

ing the psychological and the logical in *The Child and the Curriculum*, pp. 28, 29.

311.1	in moving] EE; as we move
311.12–13	because of] EE; because we know
311.13	movement] EE; growth
311.14	engaged.] EE; engaged, and the position within the function of the particular element that engages us.
311.22	doing$_\wedge$] EE; ~,
311.24	obstacle and] EE; obstacle of
311.26	sequential and] EE; sequential, efficient, and
311.27	contemporaneous and] EE; contemporaneous, correlative, and
311.31	process in which] EE; process
311.31–32	engaged.] EE; engaged with.
311.32	Operating within empirical situations we] EE; We
311.33	condition] EE; condition or state
311.34	status] EE; status or element
311.35–36	function. When . . . limitations, we] EE; function. If we do, we
312.3	attitude] EE; sort of object or material
312.8	materials] EE; terms
312.12	its problematic data as] EE; its own basis for further procedure to be
312.13	results from] EE; it secures for itself in the
312.14	inquiry] EE; its aim
312.15	before thinking began, whose] EE; at the outset, and whose
312.16	means] EE; express means
312.26	mind] EE; thought
312.26–27	situations where elements] EE; values which
312.28–29	way . . . situations can] EE; way these values can
312.30	belong.] EE; belong. It is only conditions relative to a specific period or epoch of development in a cycle of experience which enables one to tell what to do next, or to estimate the value and meaning of what is already done.
313.9	ultimate] EE; alternate
313.22	cannot] EE; can not
313.24	criticizing] EE; criticising
313.24	and organizing tools] EE; and in organizing the tools
313.24–25	research.] EE; research in these lines.
313.28	know the] EE; know in relation to its congeners the
313.28	genesis] EE; organic genesis
313.30	goods] EE; values
314.1	mass, the . . . individuality—] EE; mass—
314.2	answer] EE; *final* answer
314.6	experience] EE; genetic experience
314.12	end;] EE; ~,

314.12   we attack] EE;   attack
314.13   some interest] EE;   some other interest
314.18   occupation.] EE;   occupation in experience.
314.20   A] EE;   The
314.21   alone can] EE;   can alone
314.21   for social qualities] EE;   for the region of social values
314.25   nature of] EE;   nature either of
314.26   situations] EE;   crises
314.27   movement] EE;   growth
314.39   been found afterward] EE;   afterward been found
315.14–15   new technique] EE;   new forms of technique
315.15   inquiry] EE;   its treatment

Studies in Logical Theory 2
"The Antecedents and Stimuli of Thinking"

Copy-text is the first impression, "Thought and Its Subject-Matter: The Antecedent Conditions and Cues of the
Thought-Function," in *Studies in Logical Theory* (Chicago:
University of Chicago Press, 1903), pp. 23–48. Emendations
have been adopted from the revised new edition in *Essays in
Experimental Logic* (Chicago: University of Chicago Press,
1916), pp. 103–35.

316.1–2   2. THE ANTECEDENTS AND STIMULI OF THINK-
            ING] W; III The Antecedents and Stimuli of Think-
            ing EE;   II Thought and Its Subject-Matter: The An-
            tecedent Conditions and Cues of the Thought-Function
316.3   sense—] EE;   ~,
316.5   experience—] EE;   ~,
316.5–6   concerned with the] EE;   concerned in particular with
            description and interpretation of the
316.12   position] EE;   historic position
316.12   amid the typical functions] EE;   in the evolving
316.20   evident] EE;   apparent
316.22   meaning] EE;   inherent worth
316.22   the validity] EE;   validity
316.24   translate] EE;   translation of
316.24   acts in] EE;   terms of
316.30–31   thought in experience so] EE;   thought, so
316.31   to characterize] EE;   to select and characterize
317.4   control] EE;   transformation
317.4   experience. I] EE;   experience; and that continual con-
            fusion and inconsistency are introduced when these
            respective meanings are not identified and described
            according to their respective geneses and places. I

317.7   secondly] EE;   second
317.8   thirdly] EE;   third
317.8   *objective*] EE;   *content*
317.17   material] EE;   the material
317.17   by inquiry] EE;   into the thought-/situation,
317.17–18 as inquiry] EE;   as this
317.18   purpose. This chapter] EE;   purpose. It goes without
           saying that these are to be discriminated as stages of a
           life-process in the natural history of experience, not as
           ready-made or ontological; it is contended that, save as
           they are differentiated in connection with well-defined
           historical stages, they are either lumped off as equiva-
           lents, or else treated as absolute divisions—or as each
           by turns, according to the exigencies of the particular
           argument. In fact, this chapter
317.23–24 readjustment . . . experience] EE;   readjustment of
           experience
317.24   being thereby compelled] EE;   therefore endeavoring
317.25   historic] EE;   periodic
318.1   criticizing] EE;   criticising
318.3   Nowadays everyone] EE;   Everyone
318.5   mental] EE;   psychical
318.7–8   belonging peculiarly] EE;   belonging somehow pecul-
           iarly
318.9   the world] EE;   a world
318.13–14 anticipation with that of] EE;   anticipation of
318.14–15 perception; more generally we contrast the] EE;   per-
           ception; the
318.15   inferential] EE;   ideal
318.22   conceptions] EE;   constructs
318.27–28 meaning. Our . . . revision.] EE;   meaning.
318.30   distinctions,] EE;   ∼;
319.1   afford stuff] EE;   afford it stuff
319.1   thought may] EE;   to
319.6   this] EE;   his
319.7–9   the exercise . . . external to it;] EE;   an independent
           thought-material and an independent thought-activity;
319.10   subject-matter of thought] EE;   thought-/material
319.11   meaning and validity] EE;   worth
319.13   the fundamental] EE;   the same fundamental
319.15   always] EE;   never effecting more than
*319.18–19 as matter of fact] *stet* SLT;   as a matter of fact EE
319.20   material] EE;   specific thought-material
319.20   process of inquiry] EE;   specific thought-activity in cor-
           respondence with each other
319.23   We] EE;   1. We
319.25   giving its] EE;   giving it its

319.26–27 furnishing] EE; affording us
319.28 1. The] EE; The
319.29 impressions_∧] EE; ~,
320.37 This] EE; It is this
320.37–321.1 distinction marks] EE; distinction which marks
320n.2 *Mikrokosmus*] W; *Microkosmus*
321.2 mere] EE; receptive
321.4 the cognitive *worth*] EE; the *worth*
322.4–5 again: "Thought] EE; again:[2] "Thought
322.6 impressions."[4] W; impressions."[2] EE; impressions."
322.6 again: "The] EE; again:[3] "The
322.10–11 possible."[5] W; possible."[3] EE; possible."
322.12 ideas thus play] EE; ideas play
322.29 impressions] EE; the impressions
322.36 cause] EE; arouse
322n.2 *Logic*] W; *Ibid.*
322n.3 *Logic*] W; *Ibid.*
323.5 quality] EE; matter or quality
323.15 bald] EE; a bald
323.17–18 it characteristically qualifies content] EE; it is *meaning*, characteristic quality of content
323.34 as logical *objects*] EE; as cognitive (or logical) ob-jects
323.38 _∧objects_∧] EE; "meanings"
323n.1 *Mikrokosmus*] W; *Microkosmus*
324.6 *meaning*] EE; *worth*
324.7 process.] EE; process of valuation.
324.14 which] EE; that
324.15 that] EE; which
324.16 between (*a*)] W; (*a*) between
324.16 considering both coincidence] EE; considering coin-cidence
324.17 as psychical] EE; as both affairs of existence of psy-chical
324.19 making] EE; the inherent logic which makes
324.21 ought both] EE; both ought
324.26 frequency] EE; repetition
324.34 *say*] EE; [*rom.*]
324.35–36 connection] EE; conjunction
325.1 discount. But in] EE; discount. In
325.2–3 intellectual object] EE; idea
325.6 is a rule, specification,] EE; is really a specification_∧
325.8 treat this] EE; treat the origin of this
325.9 mental events] EE; ideas
325.10 by psycho-physical] EE; by conditions of original psy-cho-physical
325.12–13 experience involving . . . kind and] EE; experi-ence and

325.17–18   by those who held it] EE;   as an item of the experi-
            ence of those who meant it
325.22–23   experienced frame] EE;   experience-frame
325.23   world] EE;   universe
325.32   a bare] EE;   bare
325.32   a problematic] EE;   as problematic
326.6–7   not trouble] EE;   not as such trouble
326.12   contrast] EE;   may contrast
326.12   present state as bare] EE;   present bare
326.13   over against another] EE;   with a
326.13   as one which is coherent] EE;   of possible coherence
326.16–17   presents] EE;   means only
326.21–22   objective experience] EE;   experience
326.23   some] EE;   one
326.24   as mere] EE;   as bare conjunction or mere
326.26   set against] EE;   set over against
326.35   the logical] EE;   the grasp of the logical
326.38   neither] EE;   no such thing as either
326.38   nor] EE;   or
327.12   material yet] EE;   material, it yet
327.13   up,] EE;   ~:
327.15   Kantian notion] EE;   notion
327.20   avoided] EE;   really avoided
327.28   labeled] EE;   practically labeled
327.33   alternative] EE;   alternative in this dilemma
327.34   or environment] EE;   of experience
327.34   exist] EE;   are
327.35   that which is afterward] EE;   that afterward
328.3   The stimulus] EE;   It
328.5   yet which] EE;   which yet
328.8   goes] EE;   belongs
328.10   whole. To] EE;   whole. It is a case of the psychologist's
            fallacy to
328.11–12   coherence] EE;   relationship
328.13   process of inquiry is a fallacy.] EE;   thought-process.
328.19   of] EE;   which evokes
328.19   thought, giving] EE;   thought∧ and gives
328.20   activities and determining its object. On] EE;   activi-
            ties. On
328.22   so as (by insisting) to] EE;   and, by insisting,
328.25   positively, to show that] EE;   positively, that
328.29–30   reflection] EE;   thought
328.32   idea are] EE;   idea (whether as mental contents or as
            psychical existences) are
328.33   that] EE;   the
328.34   thought.] EE;   thought; while the distinction of psy-
            chical existences from external existences arises only
            within a highly elaborate technical reflection—that of

the psychologist as such.[1] . . . [1]The emphasis here is upon the term "existences," and in its plural form. Doubtless the distinction of some experiences as belonging to me, as mine in a peculiarly intimate way, from others as chiefly concerning other persons, or as having to do with things, is an early one. But this is a distinction of *concern*, of value. The distinction referred to above is that of making an *object*, or presentation, out of this felt type of value, and thereby breaking it up into distinct "events," etc., with their own laws of inner connection. This is the work of psychological analysis. Upon the whole matter of the psychical I am glad to refer to PROFESSOR GEORGE H. MEAD'S article entitled "The Definition of the Psychical," Vol. III, Part II, of *The Decennial Publications of the University of Chicago*.

328.35   continuity] EE; identity of value

328.36   inner active distraction] EE; inner distraction

328.37   each contending] EE; contending each

328.38   which] EE; that

329.4   and yet] EE; and which yet

329.6   "objective."] W; 'objective.' EE; ∧~·∧

329.11   real. The] EE; real. It is the further work of *thought* to exclude some of the contending factors from membership in experience, and thus to relegate them to the sphere of the merely subjective. But just at this epoch the

329.12   conflict among its elements.] EE; conflict.

329.15   a transition] EE; the transition

329.18   worth] EE; logical value

329.19–21   thought. Deny . . . "mental."] EE; thought.

329.32–33   stimuli to thinking] EE; stimuli

329.38   a specific] EE; an individual

329.38–40   experience. [¶] There] EE; experience. There

330.1–2   or the previously organized] EE; or organized

330.4   situation] EE; entire experience

330.5   redefinition] EE; re-definition

330.6–7   This redefining and re-relating is] EE; This is

330.7   constructive] EE; reconstructive

330.9–10   arrangement of things] EE; experience

330.29   repetition∧] EE; ~,

330.30   dialectical contradictions] EE; self-contradictions

330.31   unless] EE; save

330.34   upon doing] EE; to do

330.39   temporal phase] EE; phase

331.4–6   Now things . . . account. The] EE; Now things, objects, have already, implicitly at least, determinations of worth, of truth, reality, etc. The

331.6   etc.] EE;   etc., etc.
331.13   regarded] EE;   there
331.15   relevant to thinking as] EE;   relevant as
331.18   force and] EE; value or
331.20   (1) things] EE;   (1) value as determined by things
331.21   mere impressions] EE;   things
331.22   (2) *meaning*] EE;   (2) hence, value in the shape of *meaning*
331.23   traits] EE;   values
331.24   features] EE;   kinds of value
331.27   has been] EE;   is
331.27–28 yet is now conflicting] EE;   yet conflicting
331.30   objective] EE;   value or
331.30   validity,] EE;   ∼∧
331.32   This] EE;   Since this
331.32   attempt] EE;   deeper attempt
331.34   nevertheless] EE;   yet
331.34–35 dependent . . . it. Hence the] EE;   specifically dependent, the
331.36   avoidance] EE;   avoiding
331.36–38 secured only . . . experienced things,] EE;   found in the endeavor to characterize thought as a specific mode of valuation in the evolution of significant experience,
331.40   force] EE;   value
332.5   *daily life*] EE;   [*rom.*]
332.6   useful combinations] EE;   [*ital.*]
332.6   correct expectations] EE;   [*ital.*]
332.6–7   seasonable reactions] EE;   [*ital.*]
332.14   real state of things] EE;   type of value possessed by it
332.15   things] EE;   values
332.17   results. The] EE;   results. Even the most purely utilitarian of values are nevertheless values; not *mere* existences. But the
332.17–18 experience also is] EE;   experience is saved from reduction to just material uses and worths; for it is
332.19   goods and objects] EE;   values
332.29   environment] EE;   region of values
332.31   existences; and] EE;   existences lacking value-specifications; and
332.31   while the] EE;   the
332.33   it] EE;   but to
332.33   comes] EE;   come
332.34   realization.] EE;   realization and expression in building up a world of values.
333.4–5   criticizing] EE;   criticising
333.10   *mere*] EE;   [*rom.*]
333.11   organization and force] EE;   meaning

333.22   objects] EE;   values
333.25   form] EE;   value
333.27   scheme] EE;   scheme of values
333n.12   practical . . . course] EE;   reality appears
333n.13   thought-specifications,] EE;   thought-specifications or values,
334.1   which] EE;   that
334.2   existences] EE;   unvalued existences
334.9   idealists] EE;   us
334.40   idealist] EE;   rationalist
335.4   Lotze began] EE;   Lotze himself began
335.12   source than thought,] EE;   source,
335.15   organization] EE;   organic unity
335.32   "constitutive"] EE;   ∧~∧
335.32–33 but are prohibited] EE;   but we are absolutely prohibited
335.34   which] EE;   that
335.36⁽²⁾ constitutive] EE;   such
336.2   former!] EE;   former!¹ . . . ¹Bradley's criticisms of rationalistic idealism should have made the force of this point reasonably familiar.
336.3   not a] EE;   not meant for a
336.3   It points] EE;   It is meant to point
336.5   discovered within thinking] EE;   of the thought-function
336.6   of various] EE;   of judgment in its various
336.7   forms of judgment,] EE;   forms,
336.17–18 makes into absolute] EE;   makes absolute
336.18   distinctions] EE;   certain distinctions
336.19   things which] EE;   which
336.20   historic] EE;   wholly historic
336.20   or temporal] EE;   and relative
336.24   employ] EE;   reciprocal employ
336.25   existence] EE;   reality

Studies in Logical Theory 3
"Data and Meanings"

Copy-text is the first impression, "Thought and Its Subject-Matter: The Datum of Thinking," in *Studies in Logical Theory* (Chicago: University of Chicago Press, 1903), pp. 49–64. Emendations have been adopted from the revised new edition in *Essays in Experimental Logic* (Chicago: University of Chicago Press, 1916), pp. 136–56.

337.1–2   3. DATA AND MEANINGS [¶] We have reached the
          point] W;   IV Data and Meanings [¶] We have reached
          the point EE; III Thought and Its Subject-Matter: The
          Datum of Thinking [¶] We have now reached a second
          epochal stage in the evolution of the thought-situation,
          a crisis which forces upon us the problem of the
          distinction and mutual reference of the datum or pres-
          entation, and the ideas or "thoughts." It will economize
          and perhaps clarify discussion if we start from the
          relatively positive and constructive result just reached,
          and review Lotze's treatment from that point of regard.
          [¶] We have reached the point
337.2   matters of] EE;   matters or contents of
337.4   matters,] EE;   matters or contents,
337.4   out *as* matters] EE;   out as such
337.5   without question] EE;   without tension or question
337.5–6   "content$_\wedge$" is not] EE;   "content," or fact, is not
337.6   abstracted.] EE;   abstracted *as* content or object.
337.6   Its distinction from] EE;   Its very distinction as con-
          tent from
337.7   its matter] EE;   such
337.7   work] EE;   result
337.8   reflection] EE;   post-reflection
337.9   discriminated] EE;   conscious
337.12–337n.17   point.[1] . . . [1]This   is . . . revision.)]   EE;
          point.[1] . . . [1]The common statement that primitive
          man projects his own volitions, emotions, etc., into ob-
          jects is but a back-handed way of expressing the truth
          that "objects," etc., have only gradually emerged from
          their life-matrix. Looking back, it is almost impossible
          to avoid the fallacy of supposing that somehow such
          objects were there first and were afterward emotionally
          appreciated.
337.13   end, for it] EE;   end. It
337.15–16   in the world of the new] EE;   in the new
337.19   fold. But such] EE;   fold of the new experience; such
337.19–338.1   introduction clearly] EE;   introduction, on the
          other hand, clearly
338.2   deliberate] EE;   conscious
338.3   an organization in] EE;   the unity of
338.5   place,] EE;   place within itself,
338.5   final] EE;   deliberate final
338.10   are doubtful] EE;   are rendered doubtful
338.12–13   ideas, the *Quaesitum*, the] EE;   ideas, the ideal, the
338.13–14   the Inferential. [¶] *a*) There is] EE;   the Thought.
          For there is
338.23   conflict is] EE;   conflict as such is

338.23   immediately of] EE; immediately expressed, or felt, as of
338.24   given] EE; apprehended
338.29   terms as low] EE; as low terms
339.4   in] EE; of
339.6   [¶] *b*) It is obvious] EE; [¶] It is obvious
339.10–11 interpreted, . . . connection. The facts] EE; interpreted. The facts
339.11   presentations] EE; presentation
339.12   meanings] EE; meaning
339.20   connection‸] EE; worth,
339.21   as ideas] EE; as just ideas
339.26   external] EE; real
339.26–27 existence] EE; unreality
339.28   of *possible*, of inferred existence] EE; of *mental* existence
339.28–29 latter is regarded] EE; mental existence is in such cases regarded
339.30   existence] EE; value
339.31   regarded as] EE; regarded, from the value standpoint, as
339.31   unassured. Or,] EE; unassured. The very existence of the idea or meaning as separate *is* the partial, broken up, and hence objectively unreal (from the validity standpoint) character of the datum. Or,
339.33   facts] EE; the facts
339.35   place;] EE; place in the universe;
339.36   relative] EE; apparent
339.40   object.] EE; object in experience or reality.
340.6   mental] EE; psychical
340.9   process] EE; mental process
340.12   eliminate] EE; eliminate as false
340.14   perception] EE; apperception
340.15–23 structure. . . . In other] EE; structure. In other
340.31   world.] EE; world. It is *psychic.*
340.37   a personal] EE; psychical
340.40   existence] EE; values
341.6   prejudice] EE; pre-judice
341.6   misconception] EE; mis-conception
341.8   *validity*] EE; [*rom.*]
341.8–9   becomes . . . existence.[3]] EE; becomes mere image—subjective;[1] and finally a psychical existence.
341.13   ideatum. That] EE; ideatum, as affairs of the direction of logical movement. That
341.14–15 is still characterized] EE; is characterized
341.15–16 but real. . . . That] EE; but only in a psychical sense; that

341.17–19   in a cosmic or extra-organic sense. [¶] 1. *The*] EE;
in an objective, cosmic sense.[1]

The implication of the psychic and the logical
within both the given presentation and the thought
about it, appears in the continual shift to which
logicians of Lotze's type are put. When the psychical
is regarded as existence over against meaning as just
ideal, reality seems to reside in the psychical; it is
there anyhow, and meaning is just a curious attachment—curious because as *mere meaning* it is non-
existent as event or state—and there seems to be
nothing by which it can be even tied to the psychical
state as its bearer or representative. But when the
emphasis falls on thought as *content,* as significance,
then the psychic event, the idea as image[2] (as distinct
from idea as meaning) appears as an accidental but
necessary evil, the unfortunate irrelevant medium
through which *our* thinking has to go on.[3]

[¶] 1. *The*

1. Of course, this means that what is excluded and so left behind
in the problem of determination of *this* objective content is regarded as psychical. With reference to other problems and aims
this same psychic existence is initial, not survival. Released from
its prior absorption in some unanalyzed experience it gains
standing and momentum on its own account; *e.g.,* the "personal
equation" represents what is eliminated from a given astronomic
time-determination as being purely subjective, or "source-of-
error." But it is initiatory in reference to new modes of technique, re-readings of previous data—new considerations in psychology, even new socioethical judgments. Moreover, it remains
a fact, and even a worthful fact, as a part of one's own "inner"
experience, as an immediate *psychical reality.* That is to say,
there is a region of *personal* experience (mainly emotive or affectional) already recognized as a sphere of value. The "source
of error" is disposed of by making it a *fact* of this region. The
recognition of falsity does not *originate* the psychic (p. 38,
note).

2. Of course, this is a further reflective distinction. The plain man
and the student do not determine the extraneous, irrelevant, and
misleading matter as image in a *psychological* sense, but only
as *fanciful* or fantastic. Only to the psychologist and for *his*
purpose does it break up into image and meaning.

3. Bradley, more than any other writer, has seized upon this double
antithesis, and used it first to condemn the logical as such, and
then turned it around as the impartial condemnation of the
psychical also. See *Appearance and Reality.* In chap. 15 he
metes out condemnation to "thought" because it can never take
in the psychical existence or reality which is present; in chap.
19, he passes similar judgment upon the "psychical" because it
is brutally fragmentary. Other epistemological logicians have
wrestled—or writhed—with this problem, but I believe Bradley's
position is impregnable—from the standpoint of ready-made differences. When the antithesis is treated as part and lot of the
process of defining the truth of a particular subject-matter, and
thus as historic and relative, the case is quite otherwise.

341.26   data or material] EE;   material
341.27   counts,] EE;   ~;
341.29   arrangement] EE;   grouping
341.30   yet resembling and classed.] EE;   yet classed—as differences of a common somewhat.
341.36   data are] EE;   datum is
342.5   common~color] EE;   ~-~
342.12   datum.] EE;   datum of thought.
342.20   material] EE;   given material
342n.11   form] EE;   forms
342n.24   his] EE;   this
343.3–4   feature of spatial and temporal arrangement in contrast with] EE;   combination of coincidence and
343.4–5   coherence or connection] EE;   coherence
343.11   matters] EE;   matter
343.19   effects which] EE;   and these
343.37   isolated sensory] EE;   sensory
343.37   which are] EE;   as
343n.2–3   structures and tools] EE;   elements in and
344.3–4   selected from experienced things for that very purpose] EE;   in its own scheme
344.4   Sensory] EE;   Such
344.6   experience always] EE;   experience, as distinct from the psychologists' constructs, always
344.7   continuum.] EE;   continuum of values.
344.9–10   taken as thunder: as] EE;   taken as
344.13   a] EE;   my
344.19–20   control and use of stimuli] EE;   evolution of experience, marking a certain point in its cycle, and, consequently—having always its own conscious context and bearings—is a characteristic function of reconstruction in experience.
344.22   work] EE;   the work
344.29   clear] EE;   absolutely clear
344.33   experienced] EE;   experience
345.3   data] EE;   datum
345.4   data] EE;   datum
345.5   universal] EE;   given universal
345.8   it over] EE;   it as over
345.14   and which so] EE;   and so
345.21   ordered] EE;   organic
345.23–24   connection] EE;   transformation
345.24   dynamic continuity of existence] EE;   given sense
345.30–31   further overcomes] EE;   overcomes further
346n.22   34] W;   43
347.3   data being thoroughly] EE;   data thoroughly
347.3   connected] EE;   corrected
347.4   being] EE;   completely incarnate as

347.4   meanings] EE;   meaning
347.6–7   the description is] EE;   it is
347.9   antecedent] EE;   antecedents
347.10   somewhats extraneously brought] EE;   somewhats
             brought
347.11   thought, upon] EE;   thought, extraneously upon
347.15   facts] EE;   fact
347.16   meanings] EE;   meaning
347.26   inference] EE;   thinking
347.30–31   is discovered . . . *situation* as] EE;   is given *in* the
             thought-/situation, for the sake of accomplishing the
             aim of thought (along with a correlative discrimination
             of ideas or meanings), as
347.31–32   absolutely and in isolation, or] EE;   absolutely, or
347.37   objects),] EE;   ∼)ʌ
347.38   Lotze, like Kant, attempts] EE;   Lotze attempts
347.40–348.1 sense-data as data are] W;   senseʌdata as data
             are EE;   sense-data are
348.7   thought is] EE;   thought really is
348.16   matter given to thought] EE;   matter of thought
348.17   force] EE;   value
348.22   structural differences of] EE;   differences of structural
349.4   possible] EE;   suggested
349.26   any] EE;   and
349.34   adequate] EE;   ideal
*350.7–8   disciplines] *stet* SLT;   disciples EE

Studies in Logical Theory 4
"The Objects of Thought"

Copy-text is the first impression, "Thought and Its Subject-Matter: The Content and Object of Thought," in *Studies
in Logical Theory* (Chicago: University of Chicago Press,
1903), pp. 65–85. Emendations have been adopted from the
revised new edition in *Essays in Experimental Logic* (Chicago: University of Chicago Press, 1916), pp. 157–81.

351.1   4. THE OBJECTS OF THOUGHT] W;   V The Objects
             of Thought EE;   IV Thought and Its Subject-Matter:
             The Content and Object of Thought
351.3   repeatedly led] EE;   led repeatedly
351.4   distinctive objects] EE;   content
351.12   subject-matter] EE;   own
351.17   thought-forms] EE;   thought-form
351.25–26   bridge over] EE;   bridge

351.26   impression] EE;   impression over
352.5   *Meaning*] EE;   [*rom.*]
352.5   object] EE;   content
352.5   thought.] EE;   thought as such.
352.16   98–99] W;   99
353.9   import] EE;   meaning
353.36   sorts] EE;   kinds
354.7   arranged] EE;   ranged
354.8   one another's] EE;   each other's
354.13   each by] EE;   each in a pair, and by
354.31   *subject*;] EE;   ∼,
355.22   factors] EE;   values
355.22–23 integrated] EE;   absorptively integrated
355.23   in] EE;   into
355.23   aspects] EE;   part
355.24   coloring,] EE;   ∼;
355.25   being∧] EE;   ∼,
355.25   qualities] EE;   values
355.26   experience),] EE;   ∼)∧
355.30   matter for] EE;   object to
356.1–3   and the . . . of] EE;   and the thought-mode or idea
          as connected are the object of
356.4–5   goal. Every] EE;   goal. Exactly the same value is idea,
          as either tool or content, according as it is taken as
          instrumental or as accomplishment. Every
356.5   reflective inquiry] EE;   the thought-situation
356.7   and as] EE;   and consequently as
356.9   in] EE;   of
356.10   content or logical object.] EE;   content.
356.17   existence] EE;   possibility
356.39   meanings] EE;   its own contents
356.40   existences] EE;   that which is wholly outside itself
357.4   sense] EE;   rational meaning
357.11   defects] EE;   defects and errors
357.12–13 meanings. [¶] Our] EE;   meanings by which to
          rectify and replace themselves. Our
357.23   certain meaning] EE;   certain validity, or meaning
357.24   *object*] EE;   [*rom.*]
357.24–25 such, not merely its state or mood.] EE;   such.
357.27   valid meaning] EE;   valid idea, as a meaning
357.37   etc.,] EE;   etc., etc.,
*358.3   besides] W;   beside
358.14   the sense that] EE;   so far as
358.16   objects of knowledge] EE;   contents of consciousness
359.4   *region*] EE;   [*rom.*]
359.4   experience, to] EE;   cosmic experience, or to
359.7   a meaning] EE;   thought
359.8   found] EE;   involved

359.9   problem] EE;   metaphysical problem
359.9   existence] EE;   reality
359.12   logical] EE;   metaphysical
359.16   an object] EE;   object
359.16   a content] EE;   content
359.18–19   *determinant*] EE;   [*rom.*]
359.19   activity] EE;   experience
359.32   really] EE;   always
359.34   a] EE;   the
359.34–35   as contemplated in detachment.] EE;   as detached
            and contemplated.
359n.4   perception.] EE;   perception. See Study VII, on the
            Hypothesis.
360.1   is disorganized] EE;   is tensional as regards its exist-
            ing status, or disorganized
360.2   elements, we] EE;   elements, yet organized as emerg-
            ing out of the unified experience of the past and as
            striving as a whole, or equally in all its phases, to re-
            instate an experience harmonized in make-up, we
360.3   *held*] EE;   [*rom.*]
360.4   possible.] EE;   possible (according as they are viewed
            with reference to the past or to the future).
360.8   behavior] EE;   experience
360.10   it] EE;   the idea
360.11   it] EE;   thought
360.12   method of control] EE;   mediator
360.15   difficulty$_\wedge$] EE;   ~,
360.15   because the] EE;   because we see that the
360.18   transition.] EE;   transition from one unified form to
            another.
360.21–22   is . . . function] EE;   is such in virtue of the exer-
            cise of function
360.24–25   objectivity. It . . . with.] EE;   objectivity.
360.30   "meaning,"] EE;   "meaning" or idea as such,
360.30   made$_\wedge$up] EE;   ~-~
360n.1–2   criticized] EE;   criticised
360n.5   *feeling*] EE;   [*rom.*]
360n.5   foregoing] EE;   above
361.2   respect] EE;   aspect
361.6   property] EE;   question
361.16   connection] EE;   mutual connection
361.16   organized] EE;   individualized
361.17   meanings] EE;   meanings or ideas
361.17–18   thought sets] EE;   thought as it sets
361.18   out.] EE;   out is supplied.
361.27   that only] EE;   that it is only
361.28   issues has] EE;   issues that has
361n.3   *University*] EE;   *The University*

361n.7–8   psychical . . . logical.] EE;   psychical. Even this ex-
            plicit placing of thinking in the psychical sphere, along
            with sensations and the associative mechanism, does
            not, however, lead Lotze to reconsider his statement
            that the psychological problem is totally irrelevant and
            even corrupting as regards the logical.
361n.8   it gives] EE;   it only gives
362.19   here. The] EE;   here. It is once more the
362.19   question is whether] EE;   question whether
362.23   the phase] EE;   merely a phase
362.25–26   for . . . control.] EE;   in entering into a tensional
            status where the maintenance of its harmony of con-
            tent is problematic and hence an aim.
362.37   instrument] EE;   organ and instrument
362.41   thoroughly] EE;   so thoroughly
362.41–363.1   self-contradictory.] EE;   self-contradictory as to
            necessitate critical reconsideration of the premises
            which lead to it.
363.5–6   and which is set] EE;   and set
363.9   is *not* the] EE;   is not itself the
363.12   building] EE;   erecting
363.14–15   longitudinally, temporally viewed] EE;   longitudi-
            nally viewed
363.26   accidentally] EE;   extraneously
363.35   matters] EE;   contents or matters
363.36   existences] EE;   bare existences
363.37   from casual] EE;   from the associations of casual
363.37–38   revery by control in reference] EE;   revery in an
            element of control by reference
363.38   end,] EE;   end which determines the fitness and thus
            the selection of the associates,
363.40   other.] EE;   other, and for the sake of a redintegration
            of a conflicting experience.
*364.18   helpful.] EE;   helpful. Life proposes to maintain at all
            hazards the unity of its own process. Experience insists
            on being itself, on securing integrity even through and
            by means of conflict.[1] . . . [1]Professor James's satis-
            faction in the contemplation of bare pluralism, of dis-
            connection, of radical having-nothing-to-do-with-one-
            another, is a case in point. The satisfaction points to an
            æsthetic attitude in which the brute diversity becomes
            itself one interesting object; and thus unity asserts
            itself in its own denial. When discords are hard and
            stubborn, and intellectual and practical unification are
            far to seek, nothing is commoner than the device of
            securing the needed unity by recourse to an emotion
            which feeds on the very brute variety. Religion and
            art and romantic affection are full of examples.

364.19   place] EE;   placing
364.20   matters] EE;   matters or values
364.21   they] EE;   this
364.21   determine] EE;   determines
364.23   operations$_\wedge$] EE; $\sim$,
365.1–2   the practice of knowing when] EE;   reflective practice,
            when
365.4   experience] EE;   experiencing
365.7–8   context (see *ante*, p. 311).] EE;   context.
365.18   arises] EE;   rises
365.20–21   the notion] EE;   our notion
365.30   subject-matter] EE;   matter
365.31   validity] EE;   worth
365.31   contagiousness.] EE;   contagiousness. Or the reference
            proves that we have not as yet reached any conclusion,
            but are entertaining a hypothesis—since social validity
            is not a matter of mere common content, but of secur-
            ing participation in a commonly adjudged social experi-
            ence through action directed thereto and directed by
            consensus of judgment.
366.8   involved. . . . All] W;   involved. . . . all
366.17   original separation] EE;   original implication of a
            separation
366.21   although unknowable] EE;   unknowable
366.22   ideas. At] EE;   ideas as just subjective. The subjectiv-
            ity of the psychical event infects at the last the mean-
            ing or ideal object. Because it has been taken to be
            something "in itself," thought is also something "in
            itself," and at
366.23   began:$_\wedge$] EE; $\sim$: —
366.33   and at its termination] EE;   and termination
366.36   a *historic* or temporal meaning] EE;   a historic mean-
            ing
366.38   fulfillment,] W;   fulfilment, EE;   fulfilment in the
            drama of evolving experience,
366.38   objective] EE;   bifold objective
366.39   references] EE;   reference
366.39   transcendental] EE;   purely metaphysical
367.5   non-existent (excepting] EE; $\sim$, $\sim$
367.6   idea),] EE; $\sim_\wedge$,
367.6   he lands] EE;   Lotze lands
367.9   scepticism—] W;   skepticism— EE; $\sim$,
367.10   such$_\wedge$] EE; $\sim$,
367.10   ready-made] EE;   independent
367.11   such—] EE; $\sim$,
367.13   other. In] EE;   other: a definition which has meaning
            only in connection with the fact that experience is
            continually integrating itself into a wholeness of co-

herent meaning deepened in significance by passing through an inner distraction in which by means of conflict certain contents are rendered partial and hence objectively conscious. In

367.14	effected. The] EE; effected. In that sense the
367.15	validity of thought] EE; reality
367.15	thought, just] EE; thought, as thought, just
367.17	dependent upon thought] EE; reflectional in character
367.20	non-intellectual experiences of things, and then the] EE; functions, and the
367.23	its final test] EE; its test of final validity
367.24–25	large, . . . control, it] EE; large, it
367n.5	experience),] EE; experiencing)$_\wedge$

[On Mill and Whewell]

Copy-text is the first impression in *Studies in Logical Theory* (Chicago: University of Chicago Press, 1903), pp. 160–68.

368.6	*Logic*] W; logic
368.9	Introduction] W; [*ital.*]
369n.1	14] W; 2
372.30	$_\wedge$a "general] W; "a $_\wedge$general
374n.1	*Logic*] W; *Ibid.*
374n.2	*Logic*] W, *Ibid.*
374n.5	*Logic*] W; *Ibid.*

"Interpretation of Savage Mind"

Readings from the present volume copy-text in the *Psychological Review*, PsR, appear to the left of the bracket; following the bracket are the substantive changes introduced in PC, the new edition of the article in *Philosophy and Civilization* (New York: Minton, Balch and Co., 1931), pp. 173–87.

40.7	man] PsR; men PC
40.16	character] PsR; trait PC
40n.1	*Ibid.,*] PsR; *Sociology,* I, PC
41.10	carnivor] PsR; carnivora PC
41.10	herbivor] PsR; herbivora PC
41.16	with] PsR; to PC
42.13	the hunting] PsR; a hunting PC
42.13	or] PsR; as a PC
42.14	type] PsR; pattern PC
42.35	had] PsR; have PC
44.21	Such immediacy] PsR; Immediacy PC
45.9	or] PsR; nor PC
45n.2	Hodgkinson] W; Hodginkson PsR; Hodkinsson PC
46.15	involved] PsR; that are involved PC
48.11	by seeing] PsR; when we see PC
49.14	It] PsR; There PC

CORRECTION OF QUOTATIONS

Dewey represented source material in varying ways, from memorial paraphrase to verbatim copy, sometimes citing his source fully, in others mentioning only authors' names, and in still others, omitting documentation altogether.

To prepare the critical text, all material inside quotation marks, except that obviously being emphasized or restated, has been searched out and the documentation has been verified and emended when necessary. Steps regularly used to emend documentation are described in Textual Principles and Procedures (*Middle Works of John Dewey*, 1:347–60), but Dewey's variations from the original in his quotations have been considered important enough to warrant a special list.

All quotations have been retained within the texts as they were first published, except for corrections required by special circumstances and noted in the Emendations List. Substantive changes that restore original readings in cases of possible compositorial or typographical errors are similarly noted as "W" emendations. The variable form of quotation suggests that Dewey, like many scholars of the period, was unconcerned about precision in matters of form, but many of the changes in cited materials may have arisen in the printing process. For example, comparing Dewey's quotations with the originals reveals that some journals house-styled the quoted materials as well as Dewey's own. In the present edition, the spelling and capitalization of the source have been reproduced.

Dewey's most frequent alteration in quoted material was changing or omitting punctuation. He also often failed to use ellipses or to separate quotations to show that material had been left out. No citation of the Dewey material or of the original appears here if the changes were only of this kind—

omitted or changed punctuation, including ellipses. In the case of omitted ellipses, attention is called to short phrases; if, however, a line or more has been left out, no attention has been called to the omission.

Italics in source material have been treated as accidentals. When Dewey omitted those italics, the omission is not noted, though Dewey's added italics are listed. If changed or omitted accidentals have substantive implications, as in the capitalization of some concept words, the quotation is noted. The form of listing the quotations, from Dewey as well as from his source, is designed to assist the reader in determining whether Dewey had the book open before him or was relying on his memory.

Notations in this section follow the formula: page-line numbers from the present text, followed by the text condensed to first and last words or such as make for sufficient clarity, then a square bracket followed by the symbol identifying the Dewey item. After a semicolon comes the necessary correction, whether of one word or a longer passage, as required. Finally, in parentheses, the author's surname and shortened source-title from the Checklist of Dewey's References are followed by a comma and the page-line reference to the source.

Four quotations have been omitted because Dewey translated from the German in order to cite the material in English. The four are 181.12–14, Eduard von Hartmann, *System der Philosophie in Grundriss*, Vol. 4; 178.3–11, Gottfried Wilhelm Leibniz, *Monadologie*; 323.8–11, Hermann Lotze, *Mikrokosmus*; and 207.21, Gottlieb Fichte, *Werke*.

House-styled spelling has been changed back to the original form at 259.19 (endeavored), 259.22 (favor), 60.26 and 60.31 (although), 60.38 (though).

"Interpretation of Savage Mind"

50.26   boast,] PR;   boast and (Horn, *Scientific Expedition*, 36.10–11)
50.27   and] PR;   with (Horn, *Scientific Expedition*, 36.11)
50.27   casualties] PR;   actual casualties (Horn, *Scientific Expedition*, 36.11)

WS: *Review of* The World and the Individual, *Second Series*

122.7–8   the small] WS;   these small (Royce, *World and Individual,* 2d Ser., 58.23)

123.20   significant relations] WS;   significant, or, if you will, in essentially practical relations (Royce, *World and Individual,* 2d Ser., 125.28–29)

129.2   evolution] WS;   *the evolution* (Royce, *World and Individual,* 2d Ser., 315.6)

129.3   this same] WS;   *the same* (Royce, *World and Individual,* 2d Ser., 315.7)

132.14–15   are inseparably] WS;   are thus inseparably (Royce, *World and Individual,* 2d Ser., 389.27–28)

132.27–28   our own] WS;   my (Royce, *World and Individual,* 2d Ser., 392.22)

132.29   laid] WS;   laid out (Royce, *World and Individual,* 2d Ser., 392.23)

133.15–16   to the life] WS;   to, although not necessarily temporally continuous with, the life (Royce, *World and Individual,* 2d Ser., 443.25–26)

Contributions to Dictionary of Philosophy and Psychology, *Vol. 2*

146.21   accordance] DPP;   agreement (Erdmann, *History of Philosophy,* 189.41)

174.23   God,] DPP;   God who is the image of the intellectual, (Plato, *Timaeus,* 515.29–30)

174.24–25   perfect possible, the image of its maker] DPP;   perfect—the one only-begotten heaven (Plato, *Timaeus,* 515.31)

229.4   repugnance of our ideas] DPP;   repugnancy, of any of our ideas (Locke, *Essays,* 424.18)

236.14   conditions] DPP;   condition (Kant, *Critique of Pure Reason,* 119.32)

240.21   known] DPP;   seen (Windelband, *History of Philosophy,* 311.21)

261.17   truth of philosophy bears] DPP;   truths of Philosophy thus bear (Spencer, *First Principles,* 133.29)

Studies in Logical Theory

320.14   thus placing] SLT;   which would place (Lotze, *Logic,* 1:2.35)

320.14   others] SLT;   rest (Lotze, *Logic*, 1:2.36)

322.7   thought's] SLT;   its own (Lotze, *Logic*, 1:36.21)

322.7   procedure] SLT;   procedure in general, (Lotze, *Logic*,
           1:36.21)

342n.13   be made] SLT;   have to be made (Lotze, *Logic*, 1:34.8)

347.35   pure thought] SLT;   pure or formal logic (Lotze, *Logic*,
           1:10.35)

347.35   apart from any] SLT;   irrespective of any (Lotze,
           Logic, 1:11.2)

347.36   objects] SLT;   the objects (Lotze, *Logic*, 1:11.3)

348.33   thought's production] SLT;   its own procedure (Lotze,
           Logic, 1:36.20)

348.36   thought] SLT;   thinking (Lotze, *Logic*, 1:36.23)

349.18   but] SLT;   but with (Lotze, *Logic*, 1:34.27)

349.18   value *after*] SLT;   value, when (Lotze, *Logic*, 1:34.27)

349.18–19 somehow] SLT;   somehow or other (Lotze, *Logic*,
           1:34.27)

349.20   maintained] SLT;   maintained the opinion (Lotze,
           Logic, 2:246.25)

349.22–23 *the conditions . . . as a*] SLT; [*rom.*] (Lotze, *Logic*,
           2:246.27)

349.23   *psychological*] SLT;   psychical (Lotze, *Logic*, 2:246.27)

349.23   *process comes about*] SLT; [*rom.*] (Lotze, *Logic*, 2:
           246.28)

349.25   thought,] SLT;   thought or (Lotze, *Logic*, 2:246.31)

349.26   in the conditions] SLT;   in those productive conditions
           of thought itself (Lotze, *Logic*, 2:246.33)

349.26–27 lie back of any which produce thought] SLT;   lie
           behind (Lotze, *Logic*, 2:246.34)

349n.4–5   gulf between psychical mechanism and thought] SLT;
           gulf which (Lotze, *Logic*, 2:251.11–12)

349n.5   unfilled.] SLT;   unfilled between the psychical mecha-
           nism and thought; (Lotze, *Logic*, 2:251.12–13)

355.3   of] SLT;   of the (Lotze, *Logic*, 1:36.7)

355.4–5   universal, . . . is]   SLT;   universal,   therefore,   is
           (Lotze, *Logic*, 1:31.5–6)

358.2   the] SLT;   this (Lotze, *Logic*, 1:16.7)

358.2   of] SLT;   the (Lotze, *Logic*, 1:16.8)

366.6   is] SLT;   is in (Lotze, *Logic*, 2:185.25)

366.10   us which] SLT;   us, it matters not where they may
           have come from, which (Lotze, *Logic*, 2:186.4–5)

368.12   for] SLT;   to (Mill, *Logic*, 8:2.23)

368.12   in] SLT;   for (Mill, *Logic*, 8:2.23)

369.17   the] SLT;   on the (Mill, *Logic*, 327:1.5–6)

371.3   seem] SLT;   appear (Whewell, *Philosophy of the In-
           ductive Sciences*, 1:21.22)

372.30   perception] SLT;   our perceptions (Whewell, *Philoso-
           phy of the Inductive Sciences*, 1:26.33–34)

372.31   an act] SLT; acts (Whewell, *Philosophy of the In-ductive Sciences*, 1:26.34)

372.31   is] SLT; are (Whewell, *Philosophy of the Inductive Sciences*, 1:26.34)

373.32   most numerous] SLT; the most numerous (Mill, *Logic*, 427:2.1–2)

374.26   *particular . . . view*] SLT; [*rom.*] (Mill, *Logic*, 429:1.51–52)

375.18   can] SLT; can only (Mill, *Logic*, 432:2.21)

375.18   known only when] SLT; known when (Mill, *Logic*, 432:2.21–22)

CHECKLIST OF DEWEY'S REFERENCES

Titles and authors' names in Dewey references have been corrected and expanded to conform accurately and consistently to the original works; all corrections appear in the Emendations List.

This section gives full publication information for each work cited by Dewey. When Dewey gave page numbers for a reference, the edition he used was identified exactly by locating the citation. Similarly, the books in Dewey's personal library have been used to verify his use of a particular edition. For other references, the edition listed here is the one from among the various editions possibly available to him that was his most likely source by reason of place or date of publication, or on the evidence from correspondence and other materials, and its general accessibility during the period.

References cited internally and at the end of each entry in the *Dictionary of Philosophy and Psychology* in abbreviated form have been omitted from this list because full bibliographical information appears in Volume 3 of the *Dictionary* itself.

Angell, James Rowland. "The Relations of Structural and Functional Psychology to Philosophy." In *Investigations Representing the Departments*. University of Chicago, The Decennial Publications, vol. 3, pt. 2, pp. 55–73. Chicago: University of Chicago Press, 1903.

Ashley, Myron Lucius. "The Nature of Hypothesis." In *Studies in Logical Theory*. University of Chicago, The Decennial Publications, vol. 11, pp. 143–83. Chicago: University of Chicago Press, 1903.

Bosanquet, Bernard. *Logic; or, the Morphology of Knowledge*. Oxford: Clarendon Press, 1888.

Bradley, Francis Herbert. *Appearance and Reality: A Metaphysical Essay*. London: Swan Sonnenschein and Co., 1893.

Brownson, Orestes A. *The Works of Orestes A. Brownson*. Collected and arranged by Henry F. Brownson. Vol. 2. Detroit: Thorndike Nourse, 1883.

Dewey, John. *The Child and the Curriculum*. Chicago: University of Chicago Press, 1902. [*The Middle Works of John Dewey, 1899–1924*, edited by Jo Ann Boydston, 2:271–91. Carbondale: Southern Illinois University Press, 1976.]

————. "Evolution and Ethics." *Monist* 8(1898):321–41. [*The Early Works of John Dewey, 1882–1898*, edited by Jo Ann Boydston, 5:34–53. Carbondale: Southern Illinois University Press, 1972.]

————. "The Evolutionary Method as Applied to Morality." *Philosophical Review* 11(1902):107–24, 353–71. [*Middle Works* 2:3–38.]

————. "The Reflex Arc Concept in Psychology." *Psychological Review* 3(1896):357–70. [*Early Works* 5:96–109.]

Erdmann, J. E. *A History of Philosophy*. Edited by W. S. Hough. 3 vols. New York: Macmillan Co., 1890.

Fichte, Johann Gottlieb. *Sämmtliche Werke*. 8 vols. Berlin: Veit and Co., 1845.

Grey, Sir George. *Journals of Two Expeditions of Discovery in North-West and Western Australia, during the Years 1837, 1838, and 1839*. 2 vols. London: T. and W. Boone, 1841.

Hamilton, Sir William. *Lectures on Metaphysics and Logic*. Edited by H. L. Mansel and John Veitch. 4 vols. Edinburgh: William Blackwood and Sons, 1870–74.

Harper, William Rainey. "The Thirty-sixth Quarterly Statement of the President of the University." *University* [of Chicago] *Record* 5(1901):370–79.

Hodgkinson, Clement. *Australia, from Port Macquarie to Moreton Bay*. London: T. and W. Boone, 1845.

The Horn Scientific Expedition to Central Australia, Report on the Work of. Edited by Baldwin Spencer. Pt. 4. London: Dulau and Co., 1896.

Huxley, Thomas H., and Youmans, William J. *The Elements of Physiology and Hygiene; a Text-Book for Educational Institutions*. Rev. ed. New York: American Book Co., 1873.

Jones, Henry. *A Critical Account of the Philosophy of Lotze*. Glasgow: James Maclehose and Sons, 1895.

Kant, Immanuel. *Immanuel Kant's Critique of Pure Reason*. Translated by F. Max Müller. London: Macmillan and Co., 1881.

Külpe, Oswald. *Introduction to Philosophy*. Translated by W. B. Pillsbury and E. B. Titchener. New York: Macmillan Co., 1897.

Lecky, William Edward Hartpole. *History of the Rise and Influence of the Spirit of Rationalism in Europe*. 2 vols. London: Longman, Green, Longman, Roberts, and Green, 1865.

Locke, John. *An Essay concerning Human Understanding*. New rev. ed. Edited by Thaddeus O'Mahoney. London: Ward, Lock, and Co., 1881.

Lotze, Hermann. *Logic*. English translation, edited by Bernard Bosanquet. 2d ed. 2 vols. Oxford: Clarendon Press, 1888.

———. *Mikrokosmus*. Leipzig: G. Hirzel, 1884.

Lumholtz, Karl Sofus. *Among Cannibals*. Translated by Rasmus B. Anderson. New York: Charles Scribner's Sons, 1889.

Mead, George Herbert. "The Definition of Psychical." In *Investigations Representing the Departments*. University of Chicago, The Decennial Publications, vol. 3, pt. 2, pp. 79–112. Chicago: University of Chicago Press, 1903.

Mill, John Stuart. *A System of Logic, Ratiocinative and Inductive: Being a Connected View of the Principles of Evidence and the Methods of Scientific Investigation*. People's Edition. London: Longmans, Green, and Co., 1889.

Moore, Addison Webster. "Existence, Meaning, and Reality in Locke's Essay and in the Present Epistemology." In *Investigations Representing the Departments*. University of Chicago, The Decennial Publications, vol. 3, pt. 2, pp. 29–51. Chicago: University of Chicago Press, 1903.

Peirce, Charles S. "Evolutionary Love." *Monist* 3(1893):176–200.

———. "The Law of Mind." *Monist* 2(1892):533–59.

Plato. *Timaeus*. In *The Dialogues of Plato*, edited by B. Jowett, 3d ed., 3:339–515. New York: Macmillan Co., 1892.

Royce, Josiah. *The World and the Individual*. First Series: The Four Historical Conceptions of Being. New York: Macmillan Co., 1900.

Schurman, Jacob Gould. *The Ethical Import of Darwinism*. New York: Charles Scribner's Sons, 1888.

Seth, Andrew. "Philosophy." *Encyclopædia Britannica* (9th ed. [American Reprint]), 18:805–10.

Spencer, Herbert. *First Principles of a New System of Philosophy*. New York: D. Appleton and Co., 1864.

———. *The Principles of Psychology*. 2d ed. 2 vols. New York: D. Appleton and Co., 1877.

———. *The Principles of Sociology*. Vol. 1. New York: D. Appleton and Co., 1896.

Thomas, William I. "The Gaming Instinct." *American Journal of Sociology* 6(1901):750–63.

———. "Der Ursprung der Exogamie." *Zeitschrift für Socialwissenschaft* 5(1902):1–18.

Whewell, William. *The Philosophy of the Inductive Sciences, Founded upon Their History*. 2 vols. London: J. W. Parker, 1840.

Windelband, Wilhelm. *A History of Philosophy*. Translated by James H. Tufts. New York: Macmillan Co., 1893.

Witmer, Lightner. *Analytical Psychology*. Boston: Ginn and Co., 1902.

Youmans, William J., and Huxley, Thomas H. *The Elements of Physiology and Hygiene; a Text-Book for Educational Institutions*. Rev. ed. New York: American Book Co., 1873.

I. Copy-text list.

The following are the editorially established forms of possible compounds which were hyphenated at the ends of lines in the copy-text.

11.24	overlaid	207.20	self-assertion
23.20	pigeon-holing	208.14	non-technical
50.21	war-like	212.29	pre-established
56.31	standpoint	218.18	self-contradictory
63.37–38	standstill	226.4	coexistence
64.39	thorough-going	227.38	self-contradictory
66.1–2	intercollegiate	255.25	standpoint
70.17	schoolroom	255.37	post-office
85.38	metal-working	258.26	supersensuous
91.10	clearing-house	261.7	name-giving
99.1	shortcomings	275.1	pigeon-holed
99.8	schoolroom	276.17	subject-matter
101.39	throughout	278.19	standpoint
114.36	quasi-professional	279.24	self-explanatory
126.29	fellow-creature	284.34	well-arranged
141.35	supernatural	285.1	round-about
144.11	preoccupation	286.15	subject-matter
150.37	quasi-mythical	286.37	shorthand
156.38	*non-essere*	287.34	ready-made
157.1	non-being	288.4	subject-matter
157.16	non-being	304.3–4	thought-provoking
158.28	anti-positing	310.20	standpoint
166.4	pre-established	315.13	standpoints
166.11	coexistence	317.35	ready-made
181.16	*panpsychisme*	325.8	subject-matter
183.27	quasi-emanistic	326.5	bookshelf
188.7	subject-matter	331.19	make-up
192.25	sub-science	334.28	piecemeal
192.40	subdivision	345.18	light-waves
199.33	schoolmen	352.34	self-evident
205.17	self-caused		

II. Critical-text list.

In quotations from the present edition, no line-end hyphens are to be retained except the following:

15.26	self-explanatory	208.14	non-technical
40.23	proof-texts	218.25	death-blow
42.11	psycho-physic	227.35	self-related
60.7	self-conceit	230.5	corner-stone
71.9	subject-matter	236.2	go-between
83.5	pigeon-holed	241.19	so-called
91.35	dance-house	266.27	hyper-phenomenal
98.20	sub-title	268.1	all-receptive
99.6	text-book	275.37	self-centered
99.15	old-fashioned	276.26	starting-point
119.9	text-books	325.32	subject-matter
146.17	self-moved	327.16	ready-made
148.35	dynamic organic	327.25	subject-matter
154.1	quasi-technical	329.4	re-formation
163.10	self-differentiating	330.5	re-relation
168.36	three-sidedness	343.6	subject-matter
188.35	subject-matter	351.18	subject-matter
205.17	self-caused	358.8	self-identical

INDEX